Noreen Giffney
Katherine O'Donnell
Editors

Twenty-First Century Lesbian Studies

Twenty-First Century Lesbian Studies has been co-published simultaneously as *Journal of Lesbian Studies*, Volume 11, Numbers 1/2 and 3/4 2007.

Pre-publication
REVIEWS,
COMMENTARIES,
EVALUATIONS . . .

"Twenty-First Century Lesbian Studies alternately challenges and defends, questions and champions lesbian studies, ultimately invigorating the field."

Professor Linda Garber
Santa Clara University
California

Twenty-First Century Lesbian Studies

Twenty-First Century Lesbian Studies has been co-published simultaneously as *Journal of Lesbian Studies*, Volume 11, Numbers 1/2 and 3/4 2007.

Monographic Separates from the *Journal of Lesbian Studies*

For additional information on these and other Haworth Press titles, including descriptions, tables of contents, reviews, and prices, use the QuickSearch catalog at http://www.HaworthPress.com.

Twenty-First Century Lesbian Studies, edited by Noreen Giffney and Katherine O'Donnell (Vol. 11, No. 1/2/3/4, 2007). *"Twenty-First Century Lesbian Studies alternately challenges and defends, questions and champions lesbian studies, ultimately invigorating the field." (Professor Linda Garber, Santa Clara University, California)*

"Lesbians" in East Asia: Diversity, Identities, and Resistance, edited by Diana Khor, PhD, and Saori Kamano, PhD (Vol. 10, No. 3/4, 2006). *"An innovative and compelling collection of writings vibrant with the lives of lesbians in Japan, Korea, China, and Hong Kong." (Susan Krieger, author, The Mirror Dance: Identity in a Women's Community)*

Challenging Lesbian Norms: Intersex, Transgender, Intersectional, and Queer Perspectives, edited by Angela Pattatucci Aragón, PhD (Vol. 10, No. 1/2, 2006). *"An invaluable resource–keenly argued and passionately felt. Some readers will hate this book, some will love it, but few will find themselves able to stop thinking about it long after they put it down." (Riki Wilchins, author of* Read my Lips *and* Queer Theory/Gender Theory; *co-editor of* GenderQueer)

Lesbian Academic Couples, edited by Michelle Gibson and Deborah T. Meem (Vol. 9, No. 4, 2005) *"The writers gathered here expose the underlying currents that allow them to flourish and continue to grow—opportunity, activism, and great love: for their work, for justice, and for each other." (Chris Cuomo, PhD, Professor of Philosophy and Women's Studies, University of Cincinnati)*

Making Lesbians Visible in the Substance Use Field, edited by Elizabeth Ettorre (Vol. 9, No. 3, 2005). *"This is the book that we in the substance abuse treatment and research fields have been waiting for." (Katherine van Wormer, PhD, MSSW, Professor of Social Work, University of Iowa; co-author,* Addiction Treatment: A Strengths Perspective)

Lesbian Communities: Festivals, RVs, and the Internet, edited by Esther Rothblum and Penny Sablove (Vol. 9, No. 1/2, 2005). *"Important. . . . Challenging and compelling. . . . A fascinating assortment of diverse perspectives on just what defines a lesbian 'community,' what needs and desires they meet, and how those worlds intersect with other groups and cultures." (Diane Anderson-Minshall, Executive Editor,* Curve *Magazine)*

Lesbian Ex-Lovers: The Really Long-Term Relationships, edited by Jacqueline S. Weinstock and Esther D. Rothblum (Vol. 8, No. 3/4, 2004). *"Compelling. . . . In these heady days of legal gay marriage, this book is a good reminder of the devotion lesbians have always had to the women we've loved, and the vows we've made with our hearts, long before we demanded licenses. This book is a tribute to the long memory we have of the women's hands who have touched our most vulnerable parts, and the invisible hands that outlast our divorces." (Arlene Istar Lev, CSW-R, CSAC, Author of* Transgender Emergence *and* The Complete Lesbian and Gay Parenting Guide; *Founder and Clinical Director, Choices Counseling and Consulting)*

Lesbians, Feminism, and Psychoanalysis: The Second Wave, edited by Judith M. Glassgold and Suzanne Iasenza (Vol. 8, No. 1/2, 2004). *"This book is the first to set the tone for a lesbian psychoanalytic revolution." (Dany Nobus, PhD, Senior Lecturer in Psychology and Psychoanalytic Studies, Brunel University, United Kingdom)*

Trauma, Stress, and Resilence Among Sexual Minority Women: Rising Like the Phoenix, edited by Kimberly F. Balsam, PhD (Vol. 7, No. 4, 2003). *Provides a first-hand look at the victimization experiences that lesbian and bisexual women face as well as how they work through these challenges and emerge resilient.*

Latina Lesbian Writers and Artists, edited by María Dolores Costa, PhD (Vol. 7, No. 3, 2003). *"A fascinating journey through the Latina lesbian experience. It brings us stories of exile, assimilation, and conflict of cultures. The book takes us to the Midwest, New York, Chicana Borderlands, Mexico, Ar-*

gentina, and Spain. It succeeds at showing the diversity within the Latina lesbian experience through deeply feminist testimonials of life and struggle." (Susana Cook, performance artist and playwright)

Lesbian Rites: Symbolic Acts and the Power of Community, edited by Ramona Faith Oswald, PhD (Vol. 7, No. 2, 2003). *"Informative, enlightening, and well written . . . illuminates the range of lesbian ritual behavior in a creative and thorough manner. Ramona Faith Oswald and the contributors to this book have done scholars and students of ritual studies an important service by demonstrating the power, pervasiveness, and performative nature of lesbian ritual practices." (Cele Otnes, PhD, Associate Professor, Department of Business Administration, University of Illinois)*

Mental Health Issues for Sexual Minority Women: Redefining Women's Mental Health, edited by Tonda L. Hughes, RN, PhD, FAAN, Carrol Smith, RN, MS, and Alice Dan, PhD (Vol. 7, No. 1, 2003). *A rare look at mental health issues for lesbians and other sexual minority women.*

Addressing Homophobia and Heterosexism on College Campuses, edited by Elizabeth P. Cramer, PhD (Vol. 6, No. 3/4, 2002). *A practical guide to creating LGBT-supportive environments on college campuses.*

Femme/Butch: New Considerations of the Way We Want to Go, edited by Michelle Gibson and Deborah T. Meem (Vol. 6, No. 2, 2002). *"Disrupts the fictions of heterosexual norms. . . . A much-needed examiniation of the ways that butch/femme identitites subvert both heteronormativity and 'expected' lesbian behavior." (Patti Capel Swartz, PhD, Assistant Professor of English, Kent State University)*

Lesbian Love and Relationships, edited by Suzanna M. Rose, PhD (Vol. 6, No. 1, 2002). *"Suzanna Rose's collection of 13 essays is well suited to prompting serious contemplation and discussion about lesbian lives and how they are–or are not–different from others. . . . Interesting and useful for debunking some myths, confirming others, and reaching out into new territories that were previously unexplored." (Lisa Keen, BA, MFA, Senior Political Correspondent, Washington Blade)*

Everyday Mutinies: Funding Lesbian Activism, edited by Nanette K. Gartrell, MD, and Esther D. Rothblum, PhD (Vol. 5, No. 3, 2001). *"Any lesbian who fears she'll never find the money, time, or support for her work can take heart from the resourcefulness and dogged determination of the contributors to this book. Not only do these inspiring stories provide practical tips on making dreams come true, they offer an informal history of lesbian political activism since World War II." (Jane Futcher, MA, Reporter, Marin Independent Journal, and author of Crush, Dream Lover, and Promise Not to Tell)*

Lesbian Studies in Aotearoa/New Zealand, edited by Alison J. Laurie (Vol. 5, No. 1/2, 2001). *These fascinating studies analyze topics ranging from the gender transgressions of women passing as men in order to work and marry as they wished to the effects of coming out on modern women's health.*

Lesbian Self-Writing: The Embodiment of Experience, edited by Lynda Hall, PhD (Vol. 4, No. 4, 2000). *"Probes the intersection of love for words and love for women. . . . Luminous, erotic, evocative." (Beverly Burch, PhD, psychotherapist and author, Other Women: Lesbian/Bisexual Experience and Psychoanalytic Views of Women and On Intimate Terms: The Psychology of Difference in Lesbian Relationships)*

'Romancing the Margins'? Lesbian Writing in the 1990s, edited by Gabriele Griffin, PhD (Vol. 4, No. 2, 2000). *Explores lesbian issues through the mediums of books, movies, and poetry and offers readers critical essays that examine current lesbian writing and discuss how recent movements have tried to remove racist and antigay themes from literature and movies.*

From Nowhere to Everywhere: Lesbian Geographies, edited by Gill Valentine, PhD (Vol. 4, No. 1, 2000). *"A significant and worthy contribution to the ever growing literature on sexuality and space. . . . A politically significant volume representing the first major collection on lesbian geographies. . . . I will make extensive use of this book in my courses on social and cultural geography and sexuality and space." (Jon Binnie, PhD, Lecturer in Human Geography, Liverpool, John Moores University, United Kingdom)*

Lesbians, Levis and Lipstick: The Meaning of Beauty in Our Lives, edited by Jeanine C. Cogan, PhD, and Joanie M. Erickson (Vol. 3, No. 4, 1999). *Explores lesbian beauty norms and the effects these norms have on lesbian women.*

Twenty-First Century Lesbian Studies

Noreen Giffney
Katherine O'Donnell
Editors

Twenty-First Century Lesbian Studies has been co-published simultaneously as *Journal of Lesbian Studies*, Volume 11, Numbers 1/2 and 3/4 2007.

HPP

Harrington Park Press®
An Imprint of The Haworth Press, Inc.

www.HaworthPress.com

Published by

Harrington Park Press®, 10 Alice Street, Binghamton, NY 13904-1580 USA

Harrington Park Press® is an imprint of The Haworth Press, Inc., 10 Alice Street, Binghamton, NY 13904-1580 USA.

Twenty-First Century Lesbian Studies has been co-published simultaneously as *Journal of Lesbian Studies*, Volume 11, Numbers 1/2 and 3/4 2007.

The development, preparation, and publication of this work has been undertaken with great care. However, the publisher, employees, editors, and agents of The Haworth Press and all imprints of The Haworth Press, Inc., including The Haworth Medical Press® and The Pharmaceutical Products Press®, are not responsible for any errors contained herein or for consequences that may ensue from use of materials or information contained in this work. With regard to case studies, identities and circumstances of individuals discussed herein have been changed to protect confidentiality. Any resemblance to actual persons, living or dead, is entirely coincidental.

The Haworth Press is committed to the dissemination of ideas and information according to the highest standards of intellectual freedom and the free exchange of ideas. Statements made and opinions expressed in this publication do not necessarily reflect the views of the Publisher, Directors, management, or staff of The Haworth Press, Inc., or an endorsement by them.

Cover design by Jennifer M. Gaska

Front cover photograph: "Resting" by Lisa Fingleton

Library of Congress Cataloging-in-Publication Data

Twenty-first century lesbian studies / Noreen Giffney, Katherine O'Donnell, editors.
      p. cm.
      "Co-published simultaneously as Journal of lesbian studies, volume 11, numbers 1/2 and 3/4 2007."
      Includes bibliographical references and index.
      ISBN 978-1-56023-650-4 (hard cover : alk. paper) – ISBN 978-1-56023-651-1 (soft cover : alk. paper)
   1. Gay and lesbian studies. I. Giffney, Noreen. II. O'Donnell, Katherine, 1966- III. Journal of lesbian studies.
HQ75.15.T84 2007
306.76'601–dc22

                                                   2007004510

The HAWORTH PRESS Inc.

Abstracting, Indexing & Outward Linking

PRINT *and* ELECTRONIC BOOKS & JOURNALS

This section provides you with a list of major indexing & abstracting services and other tools for bibliographic access. That is to say, each service began covering this periodical during the the year noted in the right column. Most Websites which are listed below have indicated that they will either post, disseminate, compile, archive, cite or alert their own Website users with research-based content from this work. (This list is as current as the copyright date of this publication.)

Abstracting, Website/Indexing Coverage . . . . Year When Coverage Began

- ****Academic Search Premier (EBSCO)****
  <http://search.ebscohost.com> 2006
- ****MasterFILE Premier (EBSCO)****
  <http://search.ebscohost.com> 2006
- ****MEDLINE (National Library of Medicine)****
  <http://www.nlm.nih.gov> 2004
- ****Psychological Abstracts (PsycINFO)**** *<http://www.apa.org>* 2001
- ****PubMed**** *<http://www.ncbi.nlm.nih.gov/pubmed/>* 2004
- ****Social Services Abstracts (ProQuest CSA)****
  <http://www.csa.com> 1998
- ****Sociological Abstracts (ProQuest CSA)****
  <http://www.csa.com> 1998
- *Abstracts in Anthropology* *<http://www.baywood.com/Journals/*
  PreviewJournals.asp?Id=0001-3455> 2006
- *Academic Source Premier (EBSCO)*
  <http://search.ebscohost.com> 2006
- *British Library Inside (The British Library)*
  <http://www.bl.uk/services/current/inside.html> 2006
- *Cambridge Scientific Abstracts (now ProQuest CSA)*
  <http://www.csa.com> 2006
- *Contemporary Women's Issues (Thomson Gale)* 1998
- *Current Abstracts (EBSCO)*
  <http://search.ebscohost.com> 2007

(continued)

(continued)

Bibliographic Access

Special Bibliographic Notes related to special journal issues (separates) and indexing/abstracting:

- indexing/abstracting services in this list will also cover material in any "separate" that is co-published simultaneously with Haworth's special thematic journal issue or DocuSerial. Indexing/abstracting usually covers material at the article/chapter level.
- monographic co-editions are intended for either non-subscribers or libraries which intend to purchase a second copy for their circulating collections.
- monographic co-editions are reported to all jobbers/wholesalers/approval plans. The source journal is listed as the "series" to assist the prevention of duplicate purchasing in the same manner utilized for books-in-series.
- to facilitate user/access services all indexing/abstracting services are encouraged to utilize the co-indexing entry note indicated at the bottom of the first page of each article/chapter/contribution.
- this is intended to assist a library user of any reference tool (whether print, electronic, online, or CD-ROM) to locate the monographic version if the library has purchased this version but not a subscription to the source journal.
- individual articles/chapters in any Haworth publication are also available through the Haworth Document Delivery Service (HDDS).

As part of Haworth's continuing commitment to better serve our library patrons, we are proud to be working with the following electronic services:

AGGREGATOR SERVICES

EBSCOhost

Ingenta

J-Gate

Minerva

OCLC FirstSearch

Oxmill

SwetsWise

LINK RESOLVER SERVICES

1Cate (Openly Informatics)

ChemPort (American Chemical Society)

CrossRef

Gold Rush (Coalliance)

LinkOut (PubMed)

LINKplus (Atypon)

LinkSolver (Ovid)

LinkSource with A-to-Z (EBSCO)

Resource Linker (Ulrich)

SerialsSolutions (ProQuest)

SFX (Ex Libris)

Sirsi Resolver (SirsiDynix)

Tour (TDnet)

Vlink (Extensity, formerly Geac)

WebBridge (Innovative Interfaces)

ABOUT THE EDITORS

Noreen Giffney is a Postdoctoral Fellow in Women's Studies (WERRC), School of Social Justice at University College Dublin, Ireland, and a Research Affiliate in the Centre for the Interdisciplinary Study of Sexuality and Gender in Europe at the University of Exeter. She is the co-editor of *The Ashgate Research Companion to Queer Theory* and *Queering the Non/Human*, and is the series co-editor of the Queer Interventions book series at Ashgate Press. Her book on queer theory is forthcoming in Berg's 'The Key Concepts' series. Her next research project is a monograph on queer theory and the psychoanalyst Melanie Klein.

Address correspondence to: Women's Studies (WERRC), School of Social Justice, Hanna Sheehy-Skeffington Building, University College Dublin, Belfield, Dublin 4, Ireland.

Katherine O'Donnell teaches in Women's Studies (WERRC) at University College Dublin in Ireland. Her research interests include eighteenth-century Irish culture, the history of sexuality and Feminist and Queer Theory. Her publications include articles on the politics and speeches of Edmund Burke; she co-edited (with Michael O'Rourke) *Love, Sex, Intimacy and Friendship Between Men 1550-1800* (Palgrave Macmillan, 2003) and *Queer Masculinities 1550-1800: Sitting Same-Sex Desire in the Early Modern World* (Palgrave Macmillan, 2005).

To my young friend, Mary McAuliffe, in memory of JJ's (KOD)

For Nicole Murray, who knows more than she ever wanted to
about Lesbian Studies (NG)

Acknowledgements

We owe our thanks to Susan Bailey, Ursula Barry, Lisa Fingleton, Paula Fogarty, Mary McAuliffe, Sally Munt, Nicole Murray, Michael O'Rourke, Esther Rothblum, Ailbhe Smyth, the anonymous reviewers and contributors. Noreen Giffney is especially grateful to Nicole Murray for her assistance at the proofing stage.

Twenty-First Century Lesbian Studies

CONTENTS

Introduction

Noreen Giffney
Katherine O'Donnell

Since lesbians are materially oppressed by heterosexuality daily, it is not surprising that we have seen and understood its impact daily, it is not surprising that we have seen and understood its impact first–not because we are more moral, but because our reality is different–it is a materially different reality–heterosexuality means men first–it assumes that every woman is heterosexual; that every woman is defined by and is the property of men. Her body, her ser-

---

Noreen Giffney is a Postdoctoral Fellow in Women's Studies (WERRC), School of Social Justice at University College Dublin, Ireland, and a Research Affiliate in the Centre for the Interdisciplinary Study of Sexuality and Gender in Europe at the University of Exeter. She is the co-editor of *The Ashgate Research Companion to Queer Theory* and *Queering the Non/Human*, and is the series co-editor of the Queer Interventions book series at Ashgate Press. Her book on queer theory is forthcoming in Berg's 'The Key Concepts' series. Her next research project is a monograph on queer theory and the psychoanalyst Melanie Klein.

Katherine O'Donnell is affiliated with Women's Studies (WERRC), School of Social Justice, Hanna Sheehy-Skeffington Building, University College Dublin, Belfield, Dublin 4, Ireland.

Address correspondence to: Noreen Giffney, Women's Studies (WERRC), School of Social Justice, Hanna Sheehy-Skeffington Building, University College Dublin, Belfield, Dublin 4, Ireland (E-mail: noreen.giffney@ucd.ie).

The authors appreciate the insightful comments of Nicole Murray on an earlier draft.

[Haworth co-indexing entry note]: "Introduction." Giffney, Noreen, and Katherine O'Donnell. Co-published simultaneously in *Journal of Lesbian Studies* (Harrington Park Press, an imprint of The Haworth Press, Inc.) Vol. 11, No. 1/2, 2007, pp. 1-18; and: *Twenty-First Century Lesbian Studies* (ed: Noreen Giffney, and Katherine O'Donnell) Harrington Park Press, an imprint of The Haworth Press, Inc., 2007, pp. 1-18. Single or multiple copies of this article are available for a fee from The Haworth Document Delivery Service [1-800-HAWORTH, 9:00 a.m. - 5:00 p.m. (EST). E-mail address: docdelivery@haworthpress.com].

Available online at http://jls.haworthpress.com
doi:10.1300/J155v11n01_01

vices, her children belong to men. If you don't accept that definition, you're a queer–no matter whom you sleep with; if you do not accept that definition in this society, you're queer. (Bunch, 1975: 51)

To write or speak *as a lesbian* appears a paradoxical appearance of this 'I', one which feels neither true nor false. For it is a production, usually in response to a request, to come out or write in the name of an identity which, once produced, sometimes functions as a politically efficacious phantasm. (Butler, 1991: 13)

Currently, the most influential paradigm for analysing historical representations of homosexuality in the West is Michel Foucault's thesis that the 'species' now known as homosexual did not emerge until the late Nineteenth Century.[1] However, Foucault was focusing on that 'utterly confused category' of the male sodomite and his sources are the "ancient and civil or canonical codes–[where] sodomy was a category of forbidden acts . . . their perpetrator was nothing more than the juridical subject of them" (1978: 43). When it comes to the history of lesbians in Europe there is an embarrassment of riches in terms of the long genealogy, variety of nomenclature and narrative sources depicting women with appetites for sex with women and women who have excessive love and attachment for other women: Sapphists, fricatrices, tribades, tommies. Lesbians can be found in poetry, plays, pornography, romances, novels, sermons, journalism and essays. Contrary to Foucault's thesis, these women's engagement in homosexual love or sex is represented as being central to their identity, or rather their identification. The difficulty for scholars of lesbian history rests in the fact that these depictions are often hostile representations written by men where these gloriously freakish women get textually punished for their transgressions of the patriarchal code. Are there 'real' lesbians to be found ghosting these vivid fantasies?

What Mary McIntosh and Foucault have helped us to realize is that we have to be careful of anachronisms when talking about pre-modern people forming 'identities' of any description and when it comes to finding the lesbians in history we must pay attention to our desire to use our contemporary list of what constitutes a lesbian as a checklist of characteristics, which will lead us to lesbians of the past (Traub, 2002; Lochrie, 2005; Vanita and Sidwai, 2000; Brooten, 1996). The more difficult, but perhaps more rewarding approach is to ask how was love and sex between women constituted in the past? We can ask many more questions, such as were there conventions and boundaries that signified the limits of non-sexual love between friends? How were these limits exceeded? Were there penalties for exceeding the limits? How were these penalties avoided? Thanks to the pioneering work of literary and bibliographic scholars, such as Jeanette Foster (1985), Alison Hennegan (2000), Emma Donoghue (1997, 1993), Lillian Faderman (1994), Terry Castle (2003) and Bonnie Zimmerman (2000), at the beginning of the Twenty-First Century we know that we have an enormous amount of material with which to work.[2]

One of the striking aspects of the centuries-long depiction of love and sex between women is the focus on whether these passions were inherent desires or taught practices; was she born with unnatural desires, a deformed body or was she taught to be deviant? Perhaps it was the example of the school around the poet Sappho on Lesbos, but studious women were thought to be particularly prone to lesbianism. Jonathan Swift, writing in early eighteenth-century Ireland has his hero, Gulliver, describing homosexuality as one of "those unnatural Appetites in both Sexes, so common among us." According to Gulliver these politer Pleasures are entirely the Productions of Art and Reason, on our side of the Globe (1992: 199). Intertextuality and lesbian sex seem to go hand in hand for centuries: Anne Lister cruised prospective lovers in early nineteenth-century Yorkshire by attempting to discern if they appreciated the sixth satire of Juvenal (Lister, 268), the writings of nineteenth- and twentieth-century lesbians evince an extraordinary, often coded, knowledge of the heritage of literary representations of lesbians and into the Twenty-First Century lesbians are still finding themselves between the covers of books and on sheets of paper, while debates about what constitutes and defines a lesbian continue.

The self-reflexive questioning of lesbians and lesbian communities as to who is im/properly lesbian, how much of our sexuality is innate or learned, and how much of our identity as lesbians is in an on-going dialogue with shifting contexts, marks us in stark contrast to gay men who sometimes display a virtual lack of this epistemological and ontological anxiety. It is a questioning which animates many of the pieces in this volume. A questioning which energizes more than enervates, bringing, as it does, an awareness of the ethical risks involved in all naming which inevitably enacts the boundaries of sameness and difference, and an attendance to the gamut of violence and pleasure in such affiliations and designations.

This questioning may have roots older than the 1970s but it is in that decade that we see the clearest enunciation of debates about lesbian identity and community that continue, changed but unabated, into this new century. While the gay rights movement, inspired by the example of the Black Civil Rights movement, provided lesbians with the form and discourse for combating homophobia by coming out with pride, it was the feminist women's movement that was the crucible in which lesbian theorizing was formed. Writers, such as Jill Johnston (1973), provide us with a remarkable testimony of the brilliant exuberance of lesbians joining the women's movement and becoming the 'lavender menace' that Betty Freidan (founder of the National Organization of Women, NOW) feared would undermine Feminism. Indeed, throughout the 1970s lesbians, and African-American feminists in particular, articulated the concerns that when feminists analyzed women's oppression solely on the grounds of gender, they negated the oppression experienced by women through homophobia, classism, poverty and racism and indeed, in ignoring these sites of oppression were in danger of an unthinking replication of white middle-class privilege (Combahee River Collective, 1977; in Hull et al., 1982; Lorde, 1984). As lesbians were joining the women's movement, there were feminists who, because of their political analysis could no longer 'sleep with the enemy' and actively separated themselves, in as much as they could economically, imaginatively and certainly sexually from patriarchal heterosexist society to become 'political lesbians'.[3] As Gillian Hanscombe wittily describes it, they were head first as opposed to heat first lesbians and the internecine battle over what constituted the proper lesbian subject began.

Political lesbians deplored the false consciousness of lesbians who worked politically and made social spaces with gay men and perceived butch/femme lesbians to be aping heterosexist roles. It was on what might have seemed to be the unlikely ground of S/M sex that the political battle became pitched between the self-styled 'pro-sex lesbians' and those they reviled as 'radfemseps' (Smyth, 1992). These debates ranged over the contested territories of pornography/erotica, prostitutes/sex workers, violence/consent, safe space/censorship, gender oppression/gender play, and were subsequently termed the 'Sex Wars' of the 1980s (Allison, 1995: 105-8; Gonda, 1998; Nestle, 1987). Feminist analysis proved so congenial to lesbian theorizing that both sides understood themselves as feminist. In these turf wars lesbians argued with one another over the boundaries and correct title to the field of Feminism under the opposing camps denominated or tagged with various rubrics such as 'socialist feminist,' 'liberal feminist' and, of course, 'radical (lesbian separatist) feminist' (Bunch, 1976).

Concurrent with the sex wars throughout the 1980s, and responding to the critiques and concerns of lesbians, women of color and working-class women, feminist and lesbian theoretical debates raged, turning on the axis of how much we could depend on the idea of a female or lesbian subject (Fuss, 1990; de Lauretis, 1989). The word 'subject' carries with it that ambivalent charge of denominating not only the capacity to imagine, analyze, decide, communicate and act but also the paradoxical meaning of being the focus of a discourse, a description circumscribed by one or those elite who know; subject to a higher law in which one is spoken to or about. The split in Feminist Theory ran along the fault-line of what kinds of emphases were stressed in describing the subjectivity of women and what kind of promise for action and change seemed to be offered by the theorists. The split also had a tendency to run along disciplinary lines with the paradoxical situation that those who were trained in the Social Sciences (historians, sociologists, economists, anthropologists), who worked from the assumption that subjects and classes are formed through socialization, were generally unconcerned with problematizing further the concepts of the subjectivity of women. Those who worked in the Humanities, in Literary and Cultural Studies and in Psychoanalysis focused on the formation of interiority and severely critiqued any assumption of an *a priori* subject 'woman.' The camps were known as essentialist and social constructionist, or sometimes modernists and postmodernists, and in the theoretical disputes between the radical lesbian-feminist separatists ('lesbian feminists' were characterized as essentialist) and their critics ('feminist lesbians' on the so-called higher theoretical ground of social constructionism) both sides claimed Monique Wittig's seminal essay, "The Straight Mind" (1992), with its resonant last sentence, "Lesbians are not women" (19), as their *ur* text (Richardson, 1996; Lienert, 1996).

Increasingly radical lesbian-feminist theorizing stepped aside from the controversies and struggles around theorizing multiple identity positions to give an almost exclusive focus to sexual violence against women. This clearly demarcated territory of women's subjugation by men through domestic violence, rape, prostitution and pornography remains the key ground for radical (lesbian) feminists' theories and politics. Feminist, particularly feminist lesbians' efforts to find ways to understand and express multiple and simultaneous identity positions through political practice, community building and cultural expression can be read not so much as presaging but inciting queer theories and politics.[4] The early theorists of second-wave Feminism, thinkers, as apparently as diverse as Simone de Beauvoir, Betty Friedan, Evelyn Reed,

Monique Wittig, Adrienne Rich, Mary Daly, Kate Millet, Luce Irigaray, Juliet Mitchell and Shulamith Firestone, can be read as providing an echoing prediction to feminist-lesbian thinkers, activists and artists in their articulations of the oppression of women as giving rise to a split subjectivity. These theorists read women as alienated subjects, as fictions of historical and economic processes, *pace* Marx; as socialized constructs formed by repression and taboo, split from the unconscious, *pace* Freud, as both bodily objects and free-floating signifiers ideologically and materially pinned to pedestals, prisons, psychiatric wards, birth chambers and brothels by popular culture, high culture and religion.[5]

Judith Butler's *Gender Trouble*, published in 1990, was the zeitgeist of a new era in lesbian theorizing, politics and community-building in that throughout the 1990s the lessons from the bruising battles of the earlier decades have seen lesbians more accepting of the idea that that critique of the concept of a subject is not a negation or a repudiation of the subject, but rather a way of interrogating how it is conceived and thinks and even that there might be pleasure and freedom in deconstructing foundational premises of what it might mean to be a (lesbian or female) subject and that the opening of such space is vital to allow lesbians to think, to change and to love. Lesbian theorizing in the last decade of the previous century was described in the words of Sally R. Munt as "advocating alliance not antipathy" (1992: xiv). The former battles for total control of the field of feminism are no longer waged in that feminist lesbian theorizing is now concerned to promote pluralities of perspectives and methodologies, a 'poly-vocality' as Munt terms it. The insights and strategies advocated by feminists are now generally offered as partial, particular, provisional, contingent, contextual and the vogue for identifying oneself as one brand of feminist in distinction to others has, for many, now passed.

Where does that leave Lesbian Studies in the Twenty-First Century? This volume provides us not so much with a map to the land ahead but gives us compass readings to locate its shifting horizons.

OF ROUND PEGS AND SQUARE HOLES

Introduction: "that space where the editor does the trick with the round peg and square hole by proclaiming the magical cohesion of remarkably diverse approaches taken by individual essayists." (Doan, 1994: ix)

We have entitled this collection of essays *Twenty-First Century Lesbian Studies*. It is more properly, akin with Laura Doan's lead article, "Lesbian Studies After *The Lesbian Postmodern*," or Lesbian Studies since 1994. Our contributors share, with those of *The Lesbian Postmodern*, a commitment to interrogating the term 'lesbian' from a diverse range of perspectives, while engaging with 'postmodernism' in a multiplicity of ways. It is with the same "hesitation, discomfort, or even skepticism" (x) that the contributors to this volume undertake self-reflexive investigations into a field of knowledge-production loosely referred to as Lesbian Studies. The pieces focus more specifically on the field's institutionalization in the Humanities and Social Sciences, in addition to considering how the term 'lesbian' is employed in activist, 'community' and cultural contexts, while discussing the ways in which its usage impacts on the material lives of those who choose that label to identify themselves. Like Doan's book, the essays in this collection:

> . . . [test] the limits (of epistemology, of identity, of subjectivity, of disciplinarity) and [problematize] and [undermine] polarities (such as political efficacy and theoretical formulation, or essentialism and constructivism, or modernism and postmodernism, or margin and center) (x).

While harboring reservations at the thought of trying to pull together many radically divergent approaches, positions and views on Lesbian Studies (ix-x)–this volume showcases twenty-seven pieces–nevertheless, we think it is imperative to point to the important ways in which the authors' concerns converge, while revelling as editors in the many unresolved (perhaps irreconcilable) disjunctions between them. In this, we share Michèle Aina Barale's exuberance:

> What seems most wonderful to me about the past decade of LGBTQ writing is that it is so luxuriously, lusciously *there*. I don't have to take a vow of intellectual monogamy; I can fall in love with every single thing I read. I can also walk away when it treats me wrong.[6]

In formulating *Twenty-First Century Lesbian Studies*, we had a number of objectives. Firstly, we wanted to place the term 'lesbian' at the center of analysis, whether as a materiality, concept, category of investigation, identity, political position or object choice. In doing so, we endeavored to proliferate meanings for the word 'lesbian' specifically and generate new dialogues more generally about technologies of naming, self-identification and the significance attached to formulating new vocabularies to capture the slipperiness of acts and identities outside hetero-patriarchal norms. Secondly, we were interested in tracing the importance of the personal and strategic essentialism, and the attendant risks associated with "professions of desire" (Haggerty and Zimmerman, 1995), for those who act, write and speak 'on,' or live 'as,' 'lesbians.' Thirdly, we were eager to explore 'Lesbian Studies' as an ontology, by submitting current genealogical myths to scrutiny in an effort to open up new points of departure for future work in the area. Fourthly, our intention was to examine lesbian lives, studies and activism in a range of geographical and historical contexts to see whether the term 'lesbian' translates. Thus, we wished to consider how "situated knowledges" (Haraway, 1991)–whether geographical, temporal, social or political–might affect the current state, future development or abeyance of Lesbian Studies. And so, we sought out work that tackled the question of whether we should invest our energies in maintaining a discipline devoted to studying 'lesbian(s)' interdisciplinarily or work towards proliferating knowledge of 'lesbian(s)' throughout existing (inter-)disciplinary formations. Fifthly, we were insistent that authors put the shifting boundaries of the term 'lesbian' under interrogation in their analyses of binaries relating to insides/outsides, inclusions/exclusions and margins/centers. In more general terms, we sought to widen the contours of Lesbian Studies by actively seeking out research produced outside the US/UK axis that tends to dominate the field and on areas, such as Medieval Studies, which are often ignored in 'theoretical' discussions. We also commissioned a number of pieces by people whose main research interests lie in areas, such as bisexuality, transsexuality and transgender, intersex and queer, in an effort to facilitate dialogue about 'lesbians' and 'Lesbian Studies' between members of the LGBTTIQQA alphabet.[7]

At the time of issuing invitations and distributing a call for submissions, we asked potential contributors to consider the following questions when formulating their responses: does 'lesbian' have continued relevance as an identity descriptor or political position? Who does the term include and exclude? How does intersectional thinking impact on how we formulate 'lesbian' identities? Are we now 'post-lesbian'? Is there such a thing as Lesbian Studies? What, if anything, defines the field? Should we be concerned with defining Lesbian Studies or investing in it as a specific area of knowledge-production? What is the current state of the field? What topics or methodologies should practitioners engage most urgently with at this time? How does work grouped loosely under the 'Lesbian Studies' umbrella converge with, diverge from, draw on and enrich efforts in the areas of Feminist, Gay, Bisexual, Trans, Intersex and Queer Straight Studies? Does Lesbian Studies have a future? What are some possible futures for the field? Our efforts resulted in six full-length articles and twenty-one position pieces on a wide variety of topics. While the articles originated at two Lesbian Lives conferences,[8] the authors of the position pieces were commissioned or responded to an open call for papers.

Being in the unique position of having read all of the pieces, it seems to us that they concern themselves with what amounts to five main themes. Although almost every piece touches in some way on each of these themes, some pieces dovetail with individual themes more than others. Thus, we have divided the essays loosely into five sections: "Genealogies: Contextualizing the Field," "Readings: Desiring Fictions," "Theories: Disciplinary Challenges," "Identities: Thinking Intersectionally" and "Locations: Translating 'Lesbian'." Partly for ease of reading but more to facilitate maximal dialogue among the pieces, we have grouped together the contributors whose concerns fit most closely thematically, but whose approaches and conclusions often differ in considerable ways. As each essay is accompanied by an abstract and selection of keywords, it seems pointless either to simply summarize the arguments contained therein or allude to the contents of each section in what would function merely as a pedestrian overview. Instead, we have opted more ambitiously to briefly comment on the intricate patterns interlacing each theme more generally.

Many of the pieces adumbrate genealogies of Lesbian Studies through personal reflections and auto-ethnographies by revisiting or presenting overviews of their work and the achievements of iconic figures or groups in academic, activist and 'community' settings (Vanita, Zimmerman, Munt, Rivera-Fuentes). These personal reflections do not prove gratuitous but serve to illuminate authors' arguments, in an effort to show that the personal cannot be extricated from explorations grounded in identity politics however ambivalent authors are about their investment in identity categories. The majority of authors consider the advantages, drawbacks, personal benefits and risks involved in partaking of the academic institutionalization of Lesbian Studies. Any discussion of genealogies leads to thinking about systems of power that generate and maintain origin myths, while propelling and permeating the writing of histories. In this way, authors ask questions about who gets to write these histories. How are they circulated and by whom?

How in turn does this impact on the instantiation of hierarchies of knowledge, not to mention those who have the right or privilege to share and receive it? Who is included and excluded, at the margins and the centers, remembered or forgotten, championed or reviled, given forums to speak or silenced? All contributors engage with the shared and often thorny genealogy of Lesbian Studies and Queer Theory, some by trying to think outside, beyond or through the "collision model" (Doan) that has gained currency since the early 1990s. This "collision model" sets up Queer Theory and Lesbian Feminism as arch rivals, enemies even, in a desperate bid for the dominance of the former and the survival of the latter. Other authors offer cautionary tales about the rise to prominence of Queer Theory or its failures to fulfil what its early practitioners set out to achieve (Cruikshank). A number of authors believe that Lesbian Studies and Queer Theory can engage in more productive discussions; some see the future of Lesbian Studies within Queer Studies (Engel), while others argue that Queer Theory facilitates an encounter between Lesbian Studies and a diverse range of people (Giffney). Most pointedly, authors claim that it is only by looking back that we can begin to think forward; it is in the past that we must find new futures (Sauer). In this, the past becomes something to be cherished and not denigrated. This is in stark contrast to the presentism or flagrant ahistoricism that allows inaccuracies to circulate unchallenged or more destructively stymies the chance of productive encounters between generations of scholars and activists.

While all of the pieces undertake close readings–personal, political and/or theoretical–of texts, situations, identifications and methodological frameworks, the vast majority of them engage at some level with the idea of "Desiring Fictions" and what that might mean. In this, some of the pieces are concerned with fiction in its most literal sense–literary fiction–in their explorations of the pleasures to be gained from reading and disentangling plot twists while following the character development of lesbian/queer novels. As well as attesting to the ways in which particular lesbian/queer authors subvert norms relating to sex, gender, sexuality and desire more generally, certain contributors pay homage to one of the roots of Lesbian Studies in the Academy: Lesbian Literary Studies. Although not writing on literary fiction in this particular volume, many of the authors started out in Literary Studies or continue to work in this area. Some contributors have made notable past interventions into the area of Lesbian Literary Studies, while others are more creatively involved, reproducing excerpts from or alluding to their fictional works. The pieces also raise questions about what constitutes lesbian literature. Is it the author, the subject matter, the approach and/or or the audience? Some contributors prefer terms such as "homoaffection" (Gonda) or "lesboeroticism" (Cairns) to lend more specificity to their descriptions of the economies of affect, emotional bonds and circuits of desire emanating from and between their subjects. The subtitle, "Desiring Fictions," also works on a more abstract level in contributors' discussions of people's personal investments in the performative fictions of identity (Noble); attempts to make visible, challenge and subvert those fictions (Hemmings); and the risks associated with enacting such deconstructive moves. Authors examine in more general terms fictions relating to Lesbian Studies and what it might mean to disseminate the fruits of the field "unprofessionally" (Munt), without the constraints of egos and the Academy. Having said this, contributions also think in practical ways about what it means for the material lives of 'lesbians' to have their self-identifications exposed as strategic fictions (McNaron).

All of the pieces comment on, engage with and produce theory in their forays into the field. The term 'theory' is itself put under investigation in contributions which ask: who gets to formulate theory? Where is it produced? What are its practical uses or material effects? The submission on Medieval Studies (Sauer) also exposes the unvoiced assumption in Lesbian Studies specifically and LGBTIQ Studies more generally that theory is something produced by looking at contemporary conditions without recourse to the important research undertaken on histories and, by extension, the theories formulated by scholars working on earlier periods. The essays by contributors working outside the UK and US query the cultural contexts within which theories are produced, in addition to questioning what gets to count as Theory. Many authors submit the 'theory star system' in Queer Studies to scrutiny, in an effort to think about the ways in which certain individuals, locations and disciplines become conflated with producing theory, while others are seen as simply applying it; colonized by its ideological effects. In this, contributors interrogate a number of often unhelpful binaries circulating about theory: theory/activism, theory/application and abstract theory/material reality. While many authors write of the pleasures gained from formulating, reading or using theory, all of the pieces exhibit a belief that it is only useful if employed for interrogating assumptions and facilitating self-reflexive thought; when it attempts to become a totalizing, explanatory system or 'religion' contributors lose interest. In their engagements with the ways in which theory and postmodernism crisscross, a number of authors place the prefix 'post-'

under analysis, for example, 'post-theory' (hoogland), 'post-lesbian' (McNaron) and 'post-queer' (Schlichter, Noble) to name but three. Above all, contributors echo Bonnie Zimmerman's remark: "We need not set theories in competition one with the other, but recognize that the most interesting questions about theory may well be not what does it say, but how and why was it constructed."

In their considerations of identity, authors show that identity politics is very much a politics of the body. Thus, contributors chart the ways in which a body does not simply exist as a physical manifestation of the self (as if the self is a coherent entity), but is filtered through a prism of cultural assumptions that construct a body as normal or abnormal, depending on who is looking at it. And so, contributors point out how multiple physical signs are co-implicated in the formation of culturally-situated identities (Rivera-Fuentes). Pieces are concerned with how Critical Theory might help us to trace the embodiment, regulation and politicization of identities throughout history and in contemporary society. Many of the authors explore either directly or indirectly how bodies are constructed through discourse with the result that they become marked by race, (dis)ability, gender, sexuality and age. Some contributors explore the term 'body' in textual, geographical or genealogical terms. Others examine bodily performances from drag to self-conscious and unself-conscious, sought after and resisted modifications of the body (Holmes, Weiss). Many of the pieces ask overtly or in a more allusive way whether "any attempt to define a political, corporeal identity [might result] only in exclusion, hierarchy, silencing and oppression" (Inckle). In this way, the research gathered together here shows that it is important to consider embodiment from a number of perspectives (for example, medical, legal, educational, religious and cultural) and by using a variety of approaches (for example, Critical Race Studies, Postcolonial Theory, Psychoanalysis, Feminism, Disability Studies, Queer Theory and Gerontology). Thus, contributors are heavily invested in pursuing how intersectional thinking might lead to new avenues for working through identity, coalitional politics and scholarly work in Lesbian Studies (McCormack).

Many of the contributors are concerned with the politics of location–geographical, cultural, generational, disciplinary, temporal and political–in their engagements with the (hetero)norm generally and with the centers and margins of LGBTIQ Studies specifically (Schlichter). This collection is fortunate in having a number of pieces produced in or on locations outside of the US/UK axis which tends to occupy a hegemonic position vis-à-vis the output of research. It is telling that all of these pieces make reference to the "monopoly" (Engel) exercised by scholarly and activist work in Anglo/American contexts. While admitting that academic and activist efforts from the aforementioned have inspired and influenced work in India (Vanita), Thailand (Enteen), Germany and Europe more generally (Engel), Ireland (Giffney), Japan (Maree), the Netherlands (hoogland), Australia and New Zealand (MacBride-Stewart), Russia (Nartova) and Africa (Muthien), contributors are keen to differentiate research and direct-action politics produced in these regions from their counterparts in Britain and America. Pieces on India, Thailand, Japan and Africa also pose important questions about what the terms 'lesbian' and 'Lesbian Studies' might mean in non-Western contexts; indeed, whether they translate at all. These contributions should also give lesbian/queer scholars and activists pause for thought when waxing lyrical about the 'totalizing' effects of lesbian/queer, hetero/homo, academic/activist and essentialism/social constructionism binaries. In this, the aforementioned work points to what we in the West do not know; thus, contributors' efforts show that strategies resting on universalist principles will always fall short of the mark. These pieces, some written by authors whose first language is not English, also serve to highlight English's position as the hegemonic language of Language. The term, 'locations,' also suggests that disciplinary alignments and academic or activist credentials can play a part in whether one is listened to as opposed to just heard, and in which forums. This also rings through for political affiliations and self-identifications. In other words, contributors raise questions about who gets to speak 'as' or 'about' 'lesbians,' and to what effects? Some authors who have been involved in Lesbian Studies since its 'beginnings' exhibit anger and sadness at being misrepresented or silenced in discussions relating to Queer Theory in particular. As Margaret Cruikshank puts it, "While I do not begrudge younger LGBT scholars the career options now open to some of them, I would welcome recognition of the forerunners who, after all, produced theory ourselves." As one reads through the contributions it becomes especially evident the many potential avenues provided by the Internet for generating political alliances and facilitating dialogue between people from diverse geographical regions. In fact, it was through cyber-space that we initially made contact with contributors and later corresponded with them about their work.

All of the pieces have one striking thing in common: their oppositional relation to hetero-patriarchy. In this, an issue-based politics, attendant to the multivalent differences between and within groups, is forwarded implicitly by some, explicitly by others. Thus, contributors

writing on queer straight/lesbian, trans/lesbian, intersex/lesbian and bi-
sexual/lesbian interconnections seem to be responding already to
Michèle Aina Barale's tantalizing suggestion (and to her we give the
last word):

> . . . over the next four years every journal whose concern is sexual-
> ity [should] ask a pod of writers who do not usually read over one
> another's shoulders to do precisely that. Let five or six read the
> same text–new, old, in between–and write about it. Do that every
> year for half a decade and see where we are. I doubt that any of us
> will convert any of us. But I do suspect that such conversations in
> print will spur conversations elsewhere.

NOTES

1. The genealogy presented here is not meant to function as a comprehensive overview of the development of lesbian theorizing and political activism. Rather, it offers a
few plot markers in an effort to contextualize how Lesbian Studies in the Twenty-First
Century has been facilitated by the pioneering efforts of earlier generations.
2. Lesbian Studies in the Twenty-First Century has been facilitated by the many pioneering efforts of, for example, Wilton (1995); Cruikshank (1982); Jay and Glasgow
(1990); Zimmerman and McNaron (1996); Castle (1993); Garber (1994); Heller
(1997); Wolfe and Penelope (1993); Vanita (1996); Roof (1991); Card (1995);
Kitzinger (1987); Moraga and Anzaldúa (1984); Munt (1992); Abelove et al (1993);
Lorde (1984); Grahn (1985); Mintz and Rothblum (1997) to name but a handful.
3. Ti-Grace Atkinson's *Amazon Odyssey* chronicles her remarkable involvement
with radical feminism from 1967-72 and encapsulates in its brave and brilliant arc the
theoretical, political and artistic questions, strategies and achievements of political lesbianism. Atkinson's involvement ends as she founders on the rock of strict adherence
to separatism in supporting a male union leader and encounters virulent criticism from
other political lesbians. The book ends with an account of a scene she describes with
just the slightest hyperbole as 'Götterdämmerung', entitled "Self-Deception: AN
OPEN LETTER TO ALL THE COLLABORATORS IN 'SISTERS WILL TALK
ABOUT VIOLENCE IN THE WOMEN'S MOVEMENT'" (1974: cclix). The following two anthologies provide excellent introductions to the writings of radical lesbian
feminist separatism: Hoagland and Penelope (1988); Penelope and Wolfe (1993).
4. Linda Garber (2001) discusses the works of Judy Grahn, Pat Parker, Audre Lorde,
Adrienne Rich, and Gloria Anzaldúa as articulating not only critical lesbian feminist
theories and praxis but providing sophisticated interrogations of matters with which
queer theory currently grapples.
5. Simone de Beauvoir's *Le Deuzime sexe* (1988; orig. 1949) was quickly translated
into English. De Beauvoir explored Marxist, Freudian and Hegelian themes to uncover
the sources of the definition of women as the 'Other' of Man. Betty Friedan, a psychologist by training dedicated her book, *The Feminine Mystique*, (1963), to de Beauvoir
and led the Anglophone feminist critique of Sigmund Freud. Shulamith Firestone

opens her book *The Dialectic of Sex* (1974), with an engagement with De Beauvoir before making a Marxist analysis of women as a slave class and arguing for her freedom through complete control of reproductive technology a 'cybernetic socialism.' Kate Millet (1971) analyzed the representation of women in literature, the textual harassment of women, and marked the beginning of a new era of Feminist Literary Studies. Mary Daly's *The Church and the Second Sex* (1985) and *Beyond God the Father* (1986) moved from a devastating analysis of the misogyny of Christian religions to increasingly and poetically elaborate in her later books on the 'Background' of the 'Wild Reality' of women in contrast to the fake and sterile world of the foreground as conceived by the fathers.

6. References without quotations are to pieces in this volume.

7. Lesbian, Gay, Bisexual, Transgender, Transsexual, Intersex, Queer, Questioning, Affiliated.

8. We organized 'Lesbian Lives, Studies and Activism since *The Lesbian Postmodern*,' 13-15 February 2004; Sonja Tiernan, Mary McAuliffe and Linda Greene convened 'The Closet in Lesbian Lives, Studies and Activism', 11-13 February 2005. These conferences attracted hundreds of delegates from all over Ireland and various locations around the world, including Germany, Sweden, Australia, Italy, the UK, South Africa, the USA, Canada, Kenya, Belgium, Poland, France, Taiwan, Jamaica, Hungary, Portugal, Greece, Austria, Finland, Denmark, Norway and Spain. Over the course of three days, participants contributed to panels of academic papers, formal roundtable and informal community discussions and workshops, in addition to exhibiting their artwork, screening their films and performing their creative writings. As well as attending events at the university, delegates were treated to three days of community-organized entertainment, with a Jazz concert, a club-night and an afternoon cabaret put together by Susan Bailey. These conferences were not isolated events but the eleventh and twelfth in a series of Lesbian Lives conferences, hosted by the Women's Education, Research and Resource Centre (WERRC) at University College Dublin, Ireland since 1993.

REFERENCES

Abelove, Henry, Michèle Aina Barale and David M. Halperin, eds. *The Lesbian and Gay Studies Reader*. New York and London: Routledge, 1993.

Allison, Dorothy. *Skin: Talking About Sex, Class and Literature*. London: Pandora, 1995: 105-8.

Atkinson, Ti-Grace. *Amazon Odyssey*. New York: Links Books, 1974.

Brooten, Bernadette J. *Love Between Women: Early Christian Responses to Female Homoeroticism*. London and Chicago: University of Chicago Press, 1996.

Bunch, Charlotte. "Beyond Either/Or: Nonaligned Feminism", *Quest: A Feminist Quarterly*. 3(1), 1976: 2-17; later reprinted in Charlotte Bunch. *Passionate Politics: Feminist Theory in Action*. New York: St Martin's Press, 1987.

_____. "Not for Lesbians Only," *Quest, A Feminist Quarterly*, 2(2), 1975: 50-6; later reprinted in *Building Feminist Theory: Essays from Quest. A Feminist Quarterly*. New York and London: Longman, 1981.

Butler, Judith. *Gender Trouble: Feminism and the Subversion of Identity*. New York and London: Routledge, 1990.

_____. "Imitation and Gender Insubordination." In Diana Fuss, ed. *Inside/Out: Lesbian Theories, Gay Theories.* New York and London: Routledge, 1991: 13-31.

Card, Claudia. *Lesbian Choices.* New York: Columbia University Press, 1995.

Castle, Terry. *The Literature of Lesbianism: A Historical Anthology from Ariosto to Stonewall.* New York: Columbia University Press, 2003.

_____. *The Apparitional Lesbian: Female Homosexuality and Modern Culture.* New York: Columbia University Press, 1993.

Combahee River Collective. "A Black Feminist Statement" (1977). In Gloria T. Hull, Patricia Bell Scott and Barbara Smith, eds. *All the Women are White, All the Blacks Are Men, But Some of Us Are Brave: Black Women's Studies.* Old Westbury, New York: Feminist Press, 1982: 13-22.

Cruikshank, Margaret, ed. *Lesbian Studies: Present and Future.* New York: The Feminist Press, 1982.

Daly, Mary. *The Church and the Second Sex.* Boston: Beacon Press, 1985.

_____. *Beyond God the Father: Toward a Philosophy of Women's Liberation.* London: Women's Press, 1986.

De Beauvoir, Simone. *The Second Sex*, trans. and ed. H.M. Parshley. London: Pan Books, 1988; orig. 1949).

De Lauretis, Teresa. "The Essence of the Triangle or, Taking the Risk of Essentialism Seriously: Feminist Theory in Italy, the US and Britain," *differences: A Journal of Feminist Cultural Studies*, 1(2), 1989: 3-37.

Doan, Laura. "Preface". In Laura Doan, ed. *The Lesbian Postmodern.* New York: University of California Press, 1994: ix-xi.

Donoghue, Emma. *Passions Between Women: British Lesbian Culture 1668-1801.* New York: Harper Collins, 1993.

_____. *What Sappho Would Have Said: Four Centuries of Love Poems Between Women.* London: Hamish Hamilton, 1997.

Faderman, Lillian. *Chloe Plus Olivia: An Anthology of Lesbian Literature from the Seventeenth Century to the Present.* Harmondsworth: Penguin Books, 1994.

Firestone, Shulamith. *The Dialectic of Sex.* New York: William Morrow, 1974.

Foster, Jeannette, H. *Sex Variant Women in Literature*, 4th ed. Tallahassee, Florida: Naiad Press, 1985; orig. 1956.

Foucault, Michel. *The History of Sexuality, Volume 1: An Introduction*, trans. Robert Hurley. New York: Pantheon, 1978; orig. 1976.

Friedan, Betty. *The Feminine Mystique.* New York: W.W. Norton, 1963.

Fuss, Diana. *Essentially Speaking: Feminism, Nature and Difference.* London and New York: Routledge, 1990.

Garber, Linda, ed. *Tilting the Tower: Lesbians Teaching Queer Subjects.* New York and London: Routledge, 1994.

_____. *Identity Poetics: Race, Class, and the Lesbian-Feminist Roots of Queer Theory.* New York: Columbia University Press, 2001.

Gonda, Caroline. "Lesbian Theory." In Stevi Jackson and Jackie Jones, eds. *Contemporary Feminist Theories.* Edinburgh: Edinburgh University Press, 1998: 113-30.

Grahn, Judy. *The Highest Apple: Sappho and the Lesbian Poetic Tradition.* San Francisco: Spinsters Ink, 1985.

Haggerty, George E. and Bonnie Zimmerman, eds. *Professions of Desire: Lesbian and Gay Sexualities in Literature*. New York: The Modern Language Association of America, 1995.

Haraway, Donna J. "Situated Knowledges: The Science Question in Feminism and the Privilege of Partial Perspective," *Simians, Cyborgs, and Women: The Reinvention of Nature*. New York and London: Routledge, 1991: 183-201.

Heller, Dana, ed. *Cross-Purposes: Lesbians, Feminists, and the Limits of Alliance*. Bloomington and Indianapolis: Indiana University Press, 1997.

Hennegan, Alison. *The Lesbian Pillow Book*. London: Fourth Estate, 2000.

Hoagland, Sarah Luica and Julia Penelope, eds. *Not For Lesbians Only: A Separatist Anthology*. London: Onlywomen Press, 1988.

McIntosh, Mary. "The Homosexual Role," *Social Problems*, 16, 1968/9: 182-92.

Jay, Karla and Joanne Glasgow, eds. *Lesbian Texts and Contexts: Radical Revisions*. New York: New York University Press, 1990.

Johnston, Jill. *Lesbian Nation: The Feminist Solution*. New York: Simon and Schuster, 1973.

Kitzinger, Celia. *The Social Construction of Lesbianism*. London: Sage, 1987.

Lienert, Tania. "On Who is Calling Radical Feminists 'Cultural Feminists' and Other Historical Sleights of Hand." In Diane Bell and Renate Klein, eds. *Radically Speaking: Feminism Reclaimed*. London: Zed Books, 1996: 155-168.

Lister, Anne. *I Know My Own Heart: The Diaries of Anne Lister 1791-1840*, ed. Helena Whitbread. New York and London: New York University Press, 1988.

Lochrie, Karma. *Heterosyncrasies: Female Sexuality when Normal Wasn't*. Minneapolis and London: University of Minnesota Press, 2005.

Lorde, Audre. "An Open Letter to Mary Daly," *Sister Outsider: Essays and Speeches*. Freedom, California: The Crossing Press, 1984 : 66-71.

Millett, Kate. *Sexual Politics*. London: Hart-Davis, 1971.

Mintz, Beth and Esther Rothblum, eds. *Lesbians in Academia: Degrees of Freedom*. New York and London: Routledge, 1997.

Moraga, Cherríe and Gloria Anzaldúa, eds. *This Bridge Called My Back: Writings by Radical Women of Color*. New York: Kitchen Table/Women of Color Press, 1984.

Munt, Sally R. "Introduction." In Sally R. Munt, ed. *New Lesbian Criticism: Literary and Cultural Readings*. Hertfordshire: Harvester Wheatsheaf, 1992.

Nestle, Joan. *A Restricted Country*. Ithaca, New York: Firebrand Books, 1987.

Penelope, Julia and Susan Wolfe, eds. *Lesbian Culture: An Anthology*. Freedom, California: The Crossing Press, 1993.

Richardson, Diane. "'Misguided, Dangerous and Wrong': On the Maligning of Radical Feminism." In Diane Bell and Renate Klein, eds. *Radically Speaking: Feminism Reclaimed*. London: Zed Books, 1996: 143-54.

Roof, Judith. *A Lure of Knowledge: Lesbian Sexuality and Theory*. New York: Columbia University Press, 1991.

Smyth, Cherry. *Lesbians Talk Queer Notions*. London: Scarlet Press, 1992.

Swift, Jonathan. *Gulliver's Travels* (1719). Ware, Hertfordshire: Wordsworth Classics, 1992.

Traub, Valerie. *The Renaissance of Lesbianism in Early Modern England*. Cambridge: Cambridge University Press, 2002.

Vanita, Ruth and and Saleem Kidwai. *Same-Sex Love in India: Readings from Litera-ture and History*. New York: Palgrave Macmillan, 2000; New Delhi: Penguin, 2002.

_____. *Sappho and the Virgin Mary*: Same-Sex Love and the English Literary Imagi-nation. New York: Columbia University Press, 1996.

Wilton, Tamsin. *Lesbian Studies: Setting an Agenda*. New York and London: Routledge, 1995.

Wittig, Monique. *The Straight Mind and Other Essays*. New York: Harvester Wheatsheaf, 1992.

Wolfe, Susan J. and Julia Penelope, eds. *Sexual Practice, Textual Theory: Lesbian Cul-tural Criticism*. Oxford: Blackwell, 1993.

Zimmerman, Bonnie, ed. *Lesbian Histories and Cultures: An Encyclopedia*. New York and London: Garland Publishing, Inc., 2000.

_____ and Toni A.H. McNaron, eds. *The New Lesbian Studies: Into the Twenty-First Century*. New York: The Feminist Press, 1996.

doi:10.1300/J155v11n01_01

SECTION I

GENEALOGIES: CONTEXTUALIZING THE FIELD

I have been more interested in inviting us to continue imagining where we might go next with the genealogical project rather than figuring out why we have been complacent about the genealogy of Lesbian Studies and allowed one monolithic version to dominate for so long. Perhaps we have been too busily engaged in other important work to take much notice or overly preoccupied with the subject of 'identity.' There can be little doubt, however, that continued over-investment in the collision model [of Lesbian Studies versus Queer Theory] will hinder the success of Lesbian Studies in the decade to come. There may be no question more central to the future of Lesbian Studies than, 'how do we tell our own story?' And such a telling would, I hope, consist of multiple versions from various perspectives.

–Laura Doan

Lesbian Studies After
The Lesbian Postmodern:
Toward a New Genealogy

Laura Doan

SUMMARY. While Lesbian Studies is established as a commodity in the academic marketplace, its disciplinary contours are rather more obscure–and even more problematically, its disciplinary genealogy remains somewhat crude. The dominant genealogy of Lesbian Studies might best be characterized as a 'collision model,' a battle between politics and theory, even though much existing scholarship draws on both Lesbian-Feminist Theory and Queer Theory.[1] This article proposes that the tools and methods of a sub-field called 'Lesbian Cultural History' might be useful in generating other historical accounts of the origins and evolution of Lesbian Studies. Such a project is vi-

---

Laura Doan is Professor of Cultural History and Sexuality Studies at the University of Manchester, where she teaches in English and American Studies and co-directs the Centre for the Study of Sexuality and Culture.

Address correspondence to: Professor Laura Doan, English and American Studies, School of Arts, Histories and Cultures, The University of Manchester, Oxford Road, Manchester, M13 9PL, UK (E-mail: Laura.doan@manchester.ac.uk).

The author wishes to thank Bev Skeggs, Jackie Stacey, Chris Waters and the co-editors of this volume for their extremely helpful feedback on earlier drafts of this article.

[Haworth co-indexing entry note]: "Lesbian Studies After *The Lesbian Postmodern*: Toward a New Genealogy." Doan, Laura. Co-published simultaneously in *Journal of Lesbian Studies* (Harrington Park Press, an imprint of The Haworth Press, Inc.) Vol. 11, No. 1/2, 2007, pp. 21-35; and: *Twenty-First Century Lesbian Studies* (ed: Noreen Giffney, and Katherine O'Donnell) Harrington Park Press, an imprint of The Haworth Press, Inc., 2007, pp. 21-35. Single or multiple copies of this article are available for a fee from The Haworth Document Delivery Service [1-800-HAWORTH, 9:00 a.m. - 5:00 p.m. (EST). E-mail address: docdelivery@haworthpress.com].

Available online at http://jls.haworthpress.com
doi:10.1300/J155v11n01_02

tal because the writing of our disciplinary History clarifies how we envision a disciplinary future. doi:10.1300/J155v11n01_02 *[Article copies available for a fee from The Haworth Document Delivery Service: 1-800-HAWORTH. E-mail address: <docdelivery@haworthpress.com> Website: <http://www.HaworthPress. com> © 2007 by The Haworth Press, Inc. All rights reserved.]*

KEYWORDS. Lesbian Studies, disciplinary genealogy, 'politics versus theory,' lesbian cultural history

History can have another shape, articulated through differences that matter. (Haraway, 1992: 98)

I

Ten years have passed since the publication of a collection of fourteen essays theorizing the complex relationship between, as I described in the preface, two "highly contested" terms: "lesbian" and "postmodern" (Doan, 1994: ix). For some lesbian feminists at that time merely proposing coupling of these words was troubling enough. How, they asked, could contemporary lesbian culture be situated within a postmodern theoretical context in order to critique heteropatriarchal hegemony? Sheila Jeffreys, for instance, thought the project's attempt to *"fit lesbianism* into masculine systems of thought" deeply misguided (Jeffreys 1996: 281, emphasis mine). Yet, for others, this new direction in Lesbian Studies, with its provocative excursions into queer and postmodern theories, generated considerable excitement. A panel of papers delivered on the "lesbian postmodern" at the 1991 Modern Language Association in San Francisco attracted such a large and enthusiastic audience that it had to be shifted in mid-session to a ballroom with a capacity of over 300, and other sessions on similar topics were lively and exhilarating affairs. At the very least, such divergent responses indicate that fitting lesbians into the academy has not been a straightforward affair.

Looking back, the early 1990s were something of a heyday for what had come to be known as 'Lesbian Studies,' with publishers eager to satisfy readers' demands for innovative work in areas such as Lesbian Theory, Visual Culture, Literary Representation, Politics, Legal Theory and History. According to the historians of our small field, Lesbian

Studies grew out of Lesbian Feminism in the early 1980s, with the publication of Margaret Cruikshank's pioneering volume, *Lesbian Studies: Present and Future* (1982). In just a few years, the production of edited collections burgeoned: in 1991 literary critic Diana Fuss published her highly influential *Inside/Out: Lesbian Theories, Gay Theories*; in 1992 cultural critic Sally R. Munt made a significant addition with *New Lesbian Criticism: Literary and Cultural Readings*; and in 1993 the massive–and now classic–*Lesbian and Gay Studies Reader* appeared, edited by Henry Abelove, Michèle Barale and David Halperin. And this is to single out only a handful. That once mad clamor by publishers for work on any aspect of lesbian life or culture has now slowed down, but new scholarship grappling with the 'lesbian' or 'lesbianism' as a subject and object of academic scrutiny continues to be steadily promoted in publishers' catalogs, listed in any number of ways: under a heading of its own, or placed in the larger fields of Lesbian and Gay Studies or Sexuality Studies, or within a specific discipline. In fact, working out the politics of location is something of an interesting pastime in bookshops, with new contributions to Lesbian Studies popping up in Gender Studies, Sociology, History, Literary Studies, Visual Arts, Psychology or where we might least suspect it, as when one chain bookstore placed one of my co-edited volumes on the history of sexuality in their section on 'Intimacy'–shrink-wrapped, no less (Bland and Doan, 1998).

While Lesbian Studies has become fairly well established as a commodity in the academic marketplace, even if its location is unpredictable, its disciplinary contours are rather more obscure–and even more problematically, its disciplinary genealogy remains somewhat crude. In the mid-'90s there were three helpful attempts to make sense of this growing body of work: one single-authored book, Tamsin Wilton's *Lesbian Studies: Setting an Agenda* (1995); and two edited collections, Bonnie Zimmerman and Toni McNaron's *The New Lesbian Studies: Into the Twenty-First Century* (1996) and Gabriele Griffin and Sonya Andermahr's *Straight Studies Modified: Lesbian Interventions in the Academy* (1997). A common theme running through this body of work was that the highly fluid boundaries between the cognate disciplines of Women's Studies, Lesbian and Gay Studies or Queer Studies, had made it all the more difficult to understand 'Lesbian Studies' as a coherent academic discipline; so that, as Wilton explains, the very proposition of studying "lesbians and lesbian issues" raised "a deluge of doubts, queries and contradictions" (1995: 10). As with Women's Studies and African-American Studies, to cite other fields with roots in identity politics, Lesbian Studies was under considerable institutional and community pressure to be all things to all people, as it seemed wonderfully positioned to negotiate the interconnections of gender and sexuality, of sexism and heterosexism. This is a tall order for a field of inquiry with barely a toehold in mainstream academe, and rendered all the more challenging as we endeavored to remain responsive to the demands of 'politics' yet also engage with the cutting edge of 'theory.' These tensions came to be understood as an irreconcilable binary; while a political agenda demanded change in the material conditions of actual lives, theory appeared to undermine the stability of any self-understanding on which identity politics were based. If, in theory, a lesbian was always and already a 'lesbian,' that is, discursively unstable and shifting in terms of signifiers, political action is imperiled. No sexual practice, behavior, act or identity is fixed or locatable to enact that agenda. Implicit, then, in the formulation of 'politics versus theory' was the mistaken expectation that both should perform the same cultural work and use the same critical tools.

No sooner did this emerging field of Lesbian Studies begin to acquire academic respectability when, from the perspective of some lesbian feminists, the rug was pulled out from underneath its practitioners: the humanist assumptions on which the field was initially based (above all, the investment in the notion of a single unified sexual subject) were challenged by Queer Theory, which unsettled and destabilized categories of identity. For theorists such as Judith Butler "identity categories" were thought "to be instruments of regulatory regimes, whether as the normalizing categories of oppressive structures or as the rallying points for a liberatory contestation of that very oppression" (1991: 13-14). Here, in a nutshell, is an account of how this all happened, as concisely summarized by Sonya Andermahr:

> Since the emergence of second wave feminism in the 1960s there has been a vigorous–and sometimes rancorous–struggle for the sign 'lesbian' and it has become *commonplace* to rehearse the distinction between two critical paradigms . . . radical feminism (in anglophone and francophone forms) and queer theory . . . While the former emphasizes identity politics . . . the latter foregrounds difference, subversion and marginality. (1997: 11, emphasis mine)

Thus the genealogy of Lesbian Studies has been characterized as a 'collision model,' a battle between the pure and impure, Lesbian Feminism versus Queer Theory, even though that version of events may not adequately represent what most practitioners actually achieved in their writing and teaching. Admittedly, the model has always been seductively convenient and utterly serviceable, and it has had an impressively long shelf life which has lent it a certain credibility. And, obviously, when a story is told often enough, it is hard *not* to believe it, even if this version of events–our 'genealogy'–does not match up with actual critical practice.

Recently, this familiar version of the history of Lesbian Studies–one that assisted in generating more controversy than understanding–has come under scrutiny. Critic Linda Garber, for instance, argues convincingly that the "either/or choice of lesbian feminism versus queer theory" must be treated with skepticism: "The point is not that one is right and the other wrong", she strenuously asserts, "nor that one type of theory is smarter or more sophisticated than the other, but that either taken alone leaves great patches of the theoretical canvas bare" (2001: 6, 7). Garber's mapping of the lesbian-feminist roots of Queer Theory via the writings of "working-class/lesbians of color" is quite suggestive; however, if we are really intent on dislodging this now calcified origin narrative, and keen to develop more nuanced, complex accounts of the history of our interventions into the academy and our own critical practices, we must be open to other possible trajectories from multiple perspectives. Let me make it clear at the outset that the purpose of this article is not to manufacture a *new* genealogy–my objective is far more modest. What I wish to propose here is that–in this cultural moment of the post-'lesbian postmodern'–an eclectic and interdisciplinary subfield called 'Lesbian Cultural History' might generate other insightful and sophisticated historical accounts of the origins and evolution of Lesbian Studies. Such a project is vital not only because it is important to get things right–but because the writing of our disciplinary history also clarifies how we envision a disciplinary future.

II

Let me begin with some recollections about my experiences as a lesbian and as a lesbian academic at about the time I began to conceive of *The Lesbian Postmodern*. There was certainly a political dimension to my involvement in a scholarly endeavor that I thought allowed "lesbian theorists, writers and artists" to explore "multiple strategies of resistance" by seeing "the 'lesbian' as a powerful destabilizing agent of political culture and discourse" (Doan 1994: xi). When I wrote the preface to *The Lesbian Postmodern* I happily anticipated that the volume would stimulate debate among those with an interest in exploring 'lesbian' lived experience and cultural representation from a postmodernist perspective. I did not, however, foresee how this essay collection would seamlessly fit (then and now) into a genealogy which, for all its frayed edges, continued to make sense because the hostility expressed by *some* lesbian feminists toward Queer Theory has been intense and lingering, despite Judith Halberstam's persuasive call for a "queer lesbian studies" (1996). In one of the more polemical critiques of the lesbian engagement with Queer Theory, Jeffreys concludes her passionate, if contentious, review of *The Lesbian Postmodern* with the plaintive claim that "it will not help end the pain of lesbians to define their experience in the concepts of male theorists who have erased lesbian existence and helped create the hatred of women's bodies which is now being so ruthlessly enacted" (1996: 285). This stark passage illustrates perfectly the ubiquity of the "either/or choice," to return to Garber's critique, a choice in which "one is right and the other wrong." What happens, though, if we look at the terms of the binary in ways other than oppositional, as Halberstam intriguingly proposes. If the term "lesbian," she suggests, "modifies and qualifies 'queer,' and 'queer' is a term capable of challenging the stability of identities subsumed by the label 'lesbian'" (1996: 259), might the critical frameworks of both Lesbian-Feminist Theory *and* Queer Theory elucidate lived experience, and thus together facilitate an illuminating analysis that would work toward political ends? Looking at a specific historical example from my own life experience might test such a proposition.

In the 1980s I landed my first academic job at a southern Baptist university in central Florida. After four years of being 'out and proud' during my time in graduate school in Chicago, for the sake of financial survival I retreated back into the closet–or so I had thought. Virtually none of my colleagues, in my six years of teaching there, seemed to draw any inferences from the fact that I had moved to Florida with another woman or that I was unmarried. Some of our neighbors, though, were faster on the uptake, and one day I opened the door to greet my landlord, who told me that he thought the bumper sticker on the back of our car was quite amusing. As we'd never put a bumper sticker on our car, I didn't get the 'joke,' until I realized that someone had plastered an ad for the "Doll's House" on our Toyota–not a reference to Henrik Ibsen, as you might have momentarily wondered, but to an establishment featuring live nude female dancers. Just as Ibsen anatomizes the dreadful results of the cultural containment of female autonomy, so too did the labeling of sexuality signified by the taunting placement of the bumper sticker–ironically advertising the objectification of the female body for male sexual pleasure–work to contain and police what must have registered for the perpetrator as deviant in that otherwise quiet neighborhood. For the next month or so, we would often return home to find pornographic magazines scattered all over our lawn or, even more intrusively, slipped under our front door. Finally, one Saturday morning, I went out to collect the post to discover that placed on the top of our rural mailbox was a limp, semen-saturated condom. This was when the silly pranks started to feel more like sexual threats, and so we moved.

The experience of being hounded out of a neighborhood–the object of (presumably) male sexual fantasy–was more than unpleasant, but we possessed both the resources to relocate and the tools of political analysis from our Chicago days in a 'lesbian feminist community,' which helped us to understand that we may have been perceived as a threat to male sexual domination. A queer reading of this experience disentangles the peculiar nature of the harassment, to see that we weren't simply or merely the more or less straightforward victims of social policing or homophobia. The hate campaign against us had not consisted of bricks or eggs or mud hurled at our door, but took forms associated with male pleasure and desire, as seen in the ever shifting set of signifiers (the bumper sticker, the porn magazines, the condom), meaning that the lesbian body provoked hatred and fascination, repulsion and attraction, danger and excitement, threat and turn-on. Turning both interpretive frameworks on this brief account of harassment illustrates how nothing in our understanding of how Lesbian Studies has evolved can account for how the political analysis of Lesbian Feminism and the cultural analysis of Queer Theory work not in opposition to one another, but with complementarity.

When the English Department at the State University of New York offered me a job in the early 1990s, I made a point upon my departure from the South of 'coming out' to many of my Florida colleagues, and I left that oppressive environment with a commitment never to be closeted again in my work or daily life, and to be far more politically active in the profession and in my own scholarship; hence the willingness to move–as did Jeffreys, incidentally–from the study of spinsters to Lesbian Cultural Criticism. I now find it quite ironic that my own engagement with a conceptual terrain called the "lesbian postmodern" evolved from a political commitment to 'come out' as a professional lesbian. The act of 'coming out'–"a crucial political and psychic rallying point for gay men, *lesbians*, and queers within modernity," Valerie Traub writes–is inevitably bound up in humanist assumptions at loggerheads with Poststructuralist Theory (2002: 343). Such a political gesture is predicated, as I have already indicated, on the assumption that there is a single, coherent, intelligible sexual identity willing to be exposed to the exterior world. What Poststructuralist Theory challenges, though, is the humanist belief that a "sovereign subject" exists in the first place; as feminist political theorist Wendy Brown explains, "our nervousness about moving toward . . . postmodern political theory" emerges from the feminist anxiety of "giving up the ground of specifically *moral* claims against domination . . . and moving instead into the domain of the sheerly political" (Traub 2002: 342; Brown 1991: 75). In thinking that I could do political work in editing *The Lesbian Postmodern* I was simultaneously divesting and investing in the categories of identity–deploying theories that unsettled and destabilized identity, on behalf of a political agenda coextensive with the same lesbian feminists who have vigorously challenged Queer Theory.

Yet perhaps this isn't as strange as it sounds. As an intellectual project, Lesbian Studies has proven flexible and resilient in grappling with overlapping and even conflicting aims, as my own politicized interventions with Lesbian Cultural Studies show, but the dominant representation of our disciplinary history–with its marked tendency to construct these different critical methodologies and analytical frameworks as fundamentally oppositional–has been considerably less adept at conveying a sense of the field's interdisciplinarity or its capacity to cross over factional lines. As a result, the discipline has been characterized as being overly preoccupied with the tensions arising between politics and theory or Radical Lesbian Feminism and Queer, which has not been without intellectual cost. This, despite the fact that much of the work in the field has always been informed–to a greater or lesser extent–by both Lesbian Feminist *and* Queer Theories, so that the polarity of the 'either/or' proposition at the heart of the dominant genealogical account of the discipline has been less than competent in conveying the actual working practices within Lesbian Studies. Some recent work operating at the nexus of Cultural Studies, Modernist Studies and the history of sexuality, is already remapping possible alternative genealogies, thus pointing to the ways politics and theory intersect rather than collide. In this highly interdisciplinary scholarship, I discern evidence to support Griffin and Andermahr's optimistic view that "the mobilization of diverse discourses by lesbians, including radical feminism, social constructionism and queer, suggests that 'theory' *as* 'practice' has become more visible in the academy and has widened rather than narrowed the range" (1997: 6-7). Their project–*Straight Studies Modified*–highlights how

Lesbian Studies has made strategic interventions into traditional disciplines such as Film, History, Education, Biology, Computing, Psychology, Geography, Health Studies, and so on. Lesbian Studies, though, also stretches across disciplinary boundaries, and one area in particular, what I have termed 'Lesbian Cultural History'—a sub-field related to 'Lesbian Cultural Studies'—seems especially promising in rewriting our genealogy.

Lesbian Cultural Studies has been successful in negotiating Lesbian-Feminist Theory and Queer Theory to make significant political and intellectual contributions by its willingness to explore lived cultural experiences and mass cultural production, and to question rigorously the assumption of heteronormativity. Take *The Lesbian Postmodern*, for instance, where a number of essayists draw on important insights from Queer Theory to range over a wide aesthetic field, taking a serious look at topics such as Barbie-as-dildo or lesbian icons like Madonna, Sandra Bernhard and Jodie Foster. With its focus on the 'now,' Lesbian Cultural Studies has also produced exciting work on drag-king phenomena, butch-femme roles, lesbian 'zines and lesbians in sports, to cite a few other examples. Some lesbian cultural critics have found a rich terrain for the analysis of lesbian subjectivities in contemporary culture but, as Andermahr makes clear, while this field has had "to grapple with contemporary contestations of the sign 'lesbian,' unlike history, [it] does not have to address the problem of whether 'we existed *then*'" (1997: 9). This is where I see a problem in terms of the sub-field's potential to contribute to a new genealogical project.

To be sure, there are important exceptions to such ahistoricism within Lesbian Cultural Studies, as evident in Halberstam's groundbreaking study, *Female Masculinity* (1998), and in her argument elsewhere that Lesbian Studies must recognize "historical shifts within the social meaning of sexuality" (1996: 260). And, oddly enough, despite the lack of interest on the part of many lesbian cultural critics in questions pertaining to History, as historian Alison Oram comments, "much of the current academic work on lesbian history in the UK is not conducted within the discipline of history at all, but in related fields such as English literature and within cultural studies generally" (1997: 177). What kind of Lesbian History have lesbian cultural critics produced? Turning to my own specific area of interest, much of the historical investigation of the social, cultural, political or legal forces at play in the formation of an English lesbian subculture in the decades between the world wars has been somewhat problematic.[2] For one thing, few cultural critics undertake, as Martha Vicinus puts it, "the painstaking excavational work necessary to understand the variety of women's sexual subjectivities," and so too often much work on English lesbian subcultures in this period has been based on secondary rather than primary sources (1994: 57). With the absence of systematic and thorough archival research, familiar myths continually re-circulate about, for example, the role of sexology in the stigmatizing or legislating of same-sex relations between women or the extent of homophobia in the print media in the decade after the First World War. Secondly, not only have such accounts been unable to shake off these persistent cultural myths, but few studies have been attentive to national specificity–and, as I've argued elsewhere, there's no reason to assume that the sexual subcultures of Paris, for instance, were similar to those of Berlin or New York. A third tendency is that lesbian cultural critics have been over-reliant on modern categories of identity, and thus haven't recognized that the word 'lesbian' might not have held the same cultural meaning at earlier points in the Twentieth Century. It is commonplace, for example, to pick up lesbian histories that juxtapose well-known lesbian couples of the 1920s with butch/femme couples of the late 1950s, without acknowledging the very different kinds of subjectivities and political climates in place at specific times.

Of course, if sexual desire is embedded in social relations (including gender, race, class and nation), the "problem of whether 'we existed *then*'" cannot be so readily overlooked or sidestepped; however, while there are, as I've already mentioned, critics who situate sexuality within History, such work is too seldom based on a trawl through the archives.[3] Hence, my interest in Lesbian Cultural History, in which practitioners draw on the tools of historical inquiry, the theoretical strengths of Lesbian Cultural Studies and Queer Theory, and research methodologies of different disciplines.[4] In short, I would see Lesbian Cultural History as well positioned "to reveal connections," a phrase I take from Peter Burke's *Varieties of Cultural History*, in which he writes: "The *raison d'être* of a cultural historian is surely *to reveal connections* between different activities. If this task is impossible, one might as well leave architecture to the historians of architecture, psychoanalysis to the historians of psychoanalysis, and . . ."–here I take the liberty of extending his analogy–one might as well leave lesbianism to the historians of lesbianism (1997: 201). The most glaringly obvious problem with leaving the topic of lesbianism to the historians of lesbianism is that–at the moment, anyway–there are only a handful of such individuals in universities around the world publishing major studies specifically in this area. Instead, I would envision 'Lesbian Cultural History' as a practice akin to what's been termed the 'New Modernist Studies,' which is closely re-

lated to a North American version of Cultural Studies, but where scholars of modernist cultural production work within a historical framework
based on archival research.

Practitioners of the New Modernist Studies take a more interdisciplinary approach to cultural analysis to contextualize cultural production socially and politically. As Rita Felski explains, in her
consideration of the field specifically within the North American context, such scholars have been influenced profoundly by two distinctive
ideas that define the Cultural Studies approach. The first of these is "an
expanded notion of the aesthetic field," and the second–one far more
difficult to summarize succinctly–is a "theory of articulation," which
Felski defines as "a theory of social correspondences, non-correspon-
dences, and contradictions or alternatively as a theory of how contexts
are made, unmade, and re-made" (2003: 504, 511). For Cultural Studies, Felski continues:

> . . . culture is neither organically unified nor radically fragmented
> and dispersed; rather, it is a multi-jointed and multi-hinged com-
> posite of often disparate elements. Articulation thus seeks to ex-
> plain how segments of the social field may join together to form
> temporary unities. (511)

It is in the act of interpretation, then, that we see most vividly key differences: "Rather than reading *into* texts, cultural studies seeks to read
across texts" (2003: 512).

To characterize the preeminent interpretive method of new modernist
studies, Felski introduces what she calls "political formalism," which
consists of "a loose assemblage of reading techniques that are selec-
tively deployed in approaches ranging from neo-Marxism to feminism
to queer theory" (509). At the risk of oversimplification, this method refers to the deployment of the skills of "close reading," using "a formida-
ble array of analytical devices" (510). Above all, however: "This textual
hypervigilence is understood as not just aesthetic work, but also as political work . . . [and] can thus lead deep into the labyrinthian workings
of power" (510). This last point, from the perspective of reformulating
the genealogy of Lesbian Studies, is absolutely crucial, because it
would seem to offer a foundation on which to understand 'politics and
theory' not as oppositional, but as constitutive. What I'm calling 'Lesbian Cultural History', then, draws productively on these two key ideas
of Cultural Studies (the wide "aesthetic field" and a "model of articula-

tion," to return to Felski's terms), but situates individual texts within a larger historical framework, and subjects them to sustained and rigorous close reading. Additionally, Lesbian Cultural History shares one of the aims of Lesbian History, which is, as Traub notes, "to probe the contingency and incommensurability of contemporary identities" (2002: 327).

In my own work on modern lesbian subcultural development within English modernity, *Fashioning Sapphism* (2001), such an approach seems to have worked well. I investigated the lives of lesbians of the past by engaging–or connecting–with a range of other areas of inquiry, such as Medicine, Psychology, Sexology, Law, Visual Studies and Fashion, to demonstrate the importance of interdisciplinarity in tracking an increasingly visible subculture. Specifically, Radclyffe Hall's 1928 novel *The Well of Loneliness* operates as a hub, with spokes moving out into diverse subject areas, based on a reading of public and private documents, such as parliamentary records, diaries, letters and newspaper accounts. This methodology enabled me to unsettle many of the received understandings of Lesbian History, producing a revisionist intervention into terrain well trodden by others.

In my view, Lesbian Cultural History–its tools and methodologies–offers us *one* way to move beyond the 'collision model' that has so stymied the genealogy of Lesbian Studies. I would emphasize, however, that this is just one approach, and that there may be intellectual approaches that would be equally dynamic in drawing out strategic connections between disciplines, by scholars who likewise subject texts to close reading, and who situate their readings within larger social, cultural and political frameworks, based on primary and archival sources. Terry Castle, for instance, in a brilliant introduction to her recent anthology, *The Literature of Lesbianism*, breaks new ground in positing how 'lesbian intellectual history' might propel us well beyond the weary debates of who counts as a lesbian, the woman who acts on her sexual desires but writes mediocre prose *or* the woman who rarely sleeps with other women but writes exquisitely of Sapphic love? Castle wryly comments: "Must we conclude that [Vita] Sackville-West was a lesbian and Woolf not? Or that Sackville-West was somehow *more* of a lesbian than Woolf? If so, by how much?" (2003: 5). Instead, she proposes a boldly innovative approach in defining 'lesbian' or 'lesbianism' in tracing, as she puts it, "How (and when) did it first become possible in modern Western culture to *think* about erotic desire between women?" (5-6). Her strategy is to examine "lesbianism-as-theme . . . as site of collective imaginative inquiry, as topic of cultural conversation" (6). The concern, in other words, is on the lesbian as 'idea'; such a move could generate a provocative new formulation of our disciplinary genealogy.

In this article I have been more interested in inviting us to continue imagining where we might go next with the genealogical project rather than figuring out why we have been complacent about the genealogy of Lesbian Studies and allowed one monolithic version to dominate for so long. Perhaps we have been too busily engaged in other important work to take much notice or overly preoccupied with the subject of 'identity.' There can be little doubt, however, that continued over-investment in the collision model will hinder the success of Lesbian Studies in the decade to come. There may be no question more central to the future of Lesbian Studies than, "how do we tell our own story?" And such a telling would, I hope, consist of multiple versions from various perspectives, since, as Carolyn Steedman reminds us, "written history is a story that can only be told by the implicit understanding that *things are not over*, that the story isn't finished, can never be finished" (1993: 614). Exploring lesbian lives, cultures, identities and politics from diverse theoretical approaches has helped to shift questions about the complex interplay between gender and sexuality from the margins to the center. Emerging from the fruitful interactions of Cultural Studies, Modernist Studies, the New Cultural History, and Queer Theory, a 'Lesbian Cultural History' approach would be one method by which we could begin to write the genealogy of Lesbian Studies, as we continue to pose new questions about lesbian lives.

NOTES

1. For further discussion on how Lesbian Feminism became linked with politics and Queer Theory with theory only, see Griffin and Andermahr (1997); Duggan (1995, 1998); Garber (2001); Vicinus (1994).

2. Elsewhere I discuss in greater detail problems in earlier accounts of interwar lesbian subcultural developments in English national culture, see my *Fashioning Sapphism* (2001), particularly the introduction (xi-xxiii).

3. It should be noted, however, that historians of lesbian lives and cultures are increasingly undertaking extensive archival research, as seen in Vicinus (2004) or Jennings (Unpub. Manuscript).

4. Carolyn Dinshaw similarly rethinks how we generate new historical models and/or disciplinary genealogies in her call for a "tactile" history, which is facilitated by our "getting medieval": "The process of touching, of making partial connections between incommensurate entities . . .using ideas of the past, creating relations with the past" (1999: 54, 206).

REFERENCES

Abelove, Henry, Michèle Aina Barale and David Halperin, eds. *The Lesbian and Gay Studies Reader*. New York: Routledge, 1993.

Andermahr, Sonya. "'There's Nowt So Queer as Folk': Lesbian Cultural Studies". In Gabriele Griffin and Sonya Andermahr, eds. *Straight Studies Modified: Lesbian Interventions in the Academy*. London and Washington: Cassell, 1997: 8-23.

Bland, Lucy and Laura Doan, eds. *Sexology Uncensored: The Documents of Sexual Science*. Chicago: The University of Chicago Press, 1998.

Brown, Wendy. "Feminist Hesitations, Postmodern Exposures," *differences*, 3(1), 1991: 63-83.

Burke, Peter. *Varieties of Cultural History*. Oxford: Polity Press, 1997.

Butler, Judith. "Imitation and Gender Insubordination". In Diana Fuss, ed. *Inside/Out: Lesbian Theories, Gay Theories*. London: Routledge, 1991: 13-31.

Castle, Terry, ed. *The Literature of Lesbianism: A Historical Anthology from Ariosto to Stonewall*. New York: Columbia University Press, 2003.

Cruikshank, Margaret. *Lesbian Studies: Present and Future*. New York: The Feminist Press, 1982.

Dinshaw, Carolyn. *Getting Medieval: Sexualities and Communities, Pre- and Postmodern*. Durham: Duke University Press, 1999.

Doan, Laura. *Fashioning Sapphism: The Origins of a Modern English Lesbian Culture*. New York: Columbia University Press, 2001.

_____. ed. *The Lesbian Postmodern*. New York: Columbia University Press, 1994.

Duggan, Lisa. "Making It Perfectly Queer". In Lisa Duggan and Nan D. Hunter. *Sex Wars: Essays in Sexual Dissent and American Politics*. New York: Routledge, 1995: 155-72.

_____. "Theory in Practice: The Theory Wars, or, Who's Afraid of Judith Butler?" *Journal of Women's History*, 10(1), 1998: 9-19.

Felski, Rita. "Modernist Studies and Cultural Studies: Reflections on Method," *Modernism/Modernity*, 10(3), 2003: 501-17.

Fuss, Diana, ed. *Inside/Out: Lesbian Theories, Gay Theories*. London: Routledge, 1991.

Garber, Linda. *Identity Poetics: Race, Class, and the Lesbian Feminist Roots of Queer Theory*. New York: Columbia University Press, 2001.

Griffin, Gabriele and Sonya Andermahr, eds. *Straight Studies Modified: Lesbian Interventions in the Academy*. London and Washington: Cassell, 1997.

Halberstam, Judith. *Female Masculinity*. Durham: Duke University Press, 1998.

_____. "Queering Lesbian Studies." In Bonnie Zimmerman and Toni A.H. McNaron, eds. *The New Lesbian Studies: Into the Twenty-First Century*. New York: The Feminist Press, 1996: 256-61.

Haraway, Donna. "Ecce Homo, Ain't (Ar'n't) I a Woman, and Inappropriate/d Others: The Human in a Post-humanist Landscape." In Judith Butler and Joan W. Scott, eds. *Feminists Theorize the Political*. New York: Routledge, 1992: 86-100.

Jeffreys, Sheila. "Perverse Desire and the Postmodern Lesbian," *Women's History Review*. 5(2), 1996: 281-5.

Jennings, Rebecca. *Tomboys and Bachelor Girls: Narrating the Lesbian in Post-War Britain* (Unpub. Manuscript).

Munt, Sally R., ed. *New Lesbian Criticism: Literary and Cultural Readings*. Hemel Hempstead: Harvester Wheatsheaf, 1992.

Oram, Alison. "'Friends', Feminists and Sexual Outlaws: Lesbianism and British History." In Gabrielle Griffin and Sonya Andermahr, eds. *Straight Studies Modified: Lesbian Interventions in the Academy*. London and Washington: Cassell, 1997: 168-83.

Steedman, Carolyn. "Culture, Cultural Studies, and Historians." In Lawrence Grossberg, Cary Nelson and Paula A. Treichler, eds. *Cultural Studies*. New York and London: Routledge, 1993: 613-22.

Traub, Valerie. *The Renaissance of Lesbianism in Early Modern England*. Cambridge: Cambridge University Press, 2002.

Vicinus, Martha. *Intimate Friends: Women Who Loved Women, 1778-1928*. Chicago and London: The University of Chicago Press, 2004.

_____. "Lesbian History: All Theory and No Facts or All Facts and No Theory?" *Radical History Review*, 60, 1994: 57-75.

Wilton, Tamsin. *Lesbian Studies: Setting an Agenda*. London and New York: Routledge, 1995.

Zimmerman, Bonnie and Toni A.H. McNaron, eds. *The New Lesbian Studies: Into the Twenty-First Century*. New York: The Feminist Press, 1996.

doi:10.1300/J155v11n01_02

A Lesbian-Feminist Journey Through Queer Nation

Bonnie Zimmerman

SUMMARY. This article is an auto-ethnographical review of the political experiences and literary career of one of the early lesbian feminist critics and theorists. It poses the question: what does it mean to be shaped by one theoretical and political discourse (Lesbian Feminism) and then thrust by historical change into another (Queer Theory)? With the author's life and work as a frame and exemplar, it illustrates the de-

Bonnie Zimmerman is Professor of Women's Studies and Associate Vice President for Faculty Affairs at San Diego State University. She has been active in the women's and lesbian movements since 1969. As a graduate student, she helped to found the women's studies program at the University of Buffalo, and she began teaching Women's Studies at SDSU in 1978. She has taught several lesbian courses in the Women's Studies and English Departments, and has also been instrumental in developing the university's LGBT Studies program. She has published over two dozen articles, including "What Has Never Been: An Overview of Lesbian Feminist Literary Criticism" (1981), which has been included in *The Norton Anthology of Theory and Criticism*. She is also the author of *The Safe Sea of Women: Lesbian Fiction 1969-1989* (1990), and editor of *Professions of Desire: Lesbian and Gay Studies in Literature* (1995), *The New Lesbian Studies: Into the Twenty-First Century* (1996) and *Lesbian Histories and Cultures: An Encyclopedia* (2000). In 1998-99, she served as President of the National Women's Studies Association.

Address correspondence to: Professor Bonnie Zimmerman, Office of Faculty Affairs, San Diego State University, 5500 Campanile Drive, San Diego, CA 92182-8010 (E-mail: bzimmerm@mail.sdsu.edu).

[Haworth co-indexing entry note]: "A Lesbian-Feminist Journey Through Queer Nation." Zimmerman, Bonnie. Co-published simultaneously in *Journal of Lesbian Studies* (Harrington Park Press, an imprint of The Haworth Press, Inc.) Vol. 11, No. 1/2, 2007, pp. 37-52; and: *Twenty-First Century Lesbian Studies* (ed: Noreen Giffney, and Katherine O'Donnell) Harrington Park Press, an imprint of The Haworth Press, Inc., 2007, pp. 37-52. Single or multiple copies of this article are available for a fee from The Haworth Document Delivery Service [1-800-HAWORTH, 9:00 a.m. - 5:00 p.m. (EST). E-mail address: docdelivery@haworthpress.com].

velopment of lesbian feminist thought. Ultimately, it argues that the insights and values of Lesbian Feminism should not be suppressed by those of Queer Theory, and calls upon lesbian feminists to re-insert themselves into current scholarly and theoretical debates. doi:10.1300/ J155v11n01_03 *[Article copies available for a fee from The Haworth Document Delivery Service: 1-800-HAWORTH. E-mail address: <docdelivery@ haworthpress.com> Website: <http://www.HaworthPress.com> © 2007 by The Haworth Press, Inc. All rights reserved.]*

KEYWORDS. Lesbian feminism, lesbian studies, queer theory, feminist history, autobiography, auto-ethnography

I originally developed this essay as a presentation to a class on Queer Theory, although I have never considered myself–nor do I think I am ever considered to be–a part of that academic movement. For weeks I struggled with what I would say, and followed a slow writing path that has become quite familiar to me over my years as a scholar–one that is filled with potholes and dead ends and one-way streets pointing in the wrong direction. On this particular journey, I found that I did not even have a map; indeed, I wasn't sure what town or country I was in. In fact, over the past ten or fifteen years, I've felt quite a bit like Rip Van Winkle or one of those *Star Trek* characters who wakes up out of a coma and discovers that it's fifty years in the future. I re-read some old talks and unpublished papers as I prepared, and I came upon a confession that perfectly describes my feelings today: "I am scared to death. The territory is so treacherous, the maps so often indecipherable, my own preparation so inadequate. I'm sure I will fall flat on my face or fly right over the precipice. But I can't seem to resist trying." I know I've mixed my metaphors quite a bit so far, but I hope I have effectively expressed the sense of dislocation I experienced as my intellectual and political worlds modulated (another metaphor) from Lesbian Feminism to Queer Theory.

So, I decided, that's what I'll talk about: what it has been like to have been shaped by one theoretical and political discourse and then be thrust by historical change into another. How does one evaluate the shape of a career, the meaning of one's work–especially when that work has been instrumental in defining the parameters of a new discipline? To what degree is one's intellectual framework shaped by the material realities of the time and place in which one comes of age? What is the valence of intellectual fashion? I'm going to use my life and work today, not because it is extraordinary but precisely because of the ways in which it has been ordinary. My impetus here is not autobiographical, but auto-ethnographical; my emphasis not on the writing of a life, the *bios*, but on the writing of the culture, the *ethnos*, in which that life derives meaning. My life is fairly representative of a particular cohort in a particular place at a specific time in history, one that was rather productive and prolific and that left a noticeable mark on the culture. My set of experiences is neither unique nor universal. Through it perhaps we can understand something about why Western universities at this time have classes in Queer Theory and why I have drafted this article from a conference presentation on lesbian lives.[1]

I was born . . . no, this is not a *bildungsroman*. All that is important is that I am a quintessential United States baby boomer. More babies were born in the United States in 1947 than any other year in its history. The reason should be obvious: it took about a year after the end of World War II for the GIs to demobilize and marry, and another nine months for the babies to start coming. We were born into a world that was experiencing momentous and rapid change. The aftermath of a world war, then a cold war, wars of national liberation, civil rights movements that came close to civil war: between 1940 and 1970, the landscape of the United States was indelibly altered. There are dozens of social histories of this period, so I don't need to fill in the details. You probably have read about how the civil rights movement became the avatar and nursery of all the identity-based social justice movements of the 1970s. You also know how identity politics combined with the loosening of social and sexual mores opened up a space for the growth of women's and gay liberation. That space was my training ground; those movements, more than my doctoral work in English, inculcated in me the habits of the mind and passions of the heart that inspired my professional career for some thirty years. No matter how the social and academic landscape changes, and no matter that I am now a university administrator, I will always be a child of the '60s and '70s: a new-left, radical-feminist, counterculture, dyke intellectual.

There were many avenues that led women to lesbian activism in the early 1970s. The movement was no more unified or monolithic then than it is today. As you probably know, lesbians in the United States first organized in the mid-1950s when Del Martin and Phyllis Lyon founded the Daughters of Bilitis. Their decision was spurred in part by their disillusionment with male-dominated gay organizations, such as the Mattachine Society. Even in the 1950s, lesbian activism was shaped

by both sexual and gender interests. By 1970, the early women's liberation movement had heightened gender awareness even more, and DOB
began to experience dissension within its ranks between those who
wished to continue a homophile emphasis and those who espoused a
more radical-feminist agenda. By 1972, the feminist lesbians were leaving to join up with the lesbian feminists who were moving away from
the National Organization for Women and the small women's liberation
groups that had mushroomed across the country. These latter women–
mostly college students who had connections with the new left to varying degrees–had not, for the most part, started out as lesbians. The lesbians in DOB were indoctrinated by feminism, and the feminists from the
WLM were seduced by lesbianism. The most amusing–and dead-on
accurate–description of this process can be found in Sarah Schulman's
first novel, *The Sophie Horowitz Story*–still in my opinion her best
book: "It's so strange, you know, in the early seventies, one day, half the
women's movement came out as lesbians. It was like we were all sitting
around and the ice cream truck came and all of a sudden I looked around
and everyone ran out for ice cream" (1984: 126). That was me. I ran out
for ice cream one day, and I'm still addicted.

Of course, this is too neat and schematic. There were other women
who flocked to lesbian meetings, dances and organizations. In Buffalo,
where I first came out, some working-class women, both black and
white, joined with feminist lesbians from the university to create an organization called Lesbians Uniting. These were the very women Leslie
Feinberg writes about in *Stone Butch Blues* (1993). Some of these
women came together in relationships that continue thirty years later.
There were refugees from socialist organizations and from suburbs who
had never been involved in either homophile or feminist politics. It was
a time of high energy, high passion and high maintenance. Not surprisingly, most of these organizations and consciousness-raising groups did
not last very long. But they left a legacy in the writings and artwork that
proliferated throughout the decade, and in the subsequent careers of
most of the women who created Lesbian Feminism, Lesbian Theory
and Lesbian Studies in the 1970s and 1980s. I want to move now to
those early years of lesbian scholarship and theory-building; to what I
think of (both seriously and ironically) as the "heroic age" of Lesbian
Feminism.

I first began to do lesbian criticism and scholarship in the early
1970s, within the context of the feminist and lesbian activism I have just
mentioned. The central questions then urging themselves upon me, and
others like me, had to do with definitions, identities, canons and histo-

ries. I came out into a world in which homosexuality was at best a disease and at worst a sin or crime. The media was absolutely forbidden to represent lesbianism in any way other than as a tragedy that led to a death sentence. 'Queer' and 'dyke' were words of opprobrium, not pride. As brash young social activists, my generation demanded visibility and a voice and insisted on an end to the closet. I felt compelled by the very force of the new existence I had chosen to situate my lesbianism within a larger historical, political and cultural context. That was the major contribution of my generation of lesbian-feminist scholars and activists: to establish a public lesbian presence and a recognizable lesbian identity and culture.

Much of this early work took place outside universities, where lesbian academics were still largely closeted and silenced. Many of the first generation of lesbian scholars had little or no association with formal academia at all. I, for example, was a part-time community-college teacher when I wrote my first articles, and I began at San Diego State University in a one-year temporary position. We published our work in lesbian periodicals, like *Conditions* and *Sinister Wisdom*, or with lesbian and feminist small presses. J.R. Roberts, a librarian, community activist and my colleague on the Chicago-based lesbian newspaper, *Lavender Woman*, compiled *Black Lesbians*, a bibliography published by The Naiad Press. The second issue of *Sinister Wisdom*, in 1976, devoted entirely to lesbian literature, contains my first published academic essay, a review of Jane Rule's *Lesbian Images*. Long before Queer Theory, this article attempted to think through what it meant to use the term 'lesbian' as a unifying concept. *Sinister Wisdom* also published the proceedings of lesbian panels at the meetings of the Modern Language Association, panels that included such influential writers and theorists as Audre Lorde, Adrienne Rich, Julia Penelope Stanley and Mary Daly. In several cities, lesbian libraries or archives were established, the largest and most influential of these being the Lesbian Herstory Archives in New York. During the 1970s, classes were as likely to be offered at lesbian centers as in universities. These community-based institutions and scholars paved the way for academic Lesbian Studies.

Until women like me obtained a position and a modicum of power that allowed us to confront and change the entrenched misogyny and homophobia of the universities, academic Lesbian Studies was difficult to establish. But once lesbians entered or came out in the universities, the development of Lesbian Studies accelerated. During the 1980s, a shift occurred from a community-based Lesbian Studies to one largely though not entirely contained within academia. Lesbian scholarship began to appear in special issues of academic journals, at least the more radical and experimental ones. Lesbian scholars communicated with each other through newsletters, like *Matrices*, or through the Lesbian-Feminist Studies Clearinghouse. Caucuses and divisions flourished in many professional organizations. Yet, although lesbian scholarship was making the transition from community to university, it continued to articulate itself through a radical, community-based language on the margins.

This new Lesbian Studies was greatly facilitated by the institution-alization of Women's Studies in US colleges and universities. Through-out the 1970s and '80s, most courses on lesbianism were found in Women's Studies programs. A 1980 survey found them in over a dozen institutions. In 1982, the first anthology of academic lesbian writing, ti-tled simply, *Lesbian Studies*, included a sampling of course syllabi from nine different campuses, the earliest of which had been offered in 1972. Women's studies facilitated the growth of lesbian scholarship as well as pedagogy. To use myself as an example once more, my new position in a Women's Studies department enabled me to teach lesbian literature in 1979, my first year at San Diego State. In the same year, I began to pres-ent academic lesbian work at conferences of the National Women's Stud-ies Association, Modern Language Association and Popular Culture Association. Subsequently, I published these talks as articles on lesbian vampire films in *Jump Cut* (1981), lesbian pedagogy in *Radical Teacher* (1980), lesbian representation in feminist literary criticism in *Women's Studies International Forum* (1983), and lesbians in Women's Studies in the aforementioned *Lesbian Studies* anthology (1982).

But the article that made my reputation was "What Has Never Been: An Overview of Lesbian Feminist Criticism," which was presented at the first National Women's Studies Association conference in 1979 and published in 1981 in the pioneering academic journal, *Feminist Studies*. Back then, all I thought I was doing was synthesizing the published and unpublished articles that were beginning to establish a new sub-field of Lesbian Literary Criticism. I certainly had no idea that twenty-some-thing years later it would become part of the canon as established by *The Norton Anthology of Theory and Criticism*! I doubt that very many of us in Literary Studies begin our careers thinking that some day we will ap-pear in a Norton anthology. It seems just one step away from death. But an even bigger surprise had been to find that article a centerpiece of Jane Gallop's *Around 1981: Academic Feminist Literary Theory* (1992). It was the first time I had any idea that what I was doing might actually have an impact on the academy. And it is Gallop's discussion that creates a link to Queer Theory. Let me explain this point.

Lesbian Studies as it developed in the 1970s and early 1980s was, in reality, Lesbian-Feminist Studies. Although not every lesbian scholar identified with Lesbian Feminism, in general the field was strongly and unmistakably flavored by it. Lesbian feminism is too complex a theory–or really, a compilation of positions–to cover here, but suffice it to say that it represents more than the sum of Feminist Theory and Gay Politics. It is a particular variation of Feminism that grew from the perspective or subject position of the particular group of lesbians at a specific moment in history that I am using myself to represent. Lesbian Feminism is rooted in the specificity of lesbians. It assumes that lesbians differ from both heterosexual women and gay men. As Eve Kosofsky Sedgwick and others have argued, Lesbian Feminism proceeds from an analysis of gender interests–which situates lesbians primarily as women rather than homosexuals–thus distinguishing it from Gay Theory which proceeds from an analysis of sexual identity and interests (1990, 36-9). It also bases itself in the primacy of identity, distinguishing it further from Queer Theory, which lays emphasis upon acts and performance. Accordingly, Lesbian Feminism manifests a certain degree of essentialism–at least the nominal or strategic essentialism, as Teresa de Lauretis and Gayatri Spivak put it–that continues to assign meaning and value to names, labels and categories. As I said earlier, this focus on identity led lesbians of my generation to debate vigorously what it meant to be a lesbian, and who could lay claim to the label. Far from dismissing labels, we flaunted and reveled in them.

So it was natural that when I wrote my review of Lesbian-Feminist Criticism, I would begin with debates over the meaning of the word 'lesbian'. For me, that was where all intellectual and ontological work began. I did not understand the epistemological or political significance of my question until Jane Gallop explained it to me. For that, I will be eternally grateful to her, no matter how much we might disagree on professional boundaries and ethics. As Gallop identified 1981 as one watershed, I would point to the period between roughly 1987 and 1990 as another. Those years saw the publication of crucial texts that reshaped the theoretical landscape, as momentous social realities were transforming the political terrain. After Jane Gallop, Linda Alcoff, Gloria Anzaldúa, Judith Butler and Eve Kosofsky Sedgwick, Lesbian Theory could not be the same; after Act-Up and Queer Nation, lesbian activism would be irrevocably different. In the same way that my generation of lesbian scholars in the 1970s and early

'80s was preoccupied with identities, images, definitions, canons and histories, the new Lesbian–or, more properly, Queer–Studies would champion performativity, genealogies, deconstruction and representation. It is tempting to view this development in a linear fashion, despite our postmodern skepticism over metanarratives of progress. Inevitably, lesbian-feminist scholarship and theory seems dated, even primitive, compared to the sophisticated texts of Queer Theory. It sometimes appears to me that queer theorists treat Lesbian Feminism in the way some Christians see the Old Testament as mere foundation for the truth of the New. But I would remind us all of one of the most salutary observations of postmodernism: that all truths are socially located, contingent and partial.

With that caveat, I would like to return to my genealogy of lesbian scholarship. After a very fertile period that produced groundbreaking work on history, literature, humanities and social science, lesbian scholars, like just about everyone else, began to question the meanings we had placed upon such terms as 'identity,' 'position,' 'consciousness,' 'perspective,' 'experience' and 'knowledge.' The interventions of postmodern theories certainly made us aware to varying degrees that concepts like 'lesbian identity' or 'lesbian experience' are laden with ideological baggage. Just what is an 'identity' and how is it constructed? Upon which lesbian's experiences do we base our analyses? How do we derive 'truth' from literary or even historical texts–which, after all, are always someone's account of reality, not the thing itself? It used to be elegantly, breathtakingly simple: one's identity as a lesbian (substitute any other identity category) produced unique experiences that placed one in a certain position in relation to heteropatriarchy, thus generating a lesbian consciousness, perspective and way of knowing. The task of lesbian-feminist scholarship was to explore those experiences, as captured in literary texts, ethnographies, historical documents or sociological surveys, and then draw conclusions about the true meaning of lesbian lives.

This version of Lesbian Studies, like Women's Studies and the feminist movement in general, was developed primarily by North American and European white women who initially resisted, to one degree or another, the criticisms of marginalized groups within, such as lesbians of color, working-class lesbians and disabled lesbians. In the late 1970s, this resistance was reinforced by a tendency to focus only on similarities among all lesbians, and to posit a universal patriarchy that oppressed all women or all lesbians equally. Little attention was paid to the material differences among lesbians, or to the possibility that some lesbians might have access to power and privilege by virtue of their race or class or that others might feel commitments to men of their cultural groups. Moreover, the very concepts that gave strength to the nascent women's movement–such as "the personal is political" and "the authority of experience"–became barriers to recognizing and understanding the experiences of women different from one's self. Other theoretical and institutional developments in the 1990s also transformed the terms and interests of many lesbian scholars. Multicultural Theory, and the development of a distinct Black and Latina Feminism, challenged notions of a universal female or lesbian identity. The feminist construction of lesbianism, which emphasized gender (that lesbians are women) over sexuality (that lesbians are homosexual), increasingly came under attack, and new scholarship emphasized the sexual definition of lesbianism that some argue had been muted in earlier feminist theorizing.

At the same time, lesbians inside and outside the academy established closer ties with gay men, at first because of the need for coalition work to combat the increasing threat of right-wing activism and to agitate for increased resources in the fight against the AIDS epidemic. Bisexual and transgender movements developed that demanded recognition and representation within a newly coined LGBT umbrella movement. This coalition work began to be reflected in the academy. While lesbian academics worked to place lesbian scholarship into Women's Studies programs and courses, we did not attempt to establish separate Lesbian Studies programs. Such structural change occurred (to the extent that it has) in the form of Gay and Lesbian, LGBT or Queer Studies programs.

Finally, as I am sure you do not need to be told, 'Queer Theory' reshaped Lesbian Studies perhaps more radically than anything else. I'm not going to try to define Queer Theory here; as *Around 1981* noted, definition is inimical to the spirit of postmodern theories. But I will note a few descriptive points that mark its difference from the Lesbian Feminism that shaped my political and academic identity. Queer Theory rejects the idea of fixed sexual identities, thus questioning the assumption that lesbianism (or any other identity) can be the basis for defining any particular body of knowledge. In place of 'lesbian' or 'gay,' queer theorists posit a fluid notion of 'queer,' which may specify lesbians, gay men, bisexuals, transgendered and intersexed individuals, or may signify any and all marginality.

Many lesbians and feminists (and other historically marginalized groups) have found the stakes of this theoretical development particularly high. After all, some ask, how can we have a Lesbian Studies if 'lesbian' is an essentialist category destined for deconstruction? Does Queer Theory adequately explain differences based on gender and race? Hasn't lesbian visibility been too long and hard fought-for to lose in the amorphic notion of 'queer'? After years of exposing the lies in male or straight representations, how are we expected to feel when told that our representations are no truer than theirs? Or, to restate a popular complaint, just when marginalized people are beginning to recognize we too have a self, along comes theory to tell us it's all a liberal humanist fiction!

I'd like to speculate a bit about how these issues have influenced my own work as a lesbian critic and theorist. For example, one question raised by (and about) my book, *The Safe Sea of Women*, and about which I am most self-critical, concerns the boundaries that we place around identities and communities. Specifically, I fell too often into the uncritical use of the term 'the lesbian community' (although I do analyze its deconstruction as well). I failed to understand what Gallop had found salutary about "What Has Never Been", and attempted to define my topic, lesbian fiction, too rigidly. Since completing that book, I have grappled, both intellectually and emotionally, with the challenges presented by the notion of identities and communities that are more fragmented, multiple, and unstable. The questions I now find myself asking include: What is 'the lesbian community'? Is it an entity or a concept? A necessary or a debilitating fiction? To the extent that it exists, what discourses and ideologies shape it? Are there many lesbian communities, and if so how do they interact? How do lesbian communities interrelate with gay, bisexual, or transgender communities? How does Lesbian Nation reference the imperialism we ostensibly oppose? Who is left out when boundaries are drawn? I have also asked that question about the borders within the self: how do I experience and conceptualize myself as, in my case, lesbian and Jew and middle-class white American? How do postmodern theories of identity and community challenge my assumptions about lesbian or female textuality and reading strategies? Some theorists have offered provocative new models of self and community—I think of Anzaldúa's 'borderlands' and 'new mestiza' or de Lauretis's 'eccentric subject'—but none yet quite captures the sense of conflict, contradiction, dislocation, even alienation that I often perceive and feel—within and around myself.

Consequently, my work post-*Safe Sea* is located all over the scholarly map. As a lesbian, I continue to feel a particular need to work on the connections between identity, culture, history, and politics. I would go so far as to say that without a culture and a politics, we wouldn't have lesbians, only women who have sex with women. For that reason, I continued to write articles that are rooted in the specificity of lesbianism, although I was more likely to refer to it as a subject position than an identity. I also edited two books that are rooted in that lesbian specificity, the first a revised and expanded version of the classic 1982 anthology, *Lesbian Studies*, entitled *The New Lesbian Studies* (the title, ironically, was out of date almost before it was published). And the second is probably the culmination of my career as a scholar, *Lesbian Histories and Cultures: An Encyclopedia.* In our collaborative introductions, my colleague George Haggerty and I addressed the question of why we did not publish these two volumes as an encyclopedia of queer culture. We argued that, "as happy as we might be to 'queer' the past, we have not reached the point at which the differences that 'lesbian' and 'gay' imply can be completely ignored." On the other hand, we point out that the encyclopedia "shows that the 'normal' is nothing more than a fiction that has been challenged in various ways in varying cultures at various times with varying success. In this sense, then, it is an encyclopedia of queer histories and cultures after all" (2000: xiii). George and I also collaborated on another pre-queer collection, *Professions of Desire: Lesbian and Gay Studies in Literature* (1995). Although I do not think that I will ever publish much queer or gay and lesbian scholarship, I have also been instrumental in beginning LGBT studies on my campus, as I was in beginning Lesbian Studies within Women's Studies during the 1970s.

There is another phenomenon that happens after you begin counting your time in a profession in decades rather than years, the impulse to memoir. Whether autobiographical or auto-ethnographical in nature, people seem to want to know your story and you begin to have a compulsion to tell it. I have published three such articles (I suppose this is the fourth): one each on my experience as a literary critic (2001), as a lesbian feminist (1996) and as a Jew (1996). The last of these was perhaps the most emotionally difficult and ultimately rewarding forays into life history–but I'll have to save that for another time. And I have also rewritten my life in another way by finally publishing articles that bring together my original dissertation topic, George Eliot, and my lesbian scholarship. In 1973, I tried very hard to find a queer angle on Eliot, but could only offer a few very hesitant speculations about the character of Gwendolen Harleth in *Daniel Deronda.* In various unpublished conference papers delivered throughout the 1980s, I drew upon lesbian scholarship to offer provocative readings that never managed to get published. Finally, in the 1990s, I went back to some of these papers, and published two articles that offer lesbian or queer analyses of the novels (1993; 1990).[2]

Queer Theory and LGBT studies have also affected my teaching in deep and meaningful ways. Over the past twenty-five years, I have developed a slide collection that forms the basis of many presentations I have given in classrooms, for university functions, and to community groups. I used to present it simply as an inspirational parade of 'great lesbians in history'–from the Great Mother to Frida Kahlo–but increasingly it has become difficult to sustain such an essentialist approach. I tend now to focus more on ways in which women have resisted heterosexuality, or how they have embraced signifiers that today we consider lesbian. I am much more up-front about bisexual and transgender issues, as well. For instance, now, when I show slides of women who passed as men, I suggest multiple interpretations of their choice: the feminist desire for greater access to employment and mobility, the lesbian concern for safety in loving other women and the transgender urge to express an inner sense of masculinity. I think my understanding of these women has been greatly complicated by Transgender Theory, just as my appreciation of the lives of many celebrated historical figures is enhanced by the recognition that they can be best understood as both lesbian and bisexual.

I will conclude with a few points I consider essential as we negotiate the new minefields, to use Annette Kolodny's phrase (1985), facing us. The first is that we need to maintain or, where necessary, restore the links between academic Lesbian Feminism or Queer Theory, and LGBT communities. We need always to listen to the voices of people who do not speak in the dialects of high theory. This is particularly important if Lesbian and Queer Studies are to reflect our very real diversity of gender, race, class, physical ability, age and personal history–diversity that is not yet and may never be fully evident within the academy. Moreover, we need to ask how we can make our scholarship and criticism useful, and not just to ourselves as we climb the academic ladders of success.

The second point is that we truly appreciate that theories are not true or false, right or wrong, and certainly not absolute or 'real'. They are human constructs, and as such, they are shaped by individuals who are themselves the products of social and ideological forces. They are forged in the cauldrons of history and hammered out by the relations of social totalities like race, gender and class. I am a lesbian feminist, not a queer theorist, largely because I was born in 1947, am a white middle-class North American, came of age as an academic in the 1970s, and discovered Feminism before I constructed my lesbian self. Another woman, with a different history, reading the same texts and struggling with the same questions might define herself as a critical race scholar, a Chicana feminist, or a queer theorist. At the same time, theories do develop a currency and meaning independent of their origins, and no-one is precluded because of age or race or gender from adopting and adapting any one in fashion any time. I know twenty-year-old students who would identify themselves as lesbian feminists rather than queer theorists, just as there are women who share my history who now feel more comfortable as postmodernists. We need not set theories in competition, one with the other, but recognize that the most interesting questions about theory may well be not what does it say, but how and why was it constructed.

The third point I would like to make is that some of us need to continue exploring in our teaching and research the particularity of lesbian histories, perspectives, subjectivities and identities, just as we do so with gay, bisexual and transgendered. We have hardly, in our mere three decades of self-conscious existence, so thoroughly established the lesbian subject that we can now blithely discard her. Despite all the conflict and contradiction over the meaning of 'lesbian,' and almost thirty years after my first forays into Lesbian Theory and scholarship, I find it difficult to believe that the work we began then has been completed. I am not satisfied to embrace anti-essentialism uncritically, or to abandon entirely the politics of identity. I believe it is more than a mere convenience to speak of lesbians (or women or people of color) as a category of analysis. But neither am I willing to dismiss insights that have invigorated my understanding of how the category 'lesbian' is constructed and the way real lesbians experience themselves in relation to that category. Thus, it is still worth asking, what are we doing now to strengthen our presence as lesbians within institutions, to further the work of investigating our histories and shaping our future? A final point, one that is made particularly forcefully by the conference at University College Dublin in 2005, is that the center of Lesbian Feminism, or lesbian politics more broadly defined, is shifting from the centers in which it was born. Lesbian politics and Lesbian Studies is a global phenomenon. We can no longer speak of 'lesbian nation,' although we might, perhaps, think of a lesbian universe. As lesbian scholarship embraces this grand new reality, it grows in depth, complexity and relevance.

I do want to play a Cassandra role for a moment, however, and warn that in many locations and many ways the discourses of lesbianis–and specifically, Lesbian Feminism–have been all but silenced. This leads to the appropriation of our work and ideas (including Feminism itself) without any recognition or citation of sources, the vilification of our values and continued existence, and the misrepresentation and ahistorical construction of the past thirty years.[3] To counter this, Lesbian Feminists need to re-insert ourselves into the debates in a forceful and intellectually impeccable way. That, to me, is among the most important work facing lesbian-identified scholars today.

Claudine Herrmann, a French feminist, although not one of the 'big three', claims that "only he who constructs the discourse exists" (1989: 48). Lesbians who still value the specificity of lesbianism need to continue constructing discourses of lesbianism lest we disappear entirely. We need to expand our research into women's lives and texts and continue reading and citing the thinkers who shaped Lesbian Theory over the past two or three decades in order not to erase our historical existence. In short, we need more, not less, work at establishing a lesbian presence in the present and the past, including the recent lesbian feminist past. We need this because 'lesbian' continues to signify a unique position in society, language, and theory: one that is differentiated from 'feminist' by its sexual history and from 'gay' or 'queer' by its feminist history. It is different to exist in the world as a lesbian than as a gay man or a heterosexual woman, and I would contend that throughout history and across cultures particular subject positions and ways of being have served many of the same purposes that 'lesbian' does in the contemporary western world. We academics still have the task ahead of us of uncovering texts from the past and theorizing their meanings in the present. And we have a rich body of lesbian feminist, as well as queer, criticism and theory from which to draw as we undertake these tasks. To paraphrase Terry Castle, the work of lesbian scholars has only just begun (1993: 10).

NOTES

1. 'The Closet in Lesbian Lives, Studies and Activism,' University College Dublin, Ireland in February 2005.

2. My early attempts to publish lesbian or queer interpretations of George Eliot constitute one of the few experiences I can point to of possible homophobia, or lesbophobia, in my career. Interestingly, it was feminist audiences that seemed unwilling to entertain what is now the fairly uncontroversial notion that Eliot might have had a youthful romantic friendship with Sara Hennell or that the attraction between Eliot and Edith Simcox might not have been entirely one-sided. Some of this work was eventually published, as well as a provocatively queer reading of the relationship between Daniel and Mordecai in *Daniel Deronda*. In general, though, my career has been fur-

thered far more than hindered by my lesbian scholarship. In fact, I had the advantage of being a token lesbian throughout the 1970s and '80s. Although tokenism is in the long run damaging to the growth of political, social and intellectual equity, it can have a positive short run effect on individuals, such as myself.

3. Two examples of this phenomenon, both discussed in Garber's excellent study (2001), are many of the essays in Stein (1993) and Judith Butler's use of Adrienne Rich's term "compulsory heterosexuality" (1993) without any citation of its source. It should be noted that most of Stein's other work presents a better modulated critique of Lesbian Feminism. I think that some of the strongest vituperations against and most willful erasures of Lesbian Feminism have passed in recent years, in part because of the excellent work of lesbian-feminist/queer scholars like Garber. Perhaps what is most needed today are many varied and detailed histories and personal narratives about the lesbian-feminist past and the sources of today's LGBTQ communities.

REFERENCES

Butler, Judith. *Bodies that Matter: On the Discursive Limits of 'Sex.'* New York and London: Routledge, 1993.

Castle, Terry. *The Apparitional Lesbian Female Homosexuality and Modern Culture.* New York: Columbia University Press, 1993.

De Lauretis, Teresa. "Eccentric Subjects: Feminist Theory and Historical Consciousness," *Feminist Studies* 16(1), 1990: 115-50.

_____. "Upping the Anti (sic) in Feminist Theory." In Marianne Hirsch and Evelyn Fox Keller, eds. *Conflicts in Feminism.* New York and London: Routledge, 1990: 255-70.

Feinberg, Leslie. *Stone Butch Blues.* Ithaca, New York: Firebrand.1993.

Gallop, Jane. *Around 1981: Academic Literary Theory.* New York: Routledge, 1992.

Garber, Linda. *Identity Poetics: Race, Class, and the Lesbian-Feminist Roots of Queer Theory.* New York: Columbia University Press, 2001.

Haggerty, George E. and Bonnie Zimmerman, eds. *Professions of Desire: Lesbian and Gay Studies in Literature.* New York: The Modern Language Association of America, 1995.

Herrmann, Claudine. *The Tongue Snatchers.* Lincoln and London: University of Nebraska Press, 1989.

Kolodny, Annette. "Dancing Through the Minefield: Some Observations on the Theory, Practice, and Politics of a Feminist Literary Criticism." In Elaine Showalter, ed. *The New Feminist Criticism: Essays on Women, Literature and Theory.* New York: Pantheon, 1985: 144-67.

Schulman, Sarah. *The Sophie Horowitz Story.* Tallahassee: The Naiad Press, 1984.

Sedgwick, Eve Kosofsky. *Epistemology of the Closet.* Berkeley, University of California Press, 1990.

Spivak, Gayatri. "Subaltern Studies: Deconstructing Historiography." In Gayatri Spivak, ed. *In Other Worlds: Essays in Cultural Politics.* New York and London: Methuen, 1987: 197-221.

Stein, Arlene, ed. *Sisters, Sexperts, Queers: Beyond the Lesbian Nation.* New York: Plume, 1993.

Zimmerman, Bonnie. *The Safe Sea of Women: Lesbian Fiction 1969-1989.* Boston: Beacon, 1990.

_____. "A Changing Profession: Interview with Bonnie Zimmerman." In Donald E. Hall, ed. *Professions: Conversations on the Future of Literary and Cultural Studies.* Champaign: University of Illinois Press, 2001: 255-64.

_____. "The Challenges of Conflicting Communities: To Be Jewish and Lesbian and a Literary Critic." In Shelley Fisher Fishkin and Jeffrey Rubin-Dorsky, eds. *People of the Book: Jewish Identity in the Academy.* Wisconsin, Madison: University of Wisconsin Press, 1996: 203-16.

_____. "'Confessions' of a Lesbian Feminist." In Dana Heller, ed. *Cross Purposes: Lesbian Subjects, Feminist Studies, and the Limits of Alliance.* Illinois: Indiana University Press, 1996): 157-68.

_____., ed. *Lesbian Histories and Cultures: An Encyclopedia.* New York: Garland, 2000.

_____. "What Has Never Been: An Overview of Lesbian Feminist Literary Criticism, *Feminist Studies* 7(3), 1981: 451-75.

_____. "George Eliot's Sacred Chest of Language." In Alison Booth, ed. *Famous Last Words: Changes in Gender and Narrative Closure.* Charlottesville, Virginia: University of Virginia Press, 1993: 154-76.

_____. "Is 'Chloe Liked Olivia' a Lesbian Plot?" *Women's Studies International Forum,* 6(2), 1983: 169-75.

_____. "One Out of Thirty: Lesbianism in Women's Studies Textbooks." In Margaret Cruikshank, ed. *Lesbian Studies.* Old Westbury: The Feminist Press, 1982: 242-52.

_____. "Daughters of Darkness: The Lesbian Vampire on Film," *Jump Cut,* 24-5, 1981: 23-4.

_____. "'Lesbianism 101': Teaching Lesbian Courses," *Radical Teacher,* 17, 1980: 20-4.

_____. "The New Tradition," review of Jane Rule's *Lesbian Images, Sinister Wisdom,* 1(2), 1976: 34-41.

_____. "'The Dark Eye Beaming': Female Friendship in George Eliot's Fictions." In Joan Hartman and Ellen Messer-Davidow, eds. *(En)Gendering Knowledge: Feminists and Academia.* Knoxville, Tennessee: University of Tennessee Press, 1991: 85-99.

_____ and Toni A.H. McNaron, eds. *The New Lesbian Studies: Into the Twenty-First Century.* New York: The Feminist Press, 1996.

doi:10.1300/J155v11n01_03

A Seat at the Table:
Some Unpalatable Thoughts on Shame, Envy and Hate in Institutional Cultures

Sally R. Munt

SUMMARY. The unmentioned emotions that ghost this article include hurt, rage, loneliness and melancholia. It addresses pervasive and pernicious emotional dynamics among lesbians who work within the career structure of third-level institutions. These dynamics are like the elephant in the sitting room–we've all been to some extent a party or witness to these scenarios and hence are all implicated in the psychic life of these dramas, but we don't describe or analyze these relationships or address their emotional impact. This article uses object-relations theory to better understand these dynamics in order that we may respond more

Sally R. Munt is Professor of Media and Cultural Studies, Department of Media and Film, School of Humanities, University of Sussex, Brighton, UK. She has published several books in the field of sexuality and subculture, including *Heroic Desire: Lesbian Identity and Cultural Space*, Cassell/Continuum and New York University Press, 1998 and ed. *Butch/Femme: Inside Lesbian Gender*, Cassell/Continuum, 1998. She also writes on class, emotion, popular culture and disciplinary formations.

Address correspondence to: Professor Sally R. Munt, Department of Media and Film, School of Humanities, University of Sussex, Sussex House, Brighton, BN1 9RH, UK (E-mail: s.r.munt@sussex.ac.uk).

[Haworth co-indexing entry note]: "A Seat at the Table: Some Unpalatable Thoughts on Shame, Envy and Hate in Institutional Cultures." Munt, Sally R. Co-published simultaneously in *Journal of Lesbian Studies* (Harrington Park Press, an imprint of The Haworth Press, Inc.) Vol. 11, No. 1/2, 2007, pp. 53-67; and: *Twenty-First Century Lesbian Studies* (ed: Noreen Giffney, and Katherine O'Donnell) Harrington Park Press, an imprint of The Haworth Press, Inc., 2007, pp. 53-67. Single or multiple copies of this article are available for a fee from The Haworth Document Delivery Service [1-800-HAWORTH, 9:00 a.m. - 5:00 p.m. (EST). E-mail address: docdelivery@haworthpress.com].

Available online at http://jls.haworthpress.com
doi:10.1300/J155v11n01_04

reflectively, and hopefully ethically, to the damage they cause. doi:10.1300/J155v11n01_04 *[Article copies available for a fee from The Haworth Document Delivery Service: 1-800-HAWORTH. E-mail address: <docdelivery@haworthpress.com> Website: <http://www.HaworthPress.com> © 2007 by The Haworth Press, Inc. All rights reserved.]*

KEYWORDS. Emotions, institutional cultures, lesbian studies, shame, envy, hate

In this short reflection I intend to share some thoughts about the presence of destructive emotions such as shame, envy and hate in Lesbian Studies, and by extension, institutional life in Anglo-American universities. It is specifically about high-achieving lesbians-who-study, teach and write Lesbian Studies at third-level institutions; lesbians who become the target of envy and hate from their erstwhile colleagues. I inquire whether the institutionalization of scholarship has led to a crushing poverty of representation for both students and faculty alike, as both struggle with the psychic inevitability of shame, hatred and envy that the presence of a few powerful women can provoke. For the purpose of this essay I present a fairly one-dimensional focus on the related affects of shame, envy and hatred. The presence of lesbian (studies) stars on the horizon of academic life does not automatically and always result in this rather linear trajectory of feeling. There are indeed a whole host of other academic dyke dramas involving achievement, recognition, affirmation, fandom and fame. I want us to briefly explore the question of what becomes repressed by institutionalization, however, using primarily a framework from object-relations theory, to identify what emotional costs might be incurred in our interpellation, incorporation into *academentia*?[1]

In her essay, 'What Makes an Analyst?' published in her recent collection *On Not Being Able to Sleep*, Jacqueline Rose discusses the institutionalization, through formal training, of Psychoanalysis(ts), tracing how even Jacques Lacan's radical refusal and opposition to traditional training eventually became incorporated into academe (2003:167-97). She separates training from the process of the psychoanalytic experience, which she argues has failed to deliver Sigmund Freud's radical original vision. In Freud's political version of the future of Psychoanalysis, the process had a politically egalitarian, transformative agenda for society. As it became appropriated and professionalised during the Twentieth Century, Rose argues that its radical potential became neutralized. Likewise, we might wish to consider that lesbian political projects would be better off by being disseminated 'unprofessionally' throughout the general culture, rather than seeking the blessing of bourgeoisification through affiliation with university accreditation. The mechanism of cultural appropriation operates to neutralize the radical content of ideas that are generated by the critical edges of society. Fields of counter-cultural knowledge do become institutionalized in an unavoidably conservative absorption by the ideological state apparatus of education. We continue to consider this dilemma in all aspects of the lesbian dance in/around/of/against (use any preposition here, there is no escape!) the social, as we grapple with the disappointment that unfeasible visions provoke. At the same time, most minorities are condemned to a fantasy relationship with what is (wrongly) perceived to be 'the centre,' thus engendering projective identifications, whether longing or aggressive, toward those spectral powers. Whilst the cultural trope of the hegemonic lesbian ghost has been so eruditely explored by Terry Castle (1993), perhaps we should delve deeper and lurk about amongst the shadows of our own camera obscurae; we might do well to wonder about some self-propagating lesbian phantoms in our collective subconcious.

Whilst the institutionalization of lesbian knowledge has indisputably created specific gains in such key academic objectives as funded research, archival collections, employment and the bit-queering of the canon, I want us to explore briefly the question of what becomes repressed by these gains, and at what cost? In this harsher evaluation I am following a small tradition of fairly rueful writers who have asked similar questions (Chinn, 1994; Hughes, 2004; Valentine, 1998; Smyth, 1995; Munt, 1997; Munt 1999). Here is Sarah Chinn worrying a decade ago:

> . . . we can't help but recognise the temptations and pleasures of belonging to any institution, the safety of the office, the paycheck, the name in print. For me at least, the minefield of queer studies is strewn with fragrant flowers as well as shattering mortars, and it's impossible to intuit which I'll step on at any given juncture. (1994: 244)

The imaginings Chinn renders here are inescapably from the Great War, in which the petals crushed underfoot are presumably poppies, and she continues:

When we cross the minefield do we leave it unchanged for those who follow behind us? Do we risk losing a limb, or dodge with our eyes closed, praying, or sprinkle more explosives behind us with the rationalization that the challenge of wading through bombs builds character? Do we drop the seeds for roses and hope they grow among the rubble, even as we leave them behind?

Ten years ago there was a strong sentiment of war, battle and conflict felt by many of us entering the profession with a mindset for change.[2] To teach Lesbian Studies then was to be publicly declarative, to perform a speech act, to *profess*. Being a soldier for Sappho was then embraced as heroic, however, we know from speech-act theory that all utterances contain unforeseen consequences. The reality of any war is that all parties become brutalized in the process, and it may be that we lack a proper understanding of how those wounds turned, over time, to scars.

The 2003 annual HESA return statistics cited 14,000 full professors in British universities, of which 1,800 are women.[3] Since the growth of Women's and Feminist Studies in the past couple of decades, a small proportion of those high achievers are academics, most often to be found in the Humanities (though not exclusively) who have achieved success in some part *because of* rather than in spite of, the radical quality of their scholarship. Women of a certain age, who have maintained careers in the academy and eventually become powerful within the parameters of their home disciplines, have been raised up through a conjunction of their own efforts and a certain historical set of benevolent effects. A tiny proportion of these women work openly on non-normative sexualities, although most do not do this to the exclusiveness of other intellectual interests in their fields. In the educational economy, these women are rare creatures, predominantly to be found in Anglo-American contexts, although we know that isolated individuals do beaver away elsewhere. Nevertheless, it remains the unlikely case that their radical thought, embedded in the successful adoption of professional skills, has secured their passage to a permanent university elite.

The PhD, now well established as the core qualification for a career in academia, instils within the learning process a certain anxiety of influence, producing student subjects who learn to emulate their supervisors in mental, written and professional practices. Irrespective of their own personal position in the matrix, all academics do progress through a system of mentoring, and hence to an extent are destined to become agents with hagiographic tendencies. Models of identification and replication have particularly marked education, right back to Aristotle. The heroic individualism of contemporary academic cultures is conditioned by an oppositional impulse toward imitative and co-operative behaviors, if one is to profitably advance. Thus, to some extent an academic career has to move from emulation to individuation, through a classic psychoanalytic process of aggressive incorporation.[4] This dynamic in lesbian contexts is related to, but distinct from, T.S. Eliot's description of the relationships between (assumed to be male) poets and critics in "Tradition and the Individual Talent" (1920) or Harold Bloom's depiction of (assumed to be male) critics and poets in *The Anxiety of Influence* (1973) in which the psyches are being described as repressed, split and murderous and enmeshed in each other. The 'feminine' version circulates intensely–one might suggest shark-like–around the anxious boundaries of the ego, more permeable and thus more vulnerable in the female subject under patriarchy. This 'appetite' for intellectual recognition is commonly held to be an avaricious quality if displayed too openly, particularly in women. Hence, as the essential fuel for academic careers it must be tactically disguised if the subject is to achieve promotion. This requirement can lead, perhaps, to a surfeit of grace.

I have been involved for nearly twenty-five years in academic training and its concomitant career; over this time I have endured many disparate conversations along the lines I typify below. Surely we would do better to expose the repercussions of these negative emotions in our institutional lives, thus leading to a fuller or more mature understanding of them and our part in their proliferation? I want to suggest that having these few 'famous lesbians' in higher education ensures a hysterical identification that is destructive to both parties. Charismatic, special leaders unfortunately tend to be seduced into the belief of the myth of their own reproduction as special. Worship is rooted in affectual mires of shame and envy; shame is tendentious in the sense that it can lead to a turning away/liberation from the approving/owning gaze, however an unstable rejection is invoked. In part, this is an aim of the process, that the student, once sufficiently trained, is productively abandoned by mutual consent. The psychic child can seldom forgive its parent their limitations, however, and the parent can rarely quite relinquish its status, thus both parties can become trapped in a hopelessly undermining misrecognition. Unfortunately, whilst mentoring remains the deep structure of academic training for students, it also continues to be a naturalized part of academic life post-qualification, as hierarchy in academic institutions is fundamental. I say 'unfortunately' because this guidance model is enacted permissively without wider consciousness of its predeterminations. To say that a degree of hurt is of the essence of the student/mentor relationship is axiomatic, yet we do not seem to have found clear ways yet of articulating it.

Envy is even more problematic, based as it is, on the impulse to destroy the object of one's desire. Even more present in professional life than shame, envy seems to stalk one's university life as an inevitable consequence of formal success. Particularly virulent in its destructiveness, envy is produced when one person's progression is seen as a rejection of the collectivity of injury, in that former allies now 'raised up' are perceived to have become threats in their closer move toward power. This suspicion is correct, in that it can challenge another person's failure in conventional terms as being due to their own performance rather than a de-agentic perception of being a more dissipated result of generic oppression. Previous expectations of collegiality or *a priori* loyalties are disappointed once power intervenes; as it does, as it will. Destroying former identifications, the betrayal of equivalence can lead to an angry expulsion on the part of the communal imaginary. This pungent disidentification could be understood to produce an emotional disinvestment, but actually the opposite occurs, because of envy's close companionship with hate.

Hate is a vitally intimate force. Hate, like love, is a kind of paradoxical longing dependent upon cycles of connection. It is our own hate that forges a boundary against our fears; its presence in our inner life is so unacceptable that we externalise it as the malevolence of another, binding us to that person. There is pleasure in hatred, as well as torture. Hatred is determined to secure a relationship with someone, even if that aggression is marshalled for that person's destruction this is actually a false hope, as the hatred doesn't end there. Destroying one's object of hate means that one will live in an impoverished world, as the walls of the psyche relinquish a powerful representation of self. Hate is a preferable state to melancholy, in which we cannot identify what we have lost, and decline into depression, rather it is an externalized energy that at least superficially is not directed at the self. Hate is obviously not always 'bad' either, it is a clarifying stimulant. It is infinitely preferable to being alone and facing oneself. It is bristling with the energy of connective desires. Hatred is relishly conducted through wilfully maintained ignorance and projection built upon the partial knowledge the unconscious generates. I have encountered much hate in academia, but it is rarely named as such, nor called to account.

Understanding the hugely emotional character of these relationships remains at a facile level precisely because of the devaluing of emotion in academic cultures. The popularity of Daniel Goleman's idea of emotional intelligence outside of academia and the concomitant trashing of such ideas is a testament to its denial within. We may be able to wax lyrical upon the emotional complexity of arts and literature, but we are unable or unwilling to refocus analytically on the emotions engendered through our personal and institutional practices. The Italian psychoanalyst, Francesco Bisagni, writing on envy has this to say on its transgenerational transmission:

> . . . psychic nuclei are apparently transmitted through different generations. Sometimes they seem to remain dormant for years within a member of a group, then they erupt and become apparent in another member before becoming dormant again for a while, waiting to reappear somewhere else in a kind of endless poisonous movement. (2002:189)

The pathology of envy is that it circulates within family cultures as though waiting for a target to fix upon–envy abhors a vacuum. It makes the environment we work in toxic, it makes many of us sick. A classic cycle of envy is enacted when a good object becomes a bad object, which the good object is predestined to become as it cannot fulfil the huge expectations placed upon it; it must fail, as all our loving is ultimately inadequate to the expectations laid upon it. Envy disavows the healing potential of empathy, as in spatial terms the former is distanciating, and the latter is intimate, it has a peculiar propensity to expand and grow as it travels, inculcating those whom it touches. Cultural change is needed to dispel the envious creep; replacing rivalry with acts of kindness does much to shrivel its progression. Envy is performative, and we can act to refute envious behaviours despite accepting that this indeed can be our private feeling. What this does is draw the envious object closer, thus dispelling the threat. This endeavor can also then realize a different set of feelings. If this seems too abstract, then consider how you felt when one of your peers gained promotion, when you didn't . . . a banal prickle fundamental to academic life. As ever, it is what is publicly said that is important–further–public statements can have the force to dissipate private resentments.

These issues have been raised before during the 1990s in two previous incidents in the USA–the major critical case of Professor Jane Gallop's infamous 'lesbian kiss,' and the perhaps more subcultural, glamorous grad-student fanzine, *Judy*, an irreverential pastiche on the fame of the feminist/queer scholar, Judith Butler (Roof and Weigman, 1995).[5] More prosaically, our community of Lesbian Studies is stippled with anecdotes of vengeful colleagues, jealous and destructive competitiveness, ambitious cowards, the all too common tale of 'sisters' whose real or perceived aggression has destroyed the progress of more deserving candidates. I would argue that righteously claiming the 'outside' becomes a more and more sticky project once one's subject is conceived as core to a number of academic objectives. The romantic outside (the outside as a projected ideal), is a very different realm indeed from the material or real outside that dictates the lives of most people, and outlawism has a tendency to produce a self-aggrandizing stance that can produce more alienation than dialogue. States of injury are endemic to the perception of being outside, when often outsider status is claimed by a subject whom in other respects has an accumulation of cultural and/or material capital that has enabled her self-determination. Fantasies are provoked from both sides as the energy of the inside/outside model creates a violent oscillation, birthing an energy that perpetuates hostility, positionality, territorialism and rhetorical moves to claim space and authority.

The trajectory is not necessarily linear and predictive. In this sad economy of claims-making and breaking, those same powerful women are not always simply the victims of jealous, underachieving or up-and-coming mentees. They–or should I risk a 'we'–can frequently be patronizing, condescending, autocratic, manipulative, wilfully oblique, bullying, and self-aggrandizing in the most unattractive ways imaginable. We swear that *we* shall always remain real and grounded, but it is not so easy. The embodiment of these emotions, whether one is complicit with its origin and source, or its reception, exacts unforeseen damage on all protagonists. True non-conformity produces a large amount of anxiety, indeed, one might say a field of anxiety, that intensifies and elaborates the hurt. This can induce the shame/contempt cycle; both of these emotions are peculiarly contagious, and implicate all of those touched. Whole groups then start reproducing these elemental emotions; they lock onto us in spite of our best intentions, with all parties anxiously denying their own part. It is quite hard to accept that power is a chimera when you are injured. Envy is driven by this delusion, and once you slide up the pole the realization that there is no 'there' there, can produce trenchant disillusionment, coupled with deceptive nostalgia for the radical sisterhood left behind. One has to be careful not to inflict this epiphany on others.

Academia is a micro-culture in which shame circulates powerfully, but is rarely recognized. To acknowledge shame is often to appeal to it, to become somehow stained by it. For example, to tell someone about an incidence of humiliation reinvigorates that original feeling, similarly, to speak about one's shame often makes us re-shamed. The inexorably stepped progression of an academic career means that the shame non-dominant identities were made to feel whilst occupying more 'junior' positions (undergraduate, postgraduate, temporary lecturer, tenure-track and so on), is emblematic. Knowingly or unknowingly wearing the badge of shame causes us to be cruel to those perceived to be underneath us, and encourages us to pull up the ladder after ourselves. Paradoxically, shaming behavior can also trap those who sustain a great belief in their own benevolent powers of patronage. Their counsel and support can be dispensed to perceived (and often non-consensual) acolytes, in order to ward off feelings of their own performance as worthless or failed.

One root cause of profound disappointment is the chimera of 'Lesbian Studies.' Where is the real lesbian, the ur-lesbian, of this project? Of course, she does not exist, yet she haunts our endeavors, she is our measuring post. Fixing an academic area of study upon an identity whose essence is lodged in injury is asking for trouble. Returning to her via reverse discourse can only ever be partially successful, as the lesbian abiding in shame, envy and hate lies suspended in our institutional/social unconscious (Foucault, 1981). Idealization is a problem for shamed identities; it functions compensatorily both to reassure by providing aspirational figures and states, but paradoxically it cruelly and simultaneously secures their own denigration. All lesbians, like all gay men, suffer to a greater or lesser degree from homophobia, the category and the experience of homosexuality is inescapably permeated with it. This is the 'double-bind' of identity that we are damned to repeat. In order to call upon pride and presence we also invoke their corollary, shame and annihilation. Claiming of self entails loss of self, as making a self is predicated upon disavowal, even in its earliest, crudest forms. Thus our psychic life is always already infused by poignancy, melancholia, nostalgia, so, we must then necessarily inhabit the present with all our pasts and futures openly in mind, aiming to keep the balance between comprehending our subjection (loss) and temporal, future-driven narratives of possibility (hope).[6] Naming Lesbian Studies, and/or ourselves as lesbians-who-study, incurs queer schizophrenia.

This is the dynamic that Judith Butler addressed so cogently in her book, *Excitable Speech*, in which she argues that injury cannot be cleanly and legalistically separated from recognition. Butler turns her analysis to hate as it is embedded in speech, identifying the violence of enunciation, and the linguistic vulnerability that is its 'other' side. What is so inspirational about Butler's work is that she consistently refuses the victim position for her readers: firstly she ensures that we powerfully acknowledge the hate directed against us, but then secondly she leads us into a moral comprehension of our own complicit reproduction of that affect. Simply put: if you hate me, then that hate harms you. Indeed, as a speech act your hate can be inefficient, misfire and 'fail'; then, if I refuse to be inculcated by, and hold your hatred, that will have the delicious effect of making you hate me more. The consequence of your speech act may be more infelicitous for you than for me, despite your worst intention (so goes my revenge fantasy, anyhow). The mirrored scenes of hate wilfully occlude the need to hate, the satisfaction of hating, and the occasional necessity of hate. Hate can be pleasurable, as William Hazlitt demonstrated in his essay, first published in 1826:

> Nature seems (the more we look into it) made up of antipathies: without something to hate, we should lose the very spring of thought and action . . . The white streak in our own fortunes is brightened (or just rendered visible) by making all around it as dark as possible; so the rainbow paints its form upon the cloud. Is it pride? Is it envy? Is it the force of contrast? Is it weakness or malice? But so it is, that there is a secret affinity, a *hankering* after evil in the human mind, and that it takes a perverse, and yet a fortunate delight in mischief, since it is a never-failing source of satisfaction. (2004: 108)

The vindictive, rankling and headstrong humors of hate seem in Hazlitt's understanding to be provoked by boredom, indifference and malaise, and I do not think he is wrong. Hate, he reminds us, has a watchful compulsion, it begs to be recognized, and like shame, is potently embodied and exchanged in the face.

   In reaching some understanding of my experience and that of my peers, envious professional attacks and the inflamed wounds they cause seem to come more often from within the queer community than from the predictable quarters of patriarchy, from whom I suppose a certain amount are anticipated. I would like us to participate in open examination of hate, in Lesbian Studies, or, more accurately within lesbians-who-study. Consider how or where lesbians are fair game for other lesbians in academia–and ask is there a difference between how we treat those whom we know to be lesbian and those whom we suspect to be lesbian? This competitiveness causes the mind to close rather than open, it engages with the spirit of intellectual enmity rather than co-operation. There is an indulgence of trashing in academic life. It is a dynamic that causes us to lift ourselves up by pouring scorn on another, for example implying or explicitly reporting that someone else's work is 'untheorized,' 'derivative' or old-fashioned. These accusations are lazy indictments in the sense that the protagonist has often not bothered to consider the learning context in which they are presented, nor have they necessarily taken time to understand the nuance in the work that can offer the reader some new ways of understanding. It is a serene arrogance that assumes we have nothing to learn from another's consideration or perspective. Incidentally, this is not an argument for intellectual relativism, nor is it a defence of poor thought–I am drawing attention to the frequent occurrence of hasty judgments that drive down another's efforts in order to proselytize one's own cleverness.

Contempt is an emotion embodied in one's own shame that has enormous power to wound the giver and the receiver. Fully understanding shame-humiliation and contempt-disgust models further takes us to the work of Silvan Tompkins. Shame has ambivalent effects because it is founded upon the interruption of love, where the self is dependent upon the acceptance of the other, and yet the inception of identity is predicated upon separation from the other, even the renunciation of the other. Shame is a kind of imperative to the emergent self. It is, however, only once the lesbian makes identification with *others like her*, that she is able to gain herself an identity. She has reformed the bond, through shame, and commuted shame into love (with all its attendant aggression!).

We must not be naïve concerning the institutionalization of knowledge and its protagonists. The underlying structure of the academy is the same as any other hierarchical organization under capital, and we need more awareness of the contract we have made and the function to which we are put. The poverty of these organizations reproduce a punishing range of angry identifications and disidentifications; they have historical pathologies that intersect all too readily with our own unconscious wishes. For example, the logic of shame can be that we remain trapped in a cycle of ruthless competition. We cannot compensate adequately for these predispositions, they are always already in the life we have chosen, or had chosen for us. We need to find a ways of preventing a passive sorority that represses our thoughts and our agency. To be crude–none of us can be the permanently good breast–the strain of maintaining, sustaining these emotions gives some of us cancer.

The closet is fundamental structure underpinning these dynamics. We perpetuate aggression for the reason of a colleague's real or suspected lesbianism, not in spite of it; we need to examine internalised homophobia asking how it becomes channelled toward colleagues who are more openly (and embarrassingly) lesbian. I think we swallow huge discomfort whilst wearing the lesbian *straight*jacket, and sometimes yearn paradoxically for the anonymity of the suit. It is important to remember that the lesbian performance is temporal and thus a *duration*—meaning that some moments/movements are more constraining/closeting than others. Emotions too are temporal, and involuntary, and as mutable states are subject to the vicissitudes of the organisational unconscious. This unconscious is the 'other-space' of the institution, since emotions are so generally closeted in academia, they are eviscerated from the public discourse of professional life. But the personal cannot be escaped in a political economy whose measure of exchange is reputation. Thus the homosexual-in-the-academy is always already angry, injured and victimized, by the organizations we work for and by all levels within it. Both 'powerful' and 'weak' homosexuals are inextricably bound to anger in the university imaginary; with that imprint on our foreheads we share a level playing field, batting for the same team whether we like it or not, we endure (inwardly protesting), an angry affinity based upon the adage, 'my enemy's enemy is my friend.'[7] This is not to romanticize or reify our lesbian bonds however, as we may secure authoritative positions through other forms of financial or cultural capital.

We have, we owe, collective norms of obligation and relations of political affinity. To be successful these depend upon the candid recognition of the problematic motives that can drive us; we neither like to be confronted by our narcissistic or aggressive impulses, nor to be held responsible for nasty consequences that we have brokered by our wilful naivety. We are unwilling to own how impatient we feel with the suffering of others, how irritated and withholding we can be, as Lauren Berlant describes:

> . . . we witness . . . someone's desire to not connect, sympathise, or recognise an obligation to the sufferer; to refuse engagement with the scene or to minimize its effects; to misread it conveniently; to snuff or drown it out with pedantically shaped phrases or carefully designed apartheids; not to rescue or help; to go on blithely without conscience; to feel bad for the sufferers, but only so that they will go away quickly. (2004: 9)

The aversion we feel, and the structural and symbolic violence we can subsequently commit, is a response to the poverty of our own emotional imagination; with George Eliot we might then concur:

> If we had a keen vision and feeling of all ordinary human life, it would be like hearing the grass grow and the squirrel's heart beat, and we should die of that roar which lies on the other side of silence. As it is, the quickest of us walk about well wadded with stupidity. (1986: 226; quoted in Berlant, 2004: 13)

That 'stupidity' usefully insulates us against acknowledging our own deprivation, an insufficiency of love that results from the inevitable failure, in spiritual terms, of heroic individualism and its vaunted achievements. Rather, better to admit we are all scholars who in creatively intersubjective/ interdependent ways require the supportive empathy of others. We need therefore to find forms of altruism that are not enacted by the narcissism of the ego, beyond what Lacan described as, "what I want is the good of others provided that it remains in the image of my own" (1992:187).

Does dialogue, mutual-appreciation, admiration, learning, friendship, collegiality, peer groups, academic freedom, tenure, retirement, superannuation . . . ever cut across the predeterminations of an academic life? Whilst hatred is conducted through wilfully maintained ignorance and projection, love seems to have more dimensions and variables and expressions and developmental periods. Love is not always or even often primitive–love is often reflectively tended, sophisticated–wisely/melancholically aware of its own vulnerabilities, complexities, contradictions, bitter impossibilities, limits and processes of change. Isn't 'lesbian' also an identity created through dialogue, across differences, in a sense (however partial or unsuccessful or deluded) of creating a sustaining community, with at least a shadow of a sense of shared heritage, culture and history; an identity based in desire for one another and trying to find new models and practices of making communities, homes and love? Readers of this piece may have wished for a more constructive intervention based in 'thoughtful, positive, and reasoned alternatives' to shame, envy and hate, but I am writing against the impulse to make good, or to rationalize an exit, without fully mulling over the prolongation and complexity of these damaging emotions. Enacting this aspiration can only be realized if we are able to accept the limiting humanity of ourselves and our colleagues, daily rediscover empathy, and not confuse the laurels of academia with the loyalty due to those lesbians-who-study, and their friends.

ACKNOWLEDGEMENTS

This essay has been substantially rewritten following conversations with Noreen Giffney and Katherine O'Donnell; ultimately it has been a collaborative effort and I am deeply grateful to both editors for sensitively challenging me to tease out the implications and effects of the claims I make, in ethical and substantive ways. Their support has been vital to the completion of the article, and–as I have told them–I have never been so conscientiously edited, so thank you both. The collaborative practice of writing this article for the *Journal of Lesbian Studies* was a welcome exercise in falsification. With thanks also to John Rignell and Sue Thornham whose thoughts inform this piece, and to Julie Applin of the University of Sussex Library for finding some crucial references.

NOTES

1. The neologism belongs to Mary Daly.

2. Chinn's metaphor is also derived from a seminal essay written in the 1970s by Kolodny (1998).

3. UK Higher Education Statistics Agency Annual Report, Summer 2004.

4. This idea is based on the principle of introjection, which is the development, in the Kleinian tradition, of the internal world as a space in which external objects come and go, and are consumed and integrated as hostile or friendly parts of the self. The assimilation is more or less successful in creating an identity, through a process of *identification*.

5. *Judy*, 1(1), Spring Fever 1993 was produced by Ingrid Sischy and Grace Mirabella as a spoof on the iconoclastic reaction to the writing/persona of Judith Butler.

6. Narratives of hope, in my opinion, are more easily located in the creative rather than critical genres of writing. Creative writers, artists and activists, such as Adrienne Rich, Barbara Smith, Jeanette Winterson and Monique Wittig, have played an important role in creating, developing and maintaining Lesbian Studies. These writers' tangential relation to the academy often enriches their view.

7. Or, as Hazlitt so eloquently puts it: "Does anyone suppose that the love of country in an Englishman implies any friendly feeling or disposition to serve another, bearing the same name? No, it means only hatred to the French" (2004: 109).

REFERENCES

Berlant, Lauren, ed. *Compassion: The Culture and Politics of an Emotion*. London and New York: Routledge, 2004.

Bisagni, Francesco. "The Mother's Hatred and the Ugly Child." In David Mann, ed. *Love and Hate: Psychoanalytic Perspectives*. London: Routledge, 2002: 186-95.

Bloom, Harold. *The Anxiety of Influence: A Theory of Poetry*. New York: Oxford University Press, 1973.

Butler, Judith. *Excitable Speech: A Politics of the Performative*. London and New York: Routledge, 1997.

Castle, Terry. *The Apparitional Lesbian*. New York: Columbia University Press, 1993.

Chinn, Sarah. "Queering the Profession, or just Professionalizing Queers?" In Linda Garber, ed. *Tilting the Tower: Lesbians/Teaching/Queer Subjects*. London and New York: Routledge, 1994: 243-50.

Eliot, George. *Middlemarch* ed. David Carrol. London: Clarendon Press, 1986 (1871).

Eliot, Thomas Stearns, *The Sacred Wood: Essays on Poetry and Criticism*. London: Methune, 1920.

Foucault, Michel. *The History of Sexuality: An Introduction, Volume One*, trans. Robert Hurley. Harmondsworth: Penguin, 1981.

Goleman, Daniel. *Emotional Intelligence*. London: Bloomsbury, 1996.

Hazlitt, William. "On the Pleasure of Hating" in *On the Pleasure of Hating* London: Penguin, 2004: 104-20 (First published in *The Plain Speaker* 1826).

Hughes, Christina. "Perhaps She Was Having a Bad Hair Day! Taking Issue With Ungenerous Readings of Feminist Texts–An Open Letter," *European Journal of Women's Studies*, 11, 2004: 103-9.

Kolodny Annette. "Dancing Through the Minefield: Some Observations on the Theory, Practice, and Politics of a Feminist Literary Criticism." In David H. Richter, ed. *In the Critical Tradition: Classic Texts and Contemporary Trends*. Boston: Bedford, 1998: 1386-99.

Lacan, Jacques. *The Ethics of Psychoanalysis 1959-1960, The Seminars of Jacques Lacan Book VII*, ed. Jacques-Alain Miller; trans. Dennis Potter. New York: Norton, 1992.

Munt, Sally R. "'I Teach Therefore I Am': Lesbian Studies in the Liberal Academy," *Feminist Review*, 56, 1997: 85-99.

_____. "Power, Pedagogy and Partiality," *Feminism and Psychology*, 9(4), 1999: 422-5.

Roof, Judith and Robyn Weigman, eds. *Who Can Speak: Authority and Critical Identity*. Urbana and Chicago: University of Illinois Press, 1995

Rose, Jacqueline. *On Not Being Able to Sleep: Psychoanalysis and the Modern World*. London: Chatto & Windus, 2003.

Sedgwick, Eve Kosofsky and Adam Frank, eds. *Shame and Its Sisters: A Silvan Tomkins Reader*. Durham: Duke University Press, 1995.

Smyth, Ailbhe. "Haystacks in My Mind–or How to Stay SAFE (Sane, Angry and Feminist) in the 1990s." In Gabrielle Griffin, ed. *Feminist Activism in the 1990s*. London: Taylor and Francis, 1995: 192-207.

Valentine, Gill. "'Sticks and Stones May Break My Bones': A Personal Geography of Harassment," *Antipode: A Radical Journal of Geography*, 30(4), 1998: 305-32.

doi:10.1300/J155v11n01_04

SECTION II

READINGS:
DESIRING FICTIONS

Lesbian Studies is not just an academic phenomenon, but one rooted in real experience, including the experience of reading and self-formation through reading. The general importance of reading in lesbian self-construction is well documented . . . Fiction, including children's fiction, is particularly important because the novel is such a powerful ideological medium, one which can represent the rules, restrictions and hierarchies of the world as 'just the way things are,' or which can challenge them and offer alternative views. Much of the time what fiction does is to reinforce heterosexual norms, so works which offer something different . . . become all the more precious and to be sought after. Imaginative literature is also, crucially, a space in which important thinking can take place, and where aspects of human relations in particular may be articulated, theorized and worked through before the 'theory' exists to describe them.

–Caroline Gonda

Queer Paradox/Paradoxical Queer: Anne Garréta's *Pas un jour* (2002)

Lucille Cairns

SUMMARY. This paper shows how Anne Garréta's *Pas un jour* (2002) is a decidedly queer text, in both the new and the old sense of that contested epithet. I examine three interrelated concerns central to *Pas un jour*. First, I analyze Garréta's mediation of desire in general: her own experiences of it; modalities thereof which subvert more 'normative' models of lesbianism; and her convergences with other gay, but male writers and theorists of desire such as Guy Hocquenghem, Gilles Deleuze and Michel Foucault. Second, I interrogate Garréta's dichotomy between desire and friendship, and adumbrate contrasts with Foucauldian theory. Finally, I scrutinize the meaning and value attributed to the particular body of de-

Lucille Cairns is Professor in French at the University of Durham in the UK. She has published numerous articles and chapters on French women's writing as well as on male and female homosexuality in French literature, film and society, in addition to four monographs: *Marie Cardinal: Motherhood and Creativity* (1992); *Privileged Pariahdom: Homosexuality in the Novels of Dominique Fernandez* (1996); *Lesbian Desire in Post-1968 French Literature* (2002); and *Sapphism on Screen: Lesbian Desire in French and Francophone Cinema* (2006). She is also sole editor of *Gay and Lesbian Cultures in France* (2002). Her current research project examines constructions of diasporic Jewish female identities in female-authored French writing.

Address correspondence to: Professor Lucille Cairns, Department of French, School of Modern Languages and Cultures, University of Durham, Elvet Riverside, New Elvet, Durham, DH1 3JT, UK (E-mail: lucille.cairns@stir.ac.uk).

[Haworth co-indexing entry note]: "Queer Paradox/Paradoxical Queer: Anne Garréta's *Pas un jour* (2002)." Cairns, Lucille. Co-published simultaneously in *Journal of Lesbian Studies* (Harrington Park Press, an imprint of The Haworth Press, Inc.) Vol. 11, No. 1/2, 2007, pp. 71-87; and: *Twenty-First Century Lesbian Studies* (ed: Noreen Giffney, and Katherine O'Donnell) Harrington Park Press, an imprint of The Haworth Press, Inc., 2007, pp. 71-87. Single or multiple copies of this article are available for a fee from The Haworth Document Delivery Service [1-800-HAWORTH, 9:00 a.m. - 5:00 p.m. (EST). E-mail address: docdelivery@haworthpress.com].

Available online at http://jls.haworthpress.com
© 2007 by The Haworth Press, Inc. All rights reserved.
doi:10.1300/J155v11n01_05

sire with which Garréta is most commonly associated–homosexuality–and their links with those of a contemporary gay male writer, Dominique Fernandez. doi:10.1300/J155v11n01_05 *[Article copies available for a fee from The Haworth Document Delivery Service: 1-800-HAWORTH. E-mail address: <docdelivery@haworthpress.com> Website: <http://www. HaworthPress.com> © 2007 by The Haworth Press, Inc. All rights reserved.]*

KEYWORDS. Body, desire, gender, lesbian, lesboerotic, queer, paradox, postmodern, sex

INTRODUCTION

With its focus on a French literary text, the following article may strike some readers as something of a maverick in the present volume. Yet one of the strengths of Lesbian Studies is precisely its multi-disciplinary nature, encompassing inter alia Anthropology, Film Studies, Health Care, Literature, Media Studies, Performance Art, the Plastic Arts, Politics, Psychology, and Sociology. Whilst Literary Lesbian Studies enjoys an established position within that multi-disciplinary field, French Literary Lesbian Studies constitutes an embryonic domain that is doubly marginalized. Within France, it has virtually no academic presence. It is constituted by 'sub'-cultural forms and practises, chief amongst which are reviews of lesbian-themed books and the occasional literary-themed article in *Lesbia Magazine* (which relies entirely on an unsalaried team and yet has run since 1982, a longevity unrivalled by its French gay male counterparts). Outside France, in chiefly Anglophone academic writing, French Literary Lesbian Studies is a nascent area of inquiry that encounters perennial difficulties in finding plucky publishers–and even then, a common requirement is that to the lesbian be added a gay male element. Unsurprisingly, the latter will often come to outweigh the former. My own publications in the area have sought to redress that balance, and I am delighted to herald the publication in 2006 of a volume edited by Renate Günther and Wendy Michallat, *Lesbian Inscriptions in Francophone Society and Culture* (Cairns, 2001; 2002 a; 2002 c; 2002 d; 2004; 2003).

In her membership of the experimental French literary group OuLiPo, Anne F. Garréta in some ways typifies the popular image of the arcane French intellectual, for one of OuLiPo's main aims is formal subversion. Founded in 1960, OuLiPo (an abbreviation of 'Ouvroir de

Littérature Potentielle,' whose literal meaning is 'Workroom of Potential Literature') develops experimental writing techniques based on principles from Logic and Mathematics. OuLiPo's members, past and present, include such literary heavyweights as Georges Perec and Raymond Queneau–but tellingly in the French context, only one other woman apart from Garréta. My interest in Garréta here, however, derives not from her membership of this avant-garde literary movement, but from her position within the highly specific context of postmodern French literature as pioneer (arguably unwilling) of queer.

At least a decade before this Anglophone word began to gain currency in France–the land whose intellectual terrain had provided, ironically in exported form, much of the bedrock of Queer Theory–Garréta's *Sphinx*, published in 1986, had engaged in more than a little gender bending. The novel cunningly manipulates the gendered grammar of French to prevent the reader from ever identifying the sex/gender of either the narrator or her/his partner A***. One strategy deployed is to use the preterite tense instead of compound tenses whose past-participle endings would give the gender game away. Another is to use only grammatically invariable adjectives, such as *ivre* (drunk), *frivole* (frivolous), and *grave* (serious). Ignorance of the narrator's sex/gender operates as a form of Verfremdungseffekt, forcing the alienated and disoriented reader to confront the set of stereotypes which normatively direct and limit reading, and foregrounding the extent to which gender has become a fundamental organizing principle of human relations, a kind of false epistemological tool allegedly needed to decipher the world and human society. Since attribution of heterosexuality or homosexuality to the novel's characters also depends on knowledge of their sex/gender, the reader is forced, too, to suspend this other binaristic organizing category by which we have been conditioned to apprehend and classify human subjects.

Sixteen years later (after three further texts), Anne Garréta published *Pas un jour* (roughly translatable as *Not A Single Day*)–a more overtly queer book, in both the new and the old sense of that contested epithet (1987, 1990, 1999). In the new sense, it is written by an 'out' gay woman and gives representation not just to lesboeroticism but also to other, arguably less recuperable sexual practices such as transvestism and sadomasochism (not to mention a not-so-new but newly celebrated epigone: chronic deferral). In the old sense, its inscription of the narrator's lesboerotic desire may seem very odd indeed to her national interpretive communities, be they mainstream intellectual, lesbian, lesbian and gay, queer, or transsexual, for ultimately it is likely to alienate them all at some point, not least in its perverse self-contradictions, refusal of

allegiance to any theoretical or political body, and its constitutive un-
fixity, irony, and distanciation. Garréta expresses no sense of belonging
anywhere, and certainly not to a lesbian community; indeed, her sense
of radical outsiderhood is made plain. Josyane Savigneau, a member of
the Parisian critical establishment,[1] rightly observes Garréta's refusal to
claim membership of any group or community (Savigneau, 2002).
Garréta herself is categorical:

> I don't subscribe to any queer or gay and lesbian religion, or to a
> Women's Studies or Gender Studies religion. I believe that all
> these things have to be considered from a historical perspective,
> and to be related to material, social conditions, to institutional,
> normative constructions which mould what identities are within
> society, and, above all, to what purposes they are put . . . Queer as a
> critique, that's fine; when it turns into a religion and a new form of
> social intercourse, I lose interest. (Interview with Domeneghini,
> 2000)[2]

Notwithstanding Garréta's own, quite understandable resistance to the
doxologizing of queer as a socio-intellectual trend, I contend that her relations to sex, gender and sexuality in *Pas un jour* are profoundly queer; and
that the entire text is *conceptually* queer in its rhetorical fetishization of paradox. The model of queer underpinning my analyses is less Butlerian, with
its accent on the performativity of gender, than Halperian:

> Unlike gay identity, which, though deliberately proclaimed in an
> act of affirmation, is nonetheless rooted in the positive fact of ho-
> mosexual object-choice, queer identity need not be grounded in
> any positive truth or in any stable reality. As the very word im-
> plies, 'queer' does not name some natural kind or refer to some de-
> terminate object; it acquires its meaning from its oppositional
> relation to the norm. Queer is by definition whatever is at odds
> with the normal, the legitimate, the dominant. . . 'Queer', then, de-
> marcates not a positivity but a positionality vis-à-vis the norma-
> tive–a positionality that is not restricted to lesbians and gay men
> but is in fact available to anyone who is or feels marginalized be-
> cause of his or her sexual practices. (1995: 62)

Garréta's position vis-à-vis queer needs to be acknowledged as a profoundly ambivalent one. We have seen that she values queer much in

the same way as myself, viz. as a critical resistance to sexual norms, but has no interest in queer as "a religion and a new form of social intercourse". Indeed, her justification for this repudiation is eminently worth citing in the context of the present article–discussion of a literary text:

> I can't help but be a little suspicious about the recent praise for queerness: postmodern ideology corresponds so very well to the forms and qualities required of subjects for them to function in the coming new economic and political order that the match is practically miraculous . . . This debate is not without importance for literature because literature is one of the sites of formation and transformation of norms and identities, images, roles. (Interview with Domeneghini, 2000)

This article will examine three interrelated concerns which are, within the overarching rhetorical framework of paradox, central to *Pas un jour*. Firstly, and most fully, it will analyze Garréta's mediation of desire in general: her own experiences of it; modalities thereof which transgress more normative lesbian paradigms; her convergences with other gay, but exclusively *male*, and, notably, postmodern, writers and theorists of desire such as Gilles Deleuze, Michel Foucault, Félix Guattari and Guy Hocquenghem; and, briefly, the degradation of desire in the postmodern, late capitalist West. Secondly, as part of the broad investigation of desire in *Pas un jour*, it will note the dichotomy Garréta generates between desire and friendship, and will adumbrate comparisons with Foucauldian theory. Finally, it will scrutinize the meaning and value attributed by the text to one particular form of desire, that with which Garréta is most commonly associated–homosexuality–and their links with those of a contemporary gay male writer, Dominique Fernandez.

Garréta has been accused by at least one male critic (Jérôme Garcin) of having written a very cold text about desire, and it's significant that many of the features he condemns have a distinctly postmodern ring about them:

> Here is a very frosty kind of novel about desire . . . In it, the flesh is icy, alas! And Anne F. Garréta has read too many books . . . a twelve-piece set of recipe cards about love (from chatting up to splitting up), studded by endless puns, Americanisms and learned words–shibboleth, mantra, acedia, didascalics, procrastination, excursus . . . .The mannered and masochistic panache can't conceal

the emptiness of the venture, where desire is nothing more than a
literary strategy and the desired being a mere concept. (2002: 61)[3]

It is true that for the narrator, desire is a predominantly cerebral phenomenon, at least in its inception, and that she presents her desire for
women in a predominantly clinical, calculating mode. But in so doing,
should she not at the very least be saluted for breaking down the hackneyed old binaries–those arch-enemies of postmodernism–which
equate man with controlled intellect and woman with unbridled emotion? The 'body' of her text syncopates received ideas, so that the body
of desire is located in the brain, and the flesh-and-blood bodies which
form its ostensible object take on a secondary, quasi-immaterial status.
Is this mere intellectual erethism? If intellectual erethism it is, why
'mere'? Is the common impulse to denigrate any form of intellectual activity in a woman not simply a sign of entrenched sexist prejudices?
Interestingly, Garréta has elsewhere derided the "dreary normalizing
machine" which decrees that:

> . . . men do rhetoric, dialectics and reasoning and women do emo-
> tions . . . as soon as a woman starts to think, it's the beginning of
> the end of civilization (i.e. of the privileges reserved for men in a
> given culture and in a given society). Rhetoric and dialectics are
> supposedly masculine instruments; women have to be dissuaded
> from using them. (Garréta in Eva Domeneghini, 2001)

Pas un jour is ostensibly an autofictional novel about inter-female desire. It is, however, like Garréta's other texts, hybrid and palimpsestic,
steeped in intertextual allusions (for a detailed exposition of intertextuality in Garréta's previous works, see Dugast-Portes, 2002) as well
as borrowings from various languages, and to this extent its refusal of
discursive or linguistic unicity, its textual promiscuity again align it
with postmodernist trends. Further, desire is often discursivized as opposed to narrativized. Although labelled a "novel" on the front cover, it
does, in fact (as the Ante Scriptum establishes), comprise a series of
evocations of women whom the real-life author Garréta has desired, or
by whom she has herself been desired, only one of which, asserts the
Post Scriptum, is a fictional evocation. So, from the very incipit of the
text, in the tension between its external classification and its internal
'mission' statement, the key tenor of the text to come is established: par-
adox/contradiction/subversion. This impression is consolidated by the
anti-dedication, "To nobody/ To no woman" ("À nulle": phonetically,

this would give in French the imperative "annule", meaning "cancel"), which may also allude to the "lipo" (a prefix meaning "a missing thing") contained in the name of the experimental literary group OuLiPo to which Garréta has belonged since 2000.

And subversive this text is, though to what end is not always entirely clear. What, for instance, is the point of the second-person narrator, whom we are encouraged to equate with Garréta, confounding the reader by providing a misleading Table of Contents which indicates that the memories will be presented chronologically by the night when they were written about, whereas the text itself is structured alphabetically by order of the first initial of each woman recalled?[4] And why didn't Garréta just omit her mission statement rather than ostentatiously flag up its non-realization in the Post Scriptum, which almost smugly proclaims her failure to respect the rule she set herself for this project (141)? The author begins by stating her intention to free herself from herself (9), but within the very same page her key trope of paradox resurfaces, for the existence of her self is, in a classic postmodern move, put under erasure. She will connive in the *illusion* of a self by pretending to talk about her life under the angle of what is perceived to be life's universal key, indeed *the* master-key of subjectivity: desire (10). She will play the very old game of confession. Her lexical choices–"feign," "you'll play," "game"–all stress calculated inauthenticity, again subverting the credo of a genre valorizing honesty to, and authentic exploration of, the self; and, moreover, endorsing the postmodern problematization of stable subjecthood.

Paradox soon recurs. She sets herself the "ascesis" of excess–"not a single day without a woman"; but rather than daily consumption of female flesh, by this she means that for a whole month she will spend five hours daily writing about a different woman whom she has desired or who has desired her (and whose identity is anonymized by their being designated by the initial of their first name alone). Tellingly, neither the word 'lesbian' nor any of its cognates is used in *Pas un jour*. This is one more index to its location within an episteme labelled the 'lesbian postmodern'–a problematic and perhaps oxymoronic appellation. Immediately, her lesboerotic positioning subverts stereotypical preconceptions about that positioning: not for her any valorization of emotion, love, or equality, but quite the converse: a clinical, distancing, almost taxonomical stance, which contrasts sharply with that of virtually all, if not all, other lesbian-identified French writers in the contemporary period.

Nothing seduces her more in a woman than "certain acute forms of intelligence, a way of bringing this intelligence into play, an ease in speech, a loss of self in the pursuit of the pleasures of thinking and of understanding" (20).[5] The summation of what seduces her so much is again rather oxymoronic: "an almost sensual tendency towards analysis". In addition to eroticizing the cerebral, the narrator also hints at an erotics of ascesis/fantasy/deferral resulting in avoidance of actual corporeal realization. Yet there is also indication of bodily/sexual excess in her polygamous practices with women. The narrative creates a tension between bodily practises and intellectual aspirations, a form of ascesis superimposed upon excess.

Like Dominique Fernandez, one of France's most prominent literary portraitists of homosexuality–but male, despite his androgynous first name: a queer twist presumably not consciously intended by his latterly fascist father Ramon Fernandez (for a detailed study of this portraiture, see Cairns, 1996)–Garréta praises clandestinity for adding a piquant to seduction, which she sees as a dying art, and for providing a certain stimulus to desire. Unlike Fernandez, however, Garréta nuances this valorization by privileging stratagem and calculation; again, cerebralizing what is normatively conceptualized as a bodily response relatively free from mental calculations. Garréta's inscription of sexual desire generally appears to be more broadly aligned with French gay male writers generally than with French lesbian writers, at least in her narrative objectification and sheer accumulation of female conquests. Of course, it could be argued that this is in itself playfully parodic of traditional male Don Juanism.

As if to disrupt the hitherto serious tone of her text, Garréta introduces a burlesque comic note in her depiction of the straight-identified D*'s nymphomaniac demands on her body, which are traversed by a strong sadomasochistic current, including the woman's entreaties for rape, sodomization and being treated like a whore. The narrator flags up her failure in hyperbolic terms, humorously stressing her own lesbo-specific physical exhaustion: "Worn-out, my wrists hopelessly cramped, my fingers so stiff they could no longer hold a pen" (45-6). Ironically, given the sexual slant often put upon 'writing the body,' she is left literally unable to write when her body has been exhausted by sex.

What some readers may view as a dehumanization of desire continues as the narrator conflates an earlier literature/driving metaphor with a sex/driving metaphor (note the technologization of desire and sex so characteristic of the postmodern): when she is invited by the straight-identified E* to her hotel room, she has:

> . . . never seen a woman driver so terrorized by the route she's
> taken . . . It even seemed to you that she was witnessing her own
> terrified desire on show. You even suspected that she was imitat-
> ing the sounds of a roaring engine, like when you're sitting in a
> cardboard box you go vroom vroom, imagining you're in the 24 hr
> du Mans race. (59)

E*'s emotional stymie is so pronounced that the narrator qualifies her as
a wind-up doll–ironically, given her earlier neo-Sartrian comments
about desire being the mere terrain on which a consciousness battles
for recognition by another consciousness. And when finally the narrator's manual stimulation of E*'s labia, her teasing movement in
and out of her vagina, do elicit a strong response, the two alarm bells
carefully set by E* go off, signalling her agreed hour of departure–which she honours, despite E*'s surprise. The narrator's abiding
memories of this night are of its "obligatory coldness, paradoxical cru-
elty and pointless worry". E*'s failure to force the narrator's hand inside her in order to capture an evaporating pleasure suggests the
straight-identified woman's refusal of lesboerotic agency.

But E* is not the only one to fear the reality of sexual intercourse as
compared to fantasies thereon and the machinations of seduction (110).
The narrator recalls how, when in 1979 she had flirted with a stunning
fellow schoolgirl, she was plunged into a state of "mortal terror and excitement at the same time". Characteristically, the fear is filtered (and
tamed?) through a literary allusion, to Stendhalian panic. It is revealing
that her literary allusions to other fears of sexual fiasco with women are
to male subjects (112): first Stendhal (110), then Rousseau. And it
should be noted that her other explicit literary allusions and identifications are to, or with, male authors. The intertextual borrowing from
Rousseau, enjoining the inept young (male) lover to give up women and
study instead Mathematics (perhaps *the* most abstract intellectual pursuit of all) neatly illustrates the female narrator's masculine-connoted
identifications.

So, if desire between two subjects is so fraught, are there any other
options? Maybe. The narrator eroticizes the gestures and movements of
a whole body of women (in her self-defence class), due to the tip-off
that just one amongst them desires her. There is a paradoxical–
queer?–intensification of desire in its diffusion over a number of desire-
objects, coupled with a hinting at desire's contamination by social influences and at its inauthenticity in any social context: in this context,
desire becomes pre-scripted:

> You can't live in society and not get caught up in its net, in the threads of its fabric. Even where you believe you're most completely escaping it–in the frenzy of desire–it insinuates its laws, its playacting, its authority. Our desires are prompted to us–theatrically and vulgarly: dictated to us and taken away from us. (126)

The narrator's conceptual wrestling with desire builds up (or spirals down) into an increasingly gloomy view of its potential. She refers to the way desire is, perversely, both overrated and depreciated, immodestly and crudely vulgarized as if to resist an intimate feeling whose exposure to others would be humiliating (129-30). Yet the reader may be forgiven for wondering whether the narrator is capable of sustaining *any* connection with another subject when it is concatenated with desire. She even comes to deny deriving pleasure from anything, including women, when in her pensive Jansenist moods. Religious connotations recur a few pages later, but, by the recalcitrant logic which appears to structure *Pas un jour*, a seemingly serious point is destabilized, for the stigmata mentioned (138) are due to her having bitten a female lover in a mildly sadomasochistic scene where lesboerotic desire is 'written' (or 'bitten') upon the body.

The dark potential of desire is clearly posited in Garréta's insistence that it spelt death to friendship (89). Her potent friendship with K*, whom she retrospectively realized she loved, digressed into and was ruined by desire (91). In what may be the key to Garréta's take on desire, desire is down-graded relative to tenderness and love. It is significant that for the first time she uses the first-person pronoun 'I' in her confession of love. In contrast, her discourse on desire uses the second-person 'you', consonant with her objectifying and distancing take on desire. But the salient question here is: *why*, for the narrator, are desire on the one hand, and friendship-cum-love on the other, so irreconcilable? As I shall go on to explain, Foucault would seem to be an obvious, if unacknowledged, interlocutor in Garréta's portrait of desire hypostatized, but the two certainly do not concur on the relationship between desire and friendship. Whereas for Garréta the two are mutually exclusive, for Foucault they may be coextensive, complementary parts of a new, exciting set of relational potentialities surpassing the limits of legal alliances. The importance of friendship for gay men was foregrounded in the very title of Foucault's 1981 interview for France's gay male magazine *Gai Pied*: "De l'amitié comme mode de vie" ("Friendship as a Way of Life"), in which he made the following crucial observation:

> Homosexuality is a historic opportunity to open up affective and relation virtualities, not so much through the homosexual's intrinsic qualities, but because his off-centre position, in a way, the diagonal lines that he can trace in the social fabric allow these potentialities to appear. (1981, 166)

We should, of course, note that Foucault was writing eighteen years before French law introduced *le Pacs* (*Pacte civil de solidarité*), a partnership contract conferring a number of rights which is open to gay as well as to straight couples.

Some feminist readers have objected to the masculinist bias in Foucault's model; and at least one male reader has cautioned thus:

> . . . the ethical problem of self-stylization is based on a physiological order, and not a scientific principle or a theory of the 'subject', and hence cannot be considered independently of one's own sex. Foucault himself did not retreat into a theoretical gender-neutral position, convinced that there is an isomorphism between the elaboration of an aesthetics and ethics of existence and the sex of an individual. The consequence of this is the problematization of a virile ethos (appearing, especially to women, one-sided and misogynous). (Nilson, 1998, 136)

In fairness, Foucault did acknowledge that there would also have been close monosexual relationships between women; but, as Herman Nilson points out, "There were hardly any testimonies at all to these relationships, let alone from the women themselves" (137). Whether or not Foucault's work ignored women, his following, crucial assertion about male homosexuality could perfectly reasonably be applied to female homosexuality, though no doubt with different modalities: "What developments on the issue of homosexuality are heading towards is the issue of friendship." By this, he meant that to view homosexuality as merely about two individuals of the same sex having sex is grossly reductive, and ignores "everything that can disturb"–that is, all that may be both subversive and creative–in "affection, tenderness, friendship, fidelity, comradeship, companionship" between those two same-sex individuals (1981, 164).

Nonetheless, for Garréta, desire is fatally inimical to friendship and tender intimacy, and vice versa. Not surprisingly, anonymity and distanciation are correspondingly invested with intense eroticism. In reference to her erethizing of the self-defence class, consciously or unconsciously, Guy Hocquenghem's *Le Désir homosexuel* (translated as *Homosexual Desire*) is recalled in the validation of an erotics of dispersal (1993: 120), which subverts the normative conception of desire as a bilateral process between two sovereign subjects, and promotes instead the notion of desire as a multilateral force between potentially countless anonymous objects. It is seminally important that this is "the most arousing erotic experience" of the narrator's life: but the reason for its unique intensity is less the dispersal of desire over several objects (important though this communo-eroticization is) than, again, the semiological exercise it involves (cf. 43): what inspires passion is the attempt to intercept signs of desire in another woman, to locate the mystery admirer; and tellingly, this passion is qualified as a hermeneutic passion.

The narrator's Post Scriptum includes a dense and polemical disquisition upon desire, its commodification, exploitation and degradation in our contemporary postmodern era. In "contemporary mores tirelessly encourage a process of unveiling", we hear echoes of the Foucauldian notion that, contrary to common belief, from the modern period onwards subjects were incited to talk endlessly about sex, to discursivize it–notably, in the confessional (149). The risk is that she'll be seen as just one more of the disciples of sex (150); but why, on the other hand, should she let the discourse of desire be co-opted by so many idolatrists, fetishists and pornographers (151)? But an even greater risk is that, whilst thinking she's resisting the dominant discourse, she is in fact merely practicing that "so typically French form of resistance called collaboration". In the French context, these heavily emotive and overdetermined lexical choices posit the commerce of sex-discourse as a form of fascism.

This notion of totalitarianism is developed in the assertions that advertizing only sells, only produces propaganda for one and one thing alone, that it refers only to itself and to its "ultimate drivingforce"–desire (153); that desire has replaced work as the contemporary imperative (154), with subjects being trained to desire by a whole gamut of technological media, and being fashioned into desiring machines (note the implicit, if here less positive, parallel with Deleuze, Guattari and Hocquenghem).

As well as being assimilated to a fascistic political regime, desire is also metaphorized as a religion with its high priests and apparatus of dogma (154-5), key amongst which is the following commandment: "you will orgasm, this has been told unto you; it is promised" (155). The injunction is to "fervently celebrate the service of the godhead desire"

(155), for orgasm, our economy, our human commerce, the very possibility of our religion demand such worship (156). Do we detect a satirical tone in the question as to what one can possibly oppose to this universal religion (156)? Doubt and critique all form part of the religious circuit. The only real wrong would be to have no belief at all ("only lack of belief is a vice"); only irony is damnable. Thus, rhetorical virtuoso to the end, Garréta closes her text on an arch statement about the prohibition of irony.

Pas un jour problematizes desire as a general category to the hilt. Is it in any way more upbeat about homosexual desire? In her first direct reference to it, Garréta negatively encodes its binary opposite, heterosexuality, as a (simultaneously triumphalist and doleful) religion. The normative binary in which homosexuality is the inferior component is ludically reversed, via echoes of Marcel Proust in Garréta's designation of heterosexuals as "mere mortals." Supernatural transcendence is instead parodically attributed to lesbians, with lexical allusion to the Proustian intertext of *Sodome et Gomorrhe* II (translated as *Cities of the Plain*): Garréta says "You're standing in a crowd and, from afar, by a certain *phosphorescence in a gaze*, in a body, you receive the sign addressed to and perceptible to you alone" (Garreta, 2002 42; my emphasis); compare Proust's "Often, in the hall of the casino, when two girls were smitten with mutual desire, a luminous phenomenon occurred, a sort of *phosphorescent train* passing from one to the other" (1988, vol. 4: 245; my emphasis). This illuminating sign saves her from what she designates the blindness of heterosexuality.

Beyond this mockery of heterosexuality's transcendentalization and the ludic sacramentalizing of its binary opposite, the narrator demonstrates clearly her resistance to popular understandings of homosexuality. For the narrator, what has always exercised the greatest power over her imagination in 'homosexuality' is the strange semiotics and hermeneutics that flow from the situations involving secrecy which it (homosexuality) may imply. The approximation with Fernandez's model of homosexuality is again striking, but we should note also the dissonance: that what Garréta prizes is the *semiotic* pleasure of clandestinity–an intellectual pleasure–rather than the impression of what has elsewhere been called "privileged pariahdom" (Cairns, 1996) which are features of it. Garréta denigrates the language of the (gay) ghetto as impoverished, and shares with Fernandez a predilection for disquietude. Like Fernandez again, she admits the liberalizing benefits of 'rationalizing' desire (through, we infer, the constitution of gay pride), but laments its lack of charm and vertigo. This probably explains why she has often felt desire for largely straight women (again the undermining metaphor of religion is used: "women who, for the most part, professed the dominant religion" (44)). Very few received ideas on homosexuality are spared Garréta's discursive scalpel.

Unsurprisingly, she testifies wryly to lesbophobia (109), and also to the hackneyed and injurious conflation of homosexuality with pedophilia (100). A further target is the old theoretical chestnut that homosexuality is about attraction to the same, to indistinction, a refusal of difference (44).[6] Equally short shrift is given, however, to those who celebrate difference with religious self-righteousness and exclusiveness, ultimately coming full circle by ending up just the same as other acolytes.

Finally, the notion that sex and gender (two categories forming the *sine qua non* for any conception of homosexuality, or indeed heterosexuality) are mere mental constructs is tangentially shored up, with the suggestion that, if a subject continues to be internally bound by heteronormativity, it matters little what she does externally with her body or whether the sexual organs of her partner are internal or external. Garréta's exhausting relationship with D* remained strictly heterosexual, because D* made sure she didn't 'notice' the narrator was a woman (47). It is surmised that D* would maybe have feared or had difficulty in obtaining from a man the sexual pleasures of which she made the narrator an instrument–eminently queer practices, but no real threat because located firmly by D* within a heterosexual imaginary.

In conclusion, I return to my starting-point: the notion of queer. *Pas un jour* inscribes desires and acts which are queer in the modern, or rather, postmodern, sexualized sense of the word, viz. non-(hetero)normative; but ultimately, its treatment thereof is queer in the old sense of the word, viz. strange, for its architectonics are based on relentless paradox. Amongst its various antinomies, two predominate. Firstly, desire is mediated as above all cerebral, with the corporeal and sensual being largely evacuated from a phenomenon classically thought to have a privileged relation with the body. And secondly, the only potential dialogues opened up by *Pas un jour*'s treatment of desire are with male (some gay, some canonically straight) writers. There exists, most obviously beyond but also within France, a swelling corpus of female-authored writing on desire, be it lesbian-, bi- or straight-oriented, which has apparently been ignored by an intellectually sophisticated 'out' gay female writer of feminist convictions, however ill-recognized ("I'm very pleased to discover that someone thinks I'm feminist, and indeed, I am"), who is acutely aware of the fact that "literature already exists when we write. There is a world out there where things have already been done, landscapes and perspectives, there's no point in thinking they're not out there, they are" (Interview with Domeneghini, 2000). This is a queer aporia indeed, ripe with potential for postmodern dissection; my anxious question is, to what political effect, if any?

NOTES

1. Incidentally, Savigneau is rumoured to be lesbian herself, although in keeping with the French premium on the individual's right to privacy, this is definitely not part of her public image.

2. All translations from French texts are my own.

3. It is worth noting Eva Domeneghini's apposite riposte to this accusation: "Those who lament the mechanical *coldness* of *Pas un jour* should take a few moments to examine, beyond their own definition of the mechanical, the melancholy and the strangeness that emanate from it. This series of chapters represent so many nights given over to memory, during which, on a computer screen, the narrator undertakes to pour out and to dissect her memory . . . And if this memory isn't always painful, it is often so, leading to an admission of impotence that the text alone allows her momentarily to avoid. There are things you just can't write about. There are things that the text can only approach, can only brush up against, because they are unsayable and because the text would only distort them if it tried to dissect them. In this respect, the chapter on K* is like a symptom of this impotence. What is melancholy, moreover, if not the realization of memory's impotence to bring back to life what no longer exists and will not return?" (Domeneghini, 2002; my emphasis).

4. Despite this encouragement, it is unwise to assume that Garréta has literally lived the desires she inscribes. This is not to doubt her lesbian identification, but rather to allow for the possibility that her text may be invented and even implicitly vaunted as such.

5. A colleague has astutely remarked that this could almost be a description of Garréta herself, or at least the Garréta mediated by *Pas un jour*, with, as her object of desire, the text which she is writing. I concur, but would posit the *primary* object of desire as being, more probably, her implied reader (in Wolfgang Iser's sense of the term).

6. This narcissistic model and its treatment in lesbian-themed post-1968 French literature is investigated more fully in Cairns (2002 b, 2002 c).

REFERENCES

Cairns, Lucille. *Privileged Pariahdom: Homosexuality in the Novels of Dominique Fernandez*. Bern: Peter Lang, 1996.

_____. "Mireille Best", "Dominique Fernandez", "Jocelyne François," "Hélène de Monferrand," "Monique Wittig." In Aldrich, Robert and Wotherspoon, Gary, eds. *Who's Who in Contemporary Gay and Lesbian History, Vol. II: From World War II to the Present Day*. London and New York: Routledge, 2001: 36-7, 131-3, 145-6, 290-2, 452-4.

_____. "Dissidence sexuelle, conservatisme social? La mise en écriture du lesbianisme chez Hélène de Monferrand." In Nathalie Morello and Catherine Rodgers, eds. *Nouvelles écrivaines: nouvelles voix?* Amsterdam/ New York: Rodopi, 2002 a: 215-32.

_____. *Lesbian Desire in Post-1968 French Literature.* New York, Ontario and Lampeter: The Edwin Mellen Press, 2002 b.

_____. "Identity or Difference? The Ontology of Lesbianism in Contemporary French Realist Fiction." In Lucille Cairns, ed. *Gay and Lesbian Cultures in France.* Oxford, Bern, Berlin, Brussels, Frankfurt, New York, Vienna: Peter Lang, 2002 c: 157-171.

_____. "Le Phallus Lesbien (Bis): Lesbo-Erotic French Writing of the Late 1990s," *Nottingham French Studies*, 41(1), 2002 d: 89-101.

_____. "Michèle Causse," "Dominique Fernandez," "Jeanne Galzy," "Elula Perrin." In Didier Eribon, ed. *Dictionnaire des cultures gays et lesbiennes.* Paris: Larousse, 2003 a: 100, 193, 205-6, 358.

_____. "Lesbianisme et literature," *Les Cahiers du cercle*, 3, 10-15 March 2003 b: 10-15 (Reproduced in "Lesbianisme et literature," *Lesbia Magazine*, 237, July-August 2004: 28-33).

Deleuze, Gilles and Félix Guattari,. *Anti-Oedipus: Capitalism and Schizophrenia,* trans. Robert Hurley, Mark Seem and Helen R. Lane. London: Athlone, 1984.

Domeneghini, Eva. "Entretien avec Anne F. Garréta", http://cosmogonie@free.fr13 October 2000.

URL cosmogonie.free.fr/index2.html

_____. "Lettre à l'auteur", 24 December 2001.

URL cosmogonie.free.fr/pjcommentaire.html

_____. "Pas un jour: digression," November 2002 URL cosmogonie.free.fr/index2. html

Dugast-Portes, Francine. "Anne Garréta: jeux de construction et effets paroxystiques." In Nathalie Morello and Catherine Rodgers, eds. *Nouvelles écrivaines: nouvelles voix?* Amsterdam/ New York: Rodopi, 2002: 159-79.

Foucault, Michel. "De l'amitié comme mode de vie" (interview with R. de Ceccaty, J. Danet and J. Le Bitoux), *Gai Pied*, 25, April 1981: 38-9 (Reproduced in *Dits et Écrits*, 1994: 163-7).

_____. "Sex, Power and the Politics of Identity," *The Advocate*, 1984: 29.

_____. *Dits et Écrits. 1954-88.* Paris: Bibliothèque des Sciences humaines, 1994.

_____. *The History of Sexuality: The Care of the Self*, trans. Robert Hurley. London: Penguin, 1990.

_____. *The History of Sexuality: The Use of Pleasure*, trans. Robert Hurley. London: Penguin, 1992.

Garcin, Jérôme. "Et moi, et moi, et moi," *Le Nouvel observateur*, 19-25 September 2002: 61.

Garréta, Anne. *Sphinx.* Paris: Grasset, 1986.

_____. *Pour en finir avec le genre humain.* Paris: François Bourin, 1987.

_____. *Ciels liquides.* Paris: Grasset, 1990.

_____. *La Décomposition.* Paris: Grasset, 1999.

_____. *Pas un jour.* Paris: Grasset, 2002.

Günther, Renate and Wendy Michallat, eds. *Lesbian Inscriptions in Francophone Society and Culture*. Durham: Durham Modern Languages Series, 2007.

Halperin, David M. *Saint Foucault: Towards a Gay Hagiography*. New York and Oxford: Oxford University Press, 1995.

Hocquenghem, Guy. *Homosexual Desire*, trans. Daniella Dangoor. Durham and London: Duke University Press, 1993.

Nilson, Herman. *Michel Foucault and the Games of Truth*, trans. Rachel Clark. New York: St Martin's Press, 1998; London: Macmillan Press, 1998.

Proust, Marcel. *Sodome et Gomorrhe I, À la recherche du temps perdu*, vols. 3 and 4. Paris: Gallimard (Bibliothèque de la Pléiade), 1988.

Savigneau, Josyane. "Pas un jour: Anne Garréta à l'épreuve de la mémoire," *Le Monde des livres*, 5 September 2002.

doi:10.1300/J155v11n01_05

Being Faithful:
The Ethics of Homoaffection
in Antonia Forest's Marlow Novels

Caroline Gonda

SUMMARY. This article examines the ethical force and function of same-sex relationships in a ten-volume sequence of English children's books, published between 1948 and 1982, by Antonia Forest (pseudonym for Patricia Rubinstein, 1915-2003). From the late 1940s onwards, Forest's fiction articulates what Adrienne Rich theorizes in her classic work of lesbian ethics, "Women and Honor: Some Notes on Lying" (1975): the idea of same-sex bonds as the locus and standard of the ethical. Through the characters of the Marlow family (six sisters, two brothers) and their friends and enemies, Forest explores questions of honesty

Caroline Gonda is a Fellow and Director of Studies in English at St. Catharine's College, Cambridge. She is the author of *Reading Daughters' Fictions 1709-1834: Novels and Society from Manley to Edgeworth* (Cambridge University Press, 1996) and editor of *Tea and Leg-Irons: New Feminist Readings from Scotland* (Open Letters, 1992). She has also written essays and articles on British eighteenth-century and Romantic literature and culture, on lesbian theory and on contemporary Scottish lesbian writing. She is grateful to Emma Donoghue, Victoria Coulson and especially Alison Hennegan for their comments and encouragement in the writing of this article.

Address correspondence to: Dr. Caroline Gonda, St. Catharine's College, Cambridge, CB2 1RL, United Kingdom (E-mail: cjg29@cam.ac.uk).

[Haworth co-indexing entry note]: "Being Faithful: The Ethics of Homoaffection in Antonia Forest's Marlow Novels." Gonda, Caroline. Co-published simultaneously in *Journal of Lesbian Studies* (Harrington Park Press, an imprint of The Haworth Press, Inc.) Vol. 11, No. 1/2, 2007, pp. 89-105; and: *Twenty-First Century Lesbian Studies* (ed: Noreen Giffney, and Katherine O'Donnell) Harrington Park Press, an imprint of The Haworth Press, Inc., 2007, pp. 89-105. Single or multiple copies of this article are available for a fee from The Haworth Document Delivery Service [1-800-HAWORTH, 9:00 a.m. - 5:00 p.m. (EST). E-mail address: docdelivery@haworthpress.com].

and self-deception, fidelity (both religious and personal) and betrayal, integrity and duality, performance and the boundaries of the self. Forest's exploration of these questions is persistently inflected by a resistance to heterosexuality and by a privileging of same-sex bonds, whether female or male. Forest's resistance to the pressures of conventional pieties and expected emotions, whether about love, friendship or the family, makes these books particularly important for lesbian readers.

doi:10.1300/J155v11n01_06 *[Article copies available for a fee from The Haworth Document Delivery Service: 1-800-HAWORTH. E-mail address: <docdelivery@haworthpress.com> Website: <http://www.HaworthPress.com> © 2007 by The Haworth Press, Inc. All rights reserved.]*

KEYWORDS. Antonia Forest, children's literature, English girls' school stories, lesbian readers, ethics, homoaffection, same-sex relationships, twins

As a child I devoured English boarding-school stories, both boys' and girls', but the only ones I kept rereading into my teens were Antonia Forest's ones about the Marlow girls, because they offered a rare emotional complexity. I'm thinking of the convincing dynamics between the various sisters, between girls of different ages (for instance, Nicola's admiration of Lois that turns so sour), and the profound excitement of involvement in theatre and sports. When in a public library I discovered that Forest had written other books about the family's life in between school terms, I was so excited that I went back to that library repeatedly to borrow them, despite the fact that it was a long bus ride away.

Though some of the Marlow sequence could best be described as thrillers, some as psychodramas, and some as school stories, what they add up to is a uniquely honest narrative of the emotional life of a set of children, teenagers and adults called a family and its friends. As the youngest of eight, I can say that I've never read anything which captured so accurately that sense of the individual passionately bound up in, but isolated from, the group. And maybe it was that recurring isolation, those moments of being irredeemably misunderstood (one that sticks in my mind is when Nicola messes up a singing audition by bursting into tears because of the loss of her falcon), that made Forest's books so precious to me as a teenage lesbian in the iron closet of 1980s Ireland. (Emma Donoghue, personal communication, 2004)

Writing with characteristic passion and directness, the lesbian novelist Emma Donoghue recalls her formative encounters with the works of an English children's author, Antonia Forest. The importance of single-sex, English boarding-school stories in the imaginative life of young lesbian readers is a well-attested phenomenon (Hennegan, 1988, 175-7). As Donoghue's account suggests, however, Forest's emotional complexity and honesty, the convincing character dynamics she creates, and her acute sense of the tension between feelings of belonging and isolation, involvement and detachment, exert a continuing appeal for older readers as well. Unlike Donoghue, who as a child in the 1970s would have been part of Forest's intended audience, I first encountered Forest's fiction as an adult lesbian reader in the late 1990s, when all the novels were out of print. Like Donoghue, however, I had a very strong sense that this was an author worth pursuing; between my partner's bookshelves and the reading room of the university library, I read all of Forest's works. The novels are now being brought back into print by a splendid small British press called Girls Gone By, and part of my aim in this article is to introduce Antonia Forest's work to the wider lesbian audience it so richly deserves.

As these two very personal accounts should demonstrate, Lesbian Studies is not just an academic phenomenon, but one rooted in real experience, including the experience of reading and self-formation through reading. The general importance of reading in lesbian self-construction is well documented (Hennegan, 1988; Hastie, 1993). Fiction, including children's fiction, is particularly important because the novel is such a powerful ideological medium, one which can represent the rules, restrictions and hierarchies of the world as 'just the way things are,' or which can challenge them and offer alternative views. Much of the time what fiction does is to reinforce heterosexual norms, so works which offer something different—as Forest's do—become all the more precious and to be sought after. Imaginative literature is also, crucially, a space in which important thinking can take place, and where aspects of human relations in particular may be articulated, theorized and worked through before the 'theory' exists to describe them. Forest can be seen, from the late 1940s onwards, to be working out through her novels something that Adrienne Rich would much later theorize in her classic work of lesbian ethics, "Women and Honor: Some Notes on Lying" (1975). Here, Rich takes as her focus personal relationships, which she defines as "relationships between and among women" (186). Redefining conventional notions of "honor," Rich's essay not only stamps same-sex relationships as "personal" in a way relationships between the sexes are not; it also makes same-sex bonds both the locus and the standard of the ethical. The search for honesty in such relationships may be, will be difficult and demanding, but the goal is worthwhile: "trying, all the time, to extend the possibilities of truth between us./ The possibility of life between us" (194). In Forest's fiction this search for honesty becomes what I am calling the ethics of homoaffection.

The term "homoaffection" is one I have adopted/adapted from Susan Lanser's work on lesbian narrative, and in particular on the narratives she defines as "sapphic picaresque", narratives in which "homo-affectional or homo-erotic behaviour is bound up with some form of adventuring"(2001: 256). Lanser's term seems to me useful precisely because it keeps in play the possibilities and importance of the affections, as more constricting terms such as 'homoerotic' or 'homosocial' do not. 'Homoerotic' suggests a love which is inflected by sexual/carnal desire, *eros*, even if that desire is not acted upon; 'homosocial' suggests a relationship which is oblique, triangulated or re-routed through an ostensibly heterosexual object choice (Kosofsky Sedgwick, 1985). Both the homoerotic and the homosocial can be seen in Forest's fiction, but neither term does justice to the nuances and subtleties of same-sex emotions in her works. The language of the affections has particular importance for lesbians, as indeed it does for any group trying to live and love by other rules than those of normative heterosexuality. I choose "homoaffection" rather than, for example, Janice Raymond's term "gyn/affection" (1986), partly because in Forest's work the importance of same-sex affectional bonds is not confined to women or girls: Forest's treatment of male same-sex relations, I argue, influences and informs her increasingly subtle and complex handling of female homoaffection. The resistance to heterosexual norms implicit in the term 'homoaffection' is also important for my purposes here.

Antonia Forest (a pseudonym) published thirteen books for children, ten of them about the Marlow family (six sisters, two brothers). Four novels–*Autumn Term* (1948), *End of Term* (1959), *The Cricket Term* (1974) and *The Attic Term* (1977)–are set predominantly in the female homosocial world of the girls' boarding school, Kingscote; the other six books–*The Marlows and the Traitor* (1953), *Falconer's Lure* (1957), *Peter's Room* (1961), *The Thuggery Affair* (1965), *The Ready-Made Family* (1967) and *Run Away Home* (1982)–inhabit the heterosocial world of school holidays.[1] Both female and male same-sex bonds figure largely in Forest's Marlow novels: female homoaffection is seen mainly through the youngest Marlows, twin sisters Nicola and Lawrence (more often known as Nick and Lawrie), and their friendships; male-male relations are seen mostly through their brother Peter and their friend and neighbour Patrick Merrick, each of whom has a significant attachment to an older man.[2] Through these and other characters Forest explores questions of honesty and self-deception, fidelity (both religious and personal) and betrayal, integrity and duality, performance and the boundaries of the self. Forest's exploration of these questions, I argue, is persistently inflected by a resistance to heterosexuality and privileging of same-sex bonds, whether female or male.

Forest's novels are crucially concerned with truth and honesty in emotions, and with the gap that can open up between the emotions you really do have and the emotions you or others think you ought to have. The pressures of conventional emotion bear particularly hard on young lesbians, whose resistance to heterosexual female socialization and normative family values may not be fully articulated but is nevertheless passionately felt. Forest's detachment from convention makes these books particularly appealing to lesbian readers. In *Autumn Term*, one of Nicola's older sisters, Rowan, comments sardonically on Nicola's choice of bedside photographs: "It would show nicer feeling, Nicky dear . . . if you had Giles [the eldest Marlow] instead of his ship, and possibly an expensively framed cabinet portrait of Father and Mother instead of Nelson. Don't you think so, Ann?" (1948, 37). Rowan's comment mocks "nicer feeling" and their sister Ann's likely agreement with it as well as Nicola's obsession with Nelson and the Navy. Fen Crosbie misses the irony of Forest's tone when she states that Ann is "the kind of person who takes it for granted one loves one's relations" (Crosbie, 1998, quoting without attribution Forest 1959): nothing about love or emotion can or should be taken for granted in Forest's works. The novels frequently adopt a skeptical or ironic attitude towards conventional pieties–about the relative importance of families and friends, for example, or about how mothers should feel towards their children (indifference or actual dislike are serious possibilities here), or about what kind of letter of condolence you should write to the parents of someone nobody liked. Nicola in particular often wrestles with feelings she finds hard to articulate but which are prompted by the interplay of ethics and emotions. Emotional and moral integrity are inextricably linked in Forest's works; maintaining both is vital.

Integrity entails being true to oneself, and in Forest this truth is often measured against different kinds of performance. The most high-profile of these, as Donoghue's comment suggests, are "theatre and sports," and here a set of related ideas comes into play: taking part, or playing your part, both commendable in drama and sport, versus putting on an act, or pretending to be what you're not. Forest isn't hostile to fantasy or imagination, but she's wary about what happens when boundaries between fantasy and reality get blurred. This is the central idea of *Peter's Room*, where fantasy and role-play spill over from Gondal, the imaginary Brontë-esque setting of the children's game, into the ordinary world of snowbound Christmas holidays, with near-fatal results. Patrick later says, "That wasn't acting–that was–being someone" (1977: 16), and the distinction is an important one. Nicola, who enjoys acting and fantasy in their place ("she could still, given the right conditions, be a Polar expedition" (53)), becomes increasingly disturbed and frightened as her middle sister Ginty, Peter and Patrick are dangerously caught up in the game. For Lawrie, a born actress and a very talented one, her Gondal role is no more and no less real than any other part she plays, including that of Lawrie Marlow. When Nicola (undeservedly) and Ginty (deservedly) face impending public disgrace in *The Attic Term*, Lawrie says "I'd be someone in the French Resistance being put up against a wall and shot if it was me"; Ginty's thoughts immediately turn to her Gondal roles, "Rosina confronted by Alcona: or Crispin standing with sword drawn," but Nicola stubbornly insists, "I shall still be me" (1977: 204-5).

Repeatedly, the school stories focusing on the twins deal with possibilities of confusion, substitution and assumed interchangeability, held in tension with a strong desire for individuation–and indeed very considerable character differences. Much of the first book, *Autumn Term*, is concerned with their attempts to establish an identity not only independent of their four older sisters already at Kingscote, but also independent of each other. Performance further complicates matters: the twins star in a production of *The Prince and the Pauper* in *Autumn Term*; they swap places (illicitly) in the netball team and swap parts in the Nativity Play in *End of Term*–exchanges justified and necessitated by the good of the team or the production; and they are jointly cast as Ariel in *The Tempest* (Nicola singing, Lawrie acting) in *The Cricket Term*. Doubleness is a feature of Forest's novels, not least because of their striking double time scheme: the narrative time takes more or less three years (so Nicola and Lawrie are eleven in the first book and fourteen in the last), but the background time of each story is contemporary with the time of writing and publication–a thirty-four year span from 1948 to 1982. More significant still is the relation between the two worlds of school and holidays and the way in which the same characters can be or can become different people depending on which world they're in. Nicola notes the time it takes her friend Miranda to "slough off home-and-holidays and talk herself into her school self again" (1974: 44); Patrick thinks that "probably Nicola wouldn't recognize him at school either" (1959: 245).

Duality takes a more troubling and sinister form in Forest's second novel, *The Marlows and the Traitor* (1953), in which Nicola, Lawrie, Peter and their sister Ginty accidentally discover that one of Peter's instructors at Dartmouth College, Lieutenant Lewis Foley, is selling naval secrets to the Russians. A practical and moral dilemma ensues, as adults–both spies and counter-spies–have to weigh the importance of the young Marlows' lives against questions of national security. The intelligence agent Robert Anquetil experiences an additional conflict between two personal loyalties: his agonized sense of responsibility for Nicola, whom he has befriended, and his longstanding connection with Lewis Foley, a relationship that seems to be both more and less than friendship.

Trying to make sense of Foley's duality, Nicola asks Anquetil, "Has he got a twin? . . . He sounds as if he was so queer sometimes. As if there might be two of him," which Anquetil says is "exactly how one always did feel about Lewis" (1953: 63). In *Peter's Room*, Nicola is still wrestling with the question: "Foley was a queer person, wasn't he? . . . a two halves sort of person. If he hadn't been a traitor, the other half of him was quite like Giles really," to which Peter furiously replies, "If you're a traitor it doesn't matter what the other half of you's like" (1961: 118-19). Peter's unresolved feelings about Foley haunt the narrative of *Peter's Room* even though Foley himself is seldom mentioned: "For some things about that week-end [Peter] remembered very clearly and others were buried such fathoms deep it needed a block and tackle to haul them to the surface" (118).

The violence of Peter's reaction, as Nicola dimly recognizes, stems from his own initial attraction to Foley (revealed in his blushing and affected nonchalance when she first asks what Foley's like). In *The Marlows and the Traitor*, Anquetil, too, is far from immune to Foley's charm–however wary or uneasy he may feel about Foley's character. As he tries to explain to Nicola, "sometimes you find yourself involved with someone with whom you have all the ties of affection and habit, but for whom you have no real liking. Just as you very often like people for whom you have no affection at all" (1953: 62-3). The subtlety of this observation is characteristic of Forest. Nicola, who finds Anquetil's formulation confusing, doesn't quite know what to say when Foley, "with a queer little half-smile," asks if she's a friend of Anquetil's:

"He said he," she hesitated: "he said he'd known you a long time."
Foley smiled again, still with that little half-smile. "So he has," he
said. "A very long time. *Faithful* Robert." (122)

Forest had always intended to write for adults and had assumed that it
would be easy to make the transition from juvenile to adult fiction once
she had found a firm that published both. *The Marlows and the Traitor*,
although written for children, was inspired by the context of the Cold
War and by Rebecca West's accounts of the Nuremberg Trials (Forest,
2003: 7-8). The novel is unusual among Forest's books in the way it explores moments of adult consciousness–Anquetil's particularly– to
which the children do not have access. Yet Forest does not use those
moments to provide any clearer insight into the bond between Foley and
Anquetil; and the complexities of that relationship, like the "queer" am-
biguities of Foley's character, appear all the more strongly for being
perceived through Nicola's puzzled attempts to understand them. Whatever Forest thinks distinguishes adult fiction from children's fiction, it
clearly is not levels of complexity and ambiguity in same-sex emotions
and the language which describes them; even in those of her later novels
which more clearly declare themselves as children's fiction she continues to explore precisely those areas and with much the same mixture of
directness and obliquity.

It's easy to see how a series of novels set in a girls' boarding-school
would focus on complexity and ambiguity in same-sex emotions. As
Hennegan suggests, one of the pleasures of the girls' school story is its
representation of a self-contained, autonomous female world, in which
heterosexuality and indeed male characters are neither necessary nor
relevant (1988: 176). Patricia Duncker concurs: "Schoolgirl stories
set in women-only institutions lend themselves to lesbian ambigu-
ities and to the extension of conventional gender roles for girls"
(2002: 25). The critic Victoria Coulson, like Hennegan and
Donoghue a devotee of Forest's work, suggests a queer (rather than
specifically lesbian) reading of the Kingscote novels: "What's gay
about these books is that there's gender difference amongst the girls so
you don't need boys: the hetero is contained within the ostensibly
homo" (personal communication, 2004). Yet those gender differences,
and the gender identifications which ground them, do not necessarily
remain fixed or stable throughout the sequence. The characters'
gendered sense of self is a relational one, which may shift and change as
it encounters other gendered selves. Hennegan finds Forest "exemplary" in her "intelligent and subtle appreciation of . . . characters' con-

stantly developing sexual complexity" (1988: 176). Forest's treatment of female homoaffection in the Kingscote books, I would argue, becomes more subtle and more complex itself as the sequence progresses—and does so partly as a result of what the novels set in the school holidays have been doing with same-sex relationships in the meantime. *The Marlows and the Traitor* is one example; Forest's next novel, *Falconer's Lure* (1957), is another.

Falconer's Lure offers contrasting images of same-sex relationships as true or false. There is the true model of homoaffection presented by Patrick Merrick, whose close relationship with the Marlows' cousin, Jon, is shattered when Jon is killed test-piloting an experimental aircraft. Patrick's devotion and bereavement, observed by Nicola, are sharply contrasted with Ginty's performance of grief, egged on by her friendship with the frightful Unity Logan. One of the pleasures of *Falconer's Lure* is its refusal of conventional pieties about the rival claims of friendship and family—looking at Patrick's "white, thin" face, Nicola recognizes how much worse Jon's death is for him than for the Marlows: "They were only his relations. Patrick had been his friend" (1957: 56-7). Ginty, on the other hand, finds herself writing, quite insincerely, "*I feel as if part of me had died too*," because Unity has "not only written a tremendous letter" about Jon's death, "but also a poem called *Threnody for Icarus*. And if Unity felt all that, Ginty didn't see how she could very well feel less: after all, he was her cousin" (1957: 55). It takes a queer eye, I'd argue, to look so coolly at these things.

Ginty's (fortunately brief) relationship with the dreadful Unity Logan is a scarecrow portrait of everything same-sex friendships should not be. "One's always falling over [Unity] and the current friend of the bosom sitting on short flights of stairs, looking intense. She's a public menace", Rowan comments sardonically (1957: 40). Unity's language betrays the unhealthiness and artificiality of her feelings, as when she tells the disgusted Rowan: "I'd risk more than an order mark for a friend like Ginnie. I think she's the most beautiful thing the gods ever made" (41). Even Ginty herself is uneasily aware that the friendship is doing her no good: "It was queer how you invented something about yourself, and then had to pretend to yourself that it was true, because you wouldn't be as exciting a person if it wasn't" (206).

Despite the undeniable horror of Unity Logan, it would be a mistake to assume that Forest regards same-sex bonds as somehow acceptable for males but dangerous for females. The four books set at Kingscote all take for granted the existence and importance both of strong, close friendships with one's contemporaries and of particular attachments to

older girls. Nevertheless, Forest is well aware of the possible excesses–whether comic or destructive–of such relationships. A straight-
forwardly comic instance of excess is the furious argument between
Miranda West (a former adversary who becomes Nicola's best friend)
and the Headmistress's niece, Tim Keith (originally Nicola's friend,
now Lawrie's), about which of the twins has been more unfairly treated
by Authority; Nick and Lawrie find themselves the subject of a "battle
royal" in which they are, apparently, "neither required nor expected to
take part" (1959: 160). More serious is the "terrific row," which
Miranda recalls with relish years after the event, over the Lower Fifth's
persistent, swooning idolization of two Sixth-Formers:

> The whole school got hauled down to a special assembly and Keith
> *really* pitched into them . . . We all absolutely sat and *shuddered*
> while it was going on, and afterwards no one *spoke*, practically, for
> the rest of the day, and you couldn't *move* without falling over
> Lower Fifths in floods." (39)

Miranda, like her creator, is careful to establish a distance from this
model of attachment, indignantly repudiating Nicola's suggestion that
she is "cracked on" the prefect Janice Scott: "of *course* I'm not . . . I
mean–I like looking at her, quite, but not if you mean giving her roses in
silver paper and sleeping with her kirbigrips under my pillow" (38).
Later, in *The Cricket Term*, however, it becomes clear that Miranda's
feelings for Jan date back to her own earliest days as a junior girl:

> After a moment, partly teasing, but more in admiration, Nicola
> said, "You *have* been faithful, haven't you?"
>   "My middle name," said Miranda; and added, "As a matter
> of fact, that's almost true.
>   "Why, what is it?"
>   "Ruth. The *whither thou goest I will go* girl. Oh dear," said
> Miranda sadly, "after this term, when Jan's left, will be so drear.
> Absolutely *no* one to be interested in at *all*." (1974: 51-2)

Like Nicola's mixture of teasing and admiration, Miranda's tone is at
once playful and serious. Being "interested" in the Sixth is both a pastime and–for Miranda at least, who goes on writing to Jan after the older
girl has left school–something more. The Old Testament figure of Ruth,
the "*whither thou goest I will go* girl," is a doubly appropriate one for
Miranda, marking both her Jewish identity and her own kind of "faith-

fulness"–a matter of personal loyalties rather than religious convictions. What it means to be "faithful," in personal or religious terms, and what the connection is between the two, are important concerns for Forest; indeed, they are closely linked to her continuing preoccupation with treachery and betrayal. These issues are central to the novels Forest names as her personal favourites amongst her own works: *Peter's Room*, *The Player's Boy* and *The Players and the Rebels* (1995).

Nicola's friendship with Miranda is an important aspect of Forest's fourth novel, *End of Term* (1959). The novel is dedicated to fellow novelist G.B. Stern, whose background has similarities with Forest's own. Forest, the daughter of an Ulster Protestant mother and Russian Reform Jewish father, converted to Roman Catholicism in 1947. Stern, brought up in a tolerant, not particularly religious Reform Jewish household, converted to Roman Catholicism in the same year as Forest. Known as Peter to her friends, Stern was part of a circle of homosexual writers including Noël Coward and John Van Druten. I have long believed that Forest is the fellow-convert Stern refers to as "Pat" in her autobiographical work, *All in Good Time*, a conviction reinforced by the posthumous revelation of Forest's real name, Patricia Rubinstein.[3] Stern comically recounts an incident in which both women are thrown into a moral quandary when they realize that their Confessions have not been understood by an elderly, deaf priest whose first language is not English, and they have to rush off to ask another priest for advice (1954: 96-7). Stern's experience of exclusion from Christianity as a Jewish schoolgirl daily "banished and belonging nowhere until [school] Prayers were over" (10) clearly informs Miranda's vexed relation to Kingscote's Christmas celebrations, the Nativity Play in *End of Term* and the carol service in *The Attic Term*.

Miranda's upbringing, like Forest's and Stern's, has not been an Orthodox Jewish one; nevertheless, she is clearly set apart, an exotic in the conventional world of Kingscote. Forest repeatedly describes Miranda's face as "vivid" and "hawklike," and her difference is clearly part of her attraction for Nicola: "Nicola looked curiously at Miranda's vivid, clever little Jewish face, with its brilliantly blue eyes, thin aquiline nose, and short dark hair which curled like a diving duck's crest. She might be rather an interesting person to be friends with" (1959: 35).

Nicola's relationship with Miranda performs a number of important functions in the novels. Instead of the doubling of the twins, it makes possible a different kind of duality, with Miranda as the Jewish and Nicola as the Gentile aspects of Forest's own background. In addition to making possible the exploration of religious faith and cultural difference, Nicola's friendship with Miranda also informs Nicola's changing attitude to her own sex. Nicola, who has hitherto clearly spent much of her time being a boy in her own head, hero-worshipping Nelson and her brother Giles, and not feeling very comfortable with other girls, begins to see herself and them differently. Seeing Janice Scott through Miranda's eyes, Nicola sees her as if for the first time: "her face had the delicately modelled look of her mother's favourite Dresden figurine, her hair the ashen shine of a silkworm's cocoon, and her eyes the transparent grey of water over pebbles" (85). The intensity of this seeing affects its object: "As if she suddenly felt Nicola's rather too intense gaze, Janice broke off what she was saying to give her a quick, questioning glance" (86). As Miranda comments mournfully in *The Cricket Term*, "I do think Jan–*notices* you more than the rest of us . . . I *wish* she'd notice me" (1974: 160).

It's Miranda who provides Nicola with an acceptable image of her own femininity–looking at herself in the mirror, wearing the cream-coloured silk dress which Miranda has rejected as a disaster, Nicola unexpectedly finds pleasure in her own appearance:

> Nicola stared at a wholly unfamiliar version of herself. "I'd *never* have thought you were the demure type," marvelled Miranda. "But that yoke–it *goes* with you. So does the colour . . ."
> "It feels marvellous," said Nicola, of the silk cool against her legs. At the beginning of the autumn term, tights were optional. (1977, 64)

As in the moment when she first consciously looks at Jan Scott, Nicola sees herself as if through Miranda's eyes, reflecting Miranda's wondering and appreciative gaze. The mixture of coolness and sensuality here likewise recalls that earlier moment in a pleasure, that is both aesthetic and physical.

It's the friendship with Miranda, finally, which provides a usable model of female homoaffection, both within the same-age friendship itself and in Miranda's continuing devotion to Jan after Jan has left school. (We don't know where this relationship is going, but we do know that Jan writes back). Just as Miranda's honest and loyal friendship with Nicola is a very different matter from Unity Logan's with Ginty (Unity's name itself perhaps suggests a desire to incorporate the beloved), so Miranda's devotion to Jan is a very different matter from–say–Lawrie's wholly conventional crushes on older girls in Autumn Term. As Nicola witheringly remarks, Lawrie "never like[s] the same person for two minutes together" (1948: 105); becoming infatuated with the charming but utterly untrustworthy Lois Sanger, Lawrie confers on her "the romantic haze which had previously belonged to Margaret Jessop," the tall, dark-haired games captain (104). The novels' impatience with the conventional model of the crush reinforces the importance they accord to real, rather than fantasy, female-female relationships.

If Nicola and Miranda represent the Gentile and Jewish aspects of Forest's upbringing, Forest's Catholic faith is represented by Patrick Merrick. A cradle Catholic whose family suffered persecution under the Tudors, Patrick provides Nicola with an insight into "an older world . . . when . . . people believed–without reservation" (1959: 127). The friendship between Patrick and Nicola which develops in *Falconer's Lure* after Jon's death, and which is modulated through their shared interest in Jon's hawks, is brutally interrupted when Patrick becomes the object of Ginty's newly burgeoning heterosexual interests, something about which Forest is both dry and damning. The claims of heterosexuality, like those of conventional family piety, pale into insignificance beside those of friendship in Forest's work. The fact that it's Ginty, the arch-performer of emotion, who exemplifies female heterosexuality is its own statement: Ginty is as sincere in her love for Patrick as she is in anything else, but that's not saying much. Here, as in *Falconer's Lure*, the difference between their emotional responses is profound–a difference which sexual attraction and the confusions of Gondal role-playing have only temporarily concealed. In *Peter's Room*, Ginty's homo-erotically-couched fantasies about (herself as) Crispian and (Patrick as) Rupert quickly give way to the jointly-invented romance between Rupert and Rosina, "a secret character known only to Patrick and Ginty," as Nicola painfully realizes (1961: 175). The reverberations of this relationship continue into *The Attic Term*, where Patrick's discomfort and uncertainty about it become ever more apparent:

> [Ginty] said unpremeditatedly and for the first time, neither as Rosina nor a character in someone else's play but herself: "Oh Patrick–I do so love you–"
> "I do so love you too," he said lightly . . . but whether he said it as Rupert or a play-character or Patrick . . .
> "*Really*, do you?"
> . . . As Rupert, as a character from a play, he could have offered easy, extravagant assurance. As himself, he said, frowning, after a pause, "Yes, I think so." (1977: 16)

In *The Attic Term*, the boundaries between different worlds are once again blurred; here, the homosocial world of school and the heterosocial world of holidays, each a self-contained system with its own laws and characteristics, become disastrously enmeshed. Lacking her best friend, Monica, who is recovering from a car crash, Ginty finds herself miserably isolated and at odds with the world of school, and feverishly attempting to escape from that world via her nightly, obsessive and illicit telephone calls to Patrick from the school office. When a Kingscote staff member discovers Ginty pretending to read Patrick a question from the examination paper she has found in the office, Patrick is falsely accused of cheating and expelled from his school; he wonders how to break the news to Ginty:

> "Would she like a Rosina-Rupert letter, with lots of Gondal stuff about dungeons and exile? Or ought he to make it properly about themselves? *Rosina, heart's dearest–Dear Gin–*" (231). Apart from anything else, Patrick's growing recognition of how little he knows–or trusts–Ginty makes it hard to write "properly about themselves."

His expulsion nevertheless liberates him from another, similar confusion between substance and shadow: the clash between his Catholic school's eager adoption of Vatican II's modernizing dictates and his own need to keep faith with tradition. In *Run Away Home* it becomes clear that the disaster has also freed Patrick, at least for the time being, from the burden of his relationship with Ginty; realizing he's forgotten her birthday, he decides not to do anything about it:

> " . . . Better stay forgotten. There's no point–"
> "No point?" [Nicola] prompted him after a pause.
> "Just no point," he said, sounding almost surprised, as if he'd discovered more to the phrase than he'd known was there. Pleasantly surprised, evidently, for from then on he was suddenly gay and light-hearted in a way she'd only seen him once before that she could remember, off-hand: the time he won the show-jumping at the local gymkhana. (1982: 146)

Patrick's gay light-heartedness makes even more sense in the context of *Run Away Home*, in which the evils of premature heterosexuality are very much in evidence. The runaway child, Edward, whom the Marlows befriend, is escaping from a children's home where he has been placed against his will; the product of a teenage pregnancy, Edward becomes an object of contention when his parents split up and each of them repeatedly tries to seize him from the other.

Analyzing the pleasure she found as a young lesbian reader in girls' school stories, Hennegan notes that the books "might seem repressive of female sexuality from a heterosexual viewpoint. From my lesbian one they were perfection" (1988: 176). As Rosemary Auchmuty notes, earlier twentieth-century girls' school sequences sometimes incurred censorship because they were seen as dangerously endorsing intense female bonding and as implicitly or explicitly resisting normative views of heterosexuality, marriage and motherhood (1989). In its uncensored form, the girls' school sequence routinely contains schoolgirl crushes, passionate friendships, and so on. Forest's novels, however, present something more than these familiar delights: the "rare emotional complexity" identified by Donoghue and others, and the subtlety and moral seriousness with which Forest explores her recurring themes and examines crises of personal development. The thirty-four year period in which Forest wrote and published these novels gives them an unusual depth of maturation–it's a long time to spend thinking about a comparatively small number of characters and their relationships over a comparatively short span of their lives. The novels call forth a corresponding depth of response and recognition from lesbian and queer readers, who can bring to their reading something of the same engagement as Forest's, over time, with questions of same-sex love and friendship, the claims of family and heterosexual society. Being faithful is, finally, about being true to yourself and true to your emotions, whether you are Nicola or Patrick, "*faithful* Robert" or Miranda/Ruth, "the *whither thou goest I will go* girl."

NOTES

1. Only one of Forest's books, *The Thursday Kidnapping* (1963), written for a competition and wholly unrelated to the Marlow series, was published in America; the Marlow novels were "considered too English" to be taken up by American publishers (*Daily Telegraph*, 2003). Forest's other novels, *The Player's Boy* (1970) and *The Players and the Rebels* (1971), focus on a Marlow ancestor, Nicholas, a sixteenth-century male version of Nicola but with Lawrie's dramatic talents.

2. Male-male relations are central to *The Player's Boy* and *The Players and the Rebels*, from Nicholas's love for Will Shakespeare and his close friendship with the Earl of Southampton's page, Humfrey, to the complicated bond between Southampton and the Earl of Essex, played out against the backdrop of Essex's rebellion.

3. Patricia Giulia Caulfield Kate Rubinstein, born 26 May 1915, in Hampstead, North London; educated South Hampstead High School and University College London. A very private person who never married, she gave out very little biographical information. Her identity as Antonia Forest remained a closely-guarded secret until after her death on 28 November 2003, in Bournemouth, on the south coast of England (Eccleshare, 2003).

REFERENCES

Auchmuty, Rosemary. "You're a Dyke, Angela! Elsie J. Oxenham and the Rise and Fall of the Schoolgirl Story." In Lesbian History Group, *Not a Passing Phase: Reclaiming Lesbians in History 1840-1985*. London: The Women's Press, 1989: 119-40.

Crosbie, Fen. "A Family Failing?" *New Chalet Club Journal*, 13 1998. URL maulu. demon.co.uk/AF/articles/family failing/index.html

Daily Telegraph, "Antonia Forest," 6 December 2003. URL telegraph.co.uk/news/ main.jhtml?xml=news/2003/12/06/db0602.xml&sSheet=/portal/2003/12/06/ixportal.html

Duncker, Patricia. "The Suggestive Spectacle: Queer Passions in Charlotte Brontë's *Villette* and Muriel Spark's *The Rise of Miss Jean Brodie*," *Writing on the Wall: Selected Essays*, London: Pandora Press, Rivers Oram Publishers, 2002: 24-35.

Eccleshare, Julia. "Antonia Forest: Children's Writer with a Devoted Readership," *The Guardian*, 9 December 2003. URL books.guardian.co.uk/obituaries/story/0,11617, 1102909,00.html

Forest, Antonia. *Autumn Term*. London: Faber & Faber; reprinted Harmondsworth: Puffin Books, 1977; London: Faber Children's Classics, 2000; orig. 1948.

_____. *The Marlows and the Traitor*. London: Faber & Faber, 1953.

_____. *Falconer's Lure. The Story of a Summer Holiday*. London: Faber & Faber, 1957.

_____. *End of Term*. Faber & Faber, London; reprinted Harmondsworth: Puffin Books, 1978; orig. 1959.

_____. *Peter's Room*. London: Faber & Faber; reprinted London: Faber Fanfares, 1978; orig. 1961.

_____. *The Thuggery Affair*. London: Faber & Faber, reprinted London: Faber Fanfares, 1979; orig. 1965.

_____. *The Ready-Made Family*. London: Faber & Faber, 1967.

_____. *The Cricket Term*. London: Faber & Faber, reprinted Harmondsworth: Puffin Books, 1979; orig. 1974.

_____. *The Attic Term*. London: Faber & Faber; reprinted Harmondsworth: Puffin Books, 1982; orig. 1977.

_____. *Run Away Home*. London: Faber & Faber, 1982.

_____. *The Thursday Kidnapping*. London: Faber & Faber, 1963.

_____. *The Player's Boy*. London: Faber & Faber, 1970.

_____. *The Players and the Rebels*, London: Faber & Faber, 1971.

_____. Interview with Sue Sims, *Folly*, 15 July, 1995. URL maulu.demon.co.uk/AF/ author/interview95.html

_____. Foreword to reprint edition of her novels, in *Falconer's Lure*. Coleford, Bath, Somerset: Girls Gone By Publishers, 2003, 7-14.

Hastie, Nicki. "Lesbian Bibliomythography." In Gabriele Griffin, ed. *Outwrite: Lesbianism and Popular Culture*. London: Pluto Press, 1993: 68-85.

Hennegan, Alison. "On Becoming a Lesbian Reader." In Susannah Radstone, ed. *Sweet Dreams: Sexuality, Gender and Popular Fiction*. London: Lawrence and Wishart, 1998: 165-90.

Lanser, Susan. "Sapphic Picaresque, Sexual Difference and the Challenge of Homo-Adventuring," *Textual Practice*, 15(2), 2001: 251-68.

Raymond, Janice. *A Passion for Friends: Toward a Philosophy of Female Affection*. London: Women's Press, 1998.

Rich, Adrienne. "Women and Honor: Some Notes on Lying," *On Lies, Secrets, and Silence: Selected Prose 1966-1978*. New York: W.W. Norton, 1979; London: Virago Press, 1980: 185-94; orig. 1975.

Sedgwick, Eve Kosofsky. *Between Men: English Literature and Male Homosocial Desire*. New York: Columbia University Press, 1985.

Stern, G.B. *All in Good Time*. London and New York: Sheed and Ward, 1954.

doi:10.1300/J155v11n01_06

Fragmented Identities, Frustrated Politics: Transsexuals, Lesbians and 'Queer'[1]

Katherine Johnson

SUMMARY. This paper seeks to explore the complex position transsexualism has in relation to a range of personal identities and identity politics. In recent years there has been considerable debate over 'borderline identities' particularly between lesbians, transgenderists, and FTM and MTF transsexuals who transgress the identity category 'lesbian.'[2] Stronger political affiliations between transsexuals, lesbians and feminists are argued for, and a greater recognition of the futility in attempting to demarcate the infinitely blurred ontological boundaries between 'sex,' gender and sexuality. Rather, we should focus on 'issue' based politics that challenge heterosexist and normative gender epistemologies and practices that restrict non-conformist subjectivities. doi:10.1300/J155v11n01_07

Katherine Johnson is Senior Lecturer in Psychology, University of Brighton, UK. Her research interests include interdisciplinary approaches to theorizing self, identity and embodiment; gender, sexuality and Transgender Studies; mental health and non-normative identities; and qualitative research methods. She has recently published articles in *British Journal of Social Psychology* and *Men and Masculinities*.

Address correspondence to: Dr. Katherine Johnson, School of Applied Social Science, University of Brighton, Falmer, Brighton, BN1 9PH, UK (E-mail: k.e.johnson@brighton.ac.uk).

[Haworth co-indexing entry note]: "Fragmented Identities, Frustrated Politics: Transsexuals, Lesbians and 'Queer.'" Johnson, Katherine. Co-published simultaneously in *Journal of Lesbian Studies* (Harrington Park Press, an imprint of The Haworth Press, Inc.) Vol. 11, No. 1/2, 2007, pp. 107-125; and: *Twenty-First Century Lesbian Studies* (ed: Noreen Giffney, and Katherine O'Donnell) Harrington Park Press, an imprint of The Haworth Press, Inc., 2007, pp. 107-125. Single or multiple copies of this article are available for a fee from The Haworth Document Delivery Service [1-800-HAWORTH, 9:00 a.m. - 5:00 p.m. (EST). E-mail address: docdelivery@haworthpress.com].

KEYWORDS. Lesbian, transsexual, transgendered, queer, identity, politics

I think we all have our own little flags and own little pigeonholes to go and sit in occasionally and (. . .) I think that's quite divisive (. . .) because I think, I mean one of my theories about this is gay, lesbian, transgendered people have all come sort of through a process of finding out about their sexuality or their gender, and my argument is they should all stand shoulder to shoulder. But they don't (.) and lesbians shout at the guys, the guys shout at the lesbians, the lesbians and the guys shout at the trannies and the trannies shout back and it's all, it's all the same. Everybody slags each other off. (Sarah, MTF, 37, 2/168-175)[3]

INTRODUCTION

Historically, members of 'trans' communities are intrinsically linked to members of the lesbian and gay community–both identities, at least, being born out of the work of early sexologists (e.g. Ellis, 1936; Hirschfeld, 1938). Recently, 'trans' identities, particularly 'transgender', have been incorporated into the realms of 'different genders' under the rubric 'queer' to such an extent that it can be argued that rather than seeking to represent the 'transgenderist,' "queer studies *has made the transgendered subject*, the subject who crosses gender boundaries, a *key queer trope*" (Prosser, 1998: 5; my emphasis). The advent of Queer Theory promised the deconstruction of identity (Sedgwick, 1990; Butler, 1990) and in true queer celebratory style of the early 1990s and, paradoxically, using the same mantra that Jean Baudrillard (1992) had two years previously lamented, Judith Halberstam declared in *The Lesbian Postmodern* that "we are all transsexuals" (1994: 212). Given that many transsexual scholars and activists were at this time busy trying to establish the specificity of transsexual subjectivity (e.g., Stone, 1991; Stryker, 1994), the response to her paper was, perhaps unsurprisingly, predominantly critical and, at times, hostile, particularly from members of the San Francisco-based transsexual men's group, FTM International (Halberstam, 1998 a). To her credit, Halberstam took their criticisms seriously and endeavored to address them by "reconsider[ing] the various relations and non-relations between FTM and butch subjectivities and bodies" (1998 a: 289). She has further refined her position recently to suggest that:

> Transgender proves to be an important term not to people who want to reside outside of categories altogether but to people who want to place themselves in the way of particular forms of recognition. Transgender may indeed be considered a term of relationality; it describes not simply an identity but a relation between people, within a community, or within intimate bonds. (Halberstam, 2005 a: 49)

This may be the case, but it would be difficult to argue that any category that has a labelling effect is ever 'simply an identity.' As such, this is not something specific to 'transgender,' but to all processes of identification. For example, the same concepts 'recognition' and 'relationality' have been outlined as key to understanding *Self-Made Men* (Rubin, 2003).

The project here is to address the frequently fractious relations between a range of identity positions that to varying extents transgress 'sex', gender and sexuality. While it should be acknowledged that Psychology as a discipline has played a leading role in pathologizing and regulating gender and sexuality (Foucault, 1978) the post-structuralist turn that has dominated sociological accounts of transsexualism has promoted a theoretical engagement with this phenomenon as a 'concept' primarily for what it can tell us about the categories 'sex' and 'gender.' Despite vast differences in terms of their sympathy towards transsexual people this results in a range of largely feminist accounts critically evaluating transsexualism for the degree to which it fits with the political goal of overthrowing the existing gender system (e.g., Hausman, 1995, 2001; Wilton, 2000; Hird, 2002 a; Jeffreys, 2003). In this paper I want to hold on to a stronger sense of the narratives of transsexual people to illustrate how they can disrupt the feminist binary of uphold/overthrow the gender system and, despite the 'risk of essentialism' (Prosser, 1998; Elliot, 2001; Lloyd, 2005), I want to evoke a notion of interior life for gender and sexual identity positions (Elliot and Roen, 1998: 246). Thus, I argue that 'borderline identity battles' are as much to do with protecting self-identities that are psychologically important, as they are to do with political or conceptual conflict *between* identities. In the final section I comment on the implications of this for Queer Theory, lives and activism in the Twenty-First Century.

In order to explore these 'borderline identity battles' in more detail I draw on extracts from research on the wider theme of the experience of *Being Transsexual* (Johnson, 2001; forthcoming). The research is theoretically-informed by inter-disciplinary debates and grounded in qualitative data collected in the UK that attests to the diverse and complicated stories of identification and practises as told by a small group of transgendered (TG) and/or transsexual (TS) identified people. Fourteen participants took part in three interviews each, on a range of issues including understandings of the identity categories 'transsexual,' 'transgendered,' 'man,' 'woman'; experience of gender transition and interaction with medical practitioners; transitions in social, familial and sexual relations and sexual orientation identifications. The participants were recruited through adverts in the UK gay press, at a TG Film Festival in London, and through a support group, FTM Network. The sample is opportunistic and no claims are made that the sexual orientation identifications are representative of the TG/TS population at large. Of seven MTF TS/TG women, one identified as 'heterosexual' and six were in or seeking lesbian relationships, and would refer to themselves as 'lesbian,' of these six all had been involved with women prior to transitioning. Of seven FTM TS/TG men, only one was pursuing gay male sexual relations. The other six were in or seeking relations with women, but had varying degrees of attachment to the identity categories 'straight' or 'heterosexual.' All the FTM participants had passed through, with varying attachments to, a lesbian identity and some had difficulty positioning themselves as 'heterosexual,' preferring the term 'queer,' or a more fluid conception of their sexual identity. I will be drawing on MTF and FTM participants' accounts as the process of transition is negotiated across the identity category 'lesbian': from either 'lesbian woman' to 'heterosexual transman,'[4] or 'heterosexual man' to 'lesbian transwoman.'[4]

'LESBIAN,' 'WOMAN' AND TRANSWOMEN

The focus on the relationship between 'woman' and other identity categories, particularly 'lesbian,' and 'transsexual' is not new. Proponents in two key texts on Lesbian Studies in the 1990s (Wilton, 1995;

Vicinus, 1996) called for the opening up of identity categories to challenge oppression. Firstly, Tamsin Wilton argued, "it is only by making the position 'lesbian' available to the whole range of differently gendered, sexed and desiring subjects that the apparatus of lesbian oppression may be dismantled and the limits of the academic enterprise transcended" (1995: 8).[5] Secondly, Cheshire Calhoun develops this call and argues that the lesbian could be theorized within a feminist framework only if "feminism is about women *and* the open space of possibilities signified by 'the third sex'" (1996: 228). Here importance is given to Monique Wittig's (1981) proposal that 'a lesbian is not a woman' and Judith Butler's (1990) redeployment of this in the assertion that the category 'woman' is only stable within the structures of heterosexuality. Thus, Calhoun argued that feminism needed to welcome the lesbian as the 'lesbian not-woman' (1996: 228).

It would seem that 'lesbian' as 'lesbian not-woman' might provide a comfortable identity space for the MTF transsexual, particularly for those that may not achieve an embodiment exhibiting the stereotypical attributes of femininity. How do those MTF transsexuals who have struggled to achieve a female identification negotiate a sexual orientation identity that could lead them back to a position that is outside of the binary gender system they want to belong to? This question is important given that Zachary Nataf (1996: 32) reports that up to 50 percent of MTF transsexuals identify as lesbian. Within the accounts of the six participants in this research who identified as 'lesbian' there were two distinct forms of identity construction: lesbianism as a 'lifestyle identity' and lesbianism as a result of 'sexual practice'. For example, Caroline states: "I might identify or label myself as a lesbian all right because that's the lifestyle I chose to live" (Caroline, MTF, 29, 2/163). Sally and Emily, on the other hand, construct their lesbianism as a default sexual orientation based on sexual desire: ". . . I'm a lesbian I don't fancy you know 99.9 percent of men (.) there's probably about you know 25 percent of women that you know are physically attractive to me therefore I must be a lesbian (. . .)" (Sally, MTF, 35, 2/138-139); and ". . . when I was living as a man I only slept with women I only had umm desire for women and (. . .) now I still have desire for women so that makes me lesbian" (Emily, MTF, 33, 2/94-96).

In the last two accounts the participants assume gender as their primary identification, in this case 'woman,' whilst their identification as 'lesbian' becomes almost incidental. Certainly, in this instance at least, their sexual orientation is not constructed upon the basis of any affiliation with lesbianism as a 'lifestyle' or 'political' identity. In contrast,

Caroline's engagement with a 'lifestyle' sexual identity has led her to construct her gender identity in terms of being a particular kind of woman:

> K: does it (being lesbian) also have an influence where you go, who you, where you socialize things like that?
>
> C: mm (. . .) very much so (. . .) because I go out on the gay scene (. . .) and the sort of pubs you go to, the food you end up eating. I don't know it's strange it's (. . .) I mean you could have a look through my wardrobe and I've got virtually nothing, nothing which is really really butch. I mean you can go in there and find sort of dungarees or anything er a lot of combats, a lot of hiking boots, a lot of trainers, a lot of very androgynous sort of stuff umm very few skirts or rubbish like that umm yeah *it does very much influence you know where I go or what I am* (. . .) umm but I actually went on the straight scene for eighteen months (. . .) umm (. . .) because I changed over virtually on the gay scene the only women I hung around with were gay women right and at the end of the day, no matter how they were dressing then, they had been through a time where they'd worn skirts, they'd worn make up, you know, they'd gone through all that umm and as a result I decided to go on the straight scene for a couple of months because *I wanted to learn how to act and be accepted as a straight woman and as a result it makes me a better gay woman* if you know what I mean? (h) It helps me understand what they went through as well, you know, you go down a straight pub and there's guys leching after you . . . you know it's been good for me to go through that because now I can understand what (h) what gay women have had to put up with for years. (Caroline, MTF, 29, 2/267-285)

Caroline makes reference to how her identity as lesbian is constructed via what Michel Foucault (1985) describes as 'techniques of self.' For example, she talks about how her appearance as lesbian is constituted through various *gendered* styles of clothing, such as 'butch' and 'androgynous', her diet, which will inevitably effect her embodiment and sense of being-in-the-world, and the social spaces she interacts in. Even more interestingly, she also describes her attempt to construct a similar *history* to lesbian women. Caroline mentions how she needed to learn how to perform within the discourses of heterosexuality, particularly in terms of 'appearing as heterosexual' before she felt she would make an authentic lesbian. This is in stark contrast to the accounts of Sally and Emily who defined their orientation as lesbian purely on the fact that they found women sexually attractive; Caroline draws no recourse to sexual desire at all. Instead, Caroline explains how she learned to 'be' lesbian by re-enacting specific experiences that she believed would have fed into the construction of a biological lesbian woman's subjectivity. This is an explicit redeployment of the feminist critique that has been used to keep MTF transsexuals outside of the category 'women.' As Caroline claims, and I think the laugh shows her own knowing irony, "now I can understand what (h) what gay women have had to put up with for years." The notion of lesbian as 'lesbian not-woman' would appear to work well here as her primary identity is lesbian, not woman. However, on other occasions, when she and some of the other MTF participants have positioned themselves as 'lesbian,' rather than confirming their identities as 'woman,' it has resulted in a threat to their female identification:

> . . . I met one or two lesbians that don't like transgendered women umm their argument being that as you've not been brought up a woman so you don't understand umm it's quite hurtful. I can see where they're coming from, I can understand their point of view but even so (. . .) it's still a bit hard to accept. It's probably happened a couple of times really but as I say most people are quite accepting of me as a woman and they don't, they don't actually, I don't think they actually question whether I am or aren't umm I think they just assume I must be a woman I think they just assume that. (Sarah, MTF, 36, 2/189-195)

In this case, Sarah's identity as 'woman' has been questioned by some lesbians she has met, under the frequently cited, radical-feminist mantra that MTF transsexuals are "misguided and mistaken men," who, "are not women. They are 'deviant males'" (Raymond, 1980: 183). All non-transwomen have the potential to reject the transwoman's claim to 'woman' on a similar basis, if they so choose.

Feminists and lesbian feminists in particular have had an uneasy relationship with transsexualism. In Janice Raymond's (1980) infamous acerbic critique, Germaine Greer's (1999) sneer at 'pantomine dames' and Julie Bindell's recent drubbing in *The Guardian Weekend* (2004: 7), MTF transsexuals have been attacked as 'misguided men,' exhibiting patriarchal stereotypes of femininity and for not being 'real women.' What these accounts tend to end up offering, if we look through the emotive language, is a window into the theoretical confusions in the authors' arguments. These authors are keen to celebrate the social construction of gender in order to free women politically from stereotypical gender roles, but they all end up reverting to a form of 'gender essentialism' in order to claim a biological right to the category 'woman' and to berate the transsexual's claim. In my research the participants' relationship to the categories 'male' and 'female' were not straightforward. Certainly, some of them did claim to 'be male,' or 'be female.' Yet, for many of the participants, a conscious awareness of the fragility of their claim to a new gender identity was evident in their narrative accounts.

The following extract taken from an interview with Emily reiterates this point:

> We're not umm, in the case of male-to-female, we're not natural born women nor will we ever be so and the kind of sense and feeling of womanhood is the closest approximation to how er we are ourselves rather than actually being a woman (K: right) and so from that context I kind of feel that (. . .) we should as a body kind of accept and understand ourselves as transsexual rather than necessarily as women (. . .) because we're never quite there and you know, I can't tell you what it feels like to be a woman, all I know is that's the closest association umm in rigid gender terms. (Emily, MTF, 33, 1/99-106)

Emily acknowledges the tenuous claim that transwomen have to the identity 'woman' but highlights that while a binary-gender system is in operation, 'woman' is the closest approximation to her sense of gendered self. Thus, if we look to transsexual narratives our conceptual understanding of what transsexualism means is complicated by accounts of lived experience. This focus on transsexual narratives demands that we pay attention to transsexual subjectivity, and while it acknowledges these participants' uncritical engagement with a political identity, 'lesbian,' it asks whether the political voice of lesbian transwomen is silenced by the rejection of their seeming claim to be 'women.' Transwomen do have a tenuous claim to the identity category if you are working in a theoretical framework that advocates essentialism. Nevertheless, for those who draw on anti-essentialist, poststructuralist accounts, it would appear that all women have a tenuous claim to the identity category 'woman.' Moreover, rather than simply dismissing transsexuals' claims to 'authentic' gender as 'essentialist' it is important to recognize that these identifications are crucial to an individual's sense of self. As such, I am suggesting an understanding of the transsexual subject that lies somewhere between essentialist and anti-essentialist accounts of identity. While an essentialist notion of identity is problematic for politics, an anti-essentialist notion of self is difficult to live–particularly for those people whose claim to a gender identity is more easy to dismiss than others. This does not mean to say that I want to invoke a naïve notion of the subject as stable and independent of discourse, but as Moya Lloyd argues "the relation between the subject and politics is [thus] dynamic, unstable and messy as it moves between the impulse to fix identity and the impulse to unsettle identity" (2005: 69).

'LESBIAN' 'MAN' AND FTM TRANSMEN

As highlighted in the introduction FTMs have a different relationship with the identity category 'lesbian' than MTFs. Rather than focusing on the gender identity 'man', these borderline identity battles center on the importance of demarcating the ontological differences between lesbians and transmen. In April, 2000 the UK based FTM Network's newsletter, *Boys Own*, published a list, entitled "10 Most Damaging Myths about Transmen and FTMs." It is apparent in at least four of the ten myths that FTMs and Transmen differ from lesbians. For example, the two most common myths about Transmen and FTMs are described as:

> Myth 1. Transmen are really just butch lesbians who change sex to justify same-sex relationships or to avoid harassment. Myth 2. Historically, all women only chose to live as men to pursue careers that were otherwise unavailable to them, to seek economic opportunities, or to justify lesbian relationships. (*Boys Own*, April 2000: 9)

In a series of papers entitled "Butch/FTM Border Wars" (1998), Judith Halberstam and C. Jacob Hale debated these two recurring themes that are employed to distinguish FTM identity from 'butch lesbian.' Both caution against trying to stabilize terms such as 'transsexual,' 'transgender' and 'butch' and challenge "the practice of predicating an identity politics on the dead bodies of people who cannot answer for their own complexities" (285). The search for FTM and butch lesbian narratives that are grounded historically can be particularly problematic. The need for 'role models' or simply the delight that can be gained from recognizing your own experience in someone else's is understandable. To reclaim figures and attempt to shape them into an FTM transsexual–as has happened with the jazz musician Billy Tipton and the Nebraskan teenager 'Brandon Teena/Teena Brandon'–often results in an inaccurate portrayal of an individual's life (Halberstam 2005 b). Equally, Halberstam (1998a) argues there is nothing to substantiate a lesbian re-appropriation of these individuals' experiences within lesbian history. Here, their lives are often rationalized as lesbians who lack access to a liberating lesbian discourse. Halberstam warns that:

> . . . while a distinction between lesbian and FTM positions might be an important one to sketch out, there is always a danger that the effort to mark the territory of FTM subjectivity might fall into homophobic assertions about lesbians and sexist formulations of women generally. (1998 a: 297)

I agree. Yet this is equally the case for those claiming to protect lesbian identity and politics from what is described as the "destruction of lesbians" (Jeffreys, 2003: 122). In a vehement attack, Sheila Jeffreys explains what she believes to be the emergence of an 'epidemic' of FTM transsexualism. For someone who supposedly wants to do away with gender she certainly knows how to use it in an injurious style, by renaming people in terms of their pre-transition gender (46, 132). According to her, FTM transsexualism involves 'women' "who had previously identified as butch lesbians or been afraid to identify as lesbians despite loving women" opting instead for "surgical mutilation" (124).

I would make the same point, not as a critique, but to highlight the potential for coalitions between transment, lesbians and women. Instead, Jeffreys' argument focuses on two elements: that FTM transsexualism leads to the re-appropriation and promotion of masculine values and that it eradicates lesbians. To begin with the former: in my research the participants' exploration of masculinity was more complicated than a re-enactment of patriarchal values. This is not to say that there were no normative accounts of masculinity, but most of the participants were invested in wanting to become 'a *different* kind of a guy.' Parallels can be drawn here with Halberstam's argument that alternative forms of masculinity, female masculinity in particular, can subvert aspects of 'dominant masculinity' and thus de-naturalize the relationship between maleness and power (Halberstam, 1998 b: 2).

Many of the participants, in light of their female experiences, were embroiled in a process of gender construction as they sought out ways of being male that did not offend women. As Jason describes:

. . . one thing that umm (. . .) which I suppose yes is is advantageous is that having seen what it's like to be in, treated in a female role, does give you an insight . . . but on the flip side, is wanting to to be able to display your masculinity but without making it sound if it's derogatory against women. No I wouldn't want to be taken as female but it's not (. . .) (K: yeah?) to say female is a bad thing (K: right) and umm you do draw yourself up short about how, how do you put it more carefully? About how you do display your masculinity so that it isn't seen to offend, but also that you don't go OTT that you don't try and put on a sort of masculinity cloak that um isn't yours (K: mm) in order just so that you make sure people take you as male (K: yeah) and I hope I don't. It would be interesting to to hear your opinion on how I'm coming over in terms of what you perceive masculinity to be umm (. . .) and also in terms of, you know, getting a balanced attitude about people (K: mm) I say not not hooking up to an attitude that that will somehow make me feel better which is which is an attitude that really fits with me (. . .)

K: sorry can you say that last bit again?

J: (hh) well it's it's really you know say this cloak of masculine behaviour which some umm I have seen in a couple of transgender chaps put on I think cloaks of masculinity which aren't theirs purely you know (sighs). There is one chap who turned round and said umm I said I can't believe you said that, to his partner he said something 'oh it's it, you know, women nag nag nag' sort of thing (hhh) you know guy's joke. How can he say that? I wouldn't ever want to be like that, just to try and fit into this male, you know, stereotypical behaviour. So I'd be interested to know if you think I'm going down that path but also saying how would you see my masculinity? (Jason, FTM, 39, 2/540-556)

Given his previous gender experience of living as a female, in this extract we see Jason stumbling between wanting to be masculine enough to be perceived as male and a desire not to offend women. Thus, his past experience that undoubtedly involved an awareness of sexist behavior, gender inequality, and the power differentials between men and women, causes him concern–particularly for how he is now manifesting as a man. There appears to be an implicit belief within many of the FTM participants' accounts that to be male is not necessarily a valiant thing.

Constructing an alternative form of masculinity may have the potential to prise apart the profound relationship between masculinity and male-ness (Halberstam, 1998 b). Yet, those aspects of dominant masculinity that the FTM transsexual might want to resist are precisely those cul-tural and material signifiers *of* maleness. This leaves the FTM transsex-ual in somewhat of a quandary. Thus, Jason is seeking confirmation from me, the interviewer, on two levels. Firstly, affirmation that he is successfully materializing and passing as male, and more interestingly, that he is manifesting as an acceptable kind of guy–one who does not of-fend feminist principles that I, and he, may value.

Finally, I turn to the critique that FTM transsexualism is an attempt to eradicate lesbianism. In the aftermath of 'identity politics,' sexuality has a greater effect on many of the participants' lifestyles than simply who they have sex with. Within some of the FTM participants' ac-counts, there was a strong resistance to being positioned as 'heterosex-ual' or 'straight', even though this would be the ultimate act of stepping into 'male power' and confirmation of Jeffrey's critique (2003: 140). For example, Billy draws attention to the fact that previous life trajecto-ries continue to impact upon his lifestyle after transition:

> . . . a lot of umm transsexuals don't feel that they're queer. Quite often they were er straight before and then and if they're they're still of the same sexual persuasion afterwards they actually be-come queer (K: right) umm I'm in the position where I was lesbian before and now I've become straight (K: right) you would think so but no I haven't because I have a queer mentality so I strongly identify with that yeah. (Billy, FTM, 46, 2/43-47)

Having spent 25 years living on the margins of a heteronormative soci-ety, in and around the lesbian community, it is unlikely that the many facets of self that have been constructed through this existence will change simply because his new gender presentation repatriates him within the mainstream structures of heterosexuality. To be seen as and related to as 'male' is crucial for his sense of gendered self, and he still desires women, but in the accounts of those who have passed through a lesbian identity 'to be straight' means much more than engag-ing in heterosexual relations. Instead, Billy deploys the term 'queer' to denote a more comfortable space in which to live out his now conflict-ing practice of 'heterosexuality,' with a personally important affiliation with 'lesbian' and a non-normative way of being.

PERSONAL IDENTITY AND POLITICAL AFFILIATION

The emergence of 'Trans-Studies' has begun to provide much needed accounts of the journeys and experiences of those who live, often uncomfortably, at the gender and sexuality margins. Within these accounts we find a rich variety of feeling as identities and practices criss-cross the axes of gender and sexuality. The biological female who has always felt 'different,' uncomfortable in her body, who lives and loves in the lesbian community for a number of years and then transitions to live as male, losing her relationship with her lesbian lover, who doesn't want to be seen in a 'heterosexual' relationship. The FTM who previously had sex with women, but now identifies as a gay transman. The MTF who was married, who suffered with gender dysphoria for all his life, who used to dress in his wife's clothes and, for a time, joined a transvestite support-group, but later transitioned and now lives with her wife, as a woman, and identifies as 'lesbian.' Transsexualism, contrary to many feminist accounts doesn't uphold a binary gender system. Some transsexuals might want to disappear within a binary gender system, to be accepted as a 'woman' or as a 'man' in the way that non-transsexuals take for granted. These messy tales of gender and sexuality transition don't sit well within attempts to demarcate identity borderlines because, once lesbians and gays, transsexuals and transvestites begin to tell their stories, it is clear how enmeshed they are: by historical and medical discourses; by media sensationalism and misunderstanding; by violence and discrimination. But, also by shared experiences, trajectories and geographical spaces that provide either long or short-term respite in a search for a comfortable place to live.

For those who live out seemingly naturalized claims to hegemonic gender and sexuality identities there may be occasional cause for ambivalence, but rarely reflection or anxiety about these positions. Identity categories are often of greater consequence when they have been fought for. In this sense, I'm arguing that the importance of protecting identity positions has as much to do with 'psychic' health, as it has to do with political affiliations. This is not to promote an individualistic notion of the psychological subject, but to acknowledge our psychosocial positioning in relation to political battles. The personal is political, as the feminist mantra goes, but political movements need to be predicated on more than a single, unifying notion of 'identity.' We have multiple identities (gendered, sexual, classed, ethnic, familial, professional, social), which take on different levels of significance, depending on the social context. Effective political movements have to find a relational context for their members that avoids organising around an 'identity,' if they are to escape being stifled by debilitating internal debates of the status of that identity.·

Queer was one such move to open up identity categories and give voice to those who feel marginalized by identity politics. Despite its limitations, 'queer' may still have potential as a socially-transformative strategy. Here, identity battles have continued to concentrate on which sexual subjectivities constitute 'queer' and for whom 'queer' politics is applicable. This has created an undesirable split between the trans-community and the lesbian and gay community. As 'queer' came to be seen as primarily representing a gay and lesbian agenda, transsexual activists began to mobilize under their own banners: Press For Change in the UK and GenderPac in the US. Their primary motivations were to achieve improved health care and legal rights for 'trans'-people (Halberstam, 1998 a; *Press for Change Newsletter*, August 1999). Politically, in the UK, members of the 'trans'-community, like some lesbians and gay men, drew upon biological explanations for their 'medical condition' and provided conservative accounts of heterosexual normativity in order to achieve the long campaigned for right to change their birth certificates (e.g., Campbell, 1996). Thus, queers, lesbians and feminists (Califia, 1997; Hausman, 1995; Wilton, 2000) might critique transsexuals for their seeming failure to challenge a binary gender system. Many transsexuals may feel that an alliance with 'queer' is, at best, unhelpful, whilst they fight a 'legitimate' battle to challenge oppression on the basis of a biological birth defect. While I call for greater political affiliation between these groups, it would be an oversight to fail to acknowledge the differences between them and the need to mobilize sometimes around specific issues that may pertain only to one aspect of a broad community. However, I believe that it would be detrimental to *all* to negate the sibling type relationship these identities have with one another. The gay, lesbian, feminist and queer communities have frequently provided a respite for those exploring gender questions, and they also provide a home for many of those who have reached the end of their individual transgender journeys.

In recent years several attempts have been made within feminist politics to forge a notion of coalition politics, in order to move beyond the binary conception of essentialist/anti-essentialist identity, which has been interpreted as having a negative effect on political action. For example, Donna Haraway proposed "cyborg politics" where the cyborg is open to a variety of "monstrous and illegitimate" alliances (1991: 154). Rita Felski also invokes the image of political affiliation when writing about 'hybridity' in the case of post-colonialism and the nomadic subject. Her argument is not to valorize or essentialize hybridity as a new formulation for the radical or subversive, but to recognize 'cultural impurity as the inescapable backdrop of all contemporary struggles' (1997: 15). 'Queer' may still have the potential to be the 'cohesive identity' (Hekman, 2000) that is needed for political activity, or the metaphor for 'hybridity' important for political struggle.

Moya Lloyd names 'queer' as a specific example of 'inessential co-alitions' alongside 'women of colour' (2005: 161). Drawing on Chantelle Mouffe (1994: 108), Lloyd proposes that new political identities emerge in antagonism, between 'us' and 'them,' and that politics should be "oriented to 'defus[ing] the potential antagonism inherent in human relations,' turning antagonism to agonism" (165). For 'queer' the question remains whether it can maintain and forge new coalitions across non-normative sexual and gendered positions. To do this it will have to resist the urge to focus on 'winning' internal identity battles and recognize the conflict between a range of subject positions that carry psychological investments for the individuals involved. This last point is important. According to Susan Hekman, even Butler (1997) has conceded that "some version of a core is necessary to psychic health" (2000: 293). Hekman argues that the trend in recent postmodern theory to reject any notion of core subjectivity and define identity as a fiction is profoundly misleading. This line of thinking risks falling back into the pitfalls of essentializing identity and pathologizing transsexualism. Yet, if the goal is to address tensions between holding on to personal identifications in a range of positions while promoting an effective political identity then this is, to paraphrase Lloyd, a risk worth taking (2005: 55).

In order to maintain 'queer' as a 'political identity' which signals 'inessential coalitions' careful attention has to be paid to keeping the process of 'queering' alive. This means unsettling definitions and practises, and paying as much attention to the role of sexual identities as to gender identities. It would seem the notion of antagonism arises most vividly when 'queer,' as an 'identity,' throws into question individual attachments to other identities that have been historically, politically and personally crucial in the formation of subjectivity. Didi Khayatt describes her own uneasiness with the term 'queer,' because of its ambivalence, and because queer theorists seems to forget the importance of battles to gain recognition for terms such as 'lesbian' which was previously subsumed under 'gay' or 'homosexual.' She also notes that for others its ambiguity and inclusiveness allows "a sense of belonging . . . alerting . . . others to their non-conformity without having to specify a certain identity" (2002: 498). Queer may be useful as a personal naming category and this will have its own political effect depending on how it is deployed: be that subversively, mundanely, derogatorily or because it provides a psychologically important representation of self. We will all have different dialogues with the term 'queer' and it is these types of distinctions that need to be embraced rather than rejected. As Lloyd argues, "humans cannot escape the differential relations that mark out subject positions; this is the ontological ground of existence. They can, however, try to create the conditions in which the Other is no longer viewed as an enemy that must be eradicated (or excluded) but is transformed into an adversary or a counterpart" (2005: 165).

At the beginning of the Twenty-First Century, rather than concentrating efforts on attempts to demarcate the infinitely blurred ontological boundaries between our gendered and sexual identities, we need to find a way to create an effective political strategy to deal with the new challenges 'queer communities' face (and I use both queer and communities loosely). This would seem particularly pertinent as I finish this paper in the days after George W. Bush's re-election in the US. Described by the UK right-wing tabloids as a victory for the "moral majority" (2004: 1), Bush won on the basis of an anti-gay, anti-abortion, pro-Christian Right vote. Campaigning for 'gay marriage' seems a long way from Queer Nation's strategy to "put perversion in the public's face" and "embrace the diverse lesbian, gay, and bisexual identities that had been suppressed or marginalized by a restrictive politics of identity" (Bristow and Wilson, 1993: 9). The resurgence in anti-gay and anti-woman agendas, alongside evidence of a twenty-three percent increase in the reported number of homophobic attacks in the UK (Bloomfield and Barrett, 2004), require the re-framing of political allegiances and goals. Perhaps a good starting point would be to engage with our 'cultural impurity', acknowledge the importance of psychological investments in a range of identity positions, and forge 'inessential coalitions' that formulate issue-based challenges to heterosexist and normative gender epistemologies and practises.

ACKNOWLEDGEMENTS

I would like to thank the research participants for giving generously with their time and tales of transition. Thank you also to Maria Antoniou, Myra Hird, Noreen Giffney, Katherine O'Donnell and an anonymous reviewer for informative comments on a previous draft of this paper.

NOTES

1. Following Steven Seidman (1997), I deploy the term 'queer' as a verb, not an identity, and as a theory or tool for promoting social transformation. Queer should be more than another form of Identity politics with its own set of "insider/outsider politics" (Beasley, 2005: 170) and it should to do more than re-establish binary oppositions of essentialist/anti-essentialist, literalizing/deliteralizing or reinscriptive/transgressive through the very process of making them visible. It is important to acknowledge the limitations of this approach when it perhaps inevitably slips into these interpretations, but I will argue that it still has relevance for promoting political coalitions.

2. The term 'borderline identities' is taken from the dialogue on Butch/FTM Border Wars between Judith Halberstam and C. Jacob Hale (1998). It should be noted that while I do refer to psychological notions of identity my use of 'borderline identities' is distinct from 'borderline personality disorder' which is more commonly understood in Abnormal Psychology to represent a pathological state where the individual has an unstable personality and constructs various 'personalities' to protect a damaged 'core' self. Rather, I'm referring to contested identity categories and their relationship to particular experiences of the sexed body, gender and sexuality.

3. Transcription notes: (i) K: interviewer, occasionally referred to as KJ.(ii) (Sarah, MTF, 37): This string indicates that the participant was Sarah (pseudonym), and she is 37 years old. MTF is used to indicate for the reader that she has transitioned from male-to-female, but not to suggest that this is how she would identify. The extract is from interview 2, line 168-175. (iii) (.) pause in speech, each full stop indicates one second. (iv) . . . indicates omitted text. (vii) *italics* represents my emphasis. (viii) [ ] indicates point of clarification. (ix) (h) indicates laugh.

4. Here I use scare quotation marks around all terms to acknowledge that these are my terms rather than identifications embraced by all the participants, for example, some might reject these definitions and claim to have never been 'male' or 'female'.

5. Perhaps she was jumping on the mid-1990s 'queer' bandwagon, or had not fully thought through the implications of this statement, because while I agree it should be noted that this call is at odds with her more recent critique of transsexualism (Wilton, 2000; Hird, 2002 b; Wilton, 2002; Hird, 2002 c).

REFERENCES

Baudrillard, Jean. "Transpolitics, Transsexuality, Transaesthetics." In William Stearns and William Chaloupka, eds. *Jean Baudrillard: The Disappearance of Art and Politics.* New York: St Martin's Press, 1992: 9-26.

Beasley, Chris. *Gender & Sexuality: Critical Theories, Critical Thinkers.* London: Sage, 2005.

Bindell, Julie. "Gender Benders, Beware," *The Guardian Weekend,* 31 January 2004: 7.

Boys Own, 31, April 2000.

Bristow, Joseph and Angelia R. Wilson, eds. *Activating Theory: Lesbian, Gay, Bisexual Politics.* London: Lawrence and Wishart, 1993.

Butler, Judith. *Gender Trouble: Feminism and the Subversion of Identity.* New York: Routledge, 1990.

_____. *The Psychic Life of Power*. Stanford, CA: Stanford University Press, 1997.

Calhoun, Chesire. "The Gender Closet: Lesbian Disappearance under the Sign 'Woman'." In Martha Vicinus, ed. *Lesbian Subjects: A Feminist Studies Reader*. Bloomington and Indianapolis: Indiana University Press, 1996: 209-32.

Califia, Patrick. *Sex Changes: The Politics of Transgenderism*. San Francisco: Cleis Press, 1997.

Campbell, Clare. "Why I want to marry a man who was born a woman," *Daily Mail*, 9 October 1996: 28.

Elliot, Patricia. and Katrina Roen. "Transgenderism and the Question of Embodiment: Promising Queer Politics," *GLQ: A Journal of Lesbian and Gay*, 4(2), 1998: 231-61.

_____. "A Psychoanalytic Reading of Transsexual Embodiment," *Studies in Gender and Sexuality*, 2(4), 2001: 295-325.

Ellis, Havelock. *Sexual Inversion, Studies in Psychology of Sex*, vol. 2. New York: Random House, 1936.

Felski, Rita. "The Doxa of Difference," *Signs: Journal of Women in Culture and Society*, 23(1), 1997: 1-21.

Foucault, Michel. *The History of Sexuality: Volume 1. An Introduction*, trans. Robert Hurley. London: Random House,1978.

_____. *The Use of Pleasure: The History of Sexuality, Volume 2*, trans. Robert Hurley. London: Random House, 1985.

Greer, Germaine. *The Whole Woman*. London: Doubleday, 1999.

Halberstam, Judith. "F2M: The Making of Female Masculinity." In Laura Doan, ed., *The Lesbian Postmodern*. New York: Columbia University Press, 1994: 210-28.

_____. "Transgender Butch: Butch/FTM Border Wars and the Masculine Continuum," *GLQ: A Journal of Lesbian and Gay Studies*, 4(2), 1998 a: 287-310.

_____. and C. Jabob Hale. "Butch/FTM Border Wars: A Note on Collaboration," *GLQ: A Journal of Lesbian and Gay Studies*, 4(2), 1998: 283-5.

_____. *Female Masculinity*. Durham and London: Duke University Press, 1998 b.

_____. *In a Queer Time and Place: Transgender Bodies, Subcultural Lives*. New York and London: New York University Press, 2005 a.

_____. "Unlosing Brandon: Brandon Teena, Billy Tipton, and Transgender Biography," *In a Queer Time and Place: Transgender Bodies, Subcultural Lives*. New York and London: New York University Press, 2005 b.

Haraway, Donna. *Simians, Cyborgs, and Women: The Reinvention of Nature*. London: Free Association Books.

Hausman, Bernice. L. *Changing Sex: Transsexualism, Technology, and the Idea of Gender*. Durham and London: Duke University Press, 1995.

_____. "Recent Transgender Theory," *Feminist Studies*, 27, 2001: 465-90.

Hekman, Susan. "Beyond Identity: Feminism, Identity and Identity Politics," *Feminist Theory*, 1(3), 2000: 289-308.

Hird, Myra. J. "For a Sociology of Transsexualism," *Sociology*, 36(3), 2002 a: 577-95.

_____. "Out/Performing Our Selves: Invitation for Dialogue," *Sexualities*, 5(3), 2002 b: 337-56.

_____. "Welcoming Dialogue: A Further Response to Out/Performing Our Selves," *Sexualities*, 5(3), 2002 c: 362-6.

Hirschfeld, Magnus. *Sexual Anomolies and Perversions.* London: Encyclopaedic Press, 1938.

Jeffreys, Shelia. *Unpacking Queer Politics: A Lesbian Feminist Perspective.* Cambridge: Polity Press, 2003.

Johnson, Katherine. *Being Transsexual: Self, Identity and Embodied Subjectivity.* Unpb. PhD dissertation, Middlesex University, UK, 2001.

_____. "Changing Sex, Changing Self: Transitions in Embodied Subjectivity," *Men and Masculinities,* forthcoming.

Khayatt, Didi. "Toward a Queer Identity," *Sexualities,* 5(4), 2002: 487-501.

Lloyd, Moya. *Beyond Identity Politics: Feminism, Power and Politics.* London: Sage, 2005.

Nataf, Zachary. I. *Lesbians Talk Transgender.* London: Scarlet Press. 1996.

Press for Change. *Newsletter,* 13, August 1999.

Prosser, Jay. *Second Skins: The Body Narratives of Transsexuality.* New York: Columbia University Press, 1998.

Raymond, Janice. *The Transsexual Empire.* London: The Women's Press. 1980.

Rubin, Henry. *Self-Made Men: Identity and Embodiment among Transsexual Men.* USA: Vanderbilt University Press, 2003.

Sedgwick, Eve Kosofsky. *Epistemology of the Closet.* Berkeley: University of California Press, 1990.

Seidman, Steven. *Different Troubles: Queering Social Theory and Sexual Politics.* Cambridge: Cambridge University Press, 1997.

Stone, Sandy. "The *Empire* Strikes Back: A Posttranssexual Manifesto." In Julia Epstein and Kristina Straub, eds. *Body Guards: The Cultural Politics of Gender Ambiguity.* London: Routledge, 1991: 280-304

Stryker, Susan. "My Words to Victor Frankenstein above the Village of Chamounix: Performing Transgender Rage," *GLQ: A Journal of Lesbian and Gay Studies,* 1, 1994: 237-54.

Vicinus, Martha, ed. *Lesbian Subjects: A Feminist Studies Reader.* Bloomington and Indianapolis: Indiana University Press, 1996.

Wilton, Tamsin. *Lesbian Studies: Setting an Agenda.* London: Routledge, 1995.

_____. "Out/Performing Our Selves: Sex, Gender and Cartesian Dualism," *Sexualities,* 3(2), 2000: 237-54.

_____. "'You Think This Song is About You': Reply to Hird," *Sexualities,* 5(3), 2002: 357-61.

Wittig, Monique. *The Straight Mind and Other Essays.* Boston: Beacon Press. 1981.

doi:10.1300/J155v11n01_07

SECTION III

THEORIES:
DISCIPLINARY CHALLENGES

What seems most wonderful to me about the past decade of LGBTQ writing is that it is so luxuriously, lusciously, *there*. I don't have to take a vow of intellectual monogamy; I can fall in love with every single thing I read. I can also walk away, especially when it treats me wrong.

−Michèle Aina Barale

Of Hyacinths

Michèle Aina Barale

SUMMARY. This essay comments on the state of publishing in the field of sexuality in the years since the publication of *The Lesbian and Gay Studies Reader* (1993), which I co-edited with Henry Abelove and David M. Halperin. doi:10.1300/J155v11n01_08 *[Article copies available for a fee from The Haworth Document Delivery Service: 1-800-HAWORTH. E-mail address: <docdelivery@haworthpress.com> Website: <http://www.HaworthPress.com> © 2007 by The Haworth Press, Inc. All rights reserved.]*

KEYWORDS. Lesbian studies, queer studies, theory, bibliography

Michèle Aina Barale is Professor, Departments of English and Women's and Gender Studies, Amherst College, Amherst, Massachusetts. As well as being an editor of *The Lesbian and Gay Studies Reader* (1993), she has written articles on the movie, *Aliens*, Ann Bannon, Willa Cather, Radclyffe Hall, and a book on the novelist Mary Webb, *Daughters and Lovers* (1985). She is presently working on Willa Cather and possibly Toni Morrison while thinking about aesthetics and thereby confusing herself greatly.

Address correspondence to: Professor Michèle Aina Barale, Department of English, Amherst College, Amherst MA 01002-5000, USA (E-mail: mbarale@amherst.edu).

[Haworth co-indexing entry note]: "Of Hyacinths." Barale, Michèle Aina. Co-published simultaneously in *Journal of Lesbian Studies* (Harrington Park Press, an imprint of The Haworth Press, Inc.) Vol. 11, No. 1/2, 2007, pp. 129-136; and: *Twenty-First Century Lesbian Studies* (ed: Noreen Giffney, and Katherine O'Donnell) Harrington Park Press, an imprint of The Haworth Press, Inc., 2007, pp. 129-136. Single or multiple copies of this article are available for a fee from The Haworth Document Delivery Service [1-800-HAWORTH, 9:00 a.m. - 5:00 p.m. (EST). E-mail address: docdelivery@haworthpress.com].

I

I began this essay thinking that I would read in interesting and cross-sectional ways the last eight to ten years of publications that address one or several of the descriptive nouns that customize 'Studies' in the acronym LGBTQ. More: I would also perform a deceptively wacky because ultimately telling tally of topics: I would devise a huge chart of columns and labels into and under which I would organize articles and books in order to make emerge a sketchy but nonetheless provocative portrait of what academics interested in sexuality have been writing, publishing, reading and talking about. This seemed like an heroically useful thing to do, something that would justify the faith of the editors of this special issue in extending me their invitation to comment on the state of things since the publication of *The Lesbian and Gay Studies Reader*, which I edited with two others. Of course, I didn't think that the editors had in mind exactly this undertaking. I supposed that they hoped for something a little less breathtaking.

After three months of increasingly squirrelly effort, I had succeeded in filling an entire legal pad–and I write very, very small–with cryptic checks and squiggles and asterisks. What was immediately clear was that the study of sexuality–lesbian, gay, queer, transgender, trans-sexual, bisexual–was to be found in all the social sciences and humanities. I began to do some hideously painstaking cross-referencing. I worried over my categories, and called friends to worry with me. I was particularly pleased to note possibly less well-known journals which had special issues or collections of articles taking up the application of Queer Theory or the existence of lesbian traditions in a particular discipline or field or area: *Coronica: A Journal of Medieval Spanish Language and Literature* in the Fall of 2001, for instance; or *Scandinavica: An International Journal of Scandanavian Studies* in May of 2001; not to mention *North Carolina Literary Review* in 2000; and *Science Fiction Studies* in 1999–to name just a handful of the many special issues that have relevance for some part of the LGBTQ amalgam. I read with wild abandon and real admiration. I discovered a number of important things that I had missed: Angela Bowen's "Diving into Audre Lorde's 'Blackstudies'" in *Meridians* in 2003; a special issue of the *Journal of Women's History* in Autumn 2003 offers a retrospective on Adrienne Rich's "Compulsory Heterosexuality and Lesbian Existence"; and Margaret Homans' "Amy Lowell's Keats: Reading Straight, Writing Lesbian" in the *Yale Journal of Criticism*, in the Fall of 2001–to name three out of several hundred. And fun. I learned, for example, that a tripling of names were more frequently written about than any others: Cheryl Dunye, Cherrie Moraga and Jeanette Winterson. I re-read older things that my current reading made me wonder about all over again. I made my students read things that confused them mightily so that I would have someone to talk with. I worried about my categories and discovered that friends could not comfort me. In fact, I began to suspect that friends were growing weary of my worry. Which, of course, made me worry a whole lot more.

Thankfully, my not entirely sane attempt to know everything and organize it didn't work. Somewhere around entry 473 (Chris Dickinson's "Country Undetectable: Gay Artists in Country Music" published in *The Journal of Country Music* in 1999) I began to see the dark side of my endeavors–and I was not yet at the halfway point: I was right to worry about those categories. It was simple enough to put Dickinson's article in both the Popular Culture column and the column for Music. Dickinson used "gay"–so I would note it as G and not L or Q. But how about my handling of entry 28, "Women's Bodies of Performative Excess: Miming, Feigning, Refusing, and Rejecting the Phallus" by Jan Jagodzinski in *Journal for the Psychoanalysis of Culture and Society*, Spring 2003? The article is concerned with the cultural meaning of the built female body, makes use of Lacanian notions of originality and mimicry and cogitates on lesbian dicks. OK–I won't file it with Performance Studies, I thought, though it possibly has some legitimacy there (irrespective of how those dicks perform). Instead, I made a category called Psychoanalytic Studies into which I shifted some earlier entries; pondered the possibilities of cross-slotting number 28 in Popular Culture (the article's reference to *Flex* magazine's use of women bodybuilders as centerfolds and a discussion of a number of pop stars play important parts in its analysis); easily decided that I could put it under Queer Theory; and then decided to enter it in Lesbian Studies as well, but with an asterisk indicating that even though the article has dimensions of analysis that seem pretty pertinent to LS interest in gender, its use of Jacques Lacan, Gilles Deleuze and Judith Butler seems to be Higher Theory than LS prefers.

You see my quandary; you probably saw it coming all along: I was well on my way to becoming assistant manager in a purity dealership. I am, in fact, always more than willing to interfere with all sorts of intellectual borders and boundaries; as I understand my job, it is what I am supposed to do. But the more obsessively careful I got in my categorizing–the greater my attempt to not allow methodology or theoretical affiliation to outweigh topics or histories of interest; the harder I tried to encompass the whole of a work's breadth–the more I failed. No portrait or schematic was going to emerge from my efforts. What I had looked more like roadkill.

I had begun with the intention of mapping terrain, and I concluded, horrified, when I remembered that all mapping involves decisions based on knowledges that are firmly based in sets of judgments, histories, preferences, and peccadilloes. I could only draw a map of what I thought and knew. Of course. But why had I proceeded in this fashion? What was it that allowed me to forget something that I had thought that I knew very well: that there is no neutral or objective structuring of knowledge?

Something else, something that I had wanted to know even more, allowed me to not know the thing I truly believed. I had wanted to *not* find evidence of the endlessly unproductive Lesbian versus Gay versus Queer Studies debates. I did not want to work through, one more time, bisexual theory's meaning for lesbian understandings of transgender's offerings for queer folks' thinking. Not because I was feeling lazy, but because I find the need to make those distinctions, whether fine or gross, not all that constructive a thing to do any more. What seems most wonderful to me about the past decade of LGBTQ writing is that it is so luxuriously, lusciously, *there*. I don't have to take a vow of intellectual monogamy; I can fall in love with every single thing I read. I can also walk away, especially when it treats me wrong. I wanted to draw a map in which my cross-references would represent cross-talk. I wanted to show monologues and dialogues, interruptions and asides and possibly a couple of quartets. And it wasn't possible. LGBTQ publications over the past twelve years pretty much speak to their own letter of the alphabet.

II

> ... there is not a developed body of Black feminist political theory whose assumptions could be used in the study of Black women's art. When Black women's books are dealt with at all, it is usually in the context of Black literature which largely ignores the implications of sexual politics ... A Black feminist approach to literature that embodies the realization that the politics of sex as well as the politics of race and class are crucially interlocking factors in the works of Black women writers is an absolute necessity. Until a Black feminist criticism exists we will not even know what these writers mean.

(Barbara Smith, "Toward a Black Feminist Criticism," 1982)

Wet brain, Michèle, wet brain. . .
    (Rose R. Olver, WAGS 24[1]:Feminist Theories, 2005)

. . . frequency of citation is a mode of authority-making, and . . .re-
places historical research as a form of verification of the argument.
This is not a crude dichotomizing of theory versus praxis, valorizing the latter over the former. Rather, it is to suggest that while the
arguments of Queer Theory [Annamarie Jagose, 1996] are
grounded in a reading of social movements, those arguments take
theoretical commentary as evidence, rather than a detailed analysis of the movements themselves.
    (Peter Mitchell, "Wishing for Political Dominance:
Representations of History and Community in *Queer Theory,*" 2003)

They [Elizabeth Lapovsky Kennedy and Madeline Davis] co-
imagine a reconstruction of the past along with their interviewees,
and then assert the result to be historical truth.
    (Sue-Ellen Case, review of *The Persistent Desire*, 1993)

I have snuggled these statements together to draw attention to what
seem to me to be deficiencies of distinction between the old Lesbian
Studies–the one I was learning and teaching from in 1984[2]–and what
might today be heard in classrooms that are considerably different in the
theoretical readings that they bring to the study of literature and its sexuality. Barbara Smith's insistence more than two decades ago that theory
precedes literary meaning sounds not unlike the critical practices that
underlie Queer Studies classrooms, practices that in 2003 Peter Mitchell, in a critique of Annamarie Jagose's *Queer Theory*, finds methodologically troubling. Theory is not evidence, he grumbles. Moreover, he
says a little further on, queer theorists' frequency of self-citation "positions queer theory as a realm of knowledge held in awe by its practitioners. An essential element of this awe is the 'newness' of (the old term)
'queer'" (194-95).
    One way of parsing Mitchell's statement is to hear him tartly com-
menting on the culpable youthfulness of theorists who do not recognize
the present as the past because they are too busy talking to and reading
only the work of those their own age. But another way of hearing him is
as an historian for whom evidence has literal as well as metaphorical
heft. In that respect, he somewhat echoes Sue-Ellen Case's unhappiness

ten years earlier with a selection from Kennedy and Davis' historical study, *Boots of Leather, Slippers of Gold.* Unlike Barbara Smith, Case is suspicious of imagination's reconstructive ability to make history tell the story we most want to hear. In other words, she is not at ease with the way in which theory shapes, indeed, in history's case, *makes* evidence. And both Mitchell and Case sound like the warnings of my co-teacher, Rose R. Olver, a psychologist, whenever I seem to forget that bodies are not just minds.

Because for some years carping on theory–its use, provenance, proposed antagonism to activism, and its incomprehensibility–has separated lesbian critic/lambs from the goats of Queer Studies, I find it educational that the call for theory as the prelude to reading comes so early in Lesbian Studies, and that the resistance to it comes so late–last week to be precise. But I resist the urge to ask queer theorists to note the foremotherly intelligence of Smith's request. What Barbara Smith meant is not precisely what queer theorists do when they read the treatise before they read the novel.[3] LG Studies is not like Q Studies, just as L Studies is not like B and T Studies, which are not like Q Studies though they share an interest in thinking about categories and taxonomies. However, we might argue, as well, that transgender theorists, with their intense interest in the body's materialization of gender, share as much with lesbian and early feminist scholars as they do with queer theorists.

In the past, all our bitter warfare with one another, our declarations of newness and exaltation versus the other side's fearful prudery; all our wound licking, muscle flexing, accusations: they were bad enough. That we now talk to one another almost not at all in print: that seems far worse. As I read, that seemed to be the case. But perhaps not. No doubt that I missed lots. Certainly, I have misread. I await correction with hope.

III

Only our fierce attention
gets hyacinths out of those
hard cerebral lumps,
unwraps the wet buds down
the whole length of a stem. (Adrienne Rich, 1963)

What we do, those of us who do any of the academic Studies,[4] is not trivial. Our passionate need to understand who we are and how we got this way is the stuff of classrooms and therapies and all the books we read and write–no matter how abstract or how intimate. I know that for me, more than thirty years of teaching have barely wet my tongue: I still want more.[5] I want the hyacinths that conclude Adrienne Rich's "Like This Together" which offers me the luminous line "we have, as they say,/certain things in common./I mean: a view . . ." to better say what I have only been muttering about in this essay. I want us all to have and find that fierce attention that grows beautiful in its shared literacy.[6] I don't know why else we would carry on the hard work that we do if it is not to discover the life beneath.

NOTES

1. The acronym stands for 'Women's and Gender Studies.'

2. I offered my first course in 'Women-Identified Writers' (abbreviated to 'Womid Writers' in the course schedule) in 1985 in the Women Studies Program at the University of Colorado; it took until 1987 for the title 'Lesbian Literature' to get into print in the schedule.

3. I would include Black, Latino/a, and Asian/Pacific Rim in this statement.

4. I certainly do not want to pass haphazardly over real and important differences among these writers. Barbara Smith is asking for a way to incorporate both gender and sexuality when theorizing the writing of race. She is seeking a space–one that has the power to shape meaning– for lesbianism and Black feminist criticism. She is not writing before the great divide between theory and not-theory. And it would be a real wrenching of her text's context to make it speak for–or against–theory's entry into the field of sexuality.

5. I am consciously misusing the sharpening metaphor in the phrase 'to whet an appetite.'

6. All my manuscript readers at the journal pointed out that I offered nothing more than this vague solution: read together. I like that sort of solution because it allows each of us to do something. But I will try to be slightly more practical. I suggest that over the next four years every journal whose concern is sexuality ask a pod of writers who do not usually read over one another's shoulders to do precisely that. Let five or six read the same text–new, old, in between–and write about it. Do that every year for half a decade and see where we are. I doubt that any of us will convert any of us. But I do suspect that such conversations in print will spur conversations elsewhere. It is a very tame sort of suggestion. It's, well, it's bookish. But, as you can tell, I am someone who believes that you have to read the endnotes.

REFERENCES

Abelove, Henry, Michèle Aina Barale and David Halperin, eds. *The Lesbian and Gay Studies Reader*. New York and London: Routledge, 1993.

Bowen, Angela. "Diving into Audre Lorde's 'Blackstudies'," *Meridians*, 4(1), 2003: 109-29.

Case, Sue-Ellen. "Review of *The Persistent Desire: A Femme-Butch Reader*, by Joan Nestle," *GLQ: The Journal of Lesbian and Gay Studies*, 1:1, 1993: 79-82.

Dickinson, Chris. "Country Undetectable: Gay Artists in Country Music," *The Journal of Country Music*, 21(1), 1999: 28-39.

Homans, Margaret. "Amy Lowell's Keats: Reading Straight, Writing Lesbian," *Yale Journal of Criticism*, 14(2), 2001: 319-51.

Jagodzinski, Jan. "Women's Bodies of Performative Excess: Miming, Feigning, Refusing, and Rejecting the Phallus," *Journal for the Psychoanalysis of Culture and Society*, 8(1), Spring 2003: 23-31.

Jagose, Annamarie. *Queer Theory: An Introduction*. New York: New York University Press, 1996.

Kennedy, E.L. and Madeline Davis. "'They was No One to Mess with': The Construction of the Butch Role in the Lesbian Community of the 1940s and 1950s." In Joan Nestle, ed. *The Persistent Desire: A Femme-Butch Reader*. Boston: Alyson Publications, 1992:

Mitchell, Peter. "Wishing for Political Dominance: Representations of History and Community in *Queer Theory*," *Australian Literary Studies*, 21(2), 2003: 189-97.

Rich, Adrienne. *Poems Selected and New: 1950-1974*. New York: W.W. Norton, 1975.

Smith, Barbara. "Toward a Black Feminist Criticism." In Gloria T. Hull, Patricia Bell Scott and Barbara Smith, eds. *All the Women Are White, and All the Blacks Are Men, But Some of Us Are Brave: Black Women's Studies*. Old Westbury, New York: The Feminist Press, 1982: 157-75.

doi:10.1300/J155v11n01_08

Feminist Theorizing
as 'Transposed Autobiography'

renée c. hoogland

SUMMARY. This piece considers personal investments endemic in academic writing, more specifically, in Lesbian Studies. Taking Elizabeth Bowen's phrase, "transposed autobiography," as a starting-point, the author briefly discusses the development of lesbian/straight feminist debates, and continues to explore the relative absence of lesbianism in current feminist and queer theorizing. Three 'moments' serve to explain the casting aside of lesbian desire: the subsidence of lesbian/straight feminist debates, the prevalence of 'race'/ethnicity in critical theorizing and the emergence of post-theoretical trends of thought. doi:10.1300/J155v11n01_09 *[Article copies available for a fee from The Haworth Document Delivery Service: 1-800-HAWORTH. E-mail address: <docdelivery@haworthpress.com> Website:*

---

renée c. hoogland is Associate Professor in Cultural Sexuality Studies and American Studies, Radboud University, Nijmegen, The Netherlands. Having received her PhD in English Literature and Women's Studies from the University of Amsterdam in 1991, she is the author of *Elizabeth Bowen: A Reputation in Writing* (1994) and *Lesbian Configurations* (1997), and has published widely on Feminist and Queer Theory, Psychoanalysis, popular culture, and Anglo-American Literature. hoogland's current research centers on the function of fantasy in processes of embodiment, with a special focus on the role of cultural production in the coming-into-being of gendered, racialized and sexualized bodies.

Address correspondence to: Dr. renée c. hoogland, Cultural Sexual Studies/American Studies, Radboud University, Nijmegen, P.O. Box 9104, NL 6500 HE Nijmegen, The Netherlands (E-mail: renee.c.hoogland@planet.nl).

[Haworth co-indexing entry note]: "Feminist Theorizing as 'Transposed Autobiography.'" hoogland, renée c. Co-published simultaneously in *Journal of Lesbian Studies* (Harrington Park Press, an imprint of The Haworth Press, Inc.) Vol. 11, No. 1/2, 2007, pp. 137-143; and: *Twenty-First Century Lesbian Studies* (ed: Noreen Giffney, and Katherine O'Donnell) Harrington Park Press, an imprint of The Haworth Press, Inc., 2007, pp. 137-143. Single or multiple copies of this article are available for a fee from The Haworth Document Delivery Service [1-800-HAWORTH, 9:00 a.m. - 5:00 p.m. (EST). E-mail address: docdelivery@haworthpress.com].

KEYWORDS. Lesbian theory, intersectionality, the personal, post-theory

Always ready to exploit other people's powers of expression and conceptualization, I have borrowed the operative term in my title, the phrase "transposed autobiography", from the Anglo-Irish writer Elizabeth Bowen. Bowen uses the phrase in one of the prefaces to her collections of short stories–brief, essayistic, occasional pieces, in which she reflects on her development as an author, and on the kinds of decisions, she can, retrospectively, discern to have taken in her writing practice. The question she is grappling with here, is the "matter of the personal" (1962: 78). "Total impersonality", she claims, is, for the writer of fiction, an impossibility, for "any fiction . . . is bound to be transposed autobiography" (78, 77). Parenthetically adding that "(. . . it may be this at so many removes as to defeat ordinary recognition)", Bowen goes on to explain that she "can, and indeed if [she] would not, still must, relate any and every story [she] ha[s] written to something that happened to [her] in [her] own life," taking care to point out, however, that she is "speaking of happenings in the broad sense," i.e., ". . . to behold, and react, is where I am concerned a happening; speculations, unaccountable stirs of interest, attractions, apprehensions without knowable cause–these are happenings also" (78). Having thus established the inescapable dynamic in which writer, text and reality are mutually caught up, she is able to formulate, in a rather circular manner, precisely why "impersonality" in writing is impossible: "The short story writer is using his own, unique susceptibility to experience, in a sense, the susceptibility is the experience. The susceptibility, equally is the writer, who therefore cannot be absent from what he writes" (77).

The reason why I have gone into Bowen's ruminations on the matter of the personal to such lengths, apart from the fact that I cannot but continue to delight in her prose, is that from the moment I came across these reflections, while working on my PhD in the late 1980s, they have not lost their resonance in relation to my own writing practice, as a scholar, but more importantly, as a feminist critic and theorist, and, somewhat further along the road, as a lesbian critic and theorist. Even if Bowen insistently refers to the writer, also when she is talking explicitly about herself, in male terms, her notion of the writer's "unique susceptibility" to, and, in fact, coinciding with her/his experience, for me not so much served to legitimize, but in effect opened up a space in which I could do the kind of critical writing that I felt intellectually passionate about, but also saw as politically urgent.

Both my graduate work on Bowen, and my subsequent study of lesbian configurations in Twentieth-Century Western culture, found their ultimate motivation in what I considered my "unique susceptibility" as a lesbian feminist, coming into her scholarly own during the heydays of poststructuralist theorizing. Partly, this motivation sprang from frustration; frustration with not only the gender blindness of so-called male-stream practices of cultural analysis, but also with what were then called 'mainstream feminist' perspectives, i.e. critical/theoretical models that did not, in my view, sufficiently take into account the conceptual and epistemological implications of sexual–as distinct from gender– differences. Bowen's notion of "transposed autobiography" allowed me to take my experience of the world as a lesbian as a starting-point for my work in Feminist Theory.[1]

Let me add that I am using the term experience here in a non-essentialist sense, as something that may be partly produced by simultaneously oppressive and enabling sociocultural discourses, but that cannot be reduced to it. I see experience as the sustained negotiation of various "grids of intelligibility,"[2] that in turn, renders existence into an ongoing process of making and doing within ever-changing conditions of time and place. As such, as an active positioning, or event, experience, as I am using the term here, is a necessarily self-reflexive project, and thus not dissimilar to what Mikhael Bakhtin defines as "answerability," i.e., the fact that the individual's life amounts to nothing but a series of shifting positions in response to specific yet altering circumstances, which implies that one is not only answerable *to* the world, but also answerable *for* one's responses (1990).[3]

By assuming this stance, I entered into a debate that may be claimed to lie at the foundation of feminist criticism *per se*, i.e., the conflict of perspectives between straight feminists and lesbians, which reached its theoretical climax, or so it seems, in the course of the 1990s, with critics like Teresa de Lauretis (1994), Dana Heller (1994), Katie King (1994), Judith Roof (1990), myself (1997), and, not to forget, Judith Butler (1990), having all found inspiration in our notorious predecessor Monique Wittig (1992), each in our own way claiming pride of place for the lesbian as the 'privileged signifier' in feminist theorizing. Arguing to various degrees of persuasion that the figure of the lesbian, precisely because she appears, in the words of Marilyn Frye, to be "excluded from the scheme of phallocratic reality" (1983: 162), represents the most radical challenge to that reality, all of us as theorists took mainstream Feminism to task for perpetuating the "ontological closure against lesbians" by alternately subsuming sexual differentiation under all kinds of difference in terms other than gender (Frye, 1983: 172), or by reducing Adrienne Rich's originally radical notion of a "lesbian continuum" to comprehensive notions of female friendship, or, worse, mother-daughter relationships (1984: 212-41).

Since then, the "apparitional lesbian," to borrow a phrase of Terry Castle's (1993), seems to have once again lived up to the role traditionally assigned to her, for at least as a theoretical position, as a "unique susceptibility to experience", female same-sex desire no longer appears to hold sway–neither within feminist theorizing, where questions of sexuality have been displaced by debates on 'race'/ethnicity, diversity or intersectionality, and, especially in the Netherlands, on religious fundamentalism, with special focus on Muslim or Islamic women.[4] Nor within Lesbian and Gay Studies, where the emergence of queer not only seems to have led to somewhat fruitless debates over the viability of identity categories *per se*, and, concurrently, to endless negotiations over the naming of the field, resulting in impossible acronyms such as LGBTQ, but also to have produced a new privileged signifier in the form of transgenderism and/or female masculinity[5]–both, it appears to me, attempts at upping the ante, at the expense of the theoretical momentum generated, at least in part, by the productive conflicts among mainstream feminist, gay male, and lesbian critical susceptibilities as they emerged, and continued to develop during the last two decades of the Twentieth Century.

This brings me–finally–to the topic I would like to raise in this paper; a topic that forced itself upon me while I was thinking about my contribution to this special issue, and tried to relate my somewhat random thoughts to a number of events in my recent experience, moments of renewed awareness that in one way or another touch upon contemporary politics, both on politics in general, and on academic politics more specifically.

The first of these moments occurred when I sat down to update the reading list for a graduate course called, 'Lesbian Perspectives on Feminist Theory,' that I first taught a couple of years ago. Dutifully starting my search for current contributions to one of the founding debates of feminist theorizing, I soon discovered that the debate as such had more or less come to a halt by the end of the 1990s. The problematic relations between feminist and lesbian critical perspectives apparently no longer come in for critical discussion.

The second moment involves a conversation I had not too long ago at a conference in Louisville, Kentucky, with some American friends and colleagues, who complained about the fact that gender and sexuality simply appeared to have been struck off the political agenda within their respective English Departments, where the white men in positions of power had dutifully taken on the issue of 'race'/ethnicity, as far as hiring policies are concerned, but could no longer be bothered with either the political or the theoretical significance of gender and sexuality in neither curriculum development nor departmental research programs.

The third and final moment is, in fact, a recurring feeling of puzzlement and confusion that occurs whenever I hear somebody mention that we now live in post-theoretical times, or come across the phrase 'post-theory' in cultural critical writing. My puzzlement stems from the fact that I do not know exactly what is meant by the notion of post-theory. Does it mean that 'we' know longer *do* theory–which clearly is not the case if I consider my own, and my graduate students' research practices? Does it mean that theory once was, but no longer is one of the primary goals of scholarly activity? And if this is the case, what has taken its place?[6] Judging by recent publications within my own field, that of Cultural Sexuality Studies, it would appear that sexual minorities have not so much disappeared from the research agenda, as to have shifted their position back from being the subjects of theory, to being the objects of critical analysis, be it in film, media, literature or society at large.

This, at least, is what the bulk of titles produced by a quick internet search–mostly monographs and collections of case studies–seemed to suggest. And if Lesbian Studies can be regarded as to some extent representative of all non-dominant critical approaches, does this imply that post-theory actually means that feminist theorizing, too, has more or less abandoned its claim to a particular perspective, its "unique susceptibility" to the world that enables one to ask alternative questions, produce different knowledge, generate new modes of knowing? In other words, does the dawn of the post-theoretical age mean that all such self-consciously situated perspectives have been or have to be re-aligned with the dominant view from nowhere, which singles out certain problems of social and political difference to be worthy of critical and theoretical attention, while declaring others to be no longer relevant, passé, or outdated? In short, what does post-theory mean for a project like Feminism whose practitioners, from the outset, have not only been concerned with women–in all their various permutations–as objects of research, but first and foremost, to use their experience which, to recall Bowen, constitutes one's own, "unique susceptibility," in order to claim their position as subjects of research so as to generate alternative forms of knowledge and produce different kinds of theories?

NOTES

1. For alternative contemporary views on the problematic question of the personal in Lesbian (and Gay) Critical Studies, see Munt (1997); Lewis (1992).

2. The term is Michel Foucault's, I believe, but gained wide currency in feminist discourse when picked up and employed by Judith Butler (1990).

3. I have explored these ideas in detail in my study of Bowen (hoogland, 1994).

4. In this respect, the politicization of critical theorizing, partly produced by and within Lesbian and Gay Studies itself, appears to have produced the paradoxical result that "interethnic relations," generally regarded as one of the most urgent social problems by Dutch politicians and the overall population alike, have been raised to the top of a thoroughly politically-inspired research agenda, to the neglect of the by now putatively less socially-urgent questions of gender and sexuality, whose critical and theoretical significance has thus also become obscured.

5. I am referring here mainly to the claims to superior 'radicalness' of these categories on the part of, for example, Halberstam (1998) and Prosser (1998). See also Clare Hemmings' acute observations on this theme in her contribution.

6. Although I, to some extent, share the worries of some post-theorists that the heyday of Theory with a capital T has led to the uncritical rehearsal of certain "politicized" critical programs on the part of students and PhD candidates growing up amidst (the results of) the so-called culture wars on especially US campuses, my impression is that such heartfelt and justified worries have rapidly been turning into calls for a return to the "good old days" of traditional literary criticism, when "logical argumentation" and "empirical" reading practices prevailed, while "great works of art" could easily be identified on the basis of supposedly universal aesthetic values. Both the tone with which and the content of such arguments against Theory and its presumed proponents suggest to me that at least a number of these avowed post-theorists are trying to re-claim positions of power and authority within a field they feel to have been usurped and wrongfully overtaken by (younger) generations of scholars whose successful attempts at throwing out old orthodoxies have, perhaps inevitably, created their own sets of new orthodoxies. This, at least, is what can be gleaned from the various contributions to a recent volume of essays on the topic (Patai and Corrall, 2005). A less defensively-framed, and more balanced perspective on the potentially stultifying effects of some strains of increasingly abstract, post-structurally-informed thinking, can be seen to organize the essays in an earlier collection focusing on the same theme (McQuillan et al., 1999).

REFERENCES

Bakhtin, Mikhail. *Art and Answerability: Early Philosophical Essays by M.M. Bakhtin*, ed. Michael Holquist and Vladim Liapunov. Austin, TX: University of Texas Press, 1990.

Bowen, Elizabeth. Preface to *Stories by Elizabeth Bowen*. In *Afterthought*. London: Longmans, Geen and Company Ltd., 1962.

Butler, Judith. *Gender Trouble: Feminism and the Subversion of Identity.* New York and London: Routledge, 1990.

Castle, Terry. *The Apparitional Lesbian: Female Homosexuality and Modern Culture.* New York: Columbia University Press, 1993 a.

De Lauretis, Teresa. *The Practice of Love: Lesbian Sexuality and Perverse Desire.* Bloomington and Indianapolis: Indiana University Press, 1994.

Frye, Marilyn R. "To Be and Be Seen: The Politics of Reality," *The Politics of Reality: Essays in Feminist Theory.* Trumansberg, New York: The Crossing Press, 1983: 152-74.

Halberstam, Judith. *Female Masculinity.* Durham: Duke University Press, 1998.

Heller, Dana, ed. *Cross Purposes: Lesbians, Feminists, and the Limits of Alliance.* Bloomington and Indianapolis: Indiana University Press, 1997.

hoogland, renée c. *Elizabeth Bowen: A Reputation in Writing.* New York: New York University Press, 1994.

_____. *Lesbian Configurations.* Cambridge and Oxford: Polity Press, 1997.

King, Katie. *Theory in its Feminist Travels: Conversations in U.S. Women's Movements.* Bloomington and Indianapolis: Indiana University Press, 1994.

Lewis, Reina. "The Death of the Author and the Resurrection of the Dyke". In Sally R. Munt, ed. *New Lesbian Criticism: Literary and Cultural Readings.* New York and London: Harvester Wheatsheaf, 1992: 17-32.

McQuillan, Martin, Graeme McDonald, Robin Purves and Stephen Thomson, eds. *Post-Theory: New Directions in Criticism.* Edinburgh: Edinburgh University Press, 1999.

Munt, Sally R. "The Personal, Experience and the Self." In Andy Medhurst and Sally R. Munt, eds. *Lesbian and Gay Studies: A Critical Introduction.* London and Washington: Cassell, 1997: 186-97

Patai, Daphne and Will H. Corrall, eds. *Theory's Empire: An Anthology of Dissent.* New York: Columbia University Press, 2005.

Prosser, Jay. *Second Skins: The Body Narratives of Transsexuality.* New York: Columbia University Press, 1998.

Rich, Adrienne. "Compulsory Heterosexuality and Lesbian Existence." In Ann Snitow, Christine Stansell and Sharon Thompson, eds. *Desire: The Politics of Sexuality.* London: Virago Press, 1984: 212-41.

Roof, Judith. *A Lure of Knowledge: Lesbian Sexuality and Theory.* New York: Columbia University Press, 1991.

doi:10.1300/J155v11n01_09

Post-Lesbian?
Not Yet

Toni A. H. McNaron

SUMMARY. Though some may encourage us to consider ourselves in a 'post-lesbian' era, political cultural and academic realities suggest something quite different. Analyzing specific cases in all three of these arenas can strengthen a resolve to insist on the preservation of both the term and concept embodied by 'lesbian.' Finally, this essay suggests

Toni A. H. McNaron is Morse Alumni Distinguished Teaching Professor Emerita in English, University of Minnesota, Minneapolis. Her research has focused on Renaissance literature, feminist writing and GLBT literature and culture. Publications include *I Dwell in Possibility: A Memoir; Voices in the Night: Women Speaking About Incest; The Sister Bond: A Feminist View of a Timeless Connection; Poisoned Ivy: Lesbian and Gay Academics Confront Homophobia;* and *New Lesbian Studies: Into the Twenty-First Century.* From 1990-99, she was Co-Ordinator of the Bush Foundation Faculty Development Program on Excellence and Diversity in Teaching. Her writing specialties include feminist and lesbian feminist literary theory and practice, feminist pedagogy, William Shakespeare, Virginia Woolf and Emily Dickinson. While at the University of Minnesota, she began and chaired the Women's Studies Program, the Center for Advanced Feminist Studies and the GLBT Studies Program. Currently, she directs the College in the Schools Literature Program through the College of Continuing Education at the University of Minnesota.

Address correspondence to: Professor Toni A. H. McNaron, Professor Emeritus, Department of English, University of Minnesota, Twin Cities, Minneapolis, MN 55455 USA (E-mail: mcnar001@umn.edu).

[Haworth co-indexing entry note]: "Post-Lesbian? Not Yet." McNaron, Toni A. H. Co-published simultaneously in *Journal of Lesbian Studies* (Harrington Park Press, an imprint of The Haworth Press, Inc.) Vol. 11, No. 1/2, 2007, pp. 145-151; and: *Twenty-First Century Lesbian Studies* (ed: Noreen Giffney, and Katherine O'Donnell) Harrington Park Press, an imprint of The Haworth Press, Inc., 2007, pp. 145-151. Single or multiple copies of this article are available for a fee from The Haworth Document Delivery Service [1-800-HAWORTH, 9:00 a.m. - 5:00 p.m. (EST). E-mail address: docdelivery@haworthpress.com].

several areas open for future investigation by scholars and activists alike. doi:10.1300/J155v11n01_10 *[Article copies available for a fee from The Haworth Document Delivery Service: 1-800-HAWORTH. E-mail address: <docdelivery@haworthpress.com> Website: <http://www.HaworthPress. com> © 2007 by The Haworth Press, Inc. All rights reserved.]*

KEYWORDS. Lesbian realities, invisibility, homophobic culture, power of knowledge, theories of likeness

On 2 November 2004, approximately 3,000,000 Americans in eleven states voted against same-sex marriage. Because eight of the eleven amendments to these states' constitutions also prohibited legal acceptance of other forms of relationship recognition, such as civil unions and domestic partnerships, thousands of gay and non-gay families may lose benefits and suffer other hardships. According to the 2000 US census, in these eight states there are at least 2.1 million people living in households headed by unmarried partnered couples. The Michigan initiative makes clear just how extensive the denial of rights can be: "The proposal would amend the state constitution to provide that 'the union of one man and one woman in marriage shall be the only agreement recognized as a marriage or similar union *for any purpose.*'" (emphasis mine). For the advocates of such punitive measures, the culture is in a pre-lesbian rather than a post-lesbian era.

During the third debate of the 2004 presidential election, John Kerry, the Democratic candidate, discovered to his surprise that using the word 'lesbian' could set off a fire-storm of protest, branding him as demeaning not only of Vice-President Dick Cheney's already out lesbian daughter, but of the entire Cheney family and, according to some radio and television commentators, of all decent Christian Americans. The Cheneys must not see themselves in a 'post-lesbian' era, since the mere mention of the word covered them in shame in front of an entire nation, even though when Senator John Edwards, Democratic candidate for Vice-President, spoke positively to Cheney about his support for his gay daughter, the Vice-President thanked him for his kind words of support. Surely a 'post-lesbian' culture would be able to have someone identified as a lesbian without such a negative reaction.

When Susan Sontag died in early January 2005, the *New York Times*, in an otherwise glowing encomium to her as the country's "leading intellectual," neglected to say she was survived by her partner, noted photographer Annie Liebowitz, or that she had been involved with several other women in the world of art and letters. Granted that Sontag herself maintained public silence about her intimate relationships with women, making it complicated for obituary writers to make simple pronouncements. Nevertheless, the silence around the term 'lesbian' on the part of editors of the nation's putatively most liberal daily newspaper, clearly suggests that those editors do not see their potential readers as being in a 'post-lesbian' era.

I cite these anecdotes to point to what seems obvious to me, i.e., terms like 'post-lesbian' have little to do with the daily politics of individuals trying to live a sane and productive life. Too many Americans currently respond in a super-charged manner to any mention of lesbian reality to let me feel comfortable using such a phrase. It may be academically chic to posit an upwardly sloping curve away from such essentialized terms as lesbian, but it most certainly is not politically prudent to ignore the extreme discomfort of many in this culture with any articulation of the word, much less with examples of the life choices implied by it. At a yet deeper level of concern, I refuse to declare the notion of lesbian reality and culture irrelevant or passé, and that's exactly what I am asked to do if I assent to the present world as being 'post-lesbian.'

The prefix 'post' as used by intellectuals within and outside the academy usually implies progress in relation to the noun it precedes. That progress, furthermore, suggests improvement and even superiority over the original condition and whatever ideas and behaviors might be connected with it. This trajectory of movement away from or above whatever 'lesbian' might mean to such thinkers and theorists is what gives me pause. As a 68-year-old lesbian feminist, who taught and conducted literary research and writing at the University of Minnesota for 37 years, I simply cannot figure out why I would want to inhabit something called the 'post-lesbian era.' Acknowledging myself as a lesbian was one of the most empowering acts of my adult life, allowing me to find my voice as a critic and memoirist even as it clarified my sense of the source of many of my academic approaches to literature and other art forms as well as the national news.

The present rush to declare the Age of Lesbianism over reminds me of the 1970s when I chaired Women's Studies. Male colleagues and journalists routinely asked me if I thought we eventually would grow into (a.k.a. advance beyond) a time when universities and colleges would not 'need' women's studies. My answer, only partially facetious, was "Well, not as long as there are women." Perhaps this is my current honest response to questions about whether we inhabit a post-lesbian era: "Not as long as there are lesbians."

For a long time I have been watching with keen interest as efforts have been launched in the popular press as well as in theoretical writings to declare us not only in a post-lesbian but also a post-feminist moment. A deep skepticism persists about this urge to abandon a subject of research and a body of reality that seem to me never to have been fully considered in terms of scholarship or politics or materiality. Certainly the lot of many women has undergone a virtual sea change over the last few decades. Just as certainly, large numbers of lesbians (and gay men) have come out of our closets, making it increasingly harder for other people to say they do not know anyone like us. And for lesbians, whether we call ourselves that or women who love other women or queer women, invisibility and disapproval continue to be barriers to equality. For instance, I am still forced to lie or create an additional category on almost all official forms which list as the only options 'Married,' 'Single,' 'Divorced' or 'Widowed'; women in the U.S. workforce still make significantly less than men holding comparable jobs as revealed in a recent government study; large and powerful groups are working to erode if not overturn the Supreme Court decision legalizing abortion in the United States; many people still insist that exclusive terms like 'man' or 'mankind' refer to everyone; and Lawrence Summers, president of Harvard University in 2005, can declare at a conference on women and minorities in science and engineering held at the National Bureau of Economic Research that girls and women may not do as well in such fields because of biological differences between them and boys and men. Large portions of our society remain unwilling to allow women control over our own bodies, harking back to earlier efforts in this country to suppress women's sexuality in general and sexual independence from men in particular. Pernicious and regressive stances on the part of many individuals and institutions in our society belie all possibility of declaring our culture as being 'post' anything pertaining to women who try to exist personally and professionally in a way that is critical of heterosexist assumptions and policies.

If being able to say we are in a 'post-lesbian' era is supposed to signal progress, then my skepticism turns into anxiety for those women of any age who are just discovering their love for and commitment to other women. Any status-quo position depends upon a certain amount of denial and delusion in order to continue, so I do not want emerging lesbians to be lulled into any false sense that the world is eager to welcome us to its bosom. Though some younger women, especially those living in large metropolitan cities, currently prefer the term queer to lesbian, thousands more living in smaller locations across the country or finding themselves part of a generation not quite comfortable with the newest terminology, continue to use the word lesbian to describe who they are and what they believe. I find myself in the last group, so that I am chary about rendering women once again invisible by using either gay or queer to describe myself and those who feel as I do.

Years ago, when colleges and universities were instituting courses of study in women's history and culture, we were urged to call such programs 'Women's Studies' rather than 'Feminist Studies,' so as not to appear 'aggressive' or 'anti-male.' A few years after such programs had been put into place, academics were then urged to change the name to 'Gender Studies.' The putative reason for this was to place the study of women in context, but the visual and psychological effect was the erasure of women as a distinct category around which research and teaching could develop.

Similarly, when lesbian academics began to design courses, we were often urged to call such programs 'Gay Studies' or in more esoteric locations 'Gender Studies.' In both instances, a male patina obtains, revealed by what is included in many syllabi. Recent scholarship about 'queering' an author or historic or cultural period sometimes has won more approval within the academy than have gay or lesbian studies because administrators can assure legislators or private donors that there is no correlation between a faculty member's writing about such a topic and his or her own 'lifestyle.' The rubric 'Lesbian Studies,' on the other hand, signals an emphasis on female-female history, culture and desire. Young women just discovering their orientation toward other women need courses that give them the foundational constructs within which to place their particular experiences. Like everyone else who has been marginalized by the dominant culture, lesbian students thrive when material covered in their formal courses reflects their political and personal choices, just as they tend to shrink, hide or become unsure of their choices and their very beings when such courses fail to mirror their reality. This fact alone makes such programs more politically sensitive and, perhaps simultaneously, more strategically placed to subvert stereotypical ideas and theories about a significant segment of the population.

Since I do not see North American society as being anywhere near a state of enlightenment about or acceptance of lesbian realities, I perforce believe that it is essential that as many colleges and universities as possible design and maintain Lesbian Studies programs. We know that one salient way to combat prejudice and injustice is to educate the broadest possible group of citizens about the ideology or subgroup on whom such shoddy and hurtful attitudes are being visited. Offering courses and research opportunities as well as conferences and special lecture series, focused on the myriad facets of lesbian history and life, is a constructive way to open up genuine debate about such subjects and to foster a direct infusion of energy into those students and faculty with a personal stake in such research and teaching.

Nomenclature always has political and personal overtones, and this is nowhere truer than within academic settings. What we call the courses we offer, the articles and books we write, the research we do and the conferences we organize and attend reflect deeply held values. To erase the terms lesbian and Lesbian Studies from academic and political vocabularies would be to bury important historical and cultural research in the name of progress, a progress I do not find evidenced around me to any degree whatever. It would allow the investigative and creative lights that have been directed into the shadowed past of lesbian realities for such a very short time to be snuffed out prematurely. Such a darkening would in kind play into the remaining substantial ignorance of the general population about what it means to call oneself a lesbian while denying life-saving knowledge to that portion of the population that identifies itself as lesbian or is in relation with someone so identified. Most important of all, such a relinquishment of the concept of lesbian existence could jeopardize the very lives of future women who come to a crossroads in their lives when it is no longer possible or healthy for them to persist in some heterosexist mythology that surrounds them.

What would be lost to institutions of learning were we to stop offering lesbian studies courses and programs is no less urgent and far-reaching. Since all programs that begin from a position of recovery and redress must spend initial years doing precisely that–finding and explaining lost knowledge–many Lesbian Studies programs in North America have only just begun to have the luxury to consider more abstract and theoretical matters connected with what it might mean to critical methodologies in various disciplines if its advocates and spokespersons took same-sex female desire seriously as a defining category. Speaking only about literature and other humanities subjects, I can say that what would be lost are the many possible answers to this crucial question: given the preponderant view that opposites attract, what does it mean to the arts if their creators proceed from a position based on the powerful force of likeness, if aesthetic excitement does not exclusively result from contact with an 'other'? Lesbian Studies is a logical and major player in any such inquiry, and our scholars must be encouraged to pursue this paradigmatic question much further than time has so far made possible. We need to do more than admit that we are not yet in some 'post-lesbian' era; we need to champion and celebrate what can be learned and shared precisely because we still proudly inhabit 'lesbian' terrain.

doi:10.1300/J155v11n01_10

Through the Looking Glass:
A '70s Lesbian Feminist
Considers Queer Theory

Margaret Cruikshank

SUMMARY. Lesbian feminists who began their work in the 1970s probably share my mixed feelings about and attitudes towards Queer Theory: curiosity, envy, indignation and occasional agreement. The solar center of mostly male Queer Theory has young lesbian scholars orbiting around it. Gender used to share the stage with sexuality but now seems relegated to the wings. Like Marxists in the 1950s who remembered the heady days of the 1930s, we veteran lesbian feminists cannot help recalling the excitement and sense of possibility in Lesbian Studies twenty-five years ago. doi:10.1300/J155v11n01_12 *[Article copies available for a fee from The Haworth Document Delivery Service: 1-800-HAWORTH. E-mail address: <docdelivery@haworthpress.com> Website: <http://www. HaworthPress.com>* © 2007 by The Haworth Press, Inc. All rights reserved.]

Among Margaret Cruikshank's many publications are *The Lesbian Path* (1980); *Lesbian Studies: Present and Future* (1982); *New Lesbian Writing* (1984); *The Gay and Lesbian Liberation Movement* (1992); *Fierce with Reality* (1995, 2007); and *Learning to Be Old: Gender, Culture and Aging* (2002).

Address correspondence to: Professor Margaret Cruikshank, Box 134, Corea, ME 04624, USA (E-mail: pc26@midmaine.com).

[Haworth co-indexing entry note]: "Through the Looking Glass: A '70s Lesbian Feminist Considers Queer Theory." Cruikshank, Margaret. Co-published simultaneously in *Journal of Lesbian Studies* (Harrington Park Press, an imprint of The Haworth Press, Inc.) Vol. 11, No. 1/2, 2007, pp. 153-157; and: *Twenty-First Century Lesbian Studies* (ed: Noreen Giffney, and Katherine O'Donnell) Harrington Park Press, an imprint of The Haworth Press, Inc., 2007, pp. 153-157. Single or multiple copies of this article are available for a fee from The Haworth Document Delivery Service [1-800-HAWORTH, 9:00 a.m. - 5:00 p.m. (EST). E-mail address: docdelivery@haworthpress.com].

KEYWORDS. Lesbian feminism, queer theory, genealogy, gender, generational split, politics, critique, patriarchy

Lesbian feminists who began their work in the 1970s probably share my mixed feelings about and attitudes towards Queer Theory: curiosity, envy, indignation and occasional agreement. The solar center of mostly male Queer Theory has young lesbian scholars orbiting around it. Gender used to share the stage with sexuality but now seems relegated to the wings. Like Marxists in the 1950s who remembered the heady days of the 1930s, we veteran lesbian feminists cannot help recalling the excitement and sense of possibility in Lesbian Studies twenty-five years ago.

In academia, though, we lacked the numbers, the resources (and the male privilege) to make the kind of impact Queer Theory now seems to enjoy. The practice of Queer Theory builds careers; Lesbian Feminism was an enterprise that could end them. Lesbians were fired and denied tenure in the 1970s and 1980s, a loss that impacted LGBT Studies in ways difficult to calculate. While I do not begrudge younger LGBT scholars the career options now open to some of them, I would welcome recognition of the forerunners who, after all, produced theory ourselves. In short, Queer Theory presents itself as radical but settles more cosily into the academic nest than Lesbian Feminism ever has. 'Queer' is sometimes used ornamentally in article titles to signal the author's hipness rather than the actual content of the work. We were never hip. Feminism and Queer Theory share one striking similarity, however: both have infused the moribund Humanities, especially English, with new life.

Queer Theory seems an expression of American individualism in contrast to the collective, countercultural spirit of early Feminism and Lesbian Feminism. By discounting identity politics, making virtues of fluidity and indeterminacy and focusing on styles and representations, Queer Theory may align itself unwittingly with consumer culture. If who we are is so contested, then at least what we buy is certain. Occasionally, Queer Theory seems like an echo chamber, with writings citing only one another. They often allude totemically to Audre Lorde, without incorporating her ideas into their analysis, her concept of 'the erotic as power,' for example.

The challenge to identity politics also misses the power, drama, complexity and historical moment of the coming-out story. 'Essentialist' is a simplifying label. The stigma of lesbianism was so oppressive and forbidding before the 1970s that the act of claiming it was life-changing, and survival after coming-out required a group identity. Lesbianism could well appear to be the central fact of one's existence when embracing it was dangerous. Those who came-out in the 1990s and later have had many-layered mantles of protection–social and political–unavailable to those who came-out twenty or thirty years earlier.

An essay whose title and author I cannot cite disparaged two anthologies published in 1980, *The Lesbian Path* and *The Coming Out Stories*, because contributors experienced their lesbianism as a core identity, not as fluid and changeable, and thus were out of step with 1990s thought. It is true that some writers in these works described their coming-out with the fervor befitting a profound and transformative experience but that was exactly their experience. Their autobiographical accounts reflect the ways of interpreting lesbianism then available.

Lillian Faderman, Bonnie Zimmerman, Jacqueline Zita and others have noted the caricatures of Lesbian Feminism that sometimes inhabit Queer Theory. We were outdated, slightly embarrassing, humourless cousins, weighed down by ideology. I do recall conversations in Berkeley about whether a 'real' lesbian wore lipstick or painted her fingernails, but our support groups included women who did both, and so the question seemed settled. Furthermore, I never heard that penetration was wrong or patriarchal or that sexual pleasure between adult women needed regulating by other feminists. The granola-Birkenstock-flannel shirt stereotype was created by lesbians who were not there. They miss our diversity.

Queer Theory seems to prefer decentering heterosexuality to resurrecting a useable past or illuminating contemporary issues beyond popular culture. Gayle Rubin (2004) regrets that its ascendancy has meant less regard for empirical research and descriptive work. Rubin likes its emphasis on sexuality because she believes lesbian feminists de-emphasized sex, but she faults Queer Theory for historical amnesia. In the beginning, Lesbian/Gay Studies owed a great deal to activists who were also scholars keenly interested in history. I think of Tee Corinne's sideshows, books and erotic photography, for example, and Alan Berube's *Coming Out under Fire* (1990). He got a MacArthur grant; she should have.

The large claims made by Queer Theory are bracing, however. Early lesbian feminists strove to be included in the curriculum, and we perceived that inclusion potentially could alter the Humanities and the Social Sciences, but we (or at least I) could not have imagined the bold stance of Eve Kosofsky Sedgwick in *Epistemology of the Closet* (1990). She argues that Western culture cannot be understood without an antihomophobic analysis, one that sheds light on issues of secrecy/disclosure. It's possible, of course, that our early call to the Academy, "Let us in and you will be the better for it" had to precede, "If you don't know what we know, you cannot know yourselves."

Where Queer Theory has been especially valuable is in insisting on the limitations of dualistic thinking. Het/homo no longer works as a comprehensive description and 'lesbian' has multiple meanings. Feminist gerontology (Cruikshank, 2002) has also vigorously challenged dualisms, for example, young/old, but that is a barely visible enterprise compared to Queer theory. Feminist gerontologists unveil the dualism in 'successful aging,' a male-centered, white, middle-class, heterosexual model that need not name its opposite.

The varied kinds of analysis of sexuality inspired by Queer Theory could not have come out of Feminism alone. Gender explains far more, however, than queer theorists seem ready to acknowledge, and for all their emphasis on difference, the difference of class registers just a few weak bleeps on their radar screens. Feminism no longer seems the total explanatory system it appeared to be twenty-five years ago, but through its recent emphasis on global issues it has become less ethnocentric than Queer Theory. Introductory Women's Studies texts now include essays on international issues, for example.

On contentious area in LGBT Studies has been man-boy love. My impression is that for some gay male scholars, particularly older scholars, an attack on this practise is tantamount to an attack on all gay-male sexuality. For feminists, the prohibition against man-boy love seems absolute. In theory, we might agree that if the State has the power to regulate man-boy love, it can potentially regulate all forms of sex labelled 'deviant.' Today the State arrests men who have child pornography on their computers; tomorrow the targets may be women who possess lesbian erotic images. Even those feminists who favor laws banning pornography might agree that the State is an unreliable ally.

For feminists, the power difference between adults and children makes sex between them damaging. Even while acknowledging that sex between an adult male and an eighteen-year-old teenager differs from sex with a ten-year-old, the question of free consent remains. Where does Queer Theory stand on this issue? In celebrating 'outlaw' sexuality as enthusiastically as it does, Queer Theory appears to romanticize rule-breaking. According to a recent description of Queer Theory, "desire, the body, and sexuality have become primary. In this new space, desire is not only considered primary but autonomous" (Gunther, 2005: 23).

This new space would seem to leave open the possibility of man-boy love.

The most vociferous attacks on Queer Theory appear to come from British and Australian feminists, perhaps because the close link between Socialism and Feminism in those countries nurtures an identity politics particularly resistant to being 'queered.' Sheila Jeffreys's book, *Unpacking Queer Politics* (2003), packs quite a wallop. Jeffreys is certainly right that some young lesbians have 'mis-remembered' Feminism, but she distorts Queer Theory in the process of whacking it, and her equating sex toys with porn is unpersuasive.

Far more illuminating is Linda Garber's *Identity Poetics* (2001), a judicious re-appraisal of Lesbian Feminism that leaves ample room for alliances with Queer Theory. Her readings of Audre Lorde, Pat Parker, Gloria Anzaldúa and Judy Grahn place working-class women and women of color at the center of Lesbian Feminism. These writers express the "multiple, simultaneous identity positions and activist politics" that foreshadow Queer Theory (8).

With intermittent respect for Queer Theory laced with misgivings, with an uneasy sadness that my cohort of lesbian-feminist pioneers is waning, and with a sardonic sense that in time, Queer Theory will be supplanted by something else, I wish young lesbian scholars well. May this choice not obliterate the struggles and contributions of their foremothers.

REFERENCES

Berube, Alan. *Coming Out under Fire*. Detroit: The Free Press, 1990.

Cruikshank, Margaret, ed. *The Lesbian Path*. Mounterey, CA: Angel Press, 1980; rev. ed. Grey Fox Press, 1985.

_____. *Learning to Be Old: Gender, Culture and Aging*. New York: Rowman and Littlefield Publishers, Inc, 2002.

Garber, Linda. *Identity Poetics: Race, Class, and the Lesbian-Feminist Roots of Queer Theory*. New York: Columbia University Press, 2001.

Gunther, Scott. *"Alors,* Are We 'Queer' Yet?" *Gay and Lesbian Review*, 12(3), 2005: 23-5.

Jeffreys, Sheila. *Unpacking Queer Politics: A Lesbian Feminist Perspective*. Cambridge: Polity Press, 2003.

Rubin, Gayle S. "Geologies of Queer Studies: It's Déjà Vu All Over Again," *CLAGS News*, 14(2), 2004: 6-10.

Sedgwick, Eve Kosofsky. *Epistemology of the Closet*. Berkeley: University of California Press, 1990.

Stanley, Julia Penelope and Susan J. Wolfe, eds. *The Coming Out Stories*. Watertown, MA: Persephone Press, 1980.

doi:10.1300/J155v11n01_11

Rescuing Lesbian Camp

Clare Hemmings

SUMMARY. This paper explores the limits of lesbian camp as it is currently conceived within Lesbian Studies. I argue, in what I hope is a rather circuitous way, that a reliance on repudiative models of identity formation fixes gender as complementary and sexuality as oppositional, irrespective of intention. In this context, I imagine instead what it would take to theorize femininity itself as camp, and femme subjects as ideal for working this through at the level of praxis. doi:10.1300/J155v11n01_12 *[Article copies available for a fee from The Haworth Document Delivery Service: 1-800-HAWORTH. E-mail address: <docdelivery@haworthpress.com> Website: <http://www.HaworthPress.com> © 2007 by The Haworth Press, Inc. All rights reserved.]*

Clare Hemmings is Senior Lecturer in Gender Studies at the Gender Institute, LSE. Her teaching and research interests reflect her interdisciplinary background in literary theory, human geography, gender studies and sexuality studies. She is the author of *Bisexual Spaces: a Geography of Sexuality and Gender* (2002), and has written widely on femme subjectivity. She is co-editor of *The Bisexual Imaginary* (1997), and editor of "Stretching Queer Boundaries," a special issue of *Sexualities* (1999). She is currently completing a book, *Telling Feminist Stories*, which challenges the dominant progress narratives within Western feminism, and argues for a more nuanced engagement with the recent feminist past.

Address correspondence to: Dr. Clare Hemmings, Gender Institute, London School of Economics, Houghton Street, London, WC2A 2AE, UK (E-mail: c.hemmings@lse.ac.uk).

[Haworth co-indexing entry note]: "Rescuing Lesbian Camp." Hemmings, Clare. Co-published simultaneously in *Journal of Lesbian Studies* (Harrington Park Press, an imprint of The Haworth Press, Inc.) Vol. 11, No. 1/2, 2007, pp. 159-166; and: *Twenty-First Century Lesbian Studies* (ed: Noreen Giffney, and Katherine O'Donnell) Harrington Park Press, an imprint of The Haworth Press, Inc., 2007, pp. 159-166. Single or multiple copies of this article are available for a fee from The Haworth Document Delivery Service [1-800-HAWORTH, 9:00 a.m. - 5:00 p.m. (EST). E-mail address: docdelivery@haworthpress.com].

KEYWORDS. Lesbian, camp, drag, butch, femme, trans, bisexual

Having been asked to take a position on Lesbian Studies, it would seem perfectly reasonable for me, as a bisexual theorist, to reflect once again on Lesbian Studies' exclusion of those subjects and perspectives nestling under the term 'bisexual.'[1] But this is *Lesbian Studies* I am being asked to think about, and a focus on something, well, not lesbian, seems churlishly off topic. So I want to think about something else that has been troubling me–the subject of 'lesbian camp.' It's been troubling me, because as a good bisexual femme I should surely be pleased about which practices and subjects are being rendered as dyke camp currently: an array of female masculinities, finding perfection in drag-king parodies. But in fact I find these performances painfully labored and faintly–actually acutely–embarrassing. This discomfort, no doubt easy to dismiss as a matter of taste, acts as a starting point for me in thinking through the limits of how lesbian camp is imagined, and what this says about Lesbian Studies and its theoretical and political constraints currently. Of course, in exploring alternative subjects of lesbian camp for Lesbian Studies, I cannot help but be returned, on occasion, to the place of bisexuality at the heart of its logic.

We are probably all familiar with the legacy of lesbian camp in the 1990s at this point. It even has a critical genealogy. It's the masquerade, the play on heterosexual codes concomitant with the refusal of the same. It's not the worthy, earnest insistence on the difference between lesbian and straight desire, but the sexy, playful skirting around the edges, the dipping in and out of centre and margin, the beating around the bush, if you will. It's the derivation of pleasure from the gender codes that have been used to shore up and reinforce heteronorms, and the courting, evading and encountering of the dangers that this pleasure risks. We're familiar with how to theorize this serious play from sexy, smart writers like Sue-Ellen Case (1998/9), Joan Nestle (1992 a), Judith Butler (1990; 1993), Sally R. Munt (1998), Amber Hollibaugh and Cherríe Moraga (1992), Pamela Robertson (1996) and many more, and in the telling of its history a picture of the stylization of those moments into a cultural resource is often said to mark the difference from the hetero-gendered norms thus denaturalized. 'Lesbian camp'–the history of lesbian desire made manifest through its denaturalizing tendencies.

In this turning around and over of the desire-gender-history nexus that seems to form the basis for *queer camp* more generally, and indeed might be said to define a particular genre of Anglo-American Humanities theorizing from, let's say, 1985-1995 some key actors emerge, not just in theory but also in the cultural and political imaginary.[2] The drag queen: surely no-one disputes her role as camp prizewinner, her contentious denaturalization of womanliness, as Riviere (1986) might put it, the (more) perfect copy that she makes of femininity, as Butler (1990) might say. The gym-queen clone might also be a contender, it's true, but perhaps he's more iconic than camp. For Lesbian Studies it's the butch who makes the parallel copy of masculinity, the swaggering boy who parodies heteronorms most effectively, heroically denaturing the relationship between biology, gender and lust (Halberstam, 1998; Munt, 1998). For Queer Studies, then, the presence of drag or butch possibility (textually, historically and culturally) becomes *the sign* of disruption of heterosexual history and narrative.[3] For Lesbian Studies the task is thus clear: to track down female masculinity and transform its subject into the bearer of lesbian history, a history of risk, pleasure and danger (echoing Vance, 1984), and of course gender play.

Commentators on this parodic state of affairs have voiced concern about the effects of over-valuing one kind of gendered or sexed embodiment, in terms both of the burden of queer representation such bodies are subject to and subjected through, and the bodies, subjects and histories passed over in the process. The most high-profile of these debates is the contest over the *gender identity* of these border figures, whose mincing or swaggering in the borderlands makes them apt to be kidnapped by those patrolling the neighbouring territories. For Butler (1993) and Halberstam (1998), individuals such as Venus Xtravaganza and Billy Tipton lose their denaturalizing power and queer subject position at the point that they pass into hetero-obscurity, while for Jay Prosser (1998) their passing is a key part, indeed sometimes endpoint, of a transsexual narrative that cannot be reduced to queer performativities. Despite the fact that the camp and the genuine are frequently opposed in the contests between queer and trans commentators, these contests are ultimately contests over which 'real' takes precedence, queer (lesbian and gay) or transsexual.

If we take the figure of the poor, plucky femme, the subject of many Lesbian Studies' rescue missions, the reinstatement of lesbian identity in the name of lesbian camp becomes even clearer. While the femme is germane to the scene of lesbian camp, she remains inadequately theorized as an independent subject. Unable to trouble the body-gender-desire nexus on her own because of her unfortunate coincidence of body and gender, the femme's "not-quite-not straight" desire (Tyler, 1994) must be made visible for denaturalization to occur. Enter the butch, the femme's savior. Without her, our femme may slip unnoticed into the hetero-world, or enact that favorite male pornographic fantasy of girl-on-girl action. And these, of course, would never do. Attempts to reha-bilitate the femme frustratingly remain within the same paradigm, with considerable efforts expended on illustrating her unwavering fidelity to butch-femme intimacy and history (Califia 1992 a, 1992 b; Nestle, 1992 b; Walker, 1993). If she cannot be rehabilitated she can always be exiled to a different territory as a bisexual (Hemmings, 2002 a; Michel, 1996), or as that most awkward-sounding of subject positions, the hasbian. The most loyal, most consistent, least capricious, and least ambivalent of all, the femme doesn't stand a chance of being crowned lesbian-camp queen. Easier for the masquerades of a Mae West or a Madonna to sig-nify as part of gay camp than to engage the vexed location of queer femininities within Lesbian culture, it seems (Robertson, 1996).

To validate a specifically masculine lesbian camp then, Lesbian Studies must both resolve the sexual and gendered ambivalence of the butch/FTM borderlands by marking the limit of parody in wholly sexual terms, and domesticate the femme by reading her through a single affec-tive register. The rather cruel irony in this process of reification of les-bian masculinity is that its performative alibi remains the presumed heteronormativity or even essentialism of others, despite the fact that it is an utterly mundane understanding of lesbian identity that marks the limit of the parodic range. The imposition of a single sexual meaning on gender ambivalence reduces and simultaneously claims camp by cari-cature. One might expect such literalism–this parody must always equal this identity–to be laughed out of a more camp world. Neither does the problem of lesbian camp end with the reduction of gender ambivalence; it is instantiated in the very linking of drag queen and butch/king perfor-mances as similar kinds of queer camp. The proposition seems to work on the basis of a simple mirroring: if drag-queen femininities danger-ously and pleasurably unsettle heteronorms, then female masculinities must do the same. Or, if camp for gay male culture is understood as ap-propriation of women's culture and signification (Robertson, 1996), then camp for lesbian culture should properly be appropriation of men's. But are masculinity and femininity alike? Are they simply two sides of the same coin, as easily available for denaturing and camp occupation? Does Lesbian Studies really want to imagine gender first and foremost as complementarity?

It looks to me as though a terrible mistake has been made in trying to translate drag queen feminine camp histories directly into lesbian ter-rain: a terrible, un-camp gaff that has dominated theory since the 1990s.

If drag queens are doing femininity in/with/from male bodies, and this mismatch exposes the sexed body as the base for gender as a fiction, then the same must necessarily be true of masculinity in/with/from female bodies, ergo the butch as subject of lesbian camp and counter-cultural history. Such parallelism can only be consolidated through a 'return' to psychoanalysis, a turn that Butler (1997) was always, I think, bound to have to make. The story underpinning the lesbian parallel to drag is, in retrospect, rather a tortuous one. Masculinity in female bodies and femininities in male bodies are equivalent in a psychoanalytic fiction of object-choice repudiation, where heterosexuals embody the gender of lost homosexual object-choice, and homosexuals the gender of lost hetero object-choice. It's convenient, I'll give it that much. It guarantees that male and female engendering is structured as oppositional through sexuality first and foremost (making cross-gendered parodies analogous), and it ensures that these parodies are linked to sexual deviance, or contemporarily, identity. This way we can rest assured it will be a member of the family doing the denaturing.

There are myriad problems with this framework that spring to mind, not least of which, that heterosexuals once again emerge ever so fragile because they are unable to mourn the opposites they engender, and that bisexuality is reframed as predisposition and never identity, its abstraction the condition of Butler's theoretical reworking of sexual repudiation and engendering. But I said I'd stick to camp, and in that spirit I have to say it's hard to think of anything less camp than this narrative of repudiation. An inevitable childhood-wrestle with the object-choice you don't want, and the figurative losing of that battle over and over again through the embodying of that refusal. A clear and irrefutable gendering of both (there are always only two) repudiations, which must surely be a tautological gendering of sexuality in absolutely heterosexual terms. And to return to the femme, small wonder her devotion is in question! In gendered terms, she has already repudiated homosexuality, and so her lesbian desire only makes sense if her subsequent object choice is a masculine woman she can be loyal to in ways that provide an alibi for initial confusion. What has happened to the masquerade, the play and the ambivalence that form the core of camp sensibility (Cleto, 1999)? Does imagining multiple masculinities for lesbian camp really alter the literalism of its presumed sex/gender distinction? Must the femme always remain suspect, and the drag queen be returned with a bump to the meat and two vegetables her imaginative conviction had shown her to be of minor significance?

What if Lesbian Studies were to reject the repudiative model that underpins the similarity between drag and butch parody? Let us imagine, at least for a moment, how we might theorize the femme as a subject of lesbian camp in her own right. Against the bland assertion that all gender is masquerade that I argue relies on the above reframing of camp as "complementarity," I would ask the following: what do drag queens, femmes and radical feminists have in common? The knowledge of "womanliness as masquerade," to return to Riviere (1986), for a series of interconnected reasons that feminists have most consistently articulated; it is devalued, understood as the complement of the real (which is male and masculinity), and ultimately as superficial, as lacking in substance. Simone de Beauvoir (1949) knew this, and loathed it as evidenced by her acid attacks on bourgeois housewives. Monique Wittig (1981) knew this in her suggestions that the category 'lesbian' had nothing to do with gender opposition in the dialectical minds of the heterosexual powers that be. Luce Irigaray (1981) and Gayle Rubin (1975) know this, as suggested by their articulation of femininity as the shadow allowing for exchange between men. Femininity, that most reviled characteristic: marginal, excessive and ultimately contrived.

The difference between these marvelous earnest theorists and camp theorists is surely where they believe strategy lies. Escape! Transcendence, devotion to multiplicity over dualism, decamping to lesbiansville, you know the stories. Or camp! The gorgeous refusal to exit that condemned as vile and putrid, the holding fast in/of the abject, the loving of the loathed. (Female masculinity just isn't going to cut it here; masculinity is not melodrama, it doesn't have the immaterial credentials.) Might feminine camp, in whatever body, be a refusal to believe in escape, and, in a delightful turn, an insistence on the material, the literal if you like, as itself transient? This too will pass. If the femme rather than the butch is imagined as the subject of lesbian camp, as the unnatural sibling of the queen, femininity can be more fully theorized and enacted as embodied excess and available melodrama for all bodies, an available position from which to gaze (pretending not to be subject), and undermine (pretending to prop up). Such an approach might also allow Lesbian Studies to free itself from the more conventional psychoanalytic returns of Queer Studies; turns that fix rather than disrupt gendered meaning. 'Lesbian Camp'–that is, the taking on of styles that uphold a masculine order, the embodiment of excessive immateriality, the refusal of *gravitas*; serious play with constructed superficiality. Who knows, eventually it might be possible to imagine such a masculine lesbian-camp subject too, but not just yet.

NOTES

1. There is plenty of literature that does just this; see, for example, Ault (1996); Däumer (1992); Fraser (1999); Hemmings (2002).

2. I'm thinking here of its heyday, rather than continuing influence. An interesting feature of post-1995 Theory in this genre is its declining attention to queer, and particularly lesbian, subjects as central to its interrogation. renée c. hoogland's piece takes up this theme.

3. These figures and performances are not always called 'camp', of course–in the context of drag-king performance and culture, for example, the term 'kinging' is common (Troka et al, 2002)–but I use the term to frame the range of terms used for practices of gender parody whose aim or effect is heteronormative denaturing.

REFERENCES

Ault, Amber. "Hegemonic Discourse in an Oppositional Community: Lesbian Feminist Stigmatization of Bisexual Women." In Brett Beemyn and Mickey Eliason, eds. *Queer Studies: a Lesbian, Gay, Bisexual, and Transgender Anthology*. New York: New York University Press, 1996: 204-16.

Butler, Judith. *Gender Trouble: Feminism and the Subversion of Identity*. New York: Routledge, 1990.

_____. *Bodies That Matter: On the Discursive Limits of 'Sex.'* New York: Routledge, 1993.

_____. *The Psychic Life of Power: Theories in Subjection*. Stanford, CA: Stanford University Press, 1997.

Califia, Pat. "The Femme Poem." In Joan Nestle, ed. *The Persistent Desire*: A *Femme-Butch Reader*. Los Angeles and New York: Alyson Books, 1992 a: 417.

_____. "Diagnostic Tests." In Joan Nestle, ed. *The Persistent Desire: A Femme-Butch Reader*. Los Angeles and New York: Alyson Books, 1992 b: 484.

Case, Sue-Ellen. "Towards a Butch-Femme Aesthetic," *Discourse* 11, 1988/9: 55-73.

Cleto, Fabio, ed. *Camp: Queer Aesthetics and the Performing Subject: A Reader*. Edinburgh: Edinburgh University Press, 1999.

Däumer, Elizabeth D. "Queer Ethics; or, the Challenge of Bisexuality to Lesbian Ethics," *Hypatia: A Journal of Feminist Philosophy*, 7(4), 1992: 91-105.

De Beauvoir, Simone. *The Second Sex*. New York: Vintage, 1949.

Fraser, Mariam. *Identity Without Selfhood: Simone de Beauvoir and Bisexuality*. Cambridge: Cambridge University Press, 1999.

Halberstam, Judith. *Female Masculinity*. Durham: Duke University Press, 1998.

Hemmings, Clare. "'All My Life I've Been Waiting for Something': Theorising Femme Narrative in *The Well of Loneliness*." In Laura Doan and Jay Prosser, eds. *Palatable Poison: Critical Perspectives on* The Well of Loneliness *Past and Present*. New York: Columbia University Press, 2002 a: 179-96.

_____. *Bisexual Spaces: A Geography of Sexuality and Gender*. New York: Routledge, 2002 b.

Hollibaugh, Amber, and Cherrie Moraga. "What We're Rollin' Around in Bed With: Sexual Silences in Feminism." In Joan Nestle, ed. *The Persistent Desire: A Femme-Butch Reader.* Los Angeles and New York: Alyson Books, 1992: 243-53.

Irigaray, Luce. *Speculum of the Other Woman.* Ithaca: Cornell University Press, 1981.

Michel, Frann. "Do Bats Eat Cats? Reading What Bisexuality Does." In Donald E. Hall and Maria Pramaggiore, eds. *RePresenting Bisexuality: Subjects and Cultures of Fluid Desire.* New York: New York University Press, 1996: 55-69.

Munt, Sally R. *Heroic Desire: Lesbian Identity and Cultural Space.* London: Cassell, 1998.

Nestle, Joan, ed. *The Persistent Desire: A Femme-Butch Reader.* Los Angeles and New York: Alyson Books, 1992 a.

_____. "The Femme Question." In Joan Nestle, ed. *The Persistent Desire: A Femme-Butch Reader.* Los Angeles and New York: Alyson Books, 1992 b: 138-46.

Prosser, Jay. *Second Skins: the Body Narratives of Transsexuality.* New York: Columbia University Press, 1998.

Riviere, Joan. "Womanliness as Masquerade." In V. Burgin, J. Donald and C. Kaplan, eds. *Formations of Fantasy.* London: Methuen, 1986: 35-44.

Robertson, Pamela. *Guilty Pleasures: Feminist Camp from Mae West to Madonna.* Durham: Duke University Press, 1996.

Rubin, Gayle S. "The Traffic in Women: Notes on the 'Political Economy' of Sex." In R. Reiter, ed. *Toward an Anthropology of Women.* New York: Monthly Review Press, 1975: 157-210.

Troka, Donna, Kathleen LeBesco and J. Bobby Noble, eds. *The Drag King Anthology.* Binghampton, New York: Harrington Park Press, 2002.

Tyler, Carole-Anne. "Passing: Narcissism, Identity, and Difference," *differences: A Journal of Feminist Cultural Studies* 6 (2-3), 1994: 212-48.

Vance, Carole S., ed. *Pleasure and Danger: Exploring Female Sexuality.* Boston: Routledge and Kegan Paul, 1984.

Walker, Lisa M. "How to Recognize a Lesbian: The Cultural Politics of Looking Like What You Are," *Signs: Journal of Women in Culture and Society* 18, 1993: 866-91.

Wittig, Monique. "One Is Not Born a Woman," *The Straight Mind and Other Essays.* Hemel Hempstead: Harvester, 1981: 9-20.

doi:10.1300/J155v11n01_12

Refusing to Make Sense:
Mapping the In-Coherences of 'Trans'

J. Bobby Noble

SUMMARY. This article moves from the premise that 'lesbian' is a gendered embodiment marked and put in flux by century-long sexual politics and semiotics and asks how do we begin to map not only its own terrain but the incoherence generated by its intersections with transsexuality/transgender? The author suggests that it is precisely the

---

Bobby Noble (PhD, York University) is Assistant Professor in the new Sexuality Studies program at York University (Toronto, Canada). He completed his doctorate at York University in 2000 and after teaching on the west coast at the University of Victoria, he has returned back to join the Sexuality Studies program, housed in the School of Women's Studies at York University. His research focuses on sexuality, gender, transgender/transsexuality, anti-racist whiteness, and popular culture through cultural studies. In particular, his work looks at the intersections of masculinity, embodiment, and sexuality in the fields of transsexual/transgender studies, queer theory and cultural studies. Bobby is the author of the book *Masculinities Without Men?* (University of British Columbia Press, Winter 2004), selected as a Choice Outstanding Title, 2004; co-editor of *The Drag King Anthology*, a 2004 Lambda Literary Finalist (Haworth Press 2003); and has just published a new monograph called *Sons of the Movement: FTMs Risking Incoherence in a Post-Queer Cultural Landscape* (Toronto, Women's Press, 2006).

Address correspondence to: Professor J. Bobby Noble, Sexuality Studies Program, School of Women's Studies, 206 Founders College, York University, 4700 Keele Street, Toronto ON M3J 1P3, Canada (E-mail: jbnoble@yorku.ca).

[Haworth co-indexing entry note]: "Refusing to Make Sense: Mapping the In-Coherences of 'Trans.'" Noble, J. Bobby. Co-published simultaneously in *Journal of Lesbian Studies* (Harrington Park Press, an imprint of The Haworth Press, Inc.) Vol. 11, No. 1/2, 2007, pp. 167-175; and: *Twenty-First Century Lesbian Studies* (ed: Noreen Giffney, and Katherine O'Donnell) Harrington Park Press, an imprint of The Haworth Press, Inc., 2007, pp. 167-175. Single or multiple copies of this article are available for a fee from The Haworth Document Delivery Service [1-800-HAWORTH, 9:00 a.m. - 5:00 p.m. (EST). E-mail address: docdelivery@haworthpress.com].

— power of Trans to not make sense that provides it with its most provocative power to disrupt and displace epistemological regimes and asks that we shift our attention from what we teach in Lesbian-Trans Studies to how we teach these studies. The article concludes by suggesting that it is in surprising our students with the failure to 'know' that we can reveal how knowledge is really a regime of received ideas, ideologies, prejudices and opinions, a way of not knowing that one does not know. doi:10.1300/J155v11n01_13 *[Article copies available for a fee from The Haworth Document Delivery Service: 1-800-HAWORTH. E-mail address: <docdelivery@haworthpress.com> Website: <http://www.HaworthPress. com> © 2007 by The Haworth Press, Inc. All rights reserved.]*

KEYWORDS. Transsexuality/transgender, Judith Butler, categorical incoherence, lesbian postmodernism, the privilege of unknowing, pedagogical surprise, anti-heteronormativity, bodies and essentialism

The term 'lesbian' has almost always marked contradictory social and political spaces and has been imbricated with many other twentieth-century practices (Wiegman, 1994). In her introduction to *The Lesbian Postmodern*, Wiegman notes that the term 'lesbian' functions structurally as signifier, materially as alienated capitalist commodity and ideologically as imagined referent all at the exact same moment. But, equally puzzling if there is a fundamental instability around social and political spaces marked by the term, then attempting to convert those spaces into scholarly fields of knowledge, is an equally tenuous process. Such instabilities defy institutional practices that require coalescence and closure. How then to reconcile these divergent and contradictory imperatives?

Once more, in the shift from 'lesbian' to 'Lesbian Studies' what happens to the other categorical spaces of identity cross-cutting through, or at least, implicated by 'lesbian,' spaces in the late nineteenth, twentieth and twenty-first centuries that are dialogic enough to be marked by such contradictory nomenclature as butch/femme, 'the invert and her girl,' the mannish-woman, the woman-identified woman, the male-identified lesbian, the infamous 'feminism is the theory, lesbianism the practice' but also 'lesbians are not women' and more? Indeed, how to map the vast terrain of gendered embodiment marked by these century-long sexual politics and semiotics? More recently, these contradictory spaces have shifted in a direction anticipating, but still silent about, the most contradictory and paradoxical of all: lesbian man. Even popular culture, if the recent Showtime hit, *The L Word*, is any measure, has jumped aboard by introducing a biological-born man named Lisa who is, so she tells us, a lesbian-identified man. In part because of the butch-femme renaissance, but also because of increasing trans-deployments of medical technologies, the spaces marked, disavowed or otherwise, by 'lesbian' have undoubtedly become impossible, all the more so when they are grounded in the supposedly self-evident distinction between female versus male bodies. This was anticipated again, for instance, in Laura Doan's edited collection, *The Lesbian Postmodern*. In the introduction, Wiegman quotes from Judith Butler's *Gender Trouble* to posit the question under consideration in that volume and here as well: "It is no longer clear that feminist theory ought to try to settle the questions of primary identity in order to get on with the task of politics. Instead, we ought to ask, what political possibilities are the consequence of a radical critique of the categories of identity?" *The Lesbian Postmodern* provided one answer to that question; an answer queerly performative even if it was not quite queer yet in its grammars. My answer is alternatively 'post-queerly trans.'

Trans marks not only gender trouble but also category trouble that has the potential to reconfigure not just gender but embodiment itself. One of the results of trans trouble is a seemingly audacious but increasingly meddlesome paradox: the lesbian man. Autobiographically, I offer this rewording as my own meddlesome discourse on and through 'lesbian' studies: I am an out straight ftm guy who's half lesbian, teaching critical approaches to sexuality in a Canadian Women's Studies department. Let me position myself here. I want to articulate this work within my own personal history–as a white transsexual man–inside the feminist movement. Like many transsexuals–and despite a panic to the contrary–I come to this current border war with a long feminist history: I came out as a working-class lesbian in my last year of high school, 1978. I found the word lesbian in the very important feminist book *Lesbian Woman* by Del Martin and Phyllis Lyon, and after asking myself, "am I that name?" I answered, "yes." After a brief stay in Toronto in the late 1980s, I made my way west to Edmonton, Alberta where I spent almost a decade working inside the lesbian-feminist movement. My pre-academic resumé details much of this work: I did almost four years with the Edmonton Rape Crisis Centre; I was part of the lesbian caucus of the Alberta Status of Women Action Committee; I organized and took part in far too many Take Back the Night Marches. I was one of a very small group of people to organize and march in Edmonton's first Gay Pride

Parade (about 1987: there were seven of us; we walked for a block and then ran for our lives). I've spray-painted the sides of more buildings than I care to remember; I took the very first 'Women and Literature' course at the University of Alberta with Professor Shirley Newman; my feminist poster archive includes an original 1979 Toronto IWD poster but also a huge but very battered YES poster, which was part of the 1976 American ERA equal rights amendment campaign. I started and sustained through two Edmonton winters a sex-worker advocacy group called the Alliance for the Safety of Prostitutes, a group that met, during the coldest winter nights, in the only gay bar in Edmonton. I was 'the' out lesbian for many television and radio interviews and published many activist articles, pamphlets and tracts in a variety of feminist and lesbian feminist newspapers and magazines. I've helped build many parts of our activist movement long before I entered university and claim this history quite proudly, despite the pressures from many quarters to renounce my history and to change my official paperwork from F to M. Such a change is an example of a discursively manufactured categorical coherence that, like other taxonomies, will always already betray trans peoples even while it offers an alibi. I don't find my home in the word lesbian any longer (although that's often my dating pool) but I want to be very clear that I'm not here–as a transsexual man–knocking at the door of the feminist movement asking to be let in. I have been in, of, and indeed, have been the feminist movement and in my work on masculinity, and in my daily practice as an ftm transsexual man, I continue to occupy that space with a great sense of history.

There's much at stake in this reconfiguration of trans-ed category trouble or what I want to call post-queer, trans-ed practices of in-coherence. On the one hand, 'trans' is descriptive, marking lives lived across, against, or despite always already engendered and sexed bodies. Often collapsed into 'trans-gender,' that umbrella term which references almost all of the above practices from one degree to another, the term 'trans-sexual' for instance is thought to mark the use of medical technologies to mediate the disjunction between the body and a self which seems at odds with that body. But at its most provocative, 'trans' and the space it references can also refuse the medical and psychological categorical imperatives through which it has always been forced to confess. As Michel Foucault has taught us, confession is always already an overdetermined discursive practice, choreographed by régimes of power (1978). In the case of trans-folks, that confession and the legitimacies it accords, have often demanded congruency and coherence between desire and object choice; between gender identity and appropriate sexual expression; and most pernicious, between sex and gender themselves.

To render something in-coherent, on the other hand, means two things simultaneously: first, it means a lack of organization, or a failure of organization so as to make that thing difficult to comprehend; but it also means failing to cohere as a mass or entity. The reading of an ftm body as gendered male involves presenting signifiers within an economy where the signifiers accumulate toward the appearance of a coherently gendered body. Becoming a transsexual man, however, at its most incoherent and because of the limits of surgeries, can mean occupying the permanent space of not just becoming; that is, it is a permanent place of modulation of what came before by what comes after, never fully accomplishing either as an essentialist stable 'reality' but also of permanent in-coherence if the subject is to, well matter, at all. But it also means rendering bodies and subject positions as in-coherent as possible to refuse to let power work through bodies the way it needs to. It can, in other words, disrupt the coherence mandated by the neatly and dualistically triangulated male/female, gay/straight sex/gender binary systems.

Together, this seeming oxymoron–trans-ed incoherence–is performative and answers the productive category trouble called for in earlier works like *The Lesbian Postmodern*. That is, there is something a little vertiginous, a little bewildering, but also, something useful in not only 'not' making sense, but refusing the hegemonic bargain implicit in (common-) sense-making itself (Chen, 1999). The imperative of in-coherence, one directed at transsexual/transgender identity politics as much as lesbian, is coded into Wiegman's call for a lesbian postmodern; but the difference between lesbian and trans is the difference between deploying identity categories strategically, at best, ('lesbian'), and perhaps simply refusing their ground (coherently gendered bodies upon which those desires depend). Wiegman herself reminded us that, "there is no innocent way to wear [a] category" (3). That transed-folks need to get into the gender game is crucial; once we are there, however, we too must grapple with the stakes of coherence or we fail in our persistent disruptions. If Stuart Hall was right when he wrote, "almost every fixed inventory will betray us," then are dualistic and binary gender systems, however we find our way into them, ever in the interests of trans-folks (1981: 449)?

Quite apart from the ontological questions, would it not also be unwise to grapple with these questions without heeding the experiences of many of critical politics as they shift from social movements to discursive and scholarly fields inside dominant institutions? It may not be tactical to consider the 'what' (is the subject) of lesbian-trans studies as separate from the 'how' (how do we bring these subjects into our teaching) question. Not only are they the same question, the latter has a far greater urgency than the former if we recall precisely the ideological work accomplished by the 'institution' itself. While the inclusion of Women's Studies or Lesbian or even Trans Studies into post-secondary education as both curriculum and knowledge practices certainly gestures toward 'success', these inclusions also mark sites of tremendous struggle and conflict for teachers working with these institutionalized materials as critical pedagogy. Of other critical scholarship such as cultural studies–a sort of kissing cousin of Lesbian-Trans Studies–Hall wrote of the dangers of institutionalization: "My own feeling is that the explosion of cultural studies along with other forms of critical theory in the academy represents a moment of extraordinarily profound danger" (1992: 285-6). Hall's warning is answered in the work of many theorists of critical pedagogy who, when writing about educational institutions as Ideological State Apparatuses, concur with early Marxists:

> no other ideological state apparatus has the obligatory . . . audience of the totality of the children in the capitalist social formation, eight hours a day for 5 or 6 days out of 7 . . . This is the school [that] takes children from every class at infant-school age, and then for years . . . drums into them, *whether it uses new or old methods*, a certain amount of 'know-how' wrapped in the ruling ideologies. (Althusser, 2001: 1485, emphasis added)

By implication, the political efficacy of Lesbian-Trans Studies has to calibrate what it does inside the classroom for the social and ideological functioning of educational institutions themselves. Our twenty-first-century educational institutions produce citizens complete with hegemonic 'know-how'; moreover, they also producing young capitalist consumers purchasing, among other things, what they imagine to be whole and coherent selves, queer or otherwise, and whether they know it or not. In fact, an alibi of ignorance of those larger mechanisms of identity production is crucial to their success. In her essay called "The Privilege of Unknowing," Eve Kosofsky Sedgwick argues that ignorance is not the absence or opposite of knowledge but its silent co-creator. "Knowledge is not itself power", she writes, "although it is the magnetic field of power. Ignorance and opacity collude or compete with it in mobilizing the flows of meaning" (1993: 24). Sedgwick uses an analogy of language to illustrate her point: if, to use a slightly different example, a French Canadian knows English but an English-speaking Canadian lacks French, it is the Francophone who must negotiate meanings through an acquired tongue while the 'ignorant' Anglophone may dilate in her own Mother language. In this instance, the terms of the exchange are delimited by the interlocutor's not mutual but deficient interpretative practices or knowledge. These ignorance effects or epistemological asymmetries, are harnessed, licensed, socially sanctioned and regulated on a mass scale for what Sedgwick calls striking enforcements of meaning, or sense making activities. They are produced by and correspond to particulate knowledges and circulate not as the absence of, but as part of particular regimes of truth, so that making sense occurs on terms not of our own making. For many gay-positive and anti-homophobic heterosexual folks, the solution to heteronormative lacuna is merely the unself-conscious consumption of gay identities so that being 'in the know' replaces 'being out of the loop.' Politically, for many well-meaning and anti-homophobic straight folks, this has meant simply filling in the details rather than troubling the ground of intelligibility itself.

One practice of disturbing the ground of intelligibility can be found in recent work on queer heterosexuality such as that of Calvin Thomas (2000), Michael O'Rourke (2005) and Annette Schlichter (2004). These works, just to name a few, begin to map queerness outside of 'lesbian and gay' contexts, whether stated or assumed, by envisioning straight subjects who, in Schlichter's terms, do not fully comply with the imperatives of heteronormativity (560). Such instances of heterosexual in-coherence defamiliarize ignorance by relocating it not in the details to be consumed about the 'Other' but in what Thomas, citing Butler, maps as the labor of "working the weakness in the heterosexual norm" to "inhibit it's hegemonic dominance" (31). Admittedly with different points of entry, such queer hauntings of heterosexuality share much with trans occupations of heterosexuality and with other gender and sexual subjectivities which are perhaps heterogendered (what O'Rourke describes as "heteroerotic") but not heteronormative (O'Rourke, 2005: 112). Each seeks to resist the regimes of the normal whether those regimes work through the regulation of object choice or gender essentialism or both (Thomas, 2000: 13).

But, epistemologically, and even pedagogically, such ignorance-effects continue to be profoundly useful as staged interruptions. In "Teaching Ignorance," Barbara Johnson argues that one of the best pedagogical and epistemological tools we have is the ability to mobilize the critical energy and intellectual upheaval of surprise (1987). The existence of identity-based programs stage tactical opportunities to teach students to be surprised by what they do not–perhaps cannot ever–know. I paraphrase Johnson:

> If the deconstructive impulse [of Lesbian-Trans Studies] is to retain its vital and subversive edge, we must become ignorant of it again and again. It is only by forgetting what we know how to do, by setting aside the thoughts that have most changed us, that *those* thoughts and *that* knowledge can go on doing what a surprise encounter with otherness should do, that is, lay bare some hint of an ignorance one never knew one had. (16)

In this practice, then, we work to un-know, to become conscious of the fact that what we construct as knowledge is really a regime of received ideas, ideologies, prejudices and opinions, a way of not knowing that one does not know. So, if this is true, then our strategies shift from transmitting knowledge to suspending Knowledge.

Moreover, in *Epistemology of the Closet*, Sedgwick makes the argument that epistemological questions about sexual and gendered subjectivities have been bound by a set of epistemological contradictions (1990). On the one hand, identity has been conservatively constructed as minoritizing discourses (seeing that identity as an issue of active importance only for a small, distinct, relatively fixed group of people, for instance). On the other hand, what we need to do instead is to re-theorize identity as universalizing discourses (issues of continuing, determinative active importance in the lives of subjects across the spectrum of races or sexualities or genders). Minoritizing discourses shift the burden of identity to those always already marked as the Other; a universalizing approach decenters, denaturalizes and shifts our gaze from those objectified by these discourses back on to the subject doing the gazing who imagines themselves embodying identity innocently.

This is not shifting discursive or institutional power back to these subjects but shifts instead a destabilizing epistemological gaze back to argue that what we can best do inside Lesbian-Trans Studies is facilitate a surprise encounter not with these as minoritized identities but with universalized heterosexualities and with supposedly naturalized bodies as socially-produced and socially-reinforced imperatives. The practice is to facilitate surprise encounters with what our heterosexual students don't know about their own subjectivities, so their own ignorance becomes deconstructively mobilized. That mobilization is the place where we find the critical possibilities produced by the interruptions structured into and by the space of trans. Knowledge so mobilized by universalizing registers becomes, to poach again from Hall, not only one of the sites where this struggle for and against hegemony occurs; but it becomes also the stake to be won or lost in those battles (1981: 451).

REFERENCES

Althusser, Louis. "Ideology and Ideological State Apparatuses." In Vincent B. Leitch, ed. *The Norton Anthology of Theory and Criticism.* New York: W.W. Norton & Company, 2001: 1483-1509.

Butler, Judith. *Gender Trouble: Feminism and the Subversion of Identity.* New York and London: Routledge, 1990.

Chen, Anthony. "Lives at the Center of the Periphery, Lives at the Periphery of the Center: Chinese American Masculinities and Bargaining with Hegemony," *Gender and Society,* 13(5), 1999: 584-607.

Foucault, Michel. *The History of Sexuality. Volume 1: An Introduction.* Trans. Robert Hurley. New York: Random House, 1978.

Hall, Stuart. "Notes on Deconstructing 'The Popular'." In Raphael Samuel, ed. *People's History and Socialist Theory.* London: Routledge and Kegan Paul, Ltd., 1981: 227-40.

_____. "Cultural Studies and Its Theoretical Legacies." In Lawrence Grossberg, Cary Nelson and Paula A. Treichler, eds. *Cultural Studies.* New York: Routledge, 1992: 277-94.

Johnson, Barbara. *A World of Difference.* Baltimore and London: The Johns Hopkins University Press, 1987.

O'Rourke, Michael. "On the Eve of a Queer-Straight Future: Notes Toward an Antinormative Heteroerotic," *Feminism & Psychology,* 15(1), 2005: 111-16.

Schlichter, Annette. "Queer at Last? Straight Intellectuals and the Desire for Transgression," *GLQ: A Journal of Lesbian and Gay Studies,* 10(4), 2004: 543-64.

Sedgwick, Eve Kosofsky. *Epistemology of the Closet.* Berkeley and Los Angeles: University of California Press, 1990.

_____. "The Privilege of Unknowing." *Tendencies.* Durham: Duke University Press, 1993.

Thomas, Calvin. "Straight with a Twist: Queer Theory and the Subject of Heterosexuality." In Calvin Thomas, ed. *Straight with a Twist: Queer Theory and the Subject of Heterosexuality.* Urbana and Chicago: University of Illinois Press, 2000: 11-44.

Wiegman, Robyn. "Introduction: Mapping the Lesbian Postmodern." In Laura Doan, ed. *The Lesbian Postmodern.* New York: Columbia University Press, 1994: 1-22.

doi:10.1300/J155v11n01_13

SECTION IV

IDENTITIES: THINKING INTERSECTIONALLY

We have no patterns for relating across our human differences as equals. As a result, those differences have been misnamed and misused in the service of separation and confusion. Certainly there are very real differences between us, of race, age, and sex. But it is not those differences that are separating us. It is rather our refusal to recognize those differences, and to examine the distortions that result from our misnaming them and their effects upon human behaviour and expectation.

–Audre Lorde

Sister Outsider:
An Enduring Vision
Embracing Myself,
My Sister and the 'Other'

Consuelo Rivera-Fuentes

SUMMARY. This piece reflects on and reacts to Audre Lorde's critique of racism within Lesbian communities. One purpose of the article is to honor and rescue Lorde's wonderful insight into the power of words when uttered and shared by women, as well as her ideas about differences and connections that exist between Black and white feminisms.

Consuelo Rivera-Fuentes is a Chilean poet, activist and lecturer in Social Sciences and Spanish at the Open University in the UK. As an activist she was imprisoned and tortured for opposing Chilean Dictatorship in the 1980s. She was one of the founders of a Chilean Lesbian group called LEA.[1] She holds an MA in Sociology and Women's Studies and a PhD in Women's Studies. Her main area of research is 'Lesbian autobiographies' and she calls her way of reading and interacting with them 'Sym/bio/graphy' (2000). Besides her academic work written in English she has published three poetry books in Chile and was awarded the first prize in the 'Letras Lejanas' literary competition organized by the Chilean Embassy in London (2001) for her short story, "La Muñeca de Porcelana."

Address correspondence to: Dr. Consuelo Rivera-Fuentes, Adderley Lodge Farm, Adderley Road, Market Drayton, Shropshire, TF9 3ST, UK (E-mail: consuelo.rivera@care4free.net).

[Haworth co-indexing entry note]: "*Sister Outsider:* An Enduring Vision Embracing Myself, My Sister and the 'Other.'" Rivera-Fuentes, Consuelo. Co-published simultaneously in *Journal of Lesbian Studies* (Harrington Park Press, an imprint of The Haworth Press, Inc.) Vol. 11, No. 3/4, 2007, pp. 179-187; and: *Twenty-First Century Lesbian Studies* (ed: Noreen Giffney, and Katherine O'Donnell) Harrington Park Press, an imprint of The Haworth Press, Inc., 2007, pp. 179-187. Single or multiple copies of this article are available for a fee from The Haworth Document Delivery Service [1-800-HAWORTH, 9:00 a.m. - 5:00 p.m. (EST). E-mail address: docdelivery@haworthpress.com].

Available online at http://jls.haworthpress.com
doi:10.1300/J155v11n03_01

Lorde's insistence on a 'sisterhood,' which embraces the 'other' and ourselves at the same time, is a recurrent thought throughout this paper. The article is also firmly grounded in the author's own experience of alienation and racism in the European context of Women's Studies. The second purpose of this position piece is to offer practical suggestions for how to keep Lesbian Studies alive. doi:10.1300/J155v11n03_01 *[Article copies available for a fee from The Haworth Document Delivery Service: 1-800-HAWORTH. E-mail address: <docdelivery@haworthpress.com> Website: <http://www.HaworthPress.com> © 2007 by The Haworth Press, Inc. All rights reserved.]*

KEYWORDS. Audre Lorde, black lesbianism, difference, voice, political identity, racism, anger, individual and collective agency, 'sisterhood'

Once upon a time there was a Black Lesbian warrior. She was also a poet and believed that if women do not respect, use and celebrate our differences, then there is no future for us. She asked of her sisters to hear what 'the other' has to say because if we do not, then "someday women's blood will congeal upon a dead planet" (Lorde, 1996: 171).[2]

I met Audre Lorde's poetry and wisdom for the first time when I was doing an MA in Women's Studies at Lancaster University in the UK. I had just travelled from Chile and was full of naïve 'sisterhood' ideas and dreams I wanted to fulfill. I had experienced difference because of my lesbianism in Chile but I had never felt different in terms of culture or because of my Mixed-Race skin since many people in Latin America are descendent of Spanish and local indigenous people. So I woke up to 'race' in a very different, mostly white, academic environment which set me apart from other women and men, even when they were kind to me and did not overtly slap my face to wake me up.[3] Moreover, I felt different in the 'safe' space of Women's Studies because at the time, there were only two other students who came from non-European countries (Somalia and Malaysia). We were feeling a bit raw, confused, and alienated and could not understand what was wrong with being Mixed-Race, Black, Asian and vocal.[4] Those two women and me recognized one another immediately and were drawn together by the absence of issues in the curriculum that addressed our experiences and the need to get out of what we perceived as Western European frames of reference. Then, I read *Zami: A New Spelling of My Name* (1982) and Lorde's narrative and poetry made me thirsty for more of her work, so I read *The Audre Lorde Compendium* (1996) where *Sister Outsider, A Burst of Light* and *The Cancer Journals* filled me with emotions, feelings and knowledge of myself and the world around me that I had suppressed for a long time. And I dreamed of Audre Lorde and her voice. In that dream she smiled and told me: "I am your sister" and I believed her. She told me that "Black feminism is not white feminism in Blackface" (1996: 113) and that the power of one's own voice and words is infinitely better than a thousand articles written by white men and women on or about Black women but which "dismiss my heritage and the heritage of all other noneuropean women, and den [y] the real connections between all of us" (121).[5] Looking at me over the rim of her glasses she warned me that words can also be full of violence and that "[t]here are so many roots to the tree of /anger/ that sometimes the branches shatter/ before they bear" and that this could leave me silent.[6] But then she added that silence is also powerful and that I should not be afraid of it. Neither should I be afraid of difference, she added, because we need it to keep us alive and to form alliances.[7] So when I woke up from this dream I decided to transform myself and to be even more vocal and active than before.[8] I knew that this would create trouble with my fellow students and lecturers in Women's Studies and that I would have to swim naked in a river of unrecognized feelings and contradictions and that the coldness of the English waters could leave me numb. I did and have come out of the river, shivering but energized by a refreshing chill flowing between bone and flesh. I have come out, but from time to time I undress myself again and my brown body–sagging a bit now–plunges in icy waters knowing that when I come out of the lake, river or sea I will be greeted by smiling–sometimes grimacing–women who will just shake their heads and think that I am a crazy Latin American Mixed-Race Feminist Lesbian. But they never leave me standing there shivering, someone will always come to hug and dry me sharing her warmth with me. And this is not just compassion, it is also the recognition that we need one another to come out of the icy waters of a false sisterhood that denies and ignores our individual and collective desires. It is the reaction of these few women that makes me feel there is a future for Lesbian Studies. Not all of us are able or want to swim in icy water, not all of us "beat the same drum or play the same tune all the time," as Audre Lorde said once.[9] However, if we embrace ourselves, our sisters and 'the other' then the future will happen and it will be warm.[10]

So how can we be sure that there is a future for Lesbian Studies? In their introduction to *The Handbook of Lesbian and Gay Studies*, Richardson and Seidman (2002) give a historical and theoretical overview of the development of Lesbian and Gay Studies and tell us that before World War II there were mainly two models that theorized about homosexuality, namely, the medical and the psychiatric.[11] They go on to tell us that after World War II there was an increased visibility and the creation of gay and Lesbian research groups and organizations, which, of course, brought about increasing discrimination and harassment (1-2). In order to face this discrimination and to challenge both the medical and the psychiatric models, gay and Lesbian groups adopted two important political strategies: first they stated that if homosexuality was the result of a psychiatric disorder, then it should be treated and not punished. The aim of this strategy was to decriminalize homosexuality.[12] The second strategy was to say that homosexuals were as normal as heterosexuals. This approach both challenged and reversed the medical model. Political strategies, gave way, eventually, to the emergence of sociological approaches that viewed homosexuals as a victimized social minority. Richardson and Seidman go on to state that during the 1960s and 1970s, "women's and gays' liberation movements proposed a view of homosexuality as a social and political identity" (2). An example of this was that:

> Lesbians argued that being a lesbian is a political act that challenges both the norm of heterosexuality and men's dominance. To be a lesbian is to choose to live a life apart from men and to make women the center of one's personal and social life. (2)[13]

The political choice of a lesbian identity in a hostile heterosexual environment was not easy and created many internal conflicts in feminist and gay movements because, some people thought, it did not take into account other identities such as race, class, nationality, gender or age which cannot be separated from one's sexual identity. This gave way to other perspectives and epistemological movements, such as the social constructionist views and Queer Theory in Gay and Lesbian Studies. Queer theorists try to "expand politics beyond identity politics," as Richardson and Seidman (4) assert, by focusing on social and political structures that restrain the free expression of someone's sexuality and by emphasizing "the fluid, performative character of identities" (5). I must say that, although Queer Theory criticizes gay movements which are largely male-oriented, middle-class and which focus only on rights and social acceptance, theorists do not have a clear proposal on how to change power structures.[14] At least with identity politics one can exert individual and collective agency.

We can exert individual and collective agency by lesbianizing ourselves 'in relation.' This 'in relation' cannot happen if differences are not acknowledged. 'In relation' cannot happen if, when I go to conferences, there is the odd 'token' Black lesbian. 'In relation' will never happen if whenever women, Black people, gays and Lesbians attempt to address the oppression of sexism, racism and homophobia in academic contexts such as universities, we are described as aggressive, hostile, even violent. Why is it that when I talk to my students about my Lesbianism, my experiences of racism, rape and torture, white men and women (especially young people) comment afterwards that I am so angry, that they cannot understand because it has not been their experience and that I am trying to make them feel uncomfortable and that I am directing my anger at them? It is then, and only then, that I feel my anger rise like lava contained in the volcano of my Latino body. But then, Lorde, the Black Lesbian Warrior whispers in my ear that anger is actually "an appropriate reaction to racist attitudes" (1984: 129). These are Women's Studies students but they still think that racism is not their responsibility and that all I am achieving is make them feel guilty. Audre Lorde said that:

> . . . guilt is not a response to anger; it is a response to one's own action or lack of action. If it leads to change, then it can be useful, since it is no longer guilt but the beginning of knowledge. Yet all too often, guilt is just another name for impotence, for defensiveness destructive of communication, it becomes a device to protect ignorance and the continuation of things the way they are, the ultimate protection for changelessness. (1984: 130)

So I let myself be angry and hope that my students' feeling of guilt is the beginning of change and the development of consciousness because it is never too late to develop.

The future of Lesbian Studies has to include myself and my contradictions, my difference, my anger, my brown Mixed-Race body, my ways of changing reality from 'within.' It must respect and know of the lives and creativity of lesbians who came before us because without their 'Lesbianstories' we would be simply 'a group' of women who cannot influence or exert any changes in society. Any future needs the younger thoughts and feelings of the Lesbians who are, as I write this, growing glittering wings despite the homophobic, racist human beings still left on this earth waiting for them to come out fully so they can bully and harass them so as to undermine their sense of identity. The future of Lesbian Studies has to listen to my mother's voice, to the silent scream and making of revolution of my sisters in Latin America, to the poverty and strength of my sisters in Africa. If there is a future for Lesbian Studies this has to be full of the songs, words and stories of my sisters in the Middle East, Asia and Australasia. It is not enough to inhabit a virtual village of Lesbians somewhere in the colourful spatial wires of the Internet; the future of Lesbian Studies must also come down to earth and create a place like *Zami's* Carriacou where "women work together as friends and lovers" (225), a place where I can smell and taste the sweat, the juices, the tears and the laughter of the 'other.' If there is going to be any future in Lesbian Studies, our European and North American sisters, framed by centuries of colonial and capitalist past and present, must wake up and organize conferences where the proportion of Black and white women is similar both in presence and in active participation. Maybe the future of Lesbian Studies needs my Mixed-Race Latina and Black Lesbian sisters to begin to accept invitations to attend these conferences and thus influence what issues and actions are to be put on the agenda and programmes. The future of Lesbian Studies must have a vision, artists, allies, intellectuals and activists. We must learn to dance together and invite 'the other' to join us. We must work and "organize around our differences, neither denying them nor blowing them out of proportion" (Lorde, 1996: 251).[15] Finally, Lesbian Studies has to include all those women who have never learned to write a 'proper' article with exact references and bibliography but who can tell wonderful Lesbianstories of resistance and defiance to racist, sexist and homophobic attitudes and who, if we listen to them, can teach us the power of Black women's voices to imagine better places and times.

Each one of us has surely heard or read of other Black and white Lesbians' dreams and stories. Can you imagine the countless stories we have together and the power of all the dreams we hold? Share yours and maybe there will be a future for Lesbian Studies.

NOTES

1. The 'her-story' of the creation of this organization appears in my article, Rivera-Fuentes (1996).

2. From "Outlines," unpublished poem, cited in *The Audre Lorde Compendium* (1996).

3. For a longer explanation of this process of waking up to 'race,' refer to Rivera-Fuentes (1997).

4. I write the words Mixed-Race, Lesbian, Black and Asian in capitals to emphasize my strong political commitment to these categories, so that they stand out loud and proud.

5. From "An Open Letter to Mary Daly" in *Sister Outsider* in *The Audre Lorde Compendium* (1996).

6. From Lorde's unpublished poem, "Who Said It Was Simple?" I heard it in a conference and wrote it down, but I cannot provide more references for it.

7. Many Black women and men share this idea of difference and alliances as vital to influence and exert transformation: Moraga and Anzaldúa (1981); Brah (1992); Ahmed (1997).

8. I am, of course, not the only woman to be inspired by Lorde's work: critics such as Perrault (1995); Moraga and Anzaldúa (1981) who address the question–central to identity and relationality in feminist politics–of the construction of categories such as 'I' and 'we' have, for example started from Lorde's assertion that "If we don't name ourselves we are nothing" (Lorde, 1980). When it comes to the concept of difference and Lorde's suggestion that to exert radical change we need to examine difference and incorporate it into our lives and politics, authors such as Moraga (1983); Levins Morales and Morales (1986); Anzaldúa (1987) have concluded that what separates women is not difference in itself but the fear of recognizing it as something we have been programmed to respond to not only with fear but also with loathing. Lorde's influential *Zami*, has been an inspiration to many, amongst which I can mention Carlston (1993); Wilson (1992); King (1992) to name but a few.

9. She said this in a conference in her honor in Boston 1992. The conference was entitled: "The Edge of Each Other's Battles: The Vision of Audre Lorde."

10. I use 'the other' to signify those people who are not myself, or the ones I call my sisters but those who can become our allies in the fight against racism, 'disablism' and homophobia.

11. The medical model viewed homosexuality as an inherited or learned identity and as a form of sexual or gender deviance while the psychiatric model viewed homosexuals as a human type which was abnormal, see Richardson and Seidman (2002: 2).

12. I am using the concept of 'homosexuality' and 'homosexuals' as used in Richardson and Seidman (2002), despite my political preference for the more comprehensive categories of gay, lesbian, bisexual, trans-sexual and transgender people.

13. This reminds me of the words of a Latina called Lupita in the conference in honor of Audre Lorde in Boston. She said: "I've been in revolution for thirty years. When I fell in love with a woman, I started a revolution in myself."

14. I have not enough space for a more thorough analysis of Queer Theory (also this is not the focus of this piece) but there are various articles in Richardson and Seidman (2002), which deal with it: see, for example Adams (15-26); Valentine (145-60); Fortier (183-97).

15. From Lorde's speech, "I Am Your Sister: Black Women Organizing Across Sexualities," in "A Burst of Light" in *The Audre Lorde Compendium* (1996).

REFERENCES

Adams, Barry. "From Liberation to Transgression and Beyond: Gay, Lesbian and Queer Studies at the Turn of the Twenty-first Century." In Diane Richardson and Steven Seidman, eds. Handbook of Lesbian and Gay Studies. London: Sage, 2002: 15-26.

Ahmed, Sara. "It's a Sun-tan, Isn't It?" In Heidi Safia Mirza, ed. *Black British Feminism: A Reader*. London: Routledge, 1997: 53-67.

Anzaldúa, Gloria. Borderlands/La Frontera. San Francisco: Spinsters/Aunt Lute, 1987.

Brah, Avtar. "Difference, Diversity and Differentiation." In James Donald and Ali Rattansi, eds. *'Race', Culture and Difference*. London: Sage and The Open University, 1992: 126-45.

Carlston, Erin G. "Zami and the Politics of Plural Identity." Unpub. paper, 1993.

Cosslett, Tess, Celia Lury and Penny Summerfield, eds. *Feminism and Autobiography: Texts, Theories, Methods*. London: Routledge, 2000.

Donald, James and Ali Rattansi, eds. *'Race', Culture and Difference*. London: Sage and The Open University, 1992.

Fortier, Anne-Marie "Queer Diaspora." In Diane Richardson and Steven Seidman, eds. *Handbook of Lesbian and Gay Studies*. London: Sage, 2002: 183-97.

Garber, Linda, ed. *Tilting The Tower: Lesbians/Teaching/Queer Subjects*. New York and London: Routledge, 1994.

King, Katie. "Audre Lorde's Lacquered Layerings: The Lesbian Bar as a Site of Literary Production." In Sally R. Munt, ed. *New Lesbian Criticism: Literary and Cultural Readings*. Hemel Hempstead: Harvester and Wheatsheaf, 1992: 51-74.

Lorde, Audre. "An Interview with Karla Hammond," *American Poetry Review*, March/April 1980: 19.

_____. *Zami: A New Spelling of my Name*. London: Sheba, 1982.

_____. *Sister Outsider: Essays and Speeches*. New York: The Crossing Press, 1984.

_____. *The Audre Lorde Compendium: Essays, Speeches and Journals*. London: Pandora, 1996.

Mirza, Heidi Safia, ed. *Black British Feminism: A Reader*. London: Routledge, 1997.

Moraga, Cherríe and Gloria Anzaldúa, eds. *This Bridge Called My Back: Writings by Radical Women of Color*. Watertown, MA: Persephone Press, 1981.

Moraga, Cherríe. *Loving in the War Years: Lo Que Nunca Pasó Por Sus Labios*. Boston: South End Press, 1983.

Morales, Aurora Levins and Rosario Morales. *Getting Home Alive*. New York: Firebrand Books, 1986.

Munt, Sally, R., ed. *New Lesbian Criticism: Literary and Cultural Readings*. Hemel Hempstead: Harvester and Wheatsheaf, 1992.

Perrault, Jeanne. *Writing Selves: Contemporary Feminist Autography*. Minneapolis: University of Minnesota Press, 1995.

Reinfelder, Monica, ed. *Amazon to Zami: Towards a Global Lesbian Feminism*. London: Sage, 1996.

Richardson, Diane and Steven Seidman, eds. *Handbook of Lesbian and Gay Studies*. London: Sage, 2002.

Rivera-Fuentes, Consuelo. "Todas Locas, Todas Vivas, Todas Libres: Chilean Lesbians 1980-95." In Monica Reinfelder, ed. *Amazon to Zami: Towards a Global Lesbian Feminism*. London: Sage, 1996:138-51.

_____. "Two Stories, Three Lovers and the Creation of Meaning in a Black Lesbian Autobiography." In Heidi Safia Mirza, ed. *Black British Feminism: A Reader*. London: Routledge, 1997: 216-25.

_____. "Doing Sym/bio/graphy with Yasna." In Tess Cosslet et al. ed. *Feminism and Autobiography: Texts, Theories, Methods.* London: Routledge, 2000: 247-51.

_____ and Lynda Birke. "Reflections on Bodies Under Torture," *Women's Studies International Forum*, 24(6), 2001: 653-68.

Valentine, Gill. "Queer Bodies and the Production of Space." In Diane Richardson and Steven Seidman, eds. *Handbook of Lesbian and Gay Studies.* London: Sage, 2002: 145-60.

Wilson, Ana. "Audre Lorde and the African-American Tradition: When the Family is Not Enough." In Sally R. Munt, ed. *New Lesbian Criticism: Literary and Cultural Readings.* Hemel Hempstead: Harvester and Wheatsheaf, 1992: 75-93.

doi:10.1300/J155v11n03_01

Contesting 'Straights': 'Lesbians,' 'Queer Heterosexuals' and the Critique of Heteronormativity

Annette Schlichter

SUMMARY. The essay explores interrelations between Lesbian Theory and Queer Straight Theory. It provides a brief genealogy and an interrogation of the "discourse of queer heterosexuality." I argue that Queer Straight Theory is certainly indebted to lesbian (and) feminist critiques of institutional heterosexuality and their denaturalizations of straight and lesbian sexualities. Lesbian and Queer Straight Theories re-

Annette Schlichter is Associate Professor of Comparative Literature, University of California, Irvine. She is the author of a German-speaking study on the figure of the madwoman in feminist critiques of representation and the co-editor of a German collection on Feminism and Postmodernism. Her research interests are Feminist and Queer Theories, gender and literature, multiculturalism and contemporary American literature. Schlichter's current project focuses on constructions and critiques of 'heterosexuality' in Queer and Feminist Theory and in literature. Her most recent publication in English is the essay, "Queer at Last? Straight Intellectuals and the Desire for Transgression," which appeared in *GLQ: A Journal of Lesbian and Gay Studies* in 2004.

Address correspondence to: Professor Annette Schlichter, Department of Comparative Literature, University of California, Irvine, CA 92697-2650, USA (E-mail: aschlich@uci.edu).

[Haworth co-indexing entry note]: "Contesting 'Straights': 'Lesbians,' 'Queer Heterosexuals' and the Critique of Heteronormativity." Schlichter, Annette. Co-published simultaneously in *Journal of Lesbian Studies* (Harrington Park Press, an imprint of The Haworth Press, Inc.) Vol. 11, No. 3/4, 2007, pp. 189-201; and: *Twenty-First Century Lesbian Studies* (ed: Noreen Giffney, and Katherine O'Donnell) Harrington Park Press, an imprint of The Haworth Press, Inc., 2007, pp. 189-201. Single or multiple copies of this article are available for a fee from The Haworth Document Delivery Service [1-800-HAWORTH, 9:00 a.m. - 5:00 p.m. (EST). E-mail address: docdelivery@haworthpress.com].

main in disagreement, however, about notions of power and identity that shape their theoretical and political stances. doi:10.1300/J155v11n03_02
[Article copies available for a fee from The Haworth Document Delivery Service: 1-800-HAWORTH. E-mail address: <docdelivery@haworthpress.com> Website: <http://www.HaworthPress.com> © 2007 by The Haworth Press, Inc. All rights reserved.]

KEYWORDS. Heterosexuality, straightness, heteronormativity, queer straights, queer theory, lesbian theory

For a brief moment, I was surprised, when I received an invitation from *The Journal of Lesbian Studies* to explore possible configurations of 'lesbian' and 'queer straight' identities, theories, practices, politics and interests. Why this response to a very welcome request? Because the strongest reservations against the queer straight have come from eminent lesbian theorists, and have been put forward with a kind of polemical fervor that does not seem to leave much room for discussion. Teresa de Lauretis and Suzanna Danuta Walters, for instance, evoke the queer straight as an unwelcome intruder into a discourse of sexual minorities, launched by Queer Theory's theoretical excesses. De Lauretis reads queer heterosexuality–like "the literal becoming-male of lesbian PoMo"–as one of many absurd ideas that emerge from "the alleged 'subversion' of gender identity in queer/lesbian studies." Uncomfortable with the troubling of a discourse of specific feminine and lesbian identity and sexuality, she muses: "An announced collection of essays on 'queer theory and the subject of heterosexuality' declares itself 'straight with a twist.' Who knows, by next year's MLA, we may be reading something like 'Lesbian Heterosexuality: The Last Frontier'" (1997: 47). In a similar vein, Walters, who argues in favor of "the centrality of experience [versus] the vacuousness of positionality" has 'the queer heterosexual' personify the dangers of queer critiques of identity. She warns against the "deconstruction of identity politics (the recognition that identity categories can be regulatory regimes)" which, as she thinks, is likely to "become the vehicle for co-optation: the radical queer theorist as married heterosexual. It becomes a convenient way to avoid those questions of privilege" (1996: 841).

It is important to note that de Lauretis' and Walters' wider argument that the gender(indifferent) politics of queer discourse might (re)produce the invisibility of lesbian subjects reflects serious concerns shared by a number of lesbian scholars, including some who are sympathetic to queer critiques of identity (Butler, 1997 a; Martin, 1996: 45-96). It is, however, remarkable that they had already made up their minds about the queer straight before 'straights' even began their "ambiguous labor of queer straight aspiration" (Thomas, 2000: 15).[1] The specter of 'the queer heterosexual' haunts discourses of lesbian identity as the poster-child of Queer Theory's political sellout and as enemy of a lesbian critique of sexuality. Speaking in the name of lesbians, de Lauretis and Walters can only imagine the queer heterosexual as the unrightful appropriator of sexual minorities' specific knowledges and as a subject who uses his engagement with Queer Theory as an evasion of the interrogation of his own privileged status.[2]

Of course, such assumptions about queer straights are not representative of the whole field of Lesbian Theory or of views of lesbian theorists involved in the critique of sexuality. A number of scholars, who retain the name 'lesbian' while undermining the notion of (lesbian) identity,[3] played a significant role in queer deterritorializations of identities, politics and knowledge. They helped open up discursive channels for heterosexuals to articulate a critique of heteronormativity from a subject position inscribed as hegemonic. How, then, do those self-identified queer straights compare to the specters of straightness, which haunt discourses of lesbian identity? In other words: What do queer straights want? And how do their critical theories and practices intersect with the thinking of lesbians?

First, a brief delineation of the emergence of the "discourse of queer heterosexuality" is necessary (Schlichter, 2004). Current genealogies of the critique of sexuality like to credit Michel Foucault's crucial and influential work on the apparatus of sexuality for its central role in theorizing heterosexuality. Unfortunately, such genealogies tend to forget the revolutionary impact of feminist critiques, which since the 1960s have conceptualized heterosexuality as the symbolic kernel of patriarchy and major practice of male domination.[4] Second-wave feminists, from Betty Friedan to Kate Millett, contributed to the denaturalization of heterosexuality by "publicly marking it as problematic" (Katz, 1995: 113). The groundbreaking work of lesbian feminists, such as Adrienne Rich and Monique Wittig, has made numerous contributions to the conceptualization of institutionalized heterosexuality, including the critique of feminism's own heterocentrism.[6] A milestone in the process of denaturalizing heterosexuality, Rich's famous essay, "Compulsory Heterosexuality and Lesbian Existence," explicitly criticizes the assumption of a natural, innate female heterosexuality (characteristic, not only of dominant culture, but also of most major feminist works of the time) and insists on its institutional character (1984 (1980): 217). With the famous term "the straight mind," Wittig described heterosexuality as a "political regime" (1992: xiii), a set of "discourses" (25), a "social contract", "a fetish" and/or "an ideological form" (40) that penetrates and regulates society by totalizing and universalizing the ideology of sexual difference. Rich's and Wittig's influential texts offer examples of how Lesbian Feminism's politicization of gender and sexuality "productively informed" Queer Theory (Jagose, 1996: 57).[6]

Yet, it took some time until queer theorists acknowledged the contributions of feminist and lesbian writers of color, who challenged the white, Eurocentric features of hegemonic (lesbian and feminist) constructions of genders and sexualities. Authors, such as Patricia Hill Collins, Audre Lorde, Gloria Anzaldúa, Cherríe Moraga and Hortense Spillers, laid the groundwork for an intersectional analysis of discourses that regulate racial and sexual identities. Moraga's early critique of white (lesbian) feminist's descriptions of sexuality as "based in white-rooted interpretations of dominance, submission, power exchange etc" is exemplary of the complexity of socio-cultural formations of normativity, desires, and sexual identities and practices. Moraga announces: "What I need to explore will not be found in the lesbian feminist bedroom, but more likely in the mostly heterosexual bedrooms of South Texas, L.A., or even Sonora, México" (2000: 117). Her reflections on the difficulties of sexual and cultural identification imply the potential of a multi-dimensional critique of heteronormativity. This aspect of a lesbian (and) feminists of color critique has not yet been fully explored by either Feminist or Queer Theories.[7]

It should be beyond question that all current critiques of heterosexuality are indebted to this lesbian (and) feminist critical work. Nevertheless, queer theorists have significantly changed the "subject of heterosexuality", i.e., both the critical perspectives on the object of sexuality and the potential status of straight critics in that discourse by rethinking the critique of sexuality as a project that is generally directed "against the normal rather than the heterosexual" (Warner, 1993: xxvi). The specific queer reworking of the poststructuralist idea of normative discourses that *produce* gendered, sexual identities[8] has to be differentiated from notions of heterosexuality as a patriarchal institution (Rich) or patriarchal ideology (Wittig). Central to the queer critique is the deconstruction of the gender binary *and* of the dichotomy of hetero- versus homosexuality. These binaries characterize the hegemonic culture's attempts to produce and regulate dominant as well as marginal sexual subjects. The differentiation between a heteronormative social and philosophical matrix or a normalizing apparatus[9] and the homosexual and heterosexual identity positions produced by that apparatus significantly departs from lesbian (and) feminist theories of patriarchal heterosexuality. On the one hand, marginalized sexual subjects cannot claim to be situated outside of power, because they are also formed through normative discourses. On the other hand, the differentiation between heteronormativity and heterosexuality provides the possibility of a heterosexual's disidentification, a repositioning that might entail a critical reflection on heterosexual presumption. Queer writings also offer perspectives for a subversive resignification of straight subjectivities by implying that a straight identity position is–like all sexual identities–being regarded as unstable and incoherent (even if heteronormativity tries its best not to let it appear as such). Thus, straights, who are engaged in a critique and subversion of heteronormative theories and practices, can become potential affiliates of a queer project.

With the publication of the volume *Straight with a Twist: Queer Theory and the Subject of Heterosexuality* (2000), the discourse on queer heterosexuality entered the academic scene. Associating itself with an anti-homophobic, anti-normalizing project, the volume tries to undermine the notion of (straight) identity by producing a possibly queer position of the straight critic, i.e., her or his "straightness with a twist."[10] At their best, these queerings of straightness provide a form of opposition against both the binary of homosexuality/heterosexuality, which is foundational of normative culture, and against the dichotomy straight versus queer that has established itself in Sexuality Studies. As a third position, the queer straight might be reminiscent of Wittig's lesbian as "a not-woman, a not-man, a product of society, not nature" (1992: 13) or of the "woman-identified woman," who found her way into Rich's idea of the "lesbian continuum." In turn, those figurations suggest a politics of dis/identification and of counter-identification as a stage of resistance against heterosexual hegemony. And indeed, Calvin Thomas, editor of the collection *Straight With a Twist*, evokes Rich's "lesbian continuum" (and its critics) when discussing the "possibility of including straights in the queer mesh" (2000: 15). Moreover, contributor Jacqueline Foertsch engages Rich's concept in order to legitimize her claim to "a lesbian identity, different from that of a practicing lesbian" (2000: 50), i.e., a lesbian intellectual with a straight-sexual history. Yet, the queer straights' notions of power, sexuality and identity and their implications for the descriptions of the situation of 'the heterosexual subject' significantly differ from those of Wittig and Rich. The feminist texts' essentialized model of power understands patriarchy as the domination of the group/class of men over the group/class of women. Before that backdrop, Rich's work, while denaturalizing heterosexuality (by portraying it as an institution) and lesbianism (by offering it as a form of identification open to all women), keeps the binary of gender difference intact, i.e., it naturalizes gender (Jagose, 1996: 54). In fact, the idea of 'the lesbian subject's' solidly gendered self is central to Rich's work. Wittig, on the other hand, denaturalizes gender by revealing its function as an ideological ploy of sex. Yet, she promotes, as Judith Butler convincingly argues, another problematic binary, i.e., a "radical disjunction . . . between heterosexuality and homosexuality," which implies a "systemic integrity of heterosexuality" and a total determination of heterosexual subjects as well as a "purification of homosexuality" (1990: 120) Thus, Wittig's oppositional lesbian, who appears as fluid, unrepresentable and troubling to the gendered structures of heterosexual hegemony, is finally fixed in the problematic position of the subject outside ideology, "a lesbian persona liberated from the hegemony of heterosexuality" (Roof, 1994: 55).

Such tendencies that claim an oppositional stance for the lesbian are still common in later works of Lesbian Theory, where only the lesbian subject in its many figurations–for instance, as "eccentric subject" (de Lauretis, 1991), or as the "combo butch-femme" (Case, 1993: 295)–can claim a critical distance from patriarchal institutions of heterosexuality.[11] On the other hand, straightness appears so fully contained by the social order of heterosexuality that a critical analysis from the position of a heterosexual subject remains impossible. It is symptomatic that both Case and de Lauretis see the straight woman bound by a heterosexual contract that ties her to men and clouds her consciousness. Male critics of heteronormativity are just beyond the imaginable.

The queer (straight) approach to normativity as producing and regulating dominant and marginal sexualities not only undermines such clear-cut positionings. The oxymoronic designation 'queer straight' also indicates that heterosexuality is not a transparent category but rather an experience that needs to be interpreted. A closer reading of 'heterosexuality' has become urgently necessary. While Lesbian/ Gay and Queer Theory accomplished the making visible of heterosexuality as "an object of knowledge, the target of a possible critique" (Halperin, 1995: 47), there has been little further interrogation of 'the subject of heterosexuality', since those fields focus on marginalized sexualities. This emphasis seemed historically necessary, but at the same time the effect of such an oversight is a rather monolithic model of heteronormativity as well as a certain uncomplicated notion of a uniform straight life.[12]

The totalization of heteronormativity and of straight identity has been challenged in recent literature. Addressing the racialization of sexualities, Cathy Cohen, for instance, shows how discourses of racial and social stratification regulate a range of differentially-situated heterosexual positions within heteronormativity. Cohen argues that throughout US history African-American heterosexuality has been constituted as a deviation from the norm and that the figure of the black deviant is still reflected in recent public portrayals of the Welfare mother, the teenage mother, or the absent black father as irresponsible breeders (1997: 452). From a different perspective (which would have to include Cohen's findings on racial stratification), new work on an anti-normative heteroerotics challenges limited and normative assumptions about the lifestyles and sexual practices of straight subjects that are still operating in Queer Theory. A recurring stereotype is the white suburban couple, who is fully immersed in consumer capitalism and happily reproducing hegemonic subjects, while exuding sexual routine and boredom.[13] In response to such stereotypical representations Michael O'Rourke, for example, begins to develop a queer-straight sexual symbolic that deconstructs the binary formation of sexual masculine activity/feminine passivity through a resignification of the gendered meanings of the bodily orifices of vagina and anus. O'Rourke's work offers itself finally to open up a discussion about hetero-sexual practices, an issue that has yet been circumvented by queer straight theorists. However, in order to be effectively critical, such a project has to go beyond a general theory of a queer-straight symbolic to reflect on the specific hegemonic site of a white heterosexuality from which such a theoretical perspective is being proposed. In other words, queer straight talk about sexual desires and practices has to confront its access to and use of heterosexual "epistemological authority" (Halley, 1993: 83), which includes, for instance, the right to a private sexuality, a right that is not granted to sexual minorities.[14] O'Rourke would also have to interrogate the implications of race for his theory, insofar as the whiteness of a normalized heterosexuality is a precondition of the project of "proliferating queer theories which celebrate non-normative heterosexualities" (2005: 112).

While I find the identification as "queer straight" useful for the problematization of the normative restrictions of straight identity, it is certainly not a necessary identification for a strong critique of heterosexuality from the point of view of straights. A range of (pro-sex) feminists, who do not necessarily name themselves 'queer,' present various attacks on heteronormative presumptions.[15] For example, Carol Siegel proposes the very productive critical notion of "heterophobia" for an "understanding of erotic love that leads to a binarity in which the feelings compatible with domestic life are associated with reason while to the extent to which passion and romance move to realization outside domestic enclosure, they are associated with madness and disavowal of reality" (2000: 60-1). A reading of normative culture as a heterophobic formation that involves constraining conventions of gender and sexuality can account for a hierarchization of different "types of heterosexuality" as well as the abjection of homosexuality. Because the dyad heterophobia/homophobia "calls into question the commonplace that hostility toward homosexuality is the natural result of an excess of heterosexual feeling, and also the corollary idea that distaste for heterosexual passion reveals a closeted inclination towards homosexuality" (61), Siegel's interesting new critical perspective exceeds the hetero/homo antagonism.

Finally, a note of caution regarding the queer straight identification is necessary: this act of self-naming is fraught with ethical and political problems that are difficult to overcome, and I want to conclude my reflections by describing them in regard to Queer Theory's institutional re-formation (Cooper, 2004; Schlichter, 2004). Let me briefly elaborate two important aspects of the issue. First, the moment of the queer straight is also a "post-queer moment." This is not to say that a queer critique is outdated but that its arrival in academia (in parts of the university at least) relativizes its potential as oppositional force. At a time when Queer Theory has gained some academic clout, the straight intellectual's self-queering not only necessarily appears as an act of appropriation of critical strategies that come out of a struggle of sexual minorities but is also devoid of the former critical edge of lesbian, gay and queer interventions. Before that backdrop, the utopian enthusiasm of some queer straight writings, which seem to assume that the intellectual and/or sexual queering of straightness could in itself transform the heteronormative apparatus, have to be taken with a grain of salt.[17] I therefore suggest the use of the signifier 'queer' in straights' self-namings as a marker of one's affiliation with and of intellectual indebtedness to a specific political and intellectual project, one that continually emphasizes the precariousness of the identification 'queer straight,' e.g., I would use the name without the hyphen, which erases the tension between the terms.

Second, the assertion of a (critical) subjectivity under the name 'queer straight' or 'queer heterosexual' or 'straight with a twist' contradicts idea of the subversion of identity. I propose that we understand this contradiction as an effect of the specific location of Queer Theory: straights engaged in the identity critique of Queer Theory must ethically and politically legitimize their presence in a context that is already paradoxically configured. Queer discourse insists on the deconstruction of identities within an institutional space, which could not exist without the history of identity politics of the sexual minorities (inside and outside the academy) that created it.

History and its impacts are what finally separates queer straight from queer, lesbian and gay critiques–while, at the same time, the target of their critique, i.e., heteronormativity, situates them in a joint struggle for transformation. The proliferation of critical positions in this struggle does not necessarily make for harmonious relations among the critics. Nor does it have to. The diversity of contesting perspectives is necessary to a production of knowledge that has to remain intellectually and politically complex in order to challenge the ubiquitous forces of normative culture.

NOTES

1. Let those quotation marks indicate that I regard *all* identity positions as discursive productions–a view, which does not necessarily question their real material and psychic effects.

2. The figure of 'the male lesbian' can be regarded as a precursor of the queer straight. For an in-depth-interrogation of that figure, see Zita (1992).

3. It is symptomatic that there is no room for the feminized figure of the queer straight. Even Sedgwick becomes, if mentioned at all, fully masculinized. Ignoring the finer differences between "identification" and "identity," Walters turns Sedgwick's identification "as" gay man into her "being" a gay man. (847) Thereby, Walters wants to emphasize her point that the subject set up by Queer Theory is a "universal male subject or at least a universal gay male subject" (846).

4. See, for instance, Butler (1997 b); Fuss (1989); Grosz (1994); Stein, (1997); Wiegman (1994); Wilton (1995). Some of de Lauretis' writings could be situated in that group. See Stein (1997) and Phelan (1994) for accounts of different notions of lesbian identity.

5. A telling example is David Halperin's otherwise excellent book, *Saint Foucault: A Gay Hagiography*. (1995) Halperin attributes the critique of heterosexuality to Foucault's *History of Sexuality*, but also acknowledges some aspects of a problematization in Sigmund Freud's work as well as in Alfred Kinsey's and William Masters' sexological studies. No feminists are mentioned in his genealogy of a critique of sexuality (1995: 47-8; 204, n. 78).

6. For the complicated relationship of feminists and lesbians, see Wilton (1995: 87-109) and the contributions to the collection *Cross-Purposes* (1997). For a recontextualization of the 'gay/straight' split in feminism, see King (1990). See Dever for an illuminating analysis of the heteronormative turns of second wave discourses of sexuality (2004: 91-117) and for an interesting reading of the role of 'the dyke' in feminist theory (141-61).

7. Linda Garber characterizes Lesbian Feminism as an "intertext" of Queer Theory (2001: 176). Looking at poetic-as-theoretical writings, she particularly (but not exclusively) emphasizes overlooked contributions by working-class lesbians and lesbian writers of color. While Garber convincingly extrapolates the complexities of individual texts and concepts (such as Rich's "lesbian continuum"), which have been "disremembered" or simplified in order to establish new queer perspectives, she does not pay close attention to the crucial theoretical differences, which can make approaches incompatible. On some contradictions between Lesbian and Postmodern Theory, including the poststructuralist aspects of queer theory, see Roof (1994).

8. I want to emphasize the conceptualization and critique of heterosexuality in the work of lesbian and feminist thinkers of color, who have so far been credited mostly for their critiques of hegemonic notions of gender. One of the first authors to include them in a genealogy of a queer of color critique is Muñoz (1999); Linda Garber emphasizes the queer debt to lesbians of color, such as Gloria Anzaldúa and Audre Lorde (Garber, 2001).

9. My understanding of the term 'queer' follows Annamarie Jagose, who describes the queer production of knowledge as a "debunking of stable sexes, genders and sexualities [which] develops out of a specifically lesbian and gay reworking of the post-structuralist figuring of identity as a constellation of multiple and unstable positions" (1996: 1).

10. See Butler on the "heterosexual matrix" (1990: 151, n. 6), Berlant and Warner on "heteronormativity" (2000: 312, n. 2). For a political critique of heteronormativity, it is, however, crucial to recognize the interrelations of heteronormativity and straightness. (Fuss, 1991: 2).

11. This is clearest in the articles by Foertsch and Thomas, who attempt to theorize a queer straight critical position.

12. For critical comments on individual writings, see Foertsch (2000), Siegel (2000: 10-11), Wilton also criticizes straight women's critiques of lesbian hostility against heterosexuals (1995: 87-90).

13. Exceptions in Queer Theory's approach to heterosexuality are Gayle Rubin's differentiation of positions within the much-quoted "charmed circle" (1984), as well as Butler's writings, in particular her theses about the possible interrelatedness of homo- and heterosexual subject formations (1997 c: 132-66).

14. A telling example is Grosz, who tries to undermine the binary of queer and straight, but finally reproduces the dichotomy of non-normative queers/hypernormative straights, when she evokes the image of "the suburban couple whose rate of copulation is at least once a month" as the only representation of straights in her text (1994: 142).

15. I thank the anonymous reader, who offered an eloquent critique of the queer straight approach to the representation of straight sex.

16. This includes straight and lesbian women. For an early collection of feminist voices, see Vance (1989). For later theoretical work see, among others, Gaines (1995), Jackson (1995; 1999), Richardson (1998; 1994), Siegel (2000).

17. O'Rourke self-critically reflects on such utopianism (2005: 115, n. 9).

REFERENCES

Anzaldúa, Gloria. *Borderlands/La Frontera*. 2nd edtn. With an introduction by Sonia Saldivar-Hull. San Francisco: Aunt Lute Books, 1999.

Berlant, Lauren and Michael Warner. "Sex in Public." In Lauren Berlant, ed. *Intimacy*. Chicago: The University of Chicago Press, 2000: 311-31.

Butler, Judith. "Against Proper Objects." In Elizabeth Weed and Naomi Schor, ed. *Feminism Meets Queer Theory*. Bloomington: Indiana University Press, 1997 a: 1-30.

_____. *Gender Trouble: Feminism and the Subversion of Identity*. London: Routledge, 1990.

_____. "Imitation and Gender Subordination." In Linda Nicholson, ed. *The Second Wave: A Reader in Feminist Theory*. New York: Routledge, 1997 b. 300-16.

_____. *The Psychic Life of Power: Theories in Subjection*. Stanford: Stanford University Press, 1997 c.

Case, Sue-Ellen. "Toward a Butch-Femme Aesthetic." In Henry Abelove, Michèle Aina Barale and David M. Halperin, eds. *The Lesbian and Gay Studies Reader*. New York: Routledge, 1993: 294-306.

Cohen, Cathy. "Punks, Bulldaggers, and Welfare Queens: The Radical Potential of a Queer Politics?" *GLQ: A Journal of Lesbian and Gay Studies*, 3, 1997: 437-65.

Collins, Patricia Hill. *Black Feminist Thought: Knowledge, Consciousness, and the Politics of Empowerment*. New York: Routledge, 2000.

Cooper, Sarah. *Relating to Queer Theory: Rereading Sexual Self-Definition with Irigaray, Kristeva, Wittig and Cixous*. Frankfurt am-Main: Peter Lang, 2000.

De Lauretis, Teresa. "Eccentric Subjects: Feminist Theory and Historical Consciousness," *Feminist Studies* 16(1), 1991: 115-50.

_____. "Fem/Les Scramble." In Dana Heller, ed. *Cross-Purposes: Lesbians, Feminists, and the Limits of Alliance*. Bloomington: Indiana University Press, 1997: 42-8.

Dever, Carolyn. *Skeptical Feminism: Activist Theory, Activist Practice*. Minneapolis: University of Minnesota Press, 2004.

Foertsch, Jacqueline. "In Theory If Not In Practice: Straight Feminism's Lesbian Experience." In Calvin Thomas, ed. *Straight With a Twist: Queer Theory and the Subject of Heterosexuality*. Bloomington: Indiana University Press, 2000: 45-59.

Friedan, Betty. *The Feminine Mystique*. New York: Dell, 1984 (1963).

Fuss, Diana. *Essentially Speaking: Feminism, Nature and Difference*. New York: Routledge, 1989.

_____. "Inside/Out." In Diana Fuss, ed. *Inside/Out: Lesbian Theories/Gay Theories*. New York: Routledge, 1991: 1-12.

Gaines, Jane. "Feminist Heterosexuality and Its Politically Incorrect Pleasures," *Critical Inquiry* 21(4), 1995: 382-410.

Garber, Linda. *Identity Poetics: Race, Class, and the Lesbian-Feminist Roots of Queer Theory*. New York: Columbia University Press, 2001.

Grosz, Elizabeth. "Experimental Desire: Rethinking Queer Subjectivity." In Joan Copjec, ed. *Supposing the Subject*. London: Verso, 1994: 133-56.

Halley, Janet. "The Construction of Heterosexuality." In Michael Warner, ed. *Fear of a Queer Planet: Queer Politics and Social Theory*. Minneapolis: University of Minnesota Press, 1993. 82-104.

Halperin, David. *Saint Foucault: Towards a Gay Hagiography*. New York: Oxford University Press, 1995.

Heller, Dana, ed. *Cross-Purposes: Lesbians, Feminists, and the Limits of Alliance*. Bloomington: Indiana University Press, 1997.

Jackson, Stevi. *Heterosexuality in Question*. London: Sage, 1999.

Jagose, Annamarie. *Queer Theory: An Introduction*. New York: New York University Press, 1996.

Katz, Jonathan. *The Invention of Heterosexuality*. New York: Dutton, 1995.

King, Katie. "Producing Sex, Theory, and Culture: Gay/Straight Remappings in Contemporary Feminism." In Marianne Hirsch and Evelyne Fox Keller, eds. *Conflicts in Feminism*. New York: Routledge, 1990: 82-104.

Lorde, Audre. "The Master's Tools Will Never Dismantle the Master's House." In Gloria Anzaldúa and Cherríe Moraga, ed. *This Bridge Called My Back: Writings by Radical Women of Color*. New York: Ktchen Table P, 1981.

Martin, Biddy. *Femininity Played Straight: The Significance of Being Lesbian*. New York: Routledge, 1996.

Millett, Kate. *Sexual Politics*. Urbana: U of Illinois P, 2000 (1970).

Moraga, Cherríe. *Loving in the War Years: Lo Que Nunca Pasó por Sus Labios*. Cambridge, Mass.: South End Press, 2000 (1983).

Muñoz, José Esteban. *Disidentifications: Queers of Color and the Performance of Politics*. Minneapolis: University of Minnesota Press 1999.

O'Rourke, Michael. "On the Eve of a Queer-Straight Future: Notes Toward an Antinormative Heteroerotic," *Feminism and Psychology* 15(1), 2005: 111-16.

Phelan, Shane. *Getting Specific: Postmodern Lesbian Politics*. Minneapolis: University of Minnesota Press, 1994.

Rich, Adrienne. "Compulsory Heterosexuality and Lesbian Existence." In Ann Snitow, Christine Stansell and Sharon Thompson, eds. *Desire: The Politics of Sexuality*. London: Virago, 1984 (1980): 212-41.

Richardson, Diane, ed. *Theorising Heterosexuality: Telling It Straight*. Buckingham: Open University Press, 1998.

Roof, Judith. "Lesbians and Lyotard: Legitimation and the Politics of the Name." In Laura Doan, ed. *The Lesbian Postmodern*. New York: Columbia University Press, 1994. 47-66.

Rubin, Gayle. "Thinking Sex: Notes for a Radical Theory of the Politics of Sexuality." In Carole S. Vance, ed. *Pleasure and Danger: Exploring Female Sexuality*. Boston: Routledge, 1984: 267-319.

Schlichter, Annette. "Queer at Last?: Straight Intellectuals and the Desire for Transgression," *GLQ: A Journal of Lesbian and Gay Studies*, 10(4), 2004: 543-64.

Segal, Lynne. *Straight Sex: The Politis of Pleasure*. London: Virago, 1994.

Siegel, Carol. *New Millenial Sexstyles*. Bloomington: Indiana University Press, 2000.

Spillers, Hortense. "Mama's Baby, Papa's Maybe: An American Grammar Book." In Joy James and T. Denean Sharpley-Whiting, eds. *The Black Feminist Reader*. Oxford: Blackwell, 1988: 57-87.

Stein, Arlene. *Sex and Sensibility: Stories of a Lesbian Generation*. Berkeley: University of California Press 1997.

Thomas, Calvin. "Straight with a Twist: Queer Theory and the Subject of Heterosexuality." In Calvin Thomas, ed. *Straight with a Twist: Queer Theory and the Subject of Heterosexuality.* Urbana: University of Illinois Press, 2000: 11-44.

Vance, Carol, ed. *Pleasure and Danger: Exploring Female Sexuality.* London: Pandora, 1989 (1984).

Walters, Suzanna Danuta. "From Here to Queer: Radical Feminism, Postmodernism, and the Lesbian Menace (Or, Why Can't a Woman Be More Like a Fag?)," *Signs: Journal of Women in Culture and Society* 21(4), 1996: 830-69.

Warner, Michael. "Introduction." In Michael Warner, ed. *Fear of a Queer Planet: Queer Politics and Social Theory.* Minneapolis: University of Minnesota Press, 1993: vii-xxxi.

Wiegman, Robyn. "Introduction: Mapping the Lesbian Postmodern." In Laura Doan, ed. *The Lesbian Postmodern.* New York: Columbia University Press, 1994: 1-22.

Wilton, Tamsin. *Lesbian Studies: Setting an Agenda.* London: Routledge, 1995.

Wittig, Monique. *The Straight Mind and Other Essays.* Trans. Marlene Wildeman. Boston: Beacon, 1992.

Zita, Jacquelyn N. "Male Lesbians and the Postmodernist Body," *Hypatia: A Journal of Feminist Philosophy,* 7(4), 1992: 106-27.

doi:10.1300/J155v11n03_02

The Lesbian Community and FTMs: Détente in the Butch/FTM Borderlands

Jillian T. Weiss

SUMMARY. In 1998, Dr. Jacob Hale wrote about a "borderland" between butch lesbian identity and FTM masculinity, suggesting a "demilitarized zone." While the intervening years have brought no "demilitarized zone," the border may not have a long future. Converging trends in identity among the younger generation in their teens and twenties suggest this, such as changing meanings of 'lesbian' and 'FTM,' the blending of sexuality and gender, and understanding these as personal, rather than identity, differences. The socio-historical circumstances that gave power to anti-trans feminist attitudes and trans rejection of lesbian identity are disappearing. This is not to say that we are 'post-lesbian' or 'post-transsexual,' but the tension between identities, the need to distinguish clearly between them, and the arguments about who is 'really'

Jillian T. Weiss is Assistant Professor of Law and Society at Ramapo College of New Jersey in the USA. She has published two articles in the area of Transgender Studies: "GL vs. BT: The Archaeology of Biphobia and Transphobia within the US Gay and Lesbian Community," *Journal of Bisexuality*, 3, 2004: 25-55; and "The Gender Caste System: Identity, Privacy and Heteronormativity," *Law and Sexuality*, 10, 2001: 123-86. Her primary research interest is law and sexuality.

Address correspondence to: Dr. Jillian T. Weiss, School of Science and Human Services, Ramapo College of New Jersey, 505 Ramapo Valley Road, Mahwah, NJ 07430, USA (E-mail: jweiss@ramapo.edu).

[Haworth co-indexing entry note]: "The Lesbian Community and FTMs: Détente in the Butch/FTM Borderlands." Weiss, Jillian T. Co-published simultaneously in *Journal of Lesbian Studies* (Harrington Park Press, an imprint of The Haworth Press, Inc.) Vol. 11, No. 3/4, 2007, pp. 203-211; and: *Twenty-First Century Lesbian Studies* (ed: Noreen Giffney, and Katherine O'Donnell) Harrington Park Press, an imprint of The Haworth Press, Inc., 2007, pp. 203-211. Single or multiple copies of this article are available for a fee from The Haworth Document Delivery Service [1-800-HAWORTH, 9:00 a.m. - 5:00 p.m. (EST). E-mail address: docdelivery@haworthpress.com].

lesbian or 'really' FTM may be of supreme unimportance to the next generation. Time will tell. doi:10.1300/J155v11n03_03 *[Article copies available for a fee from The Haworth Document Delivery Service: 1-800-HAWORTH. E-mail address: <docdelivery@haworthpress.com> Website: <http://www. HaworthPress.com> © 2007 by The Haworth Press, Inc. All rights reserved.]*

KEYWORDS. Lesbian feminism, butch identity, FTM (female-to-male transsexuals), transsexuality, genderqueer

In 1998, Dr. Jacob Hale wrote "Consuming the Living, Dis(re)-membering the Dead in the Butch/FTM Borderlands." He discussed the competing claims by lesbians and FTMs regarding the gender identity of historical figures. The title refers to a 'borderland' between butch-lesbian identity and FTM masculinity, which consumes the living, "disremembers" the psychological identity of the dead, as well as "dismembering" their physical status as FTMs or lesbians (depending on which side of the line you reside). Hale suggests that, although the border cannot be eliminated, nor the concerns and emotions of those on both sides reconciled easily, perhaps a "demilitarized zone" should be created. My thesis is that the intervening years have brought no "demilitarized zone". There is no evidence that the combatants have changed their positions, or their fervor. The line is real. It is sign of difference, a line of demarcation, and an identity distinction of great importance to both lesbians and FTMs. Nonetheless, I contend that the border may not have a long future.

There are converging trends in sexual identity that suggest such a result. These changes primarily affect the younger generation in their teens and twenties. First, the old labels are shifting in meaning. 'Lesbian' is moving away from a primarily political discourse of 'woman-identified woman.' 'FTM' is moving away from a primarily medical discourse of 'sex change.' Second, sexuality and gender among the younger generation have changed and begun to blend. Many young people now identify as 'genderqueer,' a word suggesting the conjunction of both gender and gayness, and pluralistic challenges to the gender binary (Weiss 2004 a). 'Lesbians' can have sex with men–can even *be* men (born male-bodied or female-bodied). 'FTM' can mean 'female towards male' and refer to a lesbian, a woman and/or a man. Such a person may have sex with women, or men, or either. Third, differences among sexuality and gender are regarded as personal differences, not identity differences. Being a woman who has sex with women, but who considers oneself masculine does not require identification as 'butch.' Being a woman who considers herself transgender does not mean abandoning one's identity as a lesbian and taking on an FTM identity.

These trends are moves away from essentialism, though in different ways, and towards the 'universalizing view' suggested by Sedgwick (1990). In my experience, a majority of the older members of the lesbian and transsexual communities were raised with and will likely continue to espouse essentialist positions, continuing the long history of GL vs. BT politics (Weiss 2004 b). The younger members of these communities, however, have been raised on these universalizing principles, and that has formed their consciousness. I have no data to suggest that the attitude changes discussed herein are rapidly proliferating or will dominate in the future. Nor is there space in this limited format to explore fully the diverse landscape of Lesbian Feminism. I hope only to shine a light on these nascent trends.

WELCOME TO THE BORDERLANDS

The borderlands opened in the 1950s, when Christine Jorgensen burst into the headlines, and the term 'transsexual' moved into popular culture. From the beginning, the homosexual movement was uncomfortable with 'transsexuals.' This was not simply a question of whether transsexuals should be included in the community. It was a situation of active disapproval of the identity itself (Meyerowitz 2002:183).

Some lesbian feminists theorized transsexuality as driven by an essentialist, patriarchal conception of women (Raymond, 1979). They considered transsexuality an abdication of the need for social change. They derided FTMs as gender-conformists grasping at male privilege (Cromwell 1999: 40-1). They understood the gender identity of FTMs as internalized misogyny. Transsexuality was part of a continuum that includes the beauty industry, heterosexist propaganda and economic pressure, foot-binding, genital mutilation, pornography and "other institutions whereby men shape women to conform to their needs and fantasies" (Henry 1978; Sturgis 1979). Lesbians moved to erect a wall between lesbians and FTMs (Nestle, 2002).

The feminist discomfort with FTMs, however, was not a logical outcome of identity difference, because the women's movement centered on a successful challenge to Sigmund Freud's dictum that "anatomy is destiny." Rather, it seems to have derived from socio-historical factors surrounding the rise of the lesbian-feminist movement: its largely white, middle-class composition, the desire to appeal to the larger feminist movement, and the stigma of female masculinity (Califia 1999: 89-91). Lesbian feminists argued vigorously that the lesbian-feminist community was not a sexual community, but a political one. (Radicalesbians, 1970).

Butch identity, with its strong connection to sexuality and its similarity to heterosexual patterns, affronted these ideas. Lesbian feminists disapproved of a gender identity that included masculine characteristics in personality, appearance and dating roles:

> . . . it must be understood that what is crucial is that women begin disengaging from male defined response patterns. In the privacy of our own psyches, we must cut those cords to the core. For irrespective of where our love and sexual energies flow, if we are male-identified in our heads, we cannot realize our autonomy as human beings. (ibid)

It was made repeatedly clear in the 1970s that butch lesbians were no longer welcome within the lesbian-feminist movement (Meyerowitz, 2002:178; Rubin, 2003).

At this time, most FTMs distanced themselves from the lesbian community. Most FTMs felt strongly that they were men and therefore could not be lesbians, though they may have had ties with lesbians and the lesbian community. They made it clear that, unlike lesbianism, theirs was not an issue of erotic desire. Rather, their issue was internal gender identity, that part of the mind that makes one feel like a man or a woman. They felt strongly that they were neither homosexual, nor properly part of the homosexual community. Unlike Lesbian Feminism, their issue was avowedly not political, but strictly medical (Devor, 1997: 312, 333, 338, 342; Rubin, 2003). Most FTMs were uncomfortable with the feminist idea that they were supposed to take on the burden of changing society. This would have entailed championing the idea that they were females who had taken on a non-heteronormative gender role. The whole point of FTM identity, however, is that it is a male identity, *not* female. Most FTMs formed relationships with women, assuming the role of a man within a heterosexual relationship as then understood. They found it hard to relate to the strongly anti-male stance of Lesbian Feminism. Even those who could relate were completely disqualified from the ranks of Lesbian Feminism. Some FTMs *were* more open to acknowledging a lesbian history, and thereby a past female identity, but the lesbian-feminist community generally did not find this to be sufficient to qualify for a lesbian-feminist identity. Thus, they alienated even those possibly open to the idea of championing social change.

The medical establishment also played a central role in reinforcing the separation by requiring that FTMs demonstrate essentialist male attitudes in order to receive medical assistance for the change. Any FTM that identified as 'gay' or 'lesbian,' or felt identification with 'female' identity was not considered a good candidate for medical assistance (Califia, 1997:186; Cromwell, 1999:104-5). The medical establishment counseled them never to disclose a female or lesbian identity (Green, 2004). Without a strong essentialist ethic (or at least a strong pretense), FTMs were denied a fundamental rite of passage of FTM identity by the medical establishment.

SIGNALS OF CHANGE

These essentialist attitudes among some advocates of Lesbian Feminism and FTMs fueled the border wars, and created the borderlands. These debates have not disappeared, with each side continuing to charge the other with rabid gender essentialism (Wilton, 2000, 2002; Hird, 2002; Jeffreys, 2003; Sweeney, 2004). The socio-historical circumstances that gave power to anti-trans feminist attitudes and trans rejection of lesbian identity, however, are disappearing. There has been some relaxation of the social attitudes in the US and UK that punished openly lesbian identity through downward mobility. This relaxation is not equivalent to acceptance, as evidenced by the furor created in the recent US Presidential election by the mere utterance of the word 'lesbian' by candidate John Kerry, and President George W. Bush's successful harnessing of public sentiment against gay marriage. At the same time, it should be noted that the furor resulted because Mr. Kerry responded to a gay-rights question posed at a Presidential debate with a reference to Vice President Dick Cheney's lesbian daughter. The resulting furor did not cause outrage against Dick Cheney or his daughter, as it might have in the past, but against Mr. Kerry. Lesbian identity, while not socially 'approved,' is no longer generally understood as a dysfunctional gender inversion, as it was in the 1970s when many lesbians fought for acceptance by constructing lesbianism as primarily political, disavowing female masculinity. Many middle-class lesbians have been able to come-out without losing their middle-class lifestyle, particularly in large city environments. Medical attitudes towards FTMs are also less essentialist, permitting FTMs to identify as 'gay' or 'lesbian' without the concern that they will not be 'real' FTMs. A new generation has grown up with these changes, and the universalist ethic has shaped their attitudes. This universalist ethic and the fluid sex/gender system stemming from it do not require a border.

A sign of this universalist ethic is that many young people do not identify their sexuality in the same ways the previous generation did. The previously all-consuming question of whether or not butch and femme identities are compatible with feminist aims is less relevant in such an alternate universe. The "lesbian continuum" described by Adrienne Rich seems quaint from this vantage point. Younger queers of all kinds are taking seriously Judith Butler's suggestion to un-moor identity from bodies and to seek more personal and individual ways to be themselves, and thereby challenge fixed gender regimes (Wilchins, 2005). The labels 'lesbian' and 'FTM' do not mean the same thing they did a generation ago.

Many young people are embracing a more fluid role in terms of their sexual orientation and gender identity. They may or may not identify as someone who is attracted to women, or as FTM, but their self-definition often includes 'gender queer' or 'trans' as a means of challenging the gender binary (Gilliam, 2005). The sexuality based on this new identification is also fluid, and defies past expectations of lesbian and gay sexuality. Queer-identified young women are likely to have sex with queer-identified young men, and consider it a queer relationship. Masculine labels such as 'boy' and 'daddy' are not considered taboo by women's communities. Queer-identified young women have twice the rate of pregnancy of their heterosexual peers. In another study, twenty percent of lesbians reported having high-risk sexual contact, including sexual intercourse with men who have had sex with men (Szymanski, 2005). Here is how one lesbian described herself and her friends in 2002:

> One of my friends identifies as a female-bodied butch. He says he is neither a womon nor a lesbian, and he takes only womyn lovers. Another friend says that s/he is a lesbian and also a man. Yet another says s/he is a masculine womon. I know two people who identify as transgendered womyn–one is a biological man and the other a biological womon. The bioman dresses and lives as a womon; the biowoman dresses and lives as a man. Both call themselves lesbian. I have come to understand that, although there is not yet a name for my desires, I am a womon, a lesbian womon,

and a femme, who deeply desires male presence in female bodies. I love men on top of me and inside me. This is my kind of lesbianism. (Lionhart, 2002)

There are also lesbians who consider themselves transgender but want to remain women (Baird, 2002):

> I routinely speak before groups of young queers like Jesse who refuse to identify as gay or straight because they don't want to leave any of their friends behind, because they don't want to be known by something as simplistic as who they sleep with, or because they don't even select their partners by sex. (Wilchins, 2002: 289-97)

These moves away from essentialism and towards universalism may signal the beginnings of the disappearance of the 'border' between lesbian and FTM. I refer to 'border' here as a sign of difference, as a line of demarcation, and as a distinction of pure identity. This is not to say that we are 'post-lesbian' or 'post-transsexual.' The writers quoted here do not represent a majority of lesbians or FTMs today, but they may represent an emerging trend. I do not claim that no-one in the future will identify as lesbian or FTM. Nor do I mean that young people have abandoned all differences between sexualities and genders. Nor is the work of Feminism complete—women and girls all around the globe are treated as second-class citizens and property. It may indicate, however, that the "Butch/FTM Borderlands," as a 'real' line as written about by Hale and Halberstam in 1998, is now perceived as increasingly unstable and unreal by many in the younger generation. Among academics of this new generation, the effort (and perhaps the ability) to distinguish clearly a field of 'Lesbian' Studies, or any sexuality-based disciplines, may diminish. Among activists of this new generation, the need and desire for identity politics may wane. It is not that heteronormativity is splintering, but perhaps 'homonormativity' has lessened its hold on the younger generation. A vivid example is the recent turnabout at the Human Rights Campaign, the largest US gay advocacy group, which had staunchly resisted the idea of including transgender identity in its legislative agenda for federal employment protection. It has now said it will not support such legislation without trans inclusion. The fight for rights may be moving to an arena in which the tension between identities, the need to distinguish clearly between them and the arguments about who is 'really' lesbian or 'really' FTM may be of supreme unimportance to the next generation. Time will tell.

REFERENCES

Baird, Wally. "Disorderly Fashion." In Joan Nestle, Clare Howell and Riki Wilchins, eds. *GENDERqUEER: Voices from Beyond the Sexual Binary.* Los Angeles: Alyson Publications, 2002: 260-2.

Califia, Pat. *Sex Changes: The Politics of Transgenderism.* San Francisco: Cleis Press, 1997.

Cromwell, Jason. *Transmen and FTMs: Identities, Bodies, Genders and Sexualities.* Chicago: University of Illinois Press, 1999.

Devor, Holly. *FTM: Female to Male Transsexuals in Society* Bloomington, Illinois: Indiana University Press, 1997.

Gilliam, Jesse. Email Communication, 30 March, 2005.

Green, Jamison. *Becoming a Visible Man.* Nashville: Vanderbilt University Press, 2004.

Halberstam, Judith. "Transgender Butch: Butch/FTM Border Wars and the Masculine Continuum," *GLQ: A Journal of Lesbian and Gay Studies*, 4, 1998: 287-310.

Hale, Jacob. "Consuming the Living, Dis(re)membering the Dead in the Butch/FTM Borderlands," *GLQ: A Journal of Lesbian and Gay Studies*, 4, 1998: 311-28.

Henry, Alice. "Questioning Authority: Women, Science, and Politics," *Off Our Backs*, 8, 1978: 4-5.

Hird, Myra J. "Out/Performing Our Selves–Invitation for Dialogue," *Sexualities*, 5(2), 2002: 219-38.

_____. "Welcoming Dialogue–A Further Reply to Out/Performing Our Selves," *Sexualities*, 5(2), 2002: 245-9.

Jeffreys, Sheila. *Unpacking Queer Politics: A Lesbian Feminist Perspective.* Cambridge: Polity, 2003.

Lionhart. "Wanting Men." In Joan Nestle, Clare Howell and Riki Wilchins, eds. *GENDERqUEER: Voices from Beyond the Sexual Binary.* Eds.. Los Angeles: Alyson Publications, 2002: 228-237.

Meyerowitz, Joanne. *How Sex Changed: A History of Transsexuality in the United States.* Boston: Harvard University Press, 2002.

Nestle, Joan. "Genders on My Mind." In Joan Nestle, Clare Howell and Riki Wilchins, eds. *GENDERqUEER: Voices from Beyond the Sexual Binary.* Los Angeles: Alyson Publications, 2002: 3-10; quoting Karl Ericsen, *The Ladder*, 1970.

Raymond, Janice. *The Transsexual Empire: The Making of the She-Male.* Boston: Beacon Press, 1979.

Radicalesbians. "The Woman-Identified Woman." Pittsburgh: Know, Inc. (1970); from *Documents from the Women's Liberation Movement: An On-line Archival Collection.* April 1997. The Special Collections Library, Duke University. URL scriptorium.lib.duke.edu/wlm/womid

Rubin, Henry. *Self-Made Men: Identity and Embodiment among Transsexual Men.* Nashville: Vanderbilt University Press, 2003.

Sedgwick, Eve Kosofsky. *Epistemology of the Closet.* Los Angeles: University of California Press, 1990.

Sturgis, Susanna. "An Interview with Jan Raymond," *Off Our Backs*, 9, 1979: 14-16.

Sweeney, Belinda. "Trans-Ending Women's Rights: The Politics of Trans-Inclusion in the Age of Gender," *Women's Studies International Forum*, 27, 2004: 75-8.

Szymanski, Zak. "The Opposite of Opposite Sex," *Curve*, 13, 2005.

Weiss, Jillian Todd. *Sexuality: An Essential Glossary*. London: Arnold, 2004 a.

_____. "GL vs. BT: The Archaeology of Biphobia and Transphobia Within the US Gay and Lesbian Community," *Journal of Bisexuality*, 3, 2004 b: 25-55.

Wilchins, Riki. "Gender Rights Are Human Rights." In Joan Nestle, Clare Howell and Riki Wilchins, eds. *GENDERqUEER: Voices from Beyond the Sexual Binary*. Los Angeles: Alyson Publications, 2002. 289-97.

_____. Email Communication, 24 February 2005.

Wilton, Tamsin. "Out/Performing Our Selves: Sex, Gender and Cartesian Dualism," *Sexualities*, 3, 2000: 237-54.

_____. "'You Think This Song Is About You': Reply to Hird," *Sexualities*, 5, 2002: 357-61.

doi:10.1300/J155v11n03_03

Intersections of Lesbian Studies and Postcolonial Studies: One Possible Future for Class

Donna McCormack

SUMMARY. This position piece addresses the decline of class as a mode of inquiry in Lesbian Studies and Postcolonial Studies. It argues that in spite of this decline, class continues to forcibly pervade all areas of our lives and, therefore, should be fundamental to the research praxis of these fields of study. It goes on to suggest that the intersections of these two disciplines are able to open up a space where questions regarding class and its global dimension in the twenty-first century can be addressed. It concludes by reflecting on the possibility

Donna McCormack is a PhD candidate in the School of English at the University of Leeds, specializing in representations of 'sexing' bodies in postcolonial texts. She spent the past year working as a support worker at *The Big Issue* and teaching French at Brighton and Hove Children's University. Previous to that she undertook an MA in Sexual Dissidence and Cultural Change at the University of Sussex. Her dissertation focussed on modes of disempowerment in postcolonial novels. She has spent time working and studying in Francophone regions, including Quebec, Reunion and Paris.

Address correspondence to: Donna McCormack, School of English, Cavendish Road, University of Leeds, Leeds, LS2 9JT, UK (E-mail: donna_mccormack@yahoo.co.uk).

[Haworth co-indexing entry note]: "Intersections of Lesbian Studies and Postcolonial Studies: One Possible Future for Class." McCormack, Donna. Co-published simultaneously in *Journal of Lesbian Studies* (Harrington Park Press, an imprint of The Haworth Press, Inc.) Vol. 11, No. 3/4, 2007, pp. 213-221; and: *Twenty-First Century Lesbian Studies* (ed: Noreen Giffney, and Katherine O'Donnell) Harrington Park Press, an imprint of The Haworth Press, Inc., 2007, pp. 213-221. Single or multiple copies of this article are available for a fee from The Haworth Document Delivery Service [1-800-HAWORTH, 9:00 a.m. - 5:00 p.m. (EST). E-mail address: docdelivery@haworthpress.com].

of an ethical methodological approach to research. doi:10.1300/
J155v11n03_04 *[Article copies available for a fee from The Haworth Document
Delivery Service: 1-800-HAWORTH. E-mail address: <docdelivery@
haworthpress.com> Website: <http://www.HaworthPress.com> © 2007 by The
Haworth Press, Inc. All rights reserved.]*

KEYWORDS. Class, postcolonial studies, sex, lesbian, sexuality, gender, race, ethnicity

VIGNETTE ONE

I am attending a panel discussion at the Queer Matters conference at King's College, London entitled "The Intersections of Queer, Race and Class." There is a fierce debate between many audience members and the conference organizers over the lack of visibility of ethnic minorities and transsexuals on the panel (and at the conference in general). I listen attentively, sharing concerns with both sides of the debate. Yet my concerns are slightly different. I raise my hand and I am invited to speak. I express that class has failed to be mentioned throughout this whole debate, including in the papers given by the panelists. I also stress my anxiety over the fact that the discussion is focussing on visibility, as we cannot assume that ethnicity, sexuality, race, sex or gender are readable on bodies. Moreover, I feel that if we are to continue focussing on visibility, then class will fall out of the debate, as how can one see class?[1] Class is not mentioned again. (May 2004)

This "encounter" is personal (Ahmed, 2000).[2] I am changed by it, impacted upon, left thinking about what Queer Theory is working for in the present and, thus, what future it is building. The particular is not synonymous with the general and yet in Lesbian Studies, Feminist Theory and Cultural Studies, the personal is a situated knowledge that allows us to think about and theorise the general:

> . . . my own class history is central to my understanding of how culture works, and it would be disingenuous to suggest otherwise. (Medhurst, 2000: 21)

This encounter forces us to ask why it is so difficult to talk about class, especially given that class was one of the topics of debate. In this position piece I, therefore, reflect on reasons why class may be slipping out of debates and work on identities, power, relationships and bodies. I then suggest that the critical juncture of Lesbian Studies and Postcolonial Studies is one possible way of bringing class to the fore of our research methodologies and interests.

Perhaps the difficulties in talking about class stem from its elusiveness and its demise as a mode of inquiry. Critics tend to agree that there has been a steady decline in the study of class over the past thirty years. Broadly speaking, this is a move from a class-based politics in Cultural Studies to a focus on identity politics, reflecting a shift in society at large.[3] This move in Britain has been influenced by the insistent claims of many politicians, including Margaret Thatcher and Tony Blair, that Britain is a "classless" society. Yet, class continues to forcibly pervade all areas of our identities, relationships and bodies. The changing nature of class does not make it any less real but it does make it difficult to define. Some define class according to occupation, salary and education. Others suggest that it refers to aesthetic and value judgements, space, language, knowledge production and power (Storr, 2003). I agree with Beverley Skeggs, however, that "class is primarily about inequality and exploitation" (Skeggs, 1997: 75). In these terms, class is not so different from the issues of Postcolonial Studies and Lesbian Studies. The study of postcolonialism, lesbianism and class overlap insofar as there is a focus on what it means to belong, how bodies come to be experienced and represented as undesirable and abject and possible ways of avoiding violent encounters. There are, however, many differences that cannot be collapsed. In exploring their intersections, I am neither suggesting that we should ignore the different focus of each mode of inquiry nor that we should conflate their experiential differences, but rather that the point where Lesbian Studies meets Postcolonial Studies is a space which opens up new questions regarding class. Moreover, the methodological approaches of these disciplines impact upon each other in this encounter and are, thereby, changed; thus allowing class to take up a central position alongside other vectors of power and identity.

VIGNETTE TWO

I am participating in a debate at the University of Leeds on postcolonialism in Britain when the subject of class arises. It becomes a very heated discussion with lots of stereotypes relating to class being mentioned, something consciously avoided when talking about (post)colonialism. Class brings the discussion to focus on the North/South divide in Britain. I express my concern that we are overlooking issues of access to education, health and economics. It is suggested that these disparities are imagined, not real, and that we live in a classless society where, presumably, all people have equal access to equal resources. The debate comes to a close when it is suggested that people from the North should get over "it." The "it" was too loaded with meaning to untangle. (December 2004)

This was an academic space in which we debated issues around equal access to resources, economic disparities, prejudices and more 'just' ways of belonging in relation to postcolonial nations. It was never assumed either on a global level or on a particular level that all human beings were equal. Hierarchies, power relations and institutional structures were central to these postcolonial debates. In this encounter, however, we see that certain axes of analysis and power are prioritized, considered more real and, thus, more valid. Although postcolonialism, like Lesbian Studies, sees itself as rethinking power structures, it is apparent in the above example that often this is only in relation to a singular axis of power or identity.[4] In other words, it was suggested that experiences of structural prejudice could only be understood in relation to colonialism but not class. I suggest that one should not come at the expense of the other.

Some postcolonial critics, such as Ann Laura Stoler, argue that class is at the core of a race-based colonial politics. Representations of the degenerate, the outcast, the dirty and the abject body are all interwoven in discourses relating to colonialism, class, gender, sexuality and race. Colonial power was often iterated through a class-based discourse and reinforced through the racializing of bodies:

An overlapping set of discourses has provided the psychological and economic underpinnings for colonial distinctions of difference. These discourses tie fears of sexual contamination, physical danger, climate incompatibility, and moral breakdown to the security of a European national identity with a racist and class-specific core. (Stoler, 2002: 46)

These interconnections are central to our understandings of how certain bodies come to be conceived of as outsiders and as responsible for our social ills. To ignore the impact of class on experiences and representations of colonialism risks both creating a hierarchy of priorities and rendering class violence and prejudice invisible. Furthermore, to ignore the class, sexual, gendered, racial and ethnic dimensions of our lives prevents us from working towards a form of social transformation where violence against 'abject' bodies could be avoided.

Lesbian Studies has historically attempted to deal with class in relation to a set of identity practices and modes of power, specifically sexuality, sex and gender. Some critics suggest that this discipline's concern with class is due to women's experiences of class as a social fact. That is, women, especially lesbians, are most likely to feel the effects of economic shortages, poor housing and judgments regarding their class status (Skeggs, 1997; Lorde, 1994). Although historically class has a place in this discipline, it is not yet central to its research practices. I suggest that class cannot be understood as something others 'do' or something to add onto a piece of research or a debate. Rather, class is central to all work on sex, gender and sexuality. One's somatic and desiring experiences are very difficult, if not impossible, to separate from one's economic status, one's social and cultural background and one's sense of belonging.

The difficulty is clearly how class can be understood as central to Lesbian Studies and Postcolonial Studies in an increasingly global context where other vectors of power are prioritized and, thus, considered more important and valid. It is, here, that I see the intersections of Lesbian Studies and Postcolonial Studies as forcing us to maintain class as fundamental to issues of power. This disciplinary overlap permits a slightly different angle on the questions we can ask, not just regarding class, but also sex, ethnicity, gender, race, sexuality and colonialism. In other words, in bringing together issues with which Lesbian Studies and Postcolonial Studies are both concerned, each discipline will have to deal with the specificities of the other's work, but more importantly, they will also have to reconfigure their own methodological frameworks. So, Lesbian Studies cannot be content with exploring issues of sexuality in the developing world but must rethink its methodologies to make the global context central to its work.

These methodological changes will force us to address the tensions involved in defining class in the Twenty-First Century. Experiences of class have changed dramatically over the past thirty years. They have been impacted upon by the creation of a free-market economy; the closing down of industrial work places in much of Britain; the outsourcing of much labour-intensive manufacturing by Britain and America; and the bringing in of migrant workers for the underpaid service industry.[5] In this sense, we need to ask, what does class mean in a global market economy and how does it relate to (neo-)colonialism? Moreover, as moving up the class ladder is continually represented as a possibility, we need to ask, what impact does this have on working-class people who find it increasingly difficult to access resources? Finally, we must ask, how does class relate to issues of migration and how is its meaning changed in these encounters? While focussing on these overlaps we need to keep their differences in mind, to work with the tensions they create and their points of divergence. I agree with Elspeth Probyn that we need to stay with the spaces that make us feel uncomfortable in order to strive towards ethical methodological and living practices (Probyn, 2000: 143).

Although I do not offer answers to these complex questions which need serious consideration, I do propose one suggestion for how we might think about approaching these issues and, thereby, avoid both silencing certain voices and reiterating symbolic and material violence. Both Lesbian Studies and Postcolonial Studies contribute to debates around ethics. They both have as a fundamental practice to their methodologies the notion of self-reflexivity. This self-reflexivity, the ability to constantly question one's own goals, desires and actions, is essential to the ethics of both fields in thinking about social transformation. Such a way of conducting research and of living daily keeps in mind the responsibility we each have to the other. Such a responsibility is what Judith Butler calls our "corporeal vulnerability," our "interdependence" and a "relationality that is composed neither exclusively of myself nor you, but is to be conceived as *the tie* by which those terms are differentiated and related" (Butler, 2004: 19, 27, 22). Put simply, we are each dependent on the other and, thereby, responsible for what happens to the other. Ahmed sees this responsibility as a way of responding to the particular while keeping the general in mind. In doing so, we recognize that our responsibility is infinite:

> To say that responsibility is infinite, is to imply that it is a debt that cannot be paid back, and hence that there is always a call, a demand, for a future response to an other *whom I may yet approach*. To assume that I have been responsible–to this or to that–is to measure out our responsibility, to contain it, and hence to violate its conditions of possibility. To say that "I am responsible" here and now is a form of irresponsibility: it refuses to accept the possibility

of an approach of an-other other or, more simply, of another approach. (Ahmed, 2000: 146-7)

Such self-reflexive practices, based on the idea of a never-ending responsibility, serve to remind us of our wider social responsibilities in the research we undertake and in the methodological approaches we employ. It forces us to take responsibility for what we say or do not say, for the issues we ignore and for the subject matter we choose to focus on or not to focus on. It keeps in mind that, for many of us, work which focusses on a singular axis of power does not include or reflect our lived experiences, our embodied sociality or our theoretical musings (Lorde, 1994). While an ethics of self-reflexive responsibility emerges out of the fields of Feminism, Cultural Studies, Lesbian Studies and Postcolonial Studies, it needs to be a core academic and social praxis. The encounter between Lesbian Studies and Postcolonial Studies is a space where this responsibility can be kept in mind and one in which we are called upon to respond to the uncomfortable tensions of class, race, sexuality, gender, ethnicity, sex and colonialism. Such an intersection opens up a new set of contemporary questions regarding experiences of class in a global context. No axis of power can be considered more important or less valid in a self-reflexive ethical encounter.

NOTES

1. There is an excellent article on the way in which class is read on the body by Beverley Skeggs (2000: 129-150). Although I do not deal with the problematics of framing such debates around visibility in this article, I am currently working on this issue in another paper. The distinction I make is that rather than class being read on the body, it is actually constantly inscribed. Moreover, in certain spaces, such as the conference space described above, class is rendered invisible through the assumption that the space itself is middle-classed.

2. The term, "encounter," comes from Sara Ahmed's understanding of postcoloniality. It is pertinent here as it keeps in mind the idea that we are impacted upon in each encounter (be this with a person, an event or a text). Our future encounters thereby contain traces of these past encounters but are not restricted to or by these memories. Moreover, there is hope for change in the future encounters that will continually take place. Each encounter thus opens up a space of negotiation and dialogue.

3. The influence of American Cultural Studies on British Cultural Studies has also contributed to this shift from class to a focus on other modes of power and identity, specifically race, gender, ethnicity and sexuality (Munt, 2000: 1-16).

4. There is evidently work in the field of Postcolonial Studies that turns around more than one axis of power and I am not suggesting otherwise (McClintock, 1995; Stoler, 1995). What I am emphasizing is that there is a tendency for certain vectors of power to

fall more easily out of an analytical framework than others. I am suggesting here that in Postcolonial Studies this is often class, almost as if class is not at the core of experiences of colonialism. Such an argument is not limited to class, however, and can certainly be extended to include sex, sexuality, race, ethnicity and gender. Although some may argue that there is a need to focus on one specific vector of power, I believe that to assume all of these are not in play in every encounter is to remain blind to our diverse embodied social experiences.

5. Evidently, these issues have been around for longer than the past thirty years and I do not wish to undermine that migrant work forces and the outsourcing of labor have long been a part of First-World economies. Globalization, however, has normalised these practices on an international level. There is excellent postcolonial work that pays attention to the overlap of colonialism and world poverty and the gendered and racial aspects of underpaid work forces (Bartolovich, 2000; Alexander and Mohanty, 1997).

REFERENCES

Alexander, Jacqui and Chandra Talpade Mohanty, eds. *Feminist Genealogies, Colonial Legacies, Democratic Futures*. New York: Routledge, 1997.

Ahmed, Sara. *Strange Encounters: Embodied Others in Post-Coloniality*. London: Routledge, 2000.

Bartolovich, Crystal. "Global Capital and Transnationalism." In Gayatri Chakravorty Spivak, ed. *A Companion to Postcolonial Studies*. Oxford: Blackwell Publishers, 2000: 126-61.

Butler, Judith. *The Psychic Life of Power*. California: Stanford University Press, 1997.

_____. *Precarious Life of Power: The Powers of Mourning and Violence*. London: Verso, 2004.

Gilroy, Paul. *After Empire: Melancholia or Convivial Culture?* London: Routledge, 2004.

Khanna, Ranjana. *Dark Continents: Psychoanalysis and Colonialism*. Durham: Duke University Press, 2003

Lorde, Audre. "Age, Race, Class and Sex: Women Redefining Difference." In Mary Evans, ed. The Woman Question. London: Sage, 1994: 36-41.

McClintock, Anne. *Imperial Leather: Race, Gender and Sexuality in the Colonial Conquest*. New York: Routledge, 1995.

McIntosh, Mary. "Class". In Andy Medhurst and Sally R. Munt, eds. *Lesbian and Gay Studies: A Critical Introduction*. London: Cassell, 1997: 250-60.

Medhurst, Andy. "If Anywhere: Class Identification and Cultural Studies Academics." In Sally R. Munt, ed. *Cultural Studies and the Working Class: Subject to Change*. London: Cassell, 2000: 19-35.

Munt, Sally R. "Introduction." In Sally R. Munt, ed. *Cultural Studies and the Working Class: Subject to Change*. London: Cassell, 2000: 1-16.

Probyn, Elspeth. *Carnal Appetites: FoodSexIdentities*. London: Routledge, 2000.

Sinfield, Alan. *Literature, Politics and Culture in Postwar Britain*. London: The Athlone Press, 1997.

Skeggs, Beverley. *Formations of Class and Gender: Becoming Respectable*. London: Sage Publications, 1997.

_____. "The Appearance of Class: Challenges in Gay Space." In Sally R. Munt, ed. *Cultural Studies and the Working Class: Subject to Change.* London: Cassell, 2000: 129-150.

Stoler, Ann Laura. *Race and the Education of Desire: Foucault's History of Sexuality and the Colonial Order of Things.* London: Duke University Press, 1995.

_____. *Carnal Knowledge and Imperial Power: Race and the Intimate in Colonial Rule.* Berkeley: University of California Press, 2002.

Storr, Merl. *Latex and Lingerie: Shopping for Pleasure at Ann Summers Parties.* Oxford: Berg, 2003.

doi:10.1300/J155v11n03_04

Cal/liope in Love:
The 'Prescientific' Desires
of an Apolitical 'Hermaphrodite'

Morgan Holmes

SUMMARY. This article provides a critical reading of heterosexist determinism and the erasure of lesbian desire, activity and subjectivity in Jeffrey Eugenides' novel, *Middlesex*. doi:10.1300/J155v11n03_05 *[Article copies available for a fee from The Haworth Document Delivery Service: 1-800-HAWORTH. E-mail address: <docdelivery@haworthpress. com> Website: <http://www.HaworthPress.com> © 2007 by The Haworth Press, Inc. All rights reserved.]*

KEYWORDS. Lesbianism, intersex, Jeffrey Eugenides, *Middlesex*

Morgan Holmes is Associate Professor of Sociology at Wilfrid Laurier University in Canada and has been an active lobbyist for and intellectual supporter of intersex rights since 1993.

Address correspondence to: Professor Morgan Holmes, Sociology and Anthropology, Wilfrid Laurier University, Waterloo, ON N2L 3C5, Canada (E-mail: mholmes@ wlu.ca).

Thanks to JDL for editorial assistance, WLU for research support and to my anonymous readers for comments on the draft.

[Haworth co-indexing entry note]: "Cal/liope in Love: The 'Prescientific' Desires of an Apolitical 'Hermaphrodite.'" Holmes, Morgan. Co-published simultaneously in *Journal of Lesbian Studies* (Harrington Park Press, an imprint of The Haworth Press, Inc.) Vol. 11, No. 3/4, 2007, pp. 223-232; and: *Twenty-First Century Lesbian Studies* (ed: Noreen Giffney, and Katherine O'Donnell) Harrington Park Press, an imprint of The Haworth Press, Inc., 2007, pp. 223-232. Single or multiple copies of this article are available for a fee from The Haworth Document Delivery Service [1-800-HAWORTH, 9:00 a.m. - 5:00 p.m. (EST). E-mail address: docdelivery@haworthpress.com].

In the summer of 2002 I gave in, accepting the inevitable: now that Jeffrey Eugenides' *Middlesex* had won the Pulitzer Prize I could no longer willfully ignore it. Weary of writers who had contacted me for a number of years during my intersex-activist days, trying to determine if their proposed 'hermaphrodites' could do things like impregnate or have sex with themselves, I had put off reading the book.[1] Resigned to the fact that would-be authors were not really contacting me to find out 'the biological facts' but to get my blessing for their monstrous creations, I assumed the habit of telling them not to bother going through the motions of 'fact checking.' I would advise them simply to accept that they wanted their monsters to tell particular kinds of stories, usually within the genres of fantasy and science fiction, and that because my answers would only disappoint them, they ought to proceed without the farcical consultation with a 'real' intersexed person. I would also tell the would-be writers that I wasn't likely to have much interest in the ways in which they would call upon their hermaphrodites to carry whatever pieces of cultural baggage they might be trying to address in their writing. As Thea Hillman explains in her response to *Middlesex*: "While the Myth of Hermaphroditus has captured the imagination for ages, it traps real human beings in the painfully small confines of someone else's story" (www.isna.org).

At one time it may have been worth positing intersexed bodies to fulfill what Donna Haraway termed the "promise of monsters," creating patterns of interference to challenge traditional, masculinist, linear narrative structures that code power and privilege along a binary axis in which the self-contained male body always wins and the excessive, gestating female body always loses (1992: 300). The problem, however, is that the deployment of intersexed monsters as culture jammers par excellence has stalled, resulting not in the substantive interference that Julia Epstein proposed in her "Either/Or, Neither/Both" article (1990), but in the reification of the proper place of traditional visions and modes of masculinity in opposition to femininity. In short: the promise has been stolen and re-appropriated, and the intersexed body rendered as a neuter is thus re-positioned not as a disruptive agent, but beyond and outside the realm of gender altogether.[2] This paper examines the particular manner in which the spectacular monstrosity of a 'hermaphrodite' body is called upon to carry the burden of a moral and political tale of incest, genes, gender, sex and lesbian desire, tra(ns)versing the boundaries of time, place and propriety. Ultimately the story operates to effect the erasure of all such crises, and to secure the place of male heterosexuality and patriarchal power.

GROWING UP IN MIDDLESEX

"I was born twice: first as a baby girl on a remarkably smogless Detroit day in January of 1960; and then again, as a teenage boy in an emergency room near Petosky, Michigan, in August of 1974" (Eugenides, 2002: 3). So begins *Middlesex*, a finely crafted epic drama, a transcontinental and intergenerational tale of an omniscient gene who, as narrator of the story, is both its heroine and hero. Recognition that a tale is well-told, however, is not a tacit endorsement of its conclusions.

As the omniscient gene waiting in "the greenroom to the world" (11) Cal/liope can see the genetic calamity of her birth from its point of origin two generations back.[3] From that position, Cal/liope tells a family drama that encompasses the invasion of Greece by the Turkish army, an incestuous marriage drawing from a 'flawed' gene pool, immigrant ascension and the American Dream, and the Black Civil Rights Movement. Following the now well-established stereotype that all-girl schools are breeding grounds for infantile lesbian activity, Callie falls in love with a character referred to only as the "Obscure Object." However, deliberately echoing the circumstances that drove Alexina Barbin out of the convent in 1860's France, Eugenides' 'hermaphrodite,' Callie, is pushed out of her already tenuous position as a Greek child in her WASP-y Grosse Pointe school and community. As the hero/ine, Cal/liope performs nothing short of an Olympian feat, triumphing over adversities that range from ethnic and racial prejudice to violent homophobia, and a bout of 'gender dysphoria' in San Francisco (Eugenides, 2002: 459-476). Yet the narrative still negates same-sex desire by erasing lesbian, female sexuality under the sign of an abandoned childhood, and maps adult masculinity onto male heterosexual desire with each as the guarantor of the other.

Following the publication of *Middlesex*, Eugenides explained that he had first been inspired to write the novel after reading Herculine Barbin's memoirs:

> It had a lot of things in it that appealed to me: a medical mystery, an amazing personal transformation and a doomed passion at its center. The *hermaphrodite* who wrote it was a schoolgirl in a French convent, and she fell in love with her best friend. In doing that, she discovered that she was a *hermaphrodite*. Unfortunately, it was written in 19th century convent-school prose—very melodramatic, evasive about the anatomical details and really unable to render the emotional situation in any regard. I was frustrated by

this and thought, I'd like to write the story I'm not getting from this book. (Miller, 2002; emphasis added)

Eugenides' acknowledgement of his deliberate desire to improve on the first-person account of a personal history by rewriting it as a fiction is interesting for two reasons. First is the hubris of assuming that while 'truth may be stranger than fiction,' fiction can certainly tell a better tale; second is the assumption that desire can reveal something inherent and true about the inner self that no other mode can disclose. Barbin's own writing focuses on the many ways in which her youth and her body were unremarkable, and then on the torment of being forced into a role presumed by her physician and by the French courts to reflect Barbin's 'true sex.' Indeed, it was not desire itself that revealed Barbin's 'true sex' to be male, but rather, the externally imposed, social insistence that sexual desire was properly for an 'opposite sex' and that Barbin, therefore, had to be male. As Edward Stein explains, such a logic of opposition "pictured gay men as having male bodies and female 'souls' and lesbians as having female bodies and male 'souls'" (1999: 37). Barbin, of course, was not actually thought by her priest or her physician to be so inverted, but to have finally had an interior male soul exposed, and, along with it, a body that was male enough to warrant expulsion from the convent. That Barbin did not concur with the court's reassignment of her sex to male is evident in her suicide by carbon-monoxide poisoning in her twenty-sixth year.

Apparently dismissive of this horrific conclusion to Barbin's life, Eugenides repeats the nineteenth-century physicians' and courts' assertion that desire reveals something innate, and inherently true about one's sex. Eugenides' perspective is clear when he has Cal/liope look back to observe her adolescent first love:

> On certain days, when the greenhouse was lit just so and the Obscure Object's blouse unbuttoned two buttons, when the light illuminated the scapulars dangling between the cups of her brassiere, did Cal/liope feel any inkling of her *true biological nature*? (2002: 327; emphasis added)

Eugenides' writing reiterates the notion that desire can tell an outward observer something that the behaving subjects may not even know about themselves. Indeed, he even has Cal declare that desire is the basis of his achievement of male subjectivity, and that his desire is not 'deviant' but properly embodied: "Desire made me cross over to the other side, desire and the facticity of my body" (479). Appropriating the voice of his hero/ine, Eugenides forces the capitulation of Cal/liope's voice to the will of the nineteenth-century Church and magistrates who declared that a combination of desires and bodily facts rendered Barbin properly male, and improperly situated in the convent. Furthermore, by invoking John Colapinto's biography of David Reimer (2000), Eugenides erases the female subjectivity of young Callie, swallowing her complexities into a fictionalized argument that the adult Cal is 'as nature made him.'[4] Readers then, can look from the outside at Cal and say, "You're fine," a position that I argue below assumes an external observer is uniquely able to ascertain the internal truth of another person's identity based on external features of desire and practice.

Callie is an ethnically-marked tomboy who loves the Obscure Object for all the things that Callie is not: blonde, with a WASP pedigree and an insouciant affect echoing earlier depictions of bourgeois lesbians.[5] Barbara Creed points out:

> The central image used to control representation of the potentially lesbian body–to draw back the female body from entering the dark realm of lesbian desire–is that of the tomboy. The narrative of the tomboy functions as a liminal journey of discovery in which feminine sexuality is put into crisis and finally recuperated into the dominant patriarchal order. (1996: 88)

Eugenides thus builds into the narrative a mechanism to rescue their interchange from the realm of 'deviance'. Eugenides recuperates the tomboy child, Callie, who loves the Obscure Object, by transforming her into Cal, and renders infantile Callie's desire for and sexual activity with the Obscure Object. Such a framing of lesbian activity, in which it is left behind as a vestigial memory of an abandoned child subject, repeats the Freudian characterization of lesbianism as an arrested, immature state in which the girl child has failed to resolve her 'penis-envy' (Creed, 1996: 93). Cal/liope's transition from school-girl to adult male is yet another instance in a long tradition of narrative and juridical imperatives to cure, transform or otherwise 'do-away' with lesbian desire and lesbian sexuality. Callie's transition to Cal allows an escape from surgery, but accepts masculine, patriarchal desire as the appropriate adult form and plays into a behaviorist view that locates one's identity by the sex of one's object of desire. Edward Stein explains that behaviorists take the position that:

One's sexual orientation is determined by the sex of the people that he or she has sex with: if one has sex with people of the same sex-gender then one is a homosexual; if one has sex with people not of the same sex-gender then one is a heterosexual. There are three features to this view. First, it focuses on a person's behaviour as being determinate of his or her sexual orientation. Second it assumes that there are two and only two possible sexual orientations. Third, it focuses on whether the person is of the same sex-gender as that of [one's] sex partners rather than on whether [one's] sex partners are men or women. (1999: 42-3)

Crucially, Stein points out, the behaviorist view assumes that external observers know more definitively what the truth of our identities are than we do as subjects ourselves. Stein explains that this stance is humorously captured in the joke that has two behaviorists greeting each other, saying, "You're fine; how am I?" (42-3). The point is important because Eugenides structures the narrative from the outset to provide readers with a view of the end result with Cal/liope transformed from the impostor/female child, Callie, to the true male adult, Cal. Readers are thus made external guarantors who can bestow the statement, "You're fine," along with the general stamp of approval on Cal, not as a lesbian woman, but as a heterosexual man.

AN APOLITICAL HERMAPHRODITE

Following an awkwardly didactic gesture toward the aims and movement of the Intersex Society of North America (ISNA), Cal/liope declares a general apolitical stance to explain away a lack of involvement with intersex rights lobbying: "we hermaphrodites are people like everyone else. And I happen not to be a political person. Though I'm a member of the Intersex Society of North America, I have never taken part in its demonstrations" (Eugenides, 2002: 106). The declaration conveniently releases the novel from any perceived duty to move the intersex movement forward, which is fair enough. After all, fiction is not bound by any particular imperative to serve any given agenda; however, the claim to a lack of politics is specious, for whether the narrative voice does or does not declare a politics, the actual cultural product that is the novel exists within a political context. The notion, moreover, that desires reveal something 'true' about one's sex is a decidedly political stance that warrants further consideration here.

Eugenides began writing *Middlesex* around the time that ISNA was formed, and published it not long after Colapinto's book about David Reimer: *As Nature Made Him* (2000). Colapinto's title is telling, and rests on biologistic, essentializing notions about the cause and location of sexual desire that have been brought to bear on the treatment of intersexed persons with particular stridency.[6] In short, much of this work determines that the Y chromosome is most especially inclined to be true to itself and that it cannot be lied to about its sex. Because of his Y chromosome and nothing else, Colapinto suggests, David Reimer was a heterosexual male. Diamond stakes a similar claim as the rationale for his assertion that we ought not assign XY babies with intersex conditions as female.[7]

Oudshoorn explains in *Beyond the Natural Body* that culture shapes scientific practice, and, therefore, the science that seems most convincing and compelling is that which incorporates firmly-held cultural ideals. In the case of sex and gender, the ideals of character are incorporated into scientific practice and investigation, with "prescientific notions" leading scientists to "discoveries" that confirm generally held beliefs about the oppositional nature of males and females (1994: 15-24). The twinned prescientific commitment–to the 'natural' opposition of male to female, and to the basic 'normalcy' of heterosexuality–means that all the etic assumptions about kinship, incest and monstrosity that Eugenides sets into play cannot actually result in the birth of a 'hermaphrodite', nor even of a lesbian. Indeed, the narrative insists that Cal/liope need only to become comfortable as Cal in order to settle down in heterosexual domesticity with his female (opposite) companion, Julie. Cal may have a more tumultuous and Homeric journey to manhood than most men, but in the end, Cal's desire for women guarantees his maleness as the undeniable evidence of the power of hormones, genes and chromosomes to shape the truth of who he, or any one of us, is.

In an earlier version of this paper, I explored the value(s) in *Middlesex* and concluded that neither Eugenides nor anyone else was morally obligated to write a particular story of intersexuality (2004). I did not agree with Hillman's (2003) identity-based proposition that the stories of intersexed people were far more moving and powerful than any fictionalized account, and still find it a questionable claim. What is more deeply problematic about *Middlesex*, however, is the erasure of the viability and vitality of lesbian desire, lesbian sex(uality) and lesbian existence, and in the process, female desire disappears too. Callie cannot love the Obscure Object freely, but Cal can love Julie openly, albeit in a decidedly oblique and courtly manner. The Obscure Object disappears as soon as Cal/

liope's unique anatomy is discovered, and Julie never fully appears as a sexual being; her sexual activity is reduced to an act of turning off the lights, undressing in the dark and hurrying under the covers because she is "a shy, modest Oriental lady" (Eugenides, 2002: 513).

Eugenides' characterization of Cal/liope accepts the matched values of prescientific and biologistic explanations for sexual dimorphism as *the* appropriate mode of being. The characterization evacuates Cal/liope, the Obscure Object and Julie of any transgressive power, denies the legitimate place of lesbian desire, and rewrites it as male heterosexuality. Cal/liope's unique embodiment appears as a paradox that carries the burden of contradictory stances regarding monstrosity and incest, while at the same time offering a plea for the tolerance of difference in the basic humanity of the monster. The problem is that the 'hermaphrodite' can only become recognizable as human once all the queer desire, embodiment and sex vanish.

There is no reason to demand only one kind of story about intersexuality, or about lesbian sexuality, but there is reason to be deeply concerned that a great imaginative epic cannot manage to find a legitimate place for lesbian desire/practice. Eugenides' story erases lesbian desire, and restores a threatened masculinity to its 'proper' place by neutralizing Cal/liope's intersexuality under the sign of maleness. Through his inscription of a particular hinging of desire on anatomy and underlying biology, Eugenides heterosexualizes Cal/liope's desires, demonstrating the continuing salience of Elizabeth Grosz's observation that:

> . . . the body is literally written on, inscribed, by desire and signification, at the anatomical, physiological and neurological levels. The body is in no sense naturally or innately psychical, sexual, or sexed. It is indeterminate and indeterminable outside its social constitution as a body of a particular type. (1994: 60)

Callie's humanity is thrown into crisis by intersexed anatomy and a lesbian subjectivity, but is secured by the emergence of the heterosexual protagonist, Cal.[8] Cal/liope is, therefore, not an especially powerful character and the novel not especially new, revolutionary or useful, but just a retrenchant heterosexist politic. Eugenides' particular casting of Callie's youthful desires and sexual practices, hinged to a female subject position that aligns lesbianism with female sexuality, reiterates the traditional view of female sexuality as inherently 'deviant'. Callie's disappearance from the narrative at the point of her second birth and transformation into the adult, male, Cal, constitutes not simply the erasure of lesbian sexuality, but also of female sexuality more generally. The narrative insists that Cal always existed inside Callie, as the internal truth and seat of male heterosexuality. Furthermore, the courtly, asexual manifestation of Cal's romance with Julie renders a female voice mute in the closing chapters of the book. When Cal stands at the doorway of his childhood home in the book's last paragraph, he does so as the guardian patriarch of the family, not as the vulnerable girl-child of the first birth. The second birth then, is the restoration of order and certainty against an uncertain past. Cal may escape surgical intervention, but Cal/liope's desire is impoverished as a result. In this, as I have argued elsewhere regarding homophobic medical practice, Eugenides takes no less a heteronormative view than surgeons do.[9]

NOTES

1. I use the term 'hermaphrodite' where other authors or cultural producers have used it to indicate what I would refer to as intersexed persons. I find their acceptance of the term, so clearly echoing mythical creatures and invoking the mysterious, to be a telling indication of the goals artists, authors and screenwriters have in creating such popular deployments of bodies that are neither singularly male nor female as something extra-human or sub-human.

2. For a longer discussion of this neutralization process, see Chapter 2 of my dissertation, *The Doctor Will Fix Everything* (2000 b) on the spectacular neutralization of hermaphroditic monsters in a variety of popular examples.

3. When I refer to the bi-potentiate narrator of the story I use the form 'Cal/liope', but following the conventions of *Middlesex*, I use 'Callie' to refer to the girl-child and 'Cal' to refer to the adult man.

4. Eugenides has Calliope meet Dr. Peter Luce, an avatar for John Money, at the Gender Identity Disorder clinic where Luce treats Calliope in much the same way that Colapinto reports Money to have treated David Reimer. As Reimer was able to prevail upon his family to rescue him from final feminizing surgeries, Eugenides has Calliope run away from home to escape similar procedures and, finally, to take up a male subject position.

5. See, as just one example, Anais Nin's collected erotic stories in *Delta of Venus*. London: Penguin, 2004. Creed (1996) also provides a multitude of filmic and literary examples.

6. For further detailed examples of the manner in which chromosomes, hormones and genes are thought to have especially profound effects on the truth of sex and of desire, see: Diamond (1997); Ralf W. Dittmann et al (1992); Dotinga (2004).

7. While I agree with Diamond, and with Colapinto that non-interference should be the order of the day, my reasons have to do with the need to protect the developing autonomy of the infant, not to ensure that we mere mortals ignore the truth of biology.

8. I assert Callie as a lesbian subject because there is no intersex gender, only intersex anatomy. It is, therefore as a socially coherent girl-on-the-verge of adolescent womanhood that Callie falls in love with the Obscure Object and is constituted as a lesbian, if only to have that subject position nearly immediately erased.

9. Four of my previously published articles and chapters all make this point. (Holmes, 1994, 1998, 2000 a, 2002).

REFERENCES

Colapinto, John. *As Nature Made Him: The Boy Who Was Raised as a Girl.* New York: Harper Collins, 2000.

Creed, Barbara. "Lesbian Bodies: Tribades, Tomboys and Tarts." In Elizabeth Grosz and Elspeth Probyn, eds. *Sexy Bodies: On the Strange Carnalities of Feminism.* New York: Routledge, 1996: 86-103.

Diamond, Milton. "Sexual Identity and Sexual Orientation in Children with Traumatized or Ambiguous Genitalia," *Journal of Sex Research,* 34(2), 1997: 199-222.

Dittmann, Ralf W., Marianne E. Kappes and Michael H. Kappes. "Sexual Behavior in Adolescent and Adult Females with Congenital Adrenal Hyperplasia," *Psychoneuroendocrinology,* 17(2/3), 1992: 153-70.

Dotinga, Randy. "You've (Still) Got Male: Boys with Genital Defects, Raised as Girls, Revert Back to Original Gender," *HealthDay News,* 21 January 2004.

Epstein, Julia. "Either/or Neither/Both: Sexual Ambiguity and the Ideology of Gender," *Genders,* 7, 1990: 99-142.

Grosz, Elizabeth. *Volatile Bodies: Toward A Corporeal Feminism.* Indianapolis: Indiana University Press, 1994.

Haraway, Donna. "The Promise of Monsters: A Regenerative Politics for Inappropriate/D Others." In C. Nelson L. Grossberg and P. Treichler, eds. *Cultural Studies,* New York: Routledge, 1992: 295-337.

Hilman, Thea. ". . . and the Limitations of Myth," *ISNA News,* 12 March 2003. URL isna.org.

Holmes, Morgan. "Re-Membering a Queer Body," *Undercurrents,* 7, 1994: 11-14.

_____. "In(to)Visibility: Intersexuality in the Field of Queer." In Dawn Atkins, ed. *Looking Queer.* San Francisco: The Haworth Press, Inc., 1998: 110-115.

_____. "Queer Cut Bodies." In Joseph A. Boone et al., eds. *Queer Frontiers: Millennial Geographies, Genders and Generations.* Madison: University of Wisconsin Press, 2000 a: 84-110.

_____. *The Doctor Will Fix Everything: Intersexuality in Contemporary Culture.* Unpub. PhD Thesis, Concordia University, 2000 b.

_____. "Rethinking the Meaning and Management of Intersexuality," Sexualities, 5(2), 2002: 159-79.

_____. "In the Middle of Whose Sex? Reading Jeffrey Eugenides' 'Hermaphrodite': Resolutions and Ruptures." Unpub. paper, University of British Columbia, 2004.

Miller, Laura. "Sex, Fate and Zuess and Hera's Kinkiest Argument," *Salon.com,* 2002. URL salon.com/books/int/2002/10/08/eugenides/index.html

Anais Nin. *Delta of Venus.* London: Penguin, 2004.

Oudshoorn, Nelly Everdina. *Beyond the Natural Body: Archaeology of Sex Hormones.* New York and London: Routledge, 1994.

Stein, Edward. *The Mismeasure of Desire: The Science, Theory and Ethics of Sexual Orientation.* New York: Oxford University Press, 1999.

doi:10.1300/J155v11n03_05

Carved in Flesh?
Inscribing Body, Identity and Desire

Kay Inckle

SUMMARY. This paper opens up questions regarding the ways in which reading the body leads to limited and limiting notions of identity. These questions are based around a critique of an ethnography of lesbian body-modification which I problematize in a number of ways. I suggest that reading the body of another is both methodologically and politically problematic. I reflect on how this approach confuses the complexity of body and identity and the ways in which this relates to establishing problematic boundaries of lesbian identity. I suggest an embodied identity

Kay Inckle is currently a Research Associate in the Department of Sociology, Trinity College Dublin, from where in 2006 she was awarded her PhD. Her work primarily focuses on: embodiment, body politics and practices; gender and sexuality; qualitative and creative research methodologies, and intersects feminism, queer theory and disability studies within sociology. She also writes fiction and has a passion for eighteenth and nineteenth century novels. She is a Reiki Master and holistic practitioner, and lives in inner-city Dublin with her feline companion, Princess. Her publications include *Writing on the Body? Thinking Through Gendered Embodiment and Marked Flesh.* Newcastle Upon Tyne: Cambridge Scholars Publishing, 2007; "Tragic Heroines, Stinking Lilies and Fallen Women: Love and Desire in Kate O'Brien's *As Music and Splendour,*" *Irish Feminist Review* 2, 2006: 56-73; "Who's Hurting Who? The Ethics of Engaging the Marked Body." *Auto/biography* 13(3), 2005: 227-248.

Address correspondence to: Kay Inckle, Department of Sociology, The University of Dublin, Trinity College, College Green, Dublin 2, Ireland (E-mail: kinckle@tcd.ie).

[Haworth co-indexing entry note]: "Carved in Flesh? Inscribing Body, Identity and Desire." Inckle, Kay. Co-published simultaneously in *Journal of Lesbian Studies* (Harrington Park Press, an imprint of The Haworth Press, Inc.) Vol. 11, No. 3/4, 2007, pp. 233-242; and: *Twenty-First Century Lesbian Studies* (ed: Noreen Giffney, and Katherine O'Donnell) Harrington Park Press, an imprint of The Haworth Press, Inc., 2007, pp. 233-242. Single or multiple copies of this article are available for a fee from The Haworth Document Delivery Service [1-800-HAWORTH, 9:00 a.m. - 5:00 p.m. (EST). E-mail address: docdelivery@haworthpress.com].

cannot be fully understood or incorporated within any notion of the body as fixed or finite, and that neglecting the variability and mutability of the body is antithetical to political strategies of inclusion and equality. doi:10.1300/J155v11n03_06 *[Article copies available for a fee from The Haworth Document Delivery Service: 1-800-HAWORTH. E-mail address: <docdelivery@haworthpress.com> Website: <http://www.HaworthPress.com> © 2007 by The Haworth Press, Inc. All rights reserved.]*

KEYWORDS. Body-modification, embodiment, gender, sexuality

INTRODUCTION

In this paper I critically address some of the ways in which research around issues of sexuality and body-transformations constitute identity as readable from and fixed upon the body. Thus, rendering the body a spectacle of the 'other' and closing down possibilities for identifications that transgress binary limitations of gendered embodiment. This is not to imply that I de-link body and subjectivity, in fact the reverse would be true; I consider subjectivity, self and identity to be fundamentally embodied. I suggest that embodiment is subjective, fluid and temporal and certainly not restricted to the normative readings and possibilities upon which such research commonly rests. Normative readings of the body locate the body within binary, essentialist and/or fixed terms, and define gender, sex and sexuality as corporeal, interconnected and biological categories. These are conflated in, for example, sexology, which defines homosexuality as a pathology, and specifically a pathology of the body (Munt, 1998).

Thus, normative readings of corporeal interventions/practices (such as body-modification) are barely distinguishable from the early 'scientific' and 'criminological' discourses which constituted an individual and their character–specifically deviance (i.e., mad or bad)–as readable from their bodily presentation (Sullivan, 2001). Nor do they seem comfortably distant from the compulsory imperatives of gendered embodiment which read both gender (as masculine or feminine) and sexuality (as hetero or homo) from bodily deportment and display, and which recreate only a binary of possibilities.

In this vein I critically review a contemporary ethnography of body-modification and lesbian sexuality which relies on the author reading from and inscribing meaning upon the 'other's' body. I contrast this with the lived experience of the lesbian body and some of the issues that such corporeal identifications raise. Through this interrogation of the contrasts between research conducted both from 'within' and 'outside' lesbian experience/studies, I hope to raise a number of questions. These questions problematize notions of identity that are fixed and readable from the body, as well as the possibility of knowing the other from their body and the ethical and political problems inherent to this. Further, the simplified position of the researcher/knower is contrasted with the complexity of embodied subjectivity. Ultimately, I contest the validity of interpreting and fixing identity from bodily appearance in the context of hierarchical, dualistic and disembodied knowledge.

READING/RESEARCHING THE BODY AND INSCRIBING IDENTITY

James Myers' (2001)[1] research, "Nonmainstream Body-Modification," is published in the collection, *Extreme Methods*, which informs readers that "it is not just the topics studied . . . that are extreme, but also the research strategies that were used to study them" (Miller and Tewksbury, 2001: 205). For Myers the 'extreme' was to place himself, "a straight, male anthropologist" (185), in the world of "nonmainstream" body-modifiers who practice "genital-piercing, branding, burning and cutting" and where "the single largest group was composed of SM homosexuals and bi-sexuals" (183-5). The fact that Myers explains to his readers that "homosexuals" are "lesbians and gays" (185) indicates, I think, both the intended audience as well as the context for his research. Further, while he uses a range of methodologies he admits that "the largest amount of data from the workshops were gathered from observation" (185). Thus, Myers, an outsider writing to an audience of non-participants, draws conclusions on the basis of reading, interpreting and re-presenting the bodies and experiences of 'others.' Here, I focus on his descriptions of female piercing and cutting[2] and problematize the fetishized spectacle he creates, particularly in relation to lesbian sexuality.

There is of course nothing new in the reading of a woman's identity or sexuality from her body: be that in terms of normative femininity and her corresponding availability to men; or though factors of appearance which indicate deviance or improper femininity (Bartky, 1992; Bordo, 1993; Davis, 1995; Frost, 2000; Young, 1990). Improper femininity includes, for example, fatness (Bordo, 1993) and dis-ablement[3] (Morris, 1990; Shakespeare, 1996; Thomas, 1999), as well as lesbianism. The lesbian body has been described as specific and identifiable in historical and contemporary theorizations, and within perspectives which are both hostile to as well as positively invested in a notion of lesbian identity. According to Barbara Creed:

> There are at least three stereotypes of the lesbian body which are so threatening they cannot be easily applied to the body of the non-lesbian. These stereotypes are: the lesbian body as active and masculinized; the animalistic lesbian body; the narcissistic lesbian body . . . These stereotypes refer explicitly to the lesbian body, and arise from the nature of the threat lesbianism offers to patriarchal heterosexual culture. (1999: 112)

In addition to these categories there is also a specific 'lesbian-feminist' appearance which requires an unmodified body (Jeffreys, 2000: 2003)[4] as well as the more contemporary lesbian body located within a queer context.[5]

In terms of Creed's categorization of the lesbian body, Myers' work appears to be cognisant with the stereotypes of the animalistic and the narcissistic lesbian body. The animalistic body is present in Myers' work as a subtext where "abject desire makes the body abject" (Creed, 1999: 119) and 'extreme' bodily practices are connected with non-normative sexuality.

The narcissistic lesbian body has connotations with the early medicalization of sexuality, through the links between female sexuality and deviance and connections between "masturbation in women, narcissism and lesbianism" (Creed, 1999: 121). The narcissistic lesbian by definition "is on display . . . [and] appeal[s] to the voyeuristic desires of the male spectator" (Creed, 1999: 121). The narcissistic lesbian body is captured within Myers' voyeuristic gaze as he inscribes meaning upon the workshops he attends, where participants "were for the most part, barely subdued exhibitionists" (186).

The "female workshop" is primarily recreated as a sexualized spectacle for the voyeur, regardless of the strong "spiritual-psychological" (193) orientation of the practitioner, Raelynn. Myers describes how Raelynn, a lesbian like most of her clients, is known as "Queen of the Blood Sports" (193), and that she opens her workshop with the greeting "Hello, fellow blood sluts!" (194).

Myers revels in describing the spectacle of the first nipple piercing he witnesses, particularly because the volunteer is an "achondroplastic dwarf" [sic] "dressed in leather trousers and field boots" who "was extremely popular with many in the group" (193). Cleary delighted by the multiple forms of abjection and narcissism he witnesses, Myers goes on to describe other examples:

> The third volunteer, in her mid-twenties, had spent the first half of the workshop curled up in the laps of three different women. She removed her cotton skirt and hopped on to the chair. Pantyless and clean shaven, two labia rings and a clitoris hood ring were easily visible. Raelyn announced that this client would be getting a third labia ring today and with a theatrical leer, added, "And she has asked me to do it real-l-l slow and with a twist." (194)

From his observations Myers concludes that body modification has specific functions which include: "sexual enhancement" in which pain and pleasure are integral (197-8), "affiliation" and "shock value" (199-291). Thus, we are left with a depiction of a clearly identifiable group whose non-normative sexuality–animalistic and narcissistic lesbianism–is fixed upon and readable from the body.

LIVING THE BODY, EMBODYING THE SELF

I will now consider some of the ways in which the lived experience of the lesbian body contrasts with Myers' research: firstly, in terms of the ways in which a bodily lesbian identity is constructed, and secondly, in an extract from my research,[6] which articulates something of the complexity and fluidity of bodily identity which extends beyond simple notions of body-modification.

In her research on the role of the body/appearance within lesbian and bisexual women's sense of their identity, Karen G. Esterberg describes how the women felt that there was something distinct and identifiable about lesbian identity, and this very much related to visual and bodily clues.[7] They:

> . . . insisted on a distinctive lesbian presence in the community and felt that they could often spot another lesbian in a non-lesbian setting . . . They did want to assert a uniquely lesbian presence and sense of style, however shifting and changing that lesbian style might be. (1996: 264)

Styles of dress, hair and deportment; "a certain swagger when I walk" (265), as well as a masculine or "athletic body"[8] (271) were cited as identificatory clues but, significantly, never body-modifications.

Thus, it seems that the lesbian body *is* often self-identified through innate and performed characteristics, and within a limited range of what a lesbian, or indeed a woman may be. Since body-modification was entirely absent, there appears to be significant diversity between 'non-participant' and experience based readings of the lesbian body and the characteristics which identify it as "visibly queer" (Pitts, 2000).[9]

The following extract from my research highlights further complexities of bodily readings and the fluidity of bodily presentations. It also demonstrates the ways in which self-identification and presentation may at the same time contrast with, and adhere to, normative readings of the lesbian body and the possibilities of subverting and re-iterating those norms. In this way, the body in its presentation and reading are rendered far from static: even permanent modifications (i.e. tattooing, piecing, branding, scarification, sculpting) have a degree of fluidity and temporality within their embodiment.

In this extract Rene[10] describes the ways in which she works her body in the light of the normative prescriptions of appropriate gender and sexuality. While she feels that the body modifications, the tattoos, she has chosen may in some ways incline towards an identification of her sexuality, she feels more strongly that it is the body modifications with which she *does not* engage–those which create normative femininity–which are much more problematic and liable to expose her to recognition and hostility. These conventional body modifications include the range of practices and "rituals of the body" (Synott, 1993: 69) that are specifically gendered, and indeed create gendered bodies, such as shaving, plucking, waxing, make-up, body shaping undergarments, hair styling or cut, clothing, adornment, as well as the deportment and display of the body.

Rene's account articulates a level of complexity and ambiguity in the ways in which the readings of her body both conflate with the expected responses and the ways in which she tries to pre-empt and deflect them. This indicates, in contrast to the findings Myers (2001), that body-modification alone does not necessarily signify sexuality, but may do so in conjunction with other clues, specifically, the absence of conventional body-modifications:

> Where I live now is a very, in general, making *huge*, sweeping generalizations but, it's a fairly conservative area. It would be fairly homophobic and I would feel like some of things that [previously] didn't bother me as a lesbian; I would be much more conscious about now I'm not living in the city . . . I think that when I

started this job two years ago I was *much more* cautious. I went on the first day of work, and this woman I was teaching with said, "Did I see you at church? In church on Sunday? At the [name] church?" And I was like, "Oh my god" you know, I was really like, "How am I going to be able to come out to her when I can't even tell her that I'm not a Christian?!" You know? [laughs]

So I was quickly aware that I was working in an environment that wouldn't necessarily accept me as a lesbian, and where I could be fired. And I actually really needed the work, and didn't really feel like I wanted to enrage the whole political thing about being *out* . . . So I think initially I would have had this really strong sense of maybe not giving off certain signals that would be lesbian, like, [laughs] having facial hair! [laughs] And short hair! And tattoos, and no make-up! And I know this is all just so really shite! This is all based on the whole stereotypes–which are all true! But I was, I think, I was–not wanting to give off *clues,* like under-arm hair, or tattoos, or things that would identify me as a lesbian.

Thus, even permanent modifications of the body, incorporate a degree of fluidity into the way they are experienced, perceived and displayed and "visibility strategies" (Pitts, 2000: 459) can be used to resist the fixing of an identity and its consequences, depending on the specific context. The body itself has not changed and yet both the interpretation and experience of it have.

Further, the non-modifying of Rene's body also highlights the ways in which only certain bodily practices are considered 'modifications' and worthy of ethnographic investigation. Thus, normalising and making invisible the more or less compulsory body-modifications with which women engage in order to create normative femininity. These norms are so powerful that they are understood in terms of part of the 'natural' difference of 'gender' and have a much more significant impact in Rene's experiences than the body modifications she has chosen to engage with:

In this day and age to get a tattoo, as a woman it would be common enough, but to not shave is still a *really big taboo,* or not pluck your chin, or not pluck you eye-brows. It's actually more *abnormal* than any of the body-modification things because many people have tattoos now. So it's *not* body-modification, because it's letting your body be the way it naturally would be, but you *can't.* It's not acceptable.

CONCLUDING REMARKS

Overall, I have attempted to raise some questions regarding the normative assumptions upon which readings of the body rely. These assumptions not only position the author/researcher/reader in a place of knowing power over the 'other,' the subject of their discourse, but also fail to reflect the multiplicities and fluidity of embodied identifications.

Such notions resonate with medicalized, dualistic knowledge which perpetuates the limiting norms of embodiment which are, for example, at the center of the struggle for bodily and self-identification of trans-people (Butler, 2004; Whittle, 1999) and people with dis-abilities (Thomas, 1999). Further, if the history of feminism has highlighted anything, it is that any attempt to define a political, corporeal identity results only in exclusion, hierarchy, silencing and oppression. Finally, despite having attempted to engage with, and represent some kind of 'queer culture', Myers' ethnography is based on the very notions of fixing identity and corporeality which queer (academic) discourse resists. Judith Butler (1990; 1993; 2004), for example, has carefully argued that identity politics, and particularly when fixed upon a corporal category, is antithetical to the politics of queer.[11]

Overall then, I suggest that any reading of, or inscribing of meaning upon, the body is problematic in that it both appropriates and limits the embodied self-hood of some individuals, and obliterates others entirely. Further, reading the body in this way does little to progress theorizations and communities of people beyond the repressive and binary norms of gendered embodiment and sexuality.

NOTES

1. This paper was first published in 1992 in *The Journal of Contemporary Ethnography* and reprinted in Miller and Tewksbury, 2001.

2. Myers studied both male and female workshops, however, to me the descriptions of the female context are much more problematic.

3. I hyphenate in this way, following Wendell, 1996, in order to disrupt essentialist and normative readings.

4. The lesbian-feminist identity, based upon a "fairly rigid dress code," was particularly salient during the 1970s and '80s, when "the proper lesbian had short hair, wore sandshoes, jeans or a boiler suit, flannel shirt and rejected all forms of make-up" (Creed, 1999: 123)

5. This lesbian identity, subsequent to the queer analysis of gender, has involved a re-working and a re-claiming of masculinity and femininity in ways which may appear to be normatively readable from the body even if their intention or experience is sub-

versive (Kidd, 1999). Halberstam's *Female Masculinity* (1998), for example, fails to define what exactly masculinity *is*, but connects it with a specific female identity through bodily deportment, costume and taste. The masculinized lesbian body has a long history, as well as connections with the medicalization of gender and sexuality. It is recognizable within lesbian culture, particularly through the visibility as well as the ambivalence of the significations of the "butch body" (Munt, 1998).

6. My research focuses on issues around research ethics and the construction of knowledge in relation to gendered embodiment and body marking, i.e. 'body modification' and 'self-injury'.

7. There were also women who felt that "the attempt to define what was distinct about lesbians vis-à-vis heterosexual women did not make sense–that there is more variation within than there is between straight women or gay women" (Esterberg, 1996: 262-3)

8. Presumably this meaning of 'athletic' does not apply to women who may be, or resemble, Para Olympic or Special Olympic athletes.

9. In *Visibly Queer* (Pitts, 2000; which was re-printed in 2003 as part of the volume: *In The Flesh: The Cultural Politics of Body Modification*), Pitts argues that "gay, lesbian and transgenered body modifiers–permanently and visibly" (444) inscribe the body in opposition to heteronormative identity. As such "body modification in western cultures can be playful, aesthetic, artistic and narcissistic" (445). While Pitts is aware that body-modification is dependent upon "visibility strategies" which "may suggest a limit to the radicalism" (459), she does not consider the implications of strategies of visibility and choice in terms of the researcher's position, which are central to my critique in this paper.

10. Each participant is referred to by the pseudonym that she chose for herself.

11. In a recent publication she states the position as follows: "Queer opposes those who would regulate identities to establish epistemological claims of priority for those who make claims to certain kinds of identities–[and] insist[s] that sexuality is not easily summarised or unified through categorization" (Butler, 2004: 7). In a critique of an identity politics based around the "privileging of the visible," Lisa Walker offers a similar critique. She argues that, "within the constructs of a given identity that invests certain signifiers with political value, figures that do not present those signifiers are often neglected" (Walker, 1993: 868).

REFERENCES

Bartky, Sandra Lee. "Body Politics." In Alison M. Jagger and Iris Marrion Young, eds. *A Companion to Feminist Philosophy.* Oxford: Blackwell, 1992.

Bordo, Susan. *Unbearable Weight: Feminism, Western Culture and The Body.* London: California University Press, 1993.

Butler, Judith. *Gender Trouble.* New York and London: Routledge, 1990.

_____. *Bodies That Matter.* New York and London: Routledge, 1993

_____. *Undoing Gender.* New York &London: Routledge, 2004.

Caplan, Jane, ed. *Written on the Body: The Tattoo in European and American History.* London: Reaktion Books, 2000.

Creed, Barbara. "Lesbian Bodies: Tribades, Tomboys and Tarts." In Margrit Shildrick and Janet Price, eds. *Feminist Theory and The Body: A Reader.* Edinburgh: Edinburgh University Press, 1999.

Davis, Kathy. *Reshaping the Female Body: The Dilemma of Cosmetic Surgery.* New York and London: Routledge, 1995.

Esterberg, Karen.G. "A Certain Swagger When I Walk." In Steven Seidman, ed. *Queer Theory/Sociology.* Oxford: Blackwell, 1996.

Frost, Liz. *Young Women and The Body: A Feminist Sociology.* Basingstoke: Palgrave Macmillan, 2000.

Halberstam, Judith. *Female Masculinity.* Durham: Duke University Press, 1998.

Jeffreys, Sheila. "'Body Art' and Social Status: Cutting Tattooing and Piercing from a Feminist Perspective," *Feminism & Psychology,* 10(4), 2000.

_____. *Unpacking Queer Politics: A Lesbian Feminist Perspective.* Cambridge: Polity Press, 2003.

Kidd, Mandy. "The Bearded Lesbian." In Jane Arthurs and Jean Grimshaw, eds. *Women's Bodies: Discipline and Transgression.* Cassell: London and New York, 1999.

Miller, Mitchell J. and Richard Tewksbury, eds. *Extreme Methods: Innovative Approaches to Social Science Research.* Boston: Allyn and Bacon, 2001.

More, Kate and Stephen Whittle, eds. *Reclaiming Genders: Transsexual Grammas at the Fin de Siecle.* London and New York: Cassell, 1999.

Morris, Jenny. *Pride Against Prejudice.* London: Women's Press, 1991.

Munt, Sally R., ed. *Heroic Desire: Lesbian Identity and Cultural Space.* London and Washington: Cassell, 1998.

Myers, James. "Nonmainstream Body Modification: Genital Piercing, Branding, Burning and Cutting," *Journal of Contemporary Ethnography,* 21(3), 1992.

_____. "Nonmainstream Body Modification: Genital Piercing, Branding, Burning and Cutting." In Mitchell J. Miller and Richard Tewksbury, eds. *Extreme Methods: Innovative Approaches to Social Science Research.* Boston: Allyn and Bacon, 2001.

Pitts, Victoria. "Visibly Queer," *Sociological Quarterly,* 41(3), 2000.

_____. *In The Flesh: The Cultural Politics of Body Modification.* Basingstoke: Palgrave Macmillan, 2003.

Shakespeare, Tom et al., eds. *The Sexual Politics of Disability.* London and New York: Cassell, 1996.

Sullivan, Nikki. *Tattooed Bodies.* Connecticut and London: Praeger press, 2001.

Synott, Anthony. *The Body Social: Self, Society and Symbolism.* London: Routledge, 1993.

Walker, Lisa. "How to Recognise a Lesbian: The Cultural Politics of Looking Like What You Are," *Signs: Journal of Women in Culture and Society,* 18(4), 1993.

Wendell, Susan. "Towards a Feminist Theory of Disability." In Lennard J. Davis, ed. *The Disability Studies Reader.* London and New York. Routledge, 1996.

Whittle, Stephen. "The Becoming Man." In Kate More and Stephen Whittle, eds. *Reclaiming Genders: Transsexual Grammas at the Fin de Siecle.* London and Cassell, 1999.

Young, Iris Marion. "Breasted Experience: The Look and the Feeling." In Iris Marion Young, ed. *Throwing Like A Girl and Other Essays in Feminist Philosophy and Social Theory.* Bloomington: Indiana University Press, 1990.

doi:10.1300/J155v11n03_06

SECTION V

LOCATIONS:
TRANSLATING 'LESBIAN'

The future of Lesbian Studies has to listen to my mother's voice, to the silent scream and making of revolution of my sisters in Latin America, to the poverty and strength of my sisters in Africa. If there is a future for Lesbian Studies this has to be full of the songs, words and stories of my sisters in the Middle East, Asia and Australasia. It is not enough to inhabit a virtual village of Lesbians somewhere in the colourful spatial wires of the Internet; the future of Lesbian Studies must also come down to earth and create a place like *Zami's* Carriacou where 'women work together as friends and lovers,' a place where I can smell and taste the sweat, the juices, the tears and the laughter of the 'other.' If there is going to be any future in Lesbian Studies, our European and North American sisters, framed by centuries of colonial and capitalist past and present, must wake up and organize conferences where the proportion of Black and white women is similar both in presence and in active participation. Maybe the future of Lesbian Studies needs my Mixed-Race Latina and Black Lesbian sisters to begin to accept invitations to attend these conferences and thus influence what issues and actions are to be put in the agenda and programmes. The future of Lesbian Studies must have a vision, artists, allies, intellectuals and activists.

–Consuelo Rivera-Fuentes

Lesbian Studies and Activism in India

Ruth Vanita

SUMMARY. This essay surveys public debates and writings about lesbianism and the history of activism around lesbian issues in twentieth-century India. Weddings between women and joint suicides by female couples over the last twenty-five years are among the under-researched, but increasingly reported, phenomena that suggest future directions that activism and the study of lesbianism in India may take. doi:10.1300/J155v11n03_07 *[Article copies available for a fee from The Haworth Document Delivery Service: 1-800-HAWORTH. E-mail address: <docdelivery@haworthpress.com> Website: <http://www.HaworthPress.com> © 2007 by The Haworth Press, Inc. All rights reserved.]*

KEYWORDS. India, lesbians, same-sex weddings and suicides, LGBT movements, women's movements, feminist academics, *Fire*, Suniti Namjoshi

Ruth Vanita is Professor of Liberal Studies and Women's Studies at the University of Montana. She is the author of *Sappho and the Virgin Mary: Same-Sex Love and the English Literary Imagination* (1996); co-author of *Same-Sex Love in India: Readings from Literature and History* (2000); and editor of *Queering India: Same-Sex Love and Eroticism in Indian Culture and Society* (2001) among others. Her book, *Love's Rite: Same-Sex Marriage in India and the West* appeared in 2005 and was published by Palgrave Macmillan, New York, and Penguin, India.

Address correspondence to: Professor Ruth Vanita, Liberal Studies Faculty, The University of Montana, 32 Campus Drive, Missoula, MT 59812, USA (E-mail: ruth.vanita@umontana.edu, rv167184e@mail1.umt.edu).

[Haworth co-indexing entry note]: "Lesbian Studies and Activism in India." Vanita, Ruth. Co-published simultaneously in *Journal of Lesbian Studies* (Harrington Park Press, an imprint of The Haworth Press, Inc.) Vol. 11, No. 3/4, 2007, pp. 245-253; and: *Twenty-First Century Lesbian Studies* (ed: Noreen Giffney, and Katherine O'Donnell) Harrington Park Press, an imprint of The Haworth Press, Inc., 2007, pp. 245-253. Single or multiple copies of this article are available for a fee from The Haworth Document Delivery Service [1-800-HAWORTH, 9:00 a.m. - 5:00 p.m. (EST). E-mail address: docdelivery@haworthpress.com].

The experience and representation of lesbianism in India have much in common with those in the West, but also have some distinctly different dimensions. One example of a different manifestation is the phenomenon of same-sex couple suicide (as distinct from individual suicide). The first reported case occurred in June 1980, when Mallika, aged 20, and Lalithambika, aged 17, attempted suicide in Kerala. In her suicide note, Lalithambika wrote, "I cannot part with Mallika. Bury us together" (Lenous, 1980: 7). Since then, similar reports have appeared from all over India, as well as reports of women marrying each other, some with family support and by traditional rites, others despite family hostility. Almost all the couples are female, lower middle-class, young, not primarily English-speaking, with some education, but no contact with any lesbian or women's organizations. Some of the couples attempt unsuccessfully to obtain state endorsement of their weddings.

Such phenomena suggest some directions that the study of lesbianism in India might take. My book, *Love's Rite: Same-Sex Marriage in India and the West* (2005), examines Indic literary, legal, religious, political and social traditions of love, marriage, kinship, gender and death, to which these couples appeal when they make public statements of their commitment through a wedding or a suicide.

DEBATES ON LESBIANISM

In *Same-Sex Love in India* (2000, 2002), a collection of translations from texts in fifteen Indian languages, written over more than 2,000 years, Saleem Kidwai and I demonstrated that female-female and male-male sexual relations have been reflected on and debated in many different generic contexts in India. Along with other scholars, we argue that social and textual constructions of homosexuality as a sexual preference and an identity category have been going on in India for about two millennia, and Michel Foucault and his followers are wrong to claim that these constructions began in nineteenth-century Euro-America (xx-xxi, 24-28, 46-54, 107-125, 220-228).[1] Following colonial rule and nationalist attempts to reform Indic practices and texts in conformity with Victorian ideals, such debates about same-sex relations and terms used for them were stifled or went underground. Pre-Modern Indian texts, authored by men, contain some amazing representations of female-female amorous relations, for example, several fourteenth-century devotional texts tell the story of two women whose love-making, blessed by the Gods, results in one of them giving birth to a heroic child, and some early nineteenth-century texts describe unions between women, some of which were ritually formalized (Vanita, 2005; 2004).

The first public twentieth-century debate on female homosexuality occurred when Ismat Chughtai's Urdu short story, *Lihaf* (Quilt), was prosecuted for obscenity in 1942; this debate was largely confined to the press and literary forums. The second major debate took place in 1998 when right-wing extremists attacked theaters showing Deepa Mehta's film, *Fire*. This debate raged in the national and international media and on Indian streets for several months. While many women's organizations and human rights organizations defended the filmmaker's right to freedom of expression, some of them were unwilling to accept lesbianism as a women's rights issue (Patel, 2001; Bachmann, 2001). The controversy put the issue of lesbianism squarely on the political agenda, as national dailies printed photos of women holding placards that read, "Lesbianism is part of our heritage." The controversy also elicited important analyses by Indian lesbian academics (Ghosh, 1999; Kapur, 1999). Lesbian activism, which emerged in India in the early 1980s and grew in the 1990s, became widely visible through the *Fire* debate.

Before this emergence, the writings of Suniti Namjoshi (born 1941) constituted a lone voice in the wilderness. Her oeuvre constitutes a decades-long reflection on multiple dimensions of being lesbian and Indian. Writing in a variety of genres, such as poetry, fiction, fable, nonfiction, children's literature and biomythography, she explores the intersections of lesbianism with nationality, race, gender, class, caste, motherhood, age and species (Vanita, 2000; Vijayasree, 2000).

Despite its innovative brilliance and its devoted fan following across the world, including in India, Namjoshi's work has not received the attention it deserves, even though Indian writing in English is now internationally renowned. This is largely because of the lesbian content of her work. As a result of this neglect, Indian women's and lesbian movements have yet to take cognizance of her irreplaceable contribution to the idea of what it means to be an Indian lesbian (Dasgupta, 2001).

Although there have been in the past and still are words to refer to lesbians in Indian languages, these words are now not widely circulated.[2] The word, 'lesbian,' has been used in Hindi texts throughout the Twentieth Century and continues to be widely used in the Indian press and media, both in English and other languages. Some academics and activists object to the use of identity terms, such as 'gay' with reference to non-Western societies, claiming that such usage is neo-colonial or imperialist. Interestingly, 'lesbian' has not been objected to as much, probably because lesbians are less visible, lesbian organizations do not receive as much foreign and governmental funding as organizations serving gay and bisexual men do, in the wake of the AIDS crisis, and it is therefore less urgent for activists to reconstruct lesbians in ways that would be more attractive to funders.

In my view, such objections are in part constructed by homophobia, because the same theorists seem to be untroubled about using terms and concepts like 'family,' 'nation,' 'child,' 'law,' 'woman' or 'man,' when discussing non-Western societies, where the other-language approximates of these English words have substantially different meanings. If one were serious about using only indigenous terms, one would have to write about non-English texts entirely in their own languages, which is not feasible. English has now been spoken and written in India for two centuries, and there are more English speakers in India than in Canada and Australia put together.

A few Indian academics also use the term 'queer' in addition to 'lesbian.' Most Indian lesbian groups and activists identify as lesbian, even if they also use the term 'queer.' Most English-speaking Indians still understand and use the word 'queer' to mean 'strange' or 'odd,' hence 'lesbian' and 'gay' are more easily understood in the mainstream media.

LESBIANISM IN THE WOMEN'S MOVEMENT AND THE ACADEMY

Even though lesbians and bisexual women, some married to men, some single and some coupled with other women, were at the forefront of feminist organizing during the new wave of women's movements in India from the late 1970s onward, lesbians and lesbianism remained invisible in these movements. Women's movements, both in their academic and activist dimensions, focused almost entirely on redressing the problems of married women by trying to reform marriage-related and violence-related laws.[3] One reason was that most feminist activists emerged from the Left, whether from official Communist parties or Trotskyite and Maoist groups, and many remained linked to those groups, which, by and large, considered homosexuality a Western capitalist perversion (Srikanth, 1996). Most feminist scholars in the academy are Marxists or heavily influenced by orthodox Marxism, and were, until very recently, indifferent if not hostile to Lesbian and Gay Studies.

A shift took place in the 1990s, marked by the founding of India's first national-level gay-lesbian magazine, *Bombay Dost*, in 1990. Humsafar Trust, the organization that publishes it, is typical of the many mixed-gender groups that have arisen in Indian cities and towns. In the early 1990s, gay men and lesbians held Red Rose meetings at a coffee house in Delhi, placing a rose on the table to identify themselves. From 1993, a group in Delhi, called Friends of Siddhartha Gautam, organized annual festivals, largely of gay and lesbian films, in memory of a gay activist who died young; since then, similar festivals have proliferated in other cities, providing forums for discussion. Contacts with lesbian and gay groups in other countries, particularly the US and the UK, and especially with diasporic Indians involved in those groups, also provided support, for example, San Francisco-based *Trikone*, a magazine for LGBT South Asians, was available in India from its inception in 1986, and regularly carries contributions as well as Personals from Indians (Ratti, 1993). The Internet has boosted these communications, with several chat rooms, web-sites and listservs linking South Asian lesbians across the world.

The AIDS crisis increased both the visibility of homosexuality and the funding available to anti-AIDS groups, including some gay groups. Lesbians have been active in various initiatives for the revocation of Section 377, Indian Penal Code, the law passed by the British in 1860 that criminalizes intercourse "against the order of nature"; left-wing and liberal women's and human rights organizations have also joined these campaigns (Vanita, 2005). Although the law has not so far been used to convict lesbians, it has been used to threaten and harass them (Bhaskaran, 2001).

Sakhi in Delhi, now defunct, and Stree Sangam in Mumbai, still active by the name of Labia, were among the earliest lesbian groups. Giti Thadani, founder of Sakhi, published *Sakhiyani* (1996), perhaps the first book to examine lesbianism in India. Many other lesbian groups have come into being and disappeared or morphed into other groups; those currently in existence include Olava in Pune, Aanchal in Mumbai, Sahayatrika in Kerala, Sappho in Calcutta and Sangini in Delhi (Fernandez, 1999). These groups produce newsletters, reports and chapbooks. Newspapers have reported other lesbian associations that have been repressed, for example, seven schoolgirls in Kerala were expelled from school in 1992 for forming a Martina club (Author Unknown, 1992).

In December 1990, the fourth National Conference of Women's Movements for the first time held a session on 'Single Women.' A Stree Sangam activist narrates how the first workshop on lesbianism at the fifth National Conference evoked antagonism from other women delegates (Amita, 1999). Since then, LGBT conferences, seminars and festivals have proliferated.

Autonomous women's groups and non-governmental organizations working on women's issues now discuss sexuality issues at Women's Studies conferences and also conduct sexuality workshops for activists as well as rural and urban poor women. But national-level women's organizations attached to political parties and engaged in electoral politics remain wary if not hostile. For example, in the late 1990s, the All India Democratic Women's Organization (AIDWA), which is allied with the Communist Party of India (Marxist), asked lesbian groups in Delhi not to carry banners with the word 'lesbian' on them or use the word in slogans, arguing that their working-class cadre would be upset by the word.[4] This of course wrongly assumes that all working-class women are heterosexual.

Homosexuality is slowly becoming visible in the academy, largely under pressure from graduate students and young faculty. After a debate about syllabi that dragged on for years, during which *The Color Purple* was rejected for undergraduate study because of its depiction of lesbian sex, the English Department at Delhi University recently revised the BA and MA syllabi to include texts that suggest lesbianism without describing it, such as Virginia Woolf's novels, and a translation of Chughtai's *Lihaf*. This stirred up a controversy among faculty and in the press, with some instructors claiming they would be embarrassed to teach them in mixed classes. Since thousands of students now read these texts, and critical commentary published abroad is not easily available in India, Indian publishers are commissioning anthologies of criticism, including reprints of essays published in the West as well as new essays. Several of these essays come under the rubric of Lesbian Studies (Lal et al., 2004; Panja, 2002; Merli, 2004; Chandra, 2006).

A few researchers, mainly in the Humanities, Social Sciences and Media Studies, work regularly on lesbian topics. In Delhi, Shohini Ghosh has made important contributions through her research on film and television, her filmmaking and her teaching (Ghosh, 1999; 2001). In Mumbai, Bina Fernandez (2003), who compiled the report *Humjinsi*, recently co-authored a monograph on violence against lesbians. Anthologies on gender, masculinities and sexualities have begun to include essays on homosexuality and bisexuality, although most of them are about males rather than females, and women's studies anthologies now include essays on lesbianism (Bose, 2002).

CONCLUSION

Ideas about same-sex love are increasingly being discovered at the heart of culture, even as right-wing extremists claim that all civilizations have repudiated such love. Focusing on these ideas as central rather than marginal to culture involves revising the lesbian feminist position that men's writings about lesbianism are always sensationalist, pornographic or inaccurate. Both men's and women's writings have illuminated ideas of lesbianism; this is certainly the case in the Indian literary corpus, both pre-modern and modern, where some of the most evocative and radical visions of lesbianism have emerged in texts written by men.[5] The future of lesbian studies perhaps lies in focusing not so much on lesbian identities as on the circulation and transformation of ideas of lesbianism in different cultures and cross-culturally.[6]

NOTES

1. See also my Introduction to Vanita, 2002: 1-11. For taxonomies in first to fourth century Hindu and Jain texts, see Sweet and Zwilling (1993; 1996).

2. The most recent use of such a word was documented by historian Veena Talwar Oldenburg (1997), who found courtesans in Lucknow in the 1970s using the Urdu word *chapti* and its derivatives, textually attested in the Nineteenth Century, to describe themselves and their own sexual relationships with women.

3. These observations are based on my experience of working in the women's movement from 1978 to 1991, as founding co-editor of *Manushi: A Journal about Women and Society,* India's first national-level women's-rights magazine, and of studying and teaching at Delhi University from 1976 to 1997. I briefly analyzed this syndrome in Vanita (1999; reprinted 2004).

4. The AIDWA did, however, take a stand recently against the anti-sodomy law.

5. A good modern example is Rajasthani writer Vijay Dan Detha's story, *Dohri Joon* (Double Life). For a translation, see Vanita and Kidwai, 2000: 318-24, and for an analysis, Vanita (forthcoming b).

6. I have suggested and demonstrated this in much of my earlier work, beginning with Vanita (1996) where I argued that the idea of lesbianism shapes the imaginations of both male and female British writers, at least from the Romantic period onwards; Castle (2003) makes a parallel argument.

REFERENCES

Amita. "A Decade of Lesbian Hulla-Gulla." In Ashwini Sukhthankar, ed. *Facing the Mirror: Lesbian Writing from India.* New Delhi: Penguin, 1999: 349-54.

Author Unknown. "Lesbian Group in Kerala School," *Indian Express,* Madurai, 29 January 1992.

Monica Bachmann, "After the Fire." In Ruth Vanita, ed. *Queering India: Same-Sex Love and Eroticism in Indian Culture and Society*. New York and London: Routledge, 2001: 234-44.

Bhaskaran, Suparna. "The Politics of Penetration." In Ruth Vanita, ed. *Queering India: Same-Sex Love and Eroticism in Indian Culture and Society*. New York and London: Routledge, 2001: 15-29.

Bose, Brinda, ed. *Translating Desire: Literary/Cultural Crossings in India*. New Delhi: Katha Publications, 2002.

Castle, Terry, ed. *The Literature of Lesbianism: A Historical Anthology from Ariosto to Stonewall*. New York: Columbia University Press, 2003.

Chandra, Subhash, ed. *Lesbianism and Literature*. New Delhi: Allied Publishers, 2006.

Dasgupta, Anannya. "'Do I Remove My Skin'? Interrogating Identity in Suniti Namjoshi's Fables." In Ruth Vanita, ed. *Queering India: Same-Sex Love and Eroticism in Indian Culture and Society*. New York and London: Routledge, 2001: 100-11.

Fernandez, Bina, ed. *Humjinsi: A Resource Book on Lesbian, Gay and Bisexual Rights in India*. Mumbai: India Centre for Human Rights and Law, 1999; reprinted 2002.

_____ and Gomathy N.B. *The Nature of Violence Faced by Lesbian Women in India*. Mumbai: Tata Institute of Social Sciences, 2003.

Ghosh, Shohini. "From the Frying Pan to the Fire," *Communalism Combat*, January 1999: 19.

_____. "The Troubled Existence of Sex and Sexuality: Feminists Engage with Censorship." In Christiane Brosius and Melissa Butcher, eds. *Image Journeys: Audio-Visual Media and Cultural Change in India*. New Delhi: Sage, 1999.

_____. "Queer Pleasures for Queer People: Film, Television and Queer Sexuality in India." In Ruth Vanita, ed. *Queering India: Same-Sex Love and Eroticism in Indian Culture and Society*. New York and London: Routledge, 2001: 181-92.

Giti Thadani, *Sakhiyani: Lesbian Desire in Ancient and Modern India*. New York: Cassell, 1996.

Kapur, Ratna. "Cultural Politics of Fire," *Economic and Political Weekly*, 22 May 1999: 1297.

Lal, Malashri, Shormishtha Panja and Sumanyu Satpathy, eds., *Signifying the Self: Women and Literature*. New Delhi: Macmillan, 2004.

Lenous, Victor. "Girlfriends in Suicide Pact," *Blitz*, 11 July 1980: 7.

Merli, Carol, ed. *Illuminations: New Readings of Virginia Woolf*. New Delhi: Macmillan, 2004.

Panja, Shormishtha, ed. *Critical Theory, Textual Application*. New Delhi: Worldview Press, 2002.

Patel, Geeta. "Of Fire: Sexuality and Its Incitements," In Ruth Vanita, ed. *Queering India: Same-Sex Love and Eroticism in Indian Culture and Society*. New York and London: Routledge, 2001: 222-33.

Ratti, Rakesh, ed., *A Lotus of Another Color: An Unfolding of the South Asian Gay and Lesbian Experience*. Boston: Alyson Publications, 1993.

Srikanth, H. "Natural Is Not Always Rational," *Economic and Political Weekly*, 13 April 1996: 975-6.

Sweet, Michael J. and Leonard Zwilling. "The First Medicalization: The Taxonomy and Etiology of Queers in Classical Indian Medicine," *Journal of the History of Sexuality*, 3(4), 1993: 590-607.

_____. "'Like a City Ablaze': The Third Sex and the Creation of Sexuality in Jain Religious Literature," *Journal of the History of Sexuality*, 6(3), 1996: 359-84.

Talwar Oldenburg, Veena. "Lifestyle as Resistance: The Case of the Courtesans of Lucknow." In Violette Graff, ed. *Lucknow: Memories of a City*. Oxford: Oxford University Press, 1997: 136-54.

Vanita, Ruth. *Sappho and the Virgin Mary: Same-Sex Love and the English Literary Imagination*. New York: Columbia University Press, 1996.

_____. *Love's Rite: Same-Sex Marriage in India and the West*. New York: Palgrave Macmillan and New Delhi: Penguin, 2005.

_____. "Born of Two Vaginas: Love and Reproduction between Co-Wives in Some Medieval Indian Texts," *GLQ: A Journal of Lesbian and Gay Studies*, 11(4), September 2005.

_____. "Married Among their Companions: The Representation of Female Homoerotic Relations in Nineteenth-Century Urdu *Rekhti* Poetry," *Journal of Women's History*, 16(1), 2004: 12-53.

_____. "I'm an Excellent Animal: Cows, Motherhood and Love between Women." In Sonya Jones, ed. *A Sea of Stories: The Shaping Power of Narrative in the Lives of Gay Men and Lesbians*. New York: Haworth Press, 2000: 143-63.

_____. "India Considers Abolishing Sodomy Laws," in *GLBT History*. Pasadena, California: Ebsco Publishing and Salem Press, 2005.

_____, ed. *Queering India: Same-Sex Love and Eroticism in Indian Culture and Society*. New York and London: Routledge, 2001.

_____. "Thinking Beyond Gender in India." In Nivedita Menon, ed. *Gender and Politics in India*. New Delhi: Oxford University Press, 1999: 529-39; reprinted in Maitrayee Chaudhuri, ed. *Feminism in India*. New Delhi: Kali for Women and Women Unlimited, 2004: 69-79.

_____. "The Many Colors of Love: Homoerotic Tropes in Modern Indian Fiction." In Ruth Vanita, *Gandhi's Tiger and Sita's Smile: Essays on Gender, Sexuality and Culture*. New Delhi: Yoda Press, 2005.

_____ and Saleem Kidwai. *Same-Sex Love in India: Readings from Literature and History*. New York: Palgrave Macmillan, 2000; New Delhi: Penguin, 2002.

Vijayasree, C. *Suniti Namjoshi: The Artful Transgressor*. Jaipur and New Delhi: Rawat Publications, 2000.

doi:10.1300/J155v11n03_07

Lesbian Studies in Thailand

Jillana Enteen

SUMMARY. This piece provides an overview of the state of Lesbian Studies and women who love women in Thailand. It reflects on the cross-cultural limitations of the term 'lesbian' and Thai ambivalence towards Western sex and gender categorizations. doi:10.1300/J155v11n03_08 *[Article copies available for a fee from The Haworth Document Delivery Service: 1-800-HAWORTH. E-mail address: <docdelivery@haworthpress.com> Website: <http://www.HaworthPress.com> © 2007 by The Haworth Press, Inc. All rights reserved.]*

KEYWORDS. Lesbian, Thailand, lesbian studies, homosexuality, queer theory

---

Jillana Enteen is Associate Director of Gender Studies at Northwestern University. Enteen studies Thai culture and literature in English as well as non-Thai depictions of Thailand and has published essays concerning the use of English language terms for sexualities and genders in the urban cultures of Thailand. She has taught at several colleges in Thailand, conducted research as a Fulbright Junior Researcher and worked with women-centered non-government organizations. Her manuscript entitled, *Virtual English: Internet Use, English Language, Global Subjects*, is forthcoming from Routledge Press.

Address correspondence to: Professor Jillana Enteen, Gender Studies Program, Northwestern University, Kresge Hall, 2-360 1880 Campus Drive, Evanston, IL 60208-2211, USA (E-mail: jillana@jillana.net, j-enteen@northwestern.edu).

[Haworth co-indexing entry note]: "Lesbian Studies in Thailand." Enteen, Jillana. Co-published simultaneously in *Journal of Lesbian Studies* (Harrington Park Press, an imprint of The Haworth Press, Inc.) Vol. 11, No. 3/4, 2007, pp. 255-263; and: *Twenty-First Century Lesbian Studies* (ed: Noreen Giffney, and Katherine O'Donnell) Harrington Park Press, an imprint of The Haworth Press, Inc., 2007, pp. 255-263. Single or multiple copies of this article are available for a fee from The Haworth Document Delivery Service [1-800-HAWORTH, 9:00 a.m. - 5:00 p.m. (EST). E-mail address: docdelivery@haworthpress.com].

Lesbian Studies in Thailand might be said to encapsulate the continual dialogue and adaptation Thais conduct with Western ideas.[1] Lesbian Studies could be considered a flourishing discipline in Thailand: Women's Studies departments with relevant course offerings are growing, the field of Thai Studies is bursting with scholarly studies about women's non-normative sexualities, and there is a great deal of discussion about gender slippage and women who love women in the popular press. Similarly, the categories, identities and modes of expression that pertain to women who love women in Thailand are increasing exponentially, directly reflecting an interest in, yet resistance to, Western notions of gender identity, Feminism and sexuality. As part of this engagement, the words 'lesbian' and 'Lesbian Studies,' at least as understood by most readers of this journal, are by and large rejected by women who love women in Thailand. While Thai academics have expanded their levels of engagement with Western Feminist, Gender and Lesbian Theory, they are not endorsing Lesbian Studies as representative of Thai circumstances.

Among academics in the West, there is assumed an intrinsic relation between Lesbian Studies (from a theoretical perspective) and studying lesbians (as in anthropological or ethnographic inquiry). Accordingly, Gender Studies, Queer Theory and Lesbian Studies courses are expected, at some level, to be of interest to those with corresponding identities. Lesbian Studies in Thailand, however, highlights the disjuncture of these two formulations. The majority of the courses on gender and sexuality rely on Western theories of Feminism and the meanings of Western constructions, and professors direct the study of lesbians towards those 'other' lesbians–not the women of Thailand who love women. When specifically considered in these courses, Thai women who love women are still presented as exceptions to the syllabus without much integration into the course material. This schism in representation reflects the awareness among Thai academics that any consideration of Thai women who love women must take into account the capitalist nature of knowledge acquisition.

Market forces must certainly be acknowledged when considering scholarly-research production concerning Sexuality Studies in Thailand. Why are Western scholars producing the majority of accounts of non-normative Thai sexualities? What makes this field seem uninviting to Thai academics and highly interesting to Western theorists and researchers? These conundrums recall the origin of Anthropology as a discipline dedicated to studying 'others' and remembers the questioning provided by feminist anthropologists of the motivations that drive anthropological inquiry (i.e., studying lesbians). Similarly, Lesbian Studies, like Queer Theory and Gay Studies, by and large reveals a compulsion to imagine universal theories of gender and sexuality. Although this has been subjected to scrutiny by more recent theorists who complicate notions of sexual and gender identities, universalized assumptions of identity formation are often applied uncritically to non-Western cultures, losing the subtlety reflected in local conditions and articulations.[2] Specific to the understanding of women who love women in contemporary Thailand, anthropologist Megan Sinnott writes:

> Appreciation of local cultural understandings of sexual practices will be lost or subtly skewed if researchers use the categorizations of 'homosexuality' and 'heterosexuality' without conscious awareness of the implicit cultural meanings embedded within this binary construct. (2004: 17)

This can be seen in the blurring of the categories for sex when compared to current Western-based usages; the Thai word 'phet' connotes both gender and sexuality. In addition, categories such as 'man' and 'woman' are not simple oppositions. Thai usage casts these terms in a field of gendered/sexed positions. In other words, one can be a woman, or one can be a 'tom,' but a 'tom' is rarely described as woman or man.[3]

Thai Lesbian Studies may seem elusive because of the emergence of Lesbian Studies from Feminist Theory. Thai women who love women in academia and in highly public positions voice disidentification with the term lesbian.[4] Disidentification, as articulated by Michel Pêcheux, is "the third mode of dealing with dominant ideology, one that neither opts to assimilate within such a structure nor strictly opposes it; rather, disidentification is a strategy that works on and against dominant ideology" (as paraphrased by Muñoz, 1999: 11). Thais frequently adopt and adapt Western words for their own purposes. The two main Thai terms referring to the most widely recognized homosocial positions for Thai women are, in fact, derivations of English words.[5] 'Tom', derived from tomboy, refers to a woman who performs masculinity through her dress, speech and object choice (feminine-looking women). 'Dees,' derived from the English LaDY, can be discerned through their interest in and association with 'toms.' Overall, they conform to Thai cultural standards of appropriate womanhood (except for their homosocial liaisons and what that entails).[6] Neither role is directly translatable to their English language designations, nor do the women they embody refuse identification with these terms. Instead, the Thai manifestation of these terms reflects a dialogue with their origins–and, more importantly, an insertion into Thai vocabulary of a foreign (English is often perceived as more sexually tinged and exotic) sound to name something that is specifically Thai but previously had no common referent.[7] Not to be limited to this instance of adaptation, as Took Took Thongthiraj (1996), Megan Sinnott (2004), and I (2001) have discussed elsewhere, Thai women who love women are further augmenting their vocabulary to include other designations that do not reflect the masculine/feminine dichotomy inherent in 'tom' and 'dee' and endorse labels such as 'anjaree,' or women who follow non-conformist ways.[8] Yet they express an outright distaste for the word 'lesbian', which seems to many women (following the perception of English terms as persistently carrying more sexual connotations) to be explicitly sexual. 'Tom,' 'dee' and 'anjaree' do not refer specifically to sexual activity, while to most Thais, the word 'lesbian' carries with it the suggestion of sexual activities between women. The shaping of Lesbian Studies, therefore, reflects a highly critical engagement with Western fields of knowledge.

IN THE ACADEMY

Courses devoted to Gender and Sexuality Studies are taught at four major universities in Thailand. The first two, Thammasat and Mahidol Universities, house prestigious Women's Studies departments; the universities are also considered to be among the top in Thailand and South East Asia, particularly in the Social Sciences. Both are located in Bangkok and have, among their faculty, Gender Studies professors who are highly visible and well respected.[9] These professors are frequently interviewed on topics concerning women who love women in Thailand for the press, and they have served as visiting lecturers at other institutions. Two additional universities, Koen Khaen and Chiang Mai, also offer courses on gender and sexuality, although to staff the course in the northern city of Chiang Mai, the professor from Bangkok's Thammasat University made weekly appearances. The growth of these Gender Studies-based courses departs from earlier approaches to the study of homosocial behavior in Thailand that, since the 1950s and 1960s, promoted the study and deployment of quantitative research methods following the Kinsey pattern.[10] According to Peter Jackson, Thailand-based Studies about sexuality produced during these decades "emerged from contexts in which same-sex eroticism has been prefigured as a social problem to be solved or prevented, or as being associated with potential risks to health" (1999 b: 29).

Several graduate students I interviewed for this piece recounted guest-lecturing invitations from Gender and Sexuality Courses in order to discuss Thai conditions of women who love women. Thai circumstances provided the opening lecture for several Gender and Sexuality graduate courses, whereas the rest of the class meetings explored issues such as "Gender-as-Performative Theory," "Critiques of Biological Foundationalism in Feminist Theory of Gender", and "Politics of Sexual Subjectivities and Identities".[11] Megan Sinnott recalls that classes:

> . . . focus on women and development, women's rights (in politics etc.), domestic violence, but not on women's sexuality per se. Women's studies classes that I saw were introductions to feminist theory, but I'm not sure how much they covered sexuality. Some of the instructors at the women's studies program . . . taught cool, theoretically sophisticated theory on sexuality and gender, but I don't think they had a class on it.[12]

Sulaiporn Chonwilai writes,

> I don't think that there's a lesbian studies course in Thailand at all . . . As far as I know this issue is only mentioned as some small part of some sexuality courses in feminist studies . . . sometimes I was invited to teach in the feminist class but it was only a part of the course on sexuality or social movement and what could [I] say in one or two hours?[13]

Similarly, Assistant Professor Chutima Pragatwuisarn, who teaches at Bangkok's two leading universities, has discussed women who love women in her classes only once, for one hour.[14] Thai women who love women are thus clearly a marginal topic in these Western-theory focussed arenas.

There is a single textbook available dedicated to women who love women in Thailand. It is a collection of essays and journalistic pieces written about Thai women in English. The book, *A Collection of Articles on Lesbians and Lesbianism in Thailand* (2004), was produced by Chiang Mai University's Women Studies Center. The textbook is not widely circulated in Thailand because, notes Women Studies Center Research Officer Sabrina Gyorvary, a large percentage of students, both at the graduate and undergraduate level, cannot simply pick up an En-

glish-language book on gender and sexuality and read it without difficulty.[15] Why, then, is the only publication dedicated to this topic printed
in English and not Thai? As stated, many more academic publications
about women who love women in Thailand appear in English than in
Thai. The schism within academic production in English about Thailand and Thai reticence to broaden the course boundaries of gender and
sexuality to include Thai-specific conditions illustrates the discomfort
felt towards the uncritical acceptance of the place of studies of Thai
women who love women in Western-formulated environments.

INCREASING ATTENTION

Peter Jackson writes, "The study of discourses and cultural patterns
of transgenderism and homoeroticism in Thailand . . . is one of the least
developed areas within the field of Thai studies. It is no doubt because
so few scholars of Thailand have reflected upon these topics . . ." (1999
a: 240). Sulaiporn Chonwilai concurs, explaining:

> Though there are some students who might [be] interested in the
> subject of sexuality and lgbt issues and some want to do the re-
> search about lesbians, it's not easy for them to propose their pro-
> posal . . . The main reason is there are few professors who consider
> this issue, and they don't want to explore or pay attention to this
> subject.[16]

The general attitude that Sexuality Studies is not appropriate for serious
consideration among Thai Studies professors, however, seems to be
shifting as more graduate work abroad done by Thais considers these
topics. As young professors bring recent work by Westerners into their
classrooms upon returning to Thailand, they also cast their eye on their
own culture. Consequently, Thai sexuality has moved from Psychology
to Thai Cultural Studies and Women's Studies classrooms. Like the increase in classes for Thai graduate students, there has been, in the past
decade, a fostering of Thai students who wish to study issues concerning Thai women who love women. Faculty at Mahidol and Thammasat
Universities, in particular, have encouraged the topic among interested
graduate students. At least three dissertations or Masters theses have
been completed in Thai on the topic of 'toms' in Thailand.[17]

This is not to say that homosocial issues are only recently receiving
press. The Thai media has historically had a penchant for Western, and

increasingly, Thai non-normative sexuality. The advice column, "Strange But True," has been a popular place for men to write in about their homosocial desire, and occasionally women submit questions as well.[18] More recently, a popular weekly column has appeared by Domon Sukhapreecha in "A Day" weekly, Thailand's new progressive news magazine, about gender and sexuality. In addition, there are currently a few weekly talk shows on television with segments on sex and gender issues. One show features a famous TV host and a socio-psychiatrist. The show interviews specialists or celebrities about sexuality and cultural perspectives related to sexual risk and protection.

Finally, a large network of social resources exists for women who love women in Thailand. In Bangkok, there are several bars that have nights devoted to 'tom' and 'dee' clientele. At least three social/activist organizations represent women who love women: the now disbanded Anjaree, FIRE, representing Northern Thailand, and the Women's Health Advocacy Foundation. It is a flourishing time for Thai women to create their own language, community and identity. While presuming a teleological growth of Lesbian Studies in Thailand should be cautioned, a dialogic disidentification is certainly ascertainable and there will no doubt be more academic and popular accounts in the future.

NOTES

1. I would like to thank everyone involved in email correspondence with me for this piece, taking time in busy schedules to answer my persistent questions. Thanks particularly to Sabrina Gyorvary for new contacts, Adisak Chantarin for last-minute research, and to Jennifer Brody and Alexander Weheliye for editorial suggestions.

2. See Altman (2001) for an account of the tendency of Gay Studies to articulate a single understanding of the implications of a gay identity. While Altman is highly critical of a universal or 'global gay,' his work often posits the same.

3. One can also be a 'man'–another adapted term that applies specifically to incarcerated women who have sex with inmates labeled 'women' but who do not assume the prescribed masculine attire and attributes of 'toms.'

4. Here I refer to Muñoz's (1999) use of the term 'disidentification' with a twist.

5. I use the term 'homosocial' to diffuse the focus on sex acts inherent in the term homosexuality and its post-Stonewall deployment. Also, homosociality, along the lines of Sedgwick's (1985) use of the term, designates a continuum incorporating homosexuality, same-sex (male in Sedgwick's instance) bonding. Homosocial and homoerotic are both terms I've employed in this context to incorporate the desire articulated by both 'toms' and 'dees.' They gesture towards a range of same-sex-centered activities that may or may not be read as explicitly sexual.

6. Standards of appropriate Thai womanhood vary greatly between classes in Thailand. The majority of configurations for adult womanhood include mothering, running the household and controlling the money, looking and acting 'ladylike.' What

they do not entail is strong female bonds between non-relatives, gender nonconformity and articulations of same-sex desire.

7. 'Toms' and 'dees' might also be said to correspond loosely with butch and femme models of Western culture. The similarities are more superficially visual than culturally manifested, however: for example, while femmes have a visible presence in Western cultures, 'dees' are generally assumed to be not discernible, nor understandable without 'toms.' Furthermore, 'toms' are not women, nor are they imitating men. For a nuanced discussion of the intricacies of 'tom' and 'dee' identities, consult Sinnott (2004).

8. This is a term coined by Anjana Suvarnananda, the founder and president of the Thai organization of the same name. For a longer discussion of Anjaree and the meanings of "women who follow nonconformist ways," see Enteen (2001).

9. Chalidaporn Songsamphan (Women's Studies Center, School of Political Science, Thammasat University) and Kritaya Archavanitkul (Institute for Population and Social Research, Mahidol University).

10. In his survey of Thai Sexuality Studies in the 1950s and '60s, Peter Jackson (1999 b) reports that one set of studies resulting in a series of Masters theses and dissertations produced under the director Udomsin Srisaengnam, a Clinical Psychology Professor at Mahidol University, suggests a consistently higher rate of female homoerotic behavior reported by middle-class students to researchers than male. While Jackson rightly questions the methodology and discrepancies in analysis among the student researchers, he does note that this figure shows the incomparable differences between Thai and Western accounts. No such reports of greater homoerotic activity (i.e., physical expressions of same-sex desire) between females and males exist outside of Thailand.

11. The syllabus I refer to comes from A. Chalidaporn Songsamphan's excellent course taught at Thammasat University in Bangkok and Chiang Mai University in Northern Thailand.

12. Personal correspondence.

13. Personal correspondence.

14. "I do teach women courses at Chula[longkorn] and Thammasat but do not include the lesbian topic in my courses. In one of my courses at T[hammasat] U[niversity], Women and Life Narratives, we spent just one hour discussing one of the theses on Lesbian Relations in Thailand," Pragatwutisarn, personal correspondence.

15. Personal correspondence.

16. Personal correspondence.

17. For example, Manitta Chanchaim and Salikhub Chonticha wrote Masters theses and Sulaiporn Chonwilai, a dissertation, at Thammasat University.

18. *Strange*, a Thai language biweekly magazine, and the column by "Uncle Go" have been written about by Jackson (1995).

REFERENCES

Altman, Dennis. *Global Sex*. Chicago: University of Chicago Press, 2001.

Chanchai, Manitta. "Khwamphenekalakthang Sangkhom Khorng 'Dee' Lae Konlayut Nai Karn-Chai Chiwit Pracam Wan Knorng Phu-Ying Thii Mii Khu-Rak Pen Tom (Social Identity of 'Dees' in Daily Life Strategies of Women Who Have Tom Partners)." Unpub. Masters Thesis, Thammasat University, Thailand, 2003.

Chetamee, Matthana. "Concepts of the Family and Lesbian Lifestyles in Thailand." Unpub. Paper, "Gender and Sexuality in Thailand" Conference, Canberra, Australia, 1995.

Chonwilai, Sulaiporn. "Re: Studying Lesbian Issues in Thailand." E-Mail to the Author, 17 December 2004.

Enteen, Jillana. "Tom, Dii, and Anjaree: 'Women Who Follow Nonconformist Ways'," In John C. Hawley, ed. *Postcolonial, Queer: Theoretical Intersections.* Albany: State University of New York Press, 2001: 99-122.

Gyorvary, Sabrina. "Re: The State of Lesbian Studies in Thailand." E-mail to the Author, 8 December 2004.

Halberstam, Judith. *Female Masculinity.* Durham: Duke University Press, 1998.

Hawley, John C. *Postcolonial, Queer: Theoretical Intersections.* Albany: State University of New York Press, 2001.

Jackson, Peter A. *Dear Uncle Go; Male Homosexuality in Thailand.* San Francisco: Bua Luang Books, 1995.

_____. "Tolerant but Unaccepting: The Myth of a Thai 'Gay Paradise'." In Peter A. Jackson and Nerida M. Cook, eds. Genders *and Sexualities in Modern Thailand.* Chiang Mai, Thailand: Silkworm Books, 1999 a: 226-42.

_____. "Studies of Rates of Same-Sex Sexual Experience in Thailand: A Critical Survey." In Peter A. Jackson and Gerard Sullivan, eds. *Lady Boys, Tom Boys, Rent Boys: Male and Female Homosexualities in Contemporary Thailand.* New York: Harrington Park Press, 1999 b: 28-59.

_____ and Gerard Sullivan. "A Panoply of Roles: Sexual and Gender Diversity in Contemporary Thailand." In Peter A. Jackson and Gerard Sullivan, eds. *Lady Boys, Tom Boys, Rent Boys: Male and Female Homosexualities in Contemporary Thailand.* New York: Harrington Park Press, 1999: 1-27.

Muñoz, José Esteban. *Disidentifications: Queers of Color and the Performance of Politics.* Minneapolis: University of Minnesota Press, 1999.

Päecheux, Michel. *Language, Semantics, and Ideology.* New York: St Martin's Press, 1982.

Pragatwutisarn, Chutima. "Re: Women's Studies." E-mail to the Author, 9 February 2005.

Salikhub, Chonticha. "Krabuan-Karn Phathanaa Lae Thamrong Ekalak Khorng Yingrakruamphet (The Development and Maintenance Process of Lesbian Identities)." Unpub. Masters Thesis, Thammasat University, Thailand, 1989.

Sedgwick, Eve Kosofsky. *Between Men: English Literature and Male Homosocial Desire.* New York: Columbia University Press, 1985.

Sinnott, Megan. "Re: Lesbian Studies in Thailand." E-mail to the Author, 20 December 2004.

_____. *Toms and Dees: Transgender Identity and Female Same-Sex Relationships in Thailand.* Honolulu: University of Hawaii Press, 2004.

Somswasdi, Virada, and Alycia Nichols, eds. *A Collection of Articles on Lesbians and Lesbianism in Thailand.* Chiang Mai, Thailand: Women's Studies Center, Chiang Mai University, 2004.

Thongthiraj, Took Took. "Toward a Struggle against Invisibility: Love between Women in Thailand." In Russell Leong, ed. *Asian American Sexualities: Dimensions of the Gay and Lesbian Experience.* New York: Routledge, 1996: 163-74.

doi:10.1300/J155v11n03_08

Loud and Lusty Lesbian Queers: Lesbian Theory, Research and Debate in the German-Speaking Context

Antke Engel

SUMMARY. Taking into account recent developments in Germany, it seems to me that Lesbian Studies has its future within Queer Studies–and I am convinced, it can take a self-assured role; not contenting itself with a niche, but claiming its power to design queer from lesbian perspectives. doi:10.1300/J155v11n03_09 *[Article copies available for a fee from The Haworth Document Delivery Service: 1-800-HAWORTH. E-mail address: <docdelivery@ haworthpress.com> Website: <http://www.HaworthPress.com> © 2007 by The Haworth Press, Inc. All rights reserved.]*

KEYWORDS. Lesbian, queer studies, feminist self-critique, intersecting power relations, hegemonic neo-liberal society, academy, independent scholarship

Antke Engel got her PhD in Philosophy at Potsdam University in Germany. Her dissertation, *Wider die Eindeutigkeit. Sexualität und Geschlecht im Fokus queerer Politik der Repräsentation* (2002), proposes a strategy of equivocation as a means of queer cultural politics. She held a visiting Professorship at Hamburg University between 2003 and 2005. In 2006 she founded the Institute for Queer Theory (www.queer-institut.de). She is also an activist, who believes in mutual inspirations between theory and politics.

Address correspondence to: Dr. Antke Engel, Wohlwillstr 29, D 20359, Hamburg, Germany (E-mail: engel@queer-institut.de).

[Haworth co-indexing entry note]: "Loud and Lusty Lesbian Queers: Lesbian Theory, Research and Debate in the German-Speaking Context." Engel, Antke. Co-published simultaneously in *Journal of Lesbian Studies* (Harrington Park Press, an imprint of The Haworth Press, Inc.) Vol. 11, No. 3/4, 2007, pp. 265-273; and: *Twenty-First Century Lesbian Studies* (ed: Noreen Giffney, and Katherine O'Donnell) Harrington Park Press, an imprint of The Haworth Press, Inc., 2007, pp. 265-273. Single or multiple copies of this article are available for a fee from The Haworth Document Delivery Service [1-800-HAWORTH, 9:00 a.m. - 5:00 p.m. (EST). E-mail address: docdelivery@haworthpress.com].

Taking into account recent developments in Germany, it seems to me that Lesbian Studies has its future within Queer Studies–and I am convinced, it can take a self-assured role; not contenting itself with a niche, but claiming its power to design queer from lesbian perspectives. Let us defer the question of what lesbian perspectives are for a moment. I would like to take the above statement as the promise of an exciting new step that builds on a powerful tradition, rather than a frustrated, grief-stricken conclusion. Yes, there are reasons to lament and mourn: of course, it is annoying and regrettable that the lesbian theory magazine *Ihrsinn* folded in 2004 after 15 radical years,[1] that there is no group organizing the sixth German-speaking lesbian research symposium,[2] and that most of the feminist bookshops, libraries and archives,[3] which used to be networking points for lesbians, have closed down lately. This is a pity, especially, since there is not even a queer offspring yet.

QUEER EVOLVED FROM LESBIAN-FEMINIST SELF-CRITIQUE

But why am I ready to inhabit queer? Queer Theory, at least in the German-speaking context, was strongly promoted by lesbian feminists. This does not mean that all lesbian feminists have been in favor of queer. Rather, some lesbian feminists or radical lesbians, for example, the *Ihrsinn* editing board, strongly oppose(d) queer as dismissing and/or swallowing up lesbian-feminist perspectives into a neutralized field of fashionable individuality. They argued that queer, presenting itself as a sexual avant-garde, skipped the concern about hierarchical gender relations, and forgot about challenging patriarchal dominance and violence. Particularly during the early 1990s, the lesbian skepticism of Queer Theory made use of the same arguments as parts of the feminist movement: if we were to give up our political categories we would lose the instruments to articulate critiques and demands, with the result that the movement would fragment into individualized 'interests.'

At the same time other voices have promoted Queer Theory, because they understand it as a chance to develop new forms of contesting power relations and structures of domination (Hark 1993; Genschel 1996; Engel 1996). From their point of view, queer provides answers to struggles about heteronormative dominance, unreflected gender norms, homophobia, subtle (or not so) heterosexual normalities, but also racist, classist, and other exclusions–struggles which challenge the lesbian/ feminist movement from within, but which also demand complex strategies concerning political transformations of hegemonic society. The book, *Grenzen lesbischer Identitäten* (The Limits/Borders of Lesbian Identities) edited by Sabine Hark (1996), presents queer approaches which decisively criticize normative tendencies within Lesbian Feminism and identity politics, but also underline that queer theorizing by lesbians does not lead to a naïve embrace of an "everything goes, gender is fun"–approach, and focuses on the tensions that arise if Queer Theory is confronted with a feminist analysis (Engel, 1996).

QUEER/FEMINIST ANALYSIS
OF INTERSECTING POWER RELATIONS

Queer Theory cannot be merely reduced to a form of self-critique or reflection on power relations within queer communities, movements, or subcultures. It also draws on the feminist tradition of challenging and changing the dominant society. The concept of heteronormativity provides a category for analyzing social relations of power and domination. It understands sexuality and gender explicitly as moments that regulate, not only subjectivities and intimate social relations, but also society itself, its basic discourses and its institutions.[4] Since queer searches for the problem in the centre and not at the margins, the question becomes how does (hetero)sexuality structure society, rather than is sexuality structured by society (state, medicine, education)? Queer avoids posing an opposition between individual and society, public and private by asking how processes of subjectivity and processes of power intersect.

Apart from the gender hierarchy, Queer Theory takes into account, not only the binarity of sex and normative heterosexuality, but also criticizes any kind of identity category for effecting internal homogenizations and external exclusions. In the form of binary oppositions they foster hierarchies and submissions. Therefore, Queer Theory rejects definitions and looks for representations of difference that do not repeat classifications. While it obviously becomes difficult to define a lesbian relationship, if there are no longer any clear and stable genders, it is nonetheless promising to escape normative definitions of lesbian sexualities and relations. It is exactly because of this need to invent new representations apart from heteronormative imaginaries, that I interpret Queer Theory as an inviting site for Lesbian Studies–as an invitation to dedicate oneself to an open future. The challenge is to develop new political concepts and practises, which correspond to non-normative, post-identitarian differences but also to know how to fight a complex intersectionality of relations of power and domination (Engel et al., 2005).[5]

NO LONGER WHITE-STORY, NO LONGER HER-STORY?

Queer provides space for those who do not want to make use of the label lesbian, even if they openly live sexual or love relationships as women, were assigned female at birth, but do not identify with the female gender, or became female after having left behind their male birth assignment, or they represent many other dissident genders and sexualities. The critique of normative images of lesbians also implies skipping trans-phobic exclusions, and a questioning of the normative whiteness of queer communities. Queers of Color do not wait any longer to receive recognition, but take up space and articulate themselves, while still demanding the end of white racist privileges (Gutiérrez Rodríguez 2003; El-Tayeb 2003). Unfortunately, these political struggles bear fruit only very slowly in traditional lesbian contexts. The *Lesbenfrühlingstreffen* for example, an annual lesbian meeting, which has taken place since 1972 in changing cities, is on the one hand a space for self-reflection and debate, but on the other hand reiterates procedures of saving its homogenous community, hesitant to translate contest and conflict into transformative practise.[6] Again and again transsexuals are excluded from participating in the event, transgenders are policed not to transgress too far into masculinity, and women-born-women claim the exclusive right to define the space and to 'save' people from recognizing their different experiences of gendered violence.

THEORY-PRODUCTION SITES

Before the rise of queer there was barely any tradition of gay male and lesbian coalition politics in post-World War II Germany.[7] The self-understanding of a lesbian movement developed in the 1970s and 1980s not so much in opposing homophobia and discrimination against a homosexual orientation or lifestyle, but around questions of gender discrimination, sisterhood and the devaluation of female sexuality. Rather than understanding heterosexuality as independent from gender, it has been analyzed as a patriarchal, phallogocentric or heterosexist norm of submissive femininity. Here, the intersections between theory and politics, between ways of existence and ways of thinking, between visibility and politics of representation were dense. This is to say it was the lesbian-feminist movement, which provided contexts of knowledge production, theoretical exchange, research and debates. The movement has to be seen as a site of theory production, presenting the *Lesbenforschungssymposium* (Lesbian Research Symposium) as its academic branch. Most of the participants from Austria, Switzerland and Germany used to be independent scholars rather than affiliates of academic institutions.

Relying on independent structures provides a special quality, since one does not have to conform to academic standards. Within these contexts, it is on the one hand much more likely that theoretical approaches cross class, educational, disciplinary and occupational barriers and escape the norms of scientific intelligibility. This, of course, is an ambiguous situation, because on the other hand one lacks resources, acknowledgement, references, funding and media coverage. It is not very conceivable that one is taken seriously within the hegemonic academic field. Therefore the establishment of Gender Studies Centers at various universities in the 1990s definitely opened up opportunities for Lesbian Theory.[8] It is this double infra-structure of feminist activities outside and within the Academy which provided the space for seminars, workshops and conferences as well as publications, which openly focused on lesbian perspectives.[9]

Two moments come to mind if one is to characterize the conditions of theory production: first, Lesbian Studies has been related to the feminist rather than the gay and lesbian or homo-emancipation-movement, and second, they developed as part of a self-organized project structure, which is more or less independent from academic circles or universities. Queer Theory arose before Gay and Lesbian Studies ever entered German universities. Even though, of course, there were lesbian and gay students, lecturers and academics, Gay and Lesbian Studies programs did not exist apart from single lectures or seminars delivered by a few 'out' people. Though Queer Theory is not established or institutionalized either,[10] it still enjoys some kind of public visibility in the form of seminars and publications. Of course, it did not enter center stage, but it had its coming-out in various disciplines (either thanks to a new outspoken generation of gays and lesbians, or since queer provided a discourse of coming-out in university, or both) and has not disappeared unnoticed under the Gender Studies banner.

CHALLENGING THE ANGLO-AMERICAN MONOPOLY

Over the past five years an exchange has developed between Eastern European and German-speaking Queer Theory contexts, providing a platform for analyzing the workings of heterosexuality, homophobia and rigid binary sex/gender norms in heterogeneous political and socio-economic contexts. Annual queer conferences in Poland have been held since 2000, which have drawn people from various Eastern European countries and increasingly attract more international participants.[11] What seems most interesting to me is the fact that in Poland, where an open LGBT community only began to develop in the 1990s, queer perspectives have been integrated from the very beginning. People question whether political activism needs to go through all the steps of consciousness-raising, forming a homogenized movement and normative identity politics. Rather, a critique of identity constructions and mechanisms of exclusion and normalization inspire considerations on forms of political organizing (Mizielinska, 2004).

It turns out that struggles over power differences within queer contexts and over the workings of structural moments of domination like racism, anti-Semitism, classism, sexism or transphobia mean a shared terrain for Eastern and Western European scholars. For example, we find peculiar similarities in discourses structuring racist and trans-phobic exclusions (for example, silences of queers of color; dominance of white gay males) at all three of last year's major Queer Studies conferences: "Europe without Homophobia" (Wrocław), "Queer Matters" (London) and "Queering the Humanities" (Berlin).

Two workshops in Hamburg have offered another site of exchange for queer scholars from various European countries.[12] Focusing on the European integration process, regimes of migration and neo-liberal capitalist politics concerning welfare and work, these workshops asked for queer analysis, critique and perspectives of transformation in the field of hegemonic politics. Thus, it showed that the confrontation between different socio-political traditions of former socialist and former welfare countries meeting on the floor of neo-liberal capitalist transformations is highly productive.

LESBIAN PERSPECTIVES WITHIN QUEER THEORY

In all these contexts we find a strong engagement of lesbians conceptualizing and organizing the events, as well as giving lectures, defining discourses and debates. It turns out that lesbians know very well how to articulate their specific perspectives on hegemonic politics. Nevertheless there is struggle about who is occupying which space, taking which roles, preferring which kind of communication. It is no surprise that traditional gender hierarchies as well as other relations of power find their way back into queer contexts. This experience is the point from where I would like to take up the question of what lesbian perspectives are: hardly any lesbian does not know from personal experience what gender discrimination means. Many lesbians experience other forms of subordination because of their skin color, origin, abilities, age or sexual preferences. A lesbian perspective develops from reflecting on these intersecting power differences and from seeing oneself as accountable for one's agency in trans/forming these complex relations.

Taking the feminist and queer critique of hegemonic productions of knowledge and silence, as well as normative effects within the movement, we should not 'define' lesbian perspectives. Rather we can understand 'lesbian' as an open category of permanent struggle and reconsideration. But this includes being knowledgeable about the histories of exclusion and silencing of lesbian lives; about the effects of pathologizing and curing, of criminalizing and prosecuting, of resistance and counter-cultures. The lesbian future within Queer Theory consists of designing the field by expressing dissidence and discomfort, solidarity and creative critique, without producing new categories of identity or truth. It also consists of taking Queer Theory as the site from which to create disturbances in hegemonic society.

NOTES

1. URL www.ihrsinn.net

2. Find reference to the 5th (Bielefeld 2000) at: www.uni-bielefeld.de/IFF/forsch/lfs.htm. The others took place in Berlin 1991, Zürich 1994, Hamburg 1996, Berlin 1998. See also publications: Initiative (1991), Marti et al. (1994)

3. www.ida-dachverband.de gives an overview of women- and lesbian-archives and libraries in Austria, Switzerland, and Germany.

4. The international queer conference "Queering Democracy" (Berlin 1998) asked how political concepts of, e.g. nation, citizenship, human rights, participation, market, . . . are organized according to the heterosexual norm, and how they can be queered (quaestio eds. 2000).

5. Apart from this focus on political struggles and not necessarily in opposition to that there are also lesbian approaches, which focus rather on lesbian erotics and sexualities, e.g. series of books called Mein lesbisches Auge (My Lesbian Eye), (Nössler et al. 2004) or (Kuhnen 1997).

6. www.lesbenfruehling.de/hannover2002/seiten/lft2002/chronik.html

7. During the Weimar Republic a vivid homophile culture and politics existed, which included 'lesbians' as well as 'gay males'. But even then political coalitions were rare and dominated by males, e.g. the Wissenschaftlich-humanitäres Kommitee of Magnus Hirschfeld (Lindemann 1993: 101; Schlüpman 1993: 106ff.). Schader

(2004) focuses on 'lesbian life' during the 1920s. Schopman (1993) explains the specific situations of lesbians during National Socialism. When Etgeton and Hark published Freundschaft unter Vorbehalt (Friendship With the Reservation that . . .) in 1997 this was one of the first attempts to reflect on lesbian and gay coalitions and their political potential.

8. Gender Studies programmes have been installed for example at the universities of Bielefeld, Frankfurt, Bremen, Berlin, Hamburg, Oldenburg, Freiburg, Basel (Switzerland), Innsbruck (Austria).

9. Academic books on lesbian lives have been published only after Gender Studies found a place at universities and queer theory had been already on the horizon: Hacker (1987); beiträge (1989); Schoppmann (1993); Hark (1996); Bührmann (1997); Kuhnen (1997); Engel (2002); Hänsch (2003); Schader (2004).

10. In 2002 Hamburg University was close to the point of establishing the first professorship of queer theory in Germany, but then gave up on this project due to political stumbling-blocks.

11. 3rd Polish queer conference "Difference and Identity" (Warsaw 2003), 4th, "Parameters of Desire" (Bielsko-Bialas 2003), 5th, "Europe without Homophobia" (Wroclaw 2004). Basiuk et al. (2002) covers the first two, Basiuk et al. (2005) the following conferences. Also the web-magazine *inter alia. journal of queer studies* is about to go online as a forum for queer studies. The networks of exchange also inspired the Belgrade international queer conference "Coming Out With Nick 2" (2003), which, apart from cross-relations with the Polish conferences, also attracted lesbians from Austria and Finland.

12. "Intervention Rather than Integration. Queer/feminist Critique of European Politics and Globalization" (2003), "Re/working Conditions. Queer/feminist Perspectives on Resistance Against Precarious Work" (2004). URL www.queerworking.de

REFERENCES

"Nirgendwo und überall. Lesben," *beiträge zur feministischen Theorie und Praxis*, 12, 1989: 25-6.

Bührmann, Andrea. *Das authentische Geschlecht. Die Sexualitätsdebatte der Neuen Frauenbewegung und die Foucaultsche Machtanalyse*. Münster: Westfäl. Dampfboot, 1995.

Basiuk, Tomasz, Dominika Ferens and Tomasz Sikora, eds. *A Queer Mixture: Gender Perspectives on Minority Sexual Identities*. Odmiany Odmienca: Katowice, 2002.

_____. eds. *Parameters of Desire*. Krakow: Universitas, forthcoming 2005.

El-Tayeb, Fatima. "Rassismus als Nebenwiderspruch. Ausgrenzungspraktiken in der queer community." iz3w. *informationszentrum* 3. welt., 280, 2004: 20-3.

Engel, Antke. "Verqueeres Begehren." In Sabine Hark, ed. *Grenzen lesbischer Identitäten*. Berlin: Querverlag, 1996: 73-95.

_____. *Wider die Eindeutigkeit. Sexualität und Geschlecht im Fokus queerer Politik der Repräsentation*. Frankfurt/M: Campus, 2002.

_____. "Traveling Images. Desire as Movement. Desire as Method." In Tomasz Basiuk, Dominika Ferens and Tomasz Sikora, eds. *Parameters of Desire*. Krakow: Universitas, forthcoming 2005.

_____. Nina Schulz and Juliette Wedl, eds. "Queere Politiken. Analysen, Kritik, Perspektiven," *femina politica. Zeitschrift für feministische Politikwissenschaft,* 14(1), 2005, forthcoming.

Etgeton, Stefan and Sabine Hark, eds. *Freundschaft unter Vorbehalt. Chancen und Grenzen lesbisch-schwuler Bündnisse.* Berlin: Querverlag, 1997.

Genschel, Corinna. "Fear of a Queer Planet. Dimensionen lesbisch-schwuler Gesellschaftskritik," *Das Argument,* 216(4), 1996: 525-37.

Gutiérrez Rodríguez, Encarnación. "Repräsentation, Subalternität und Postkoloniale Kritik." In Encarnación Gutiérrez Rodríguez and Hito Steyerl, eds. *Spricht die Subalterne deutsch? Migration und postkoloniale Kritik.* Münster: Unrast, 2003: 17-37.

Hacker, Hanna. *Frauen und Freundinnen. Studien zur "weiblichen Homosexualität" am Beispiel Österreich 1870-1938.* Berlin: Beltz, 1987.

Hänsch, Ulrike. *Individuelle Freiheiten–heterosexuelle Normen in Lebensgeschichten lesbischer Frauen.* Opladen: Leske and Budrich, 2003.

Hark, Sabine. "Queer Interventionen," *Feministische Studien,* 11(2), 1993: 103-9.

_____, ed. *Grenzen lesbischer Identitäten.* Berlin: Querverlag, 1996.

_____. *Deviante Subjekte. Die paradoxe Politik der Identität,* Opladen: Leske and Budrich, 1996.

Initiative für ein Symposium. "Facetten deutschsprachiger Lesbenforschung," ed. *Thesenpapiere.* Berlin, 1991.

Kuhnen, Stephanie, ed. *Butch/Femme. Eine erotische Kultur.* Berlin: Querverlag, 1997.

Lindemann, Gesa. "Magnus Hirschfeld." In Rüdiger Lautmann, ed. *Homosexualität. Handbuch der Theorie-und Forschungsgeschichte.* Frankfurt/M: Campus, 1993: 91-104.

Marti, M., A. Schneider, I. Sgier and A. Wymann, eds. *Querfeldein–Beiträge zur Lesbenforschung.* Bern, Zürich, Dortmund 1994.

Mizielinska, Joanna. "'You Are Not That Name': The Problem of the Exclusion of Male-To-Female Transsexuals From The Lesbian Movement." In Tomasz Basiuk, Dominika Ferens and Tomasz Sikora eds. *A Queer Mixture: Gender Perspectives on Minority Sexual Identities. Odmiany Odmienca.* Katowice, 2002: 205-13.

_____. "Poland Meets Queer Theory." In K. Slany, B. Kowalska and M. Smietana, eds. *Homoseksualizm. Perspektywa interdyscyplinarna* (Homosexuality Interdisciplinary Perspective). Krakow: Zaklad Wydawniczy NOMOS, forthcoming 2005.

Nössler, Regina and Laura Merrit, eds.. *Mein lesbisches Auge 4. Das Jahrbuch der Erotik XIXa,* Tübingen: konkursbuch, 2004.

quaestio, eds.. *Queering Demokratie. Sexuelle Politiken.* Berlin: Querverlag, 2000.

Schader, Heike: *Virile, Vamps und wilde Veilchen. Sexualität, Begehren und Erotik in den Zeitschriften homosexueller Frauen im Berlin der 20er Jahre.* Königstein: Ulrike Helmer, 2004.

Schlüpmann, Heide. "Helene Stöcker." In Rüdiger Lautmann, ed. *Homosexualität. Handbuch der Theorie-und Forschungsgeschichte.* Frankfurt/M: Campus, 1993: 105-10.

Schoppmann, Claudia. *Zeit der Maskierung. Lebensgeschichten lesbischer Frauen im "Dritten Reich."* Berlin: Orlanda, 1993.

doi:10.1300/J155v11n03_09

Quare Éire

Noreen Giffney

SUMMARY. In this position piece we will briefly introduce The(e)ories: Advanced Seminars for Queer Research, which we founded and have convened at University College Dublin, Ireland, since January 2003. We will do this in an effort to illustrate how the aims and development of The(e)ories have mirrored, but also deviated from the US/UK-centric model of Queer Theory which (although largely a myth) continues to dominate discussions of sexuality. In this, we endeavor here to show how Queer Theory and Lesbian Studies, while not interchangeable, intersect with each other in important ways in our praxis in Ireland and thus, are not reducible to the "collision model" (Doan, this volume) forwarded by proponents and critics alike. doi:10.1300/J155v11n03_10

Author Note: The 'we' in this piece refers to my collaborations with Michael O'Rourke. The piece was written after discussion with him.

Noreen Giffney is a Postdoctoral Fellow in Women's Studies (WERRC), School of Social Justice at University College Dublin, Ireland, and a Research Affiliate in the Centre for the Interdisciplinary Study of Sexuality and Gender in Europe at the University of Exeter. She is the co-editor of *The Ashgate Research Companion to Queer Theory* and *Queering the Non/Human*, and is the series co-editor of the Queer Interventions book series at Ashgate Press. Her book on queer theory is forthcoming in Berg's 'The Key Concepts' series. Her next research project is a monograph on queer theory and the psychoanalyst Melanie Klein.

Address correspondence to: Dr. Noreen Giffney, Women's Studies (WERRC), School of Social Justice, Hanna Sheehy-Skeffington Building, University College Dublin, Belfield, Dublin 4, Ireland (E-mail: noreen.giffney@ucd.ie).

[Haworth co-indexing entry note]: "Quare Éire." Giffney, Noreen. Co-published simultaneously in *Journal of Lesbian Studies* (Harrington Park Press, an imprint of The Haworth Press, Inc.) Vol. 11, No. 3/4, 2007, pp. 275-289; and: *Twenty-First Century Lesbian Studies* (ed: Noreen Giffney, and Katherine O'Donnell) Harrington Park Press, an imprint of The Haworth Press, Inc., 2007, pp. 275-289. Single or multiple copies of this article are available for a fee from The Haworth Document Delivery Service [1-800-HAWORTH, 9:00 a.m. - 5:00 p.m. (EST). E-mail address: docdelivery@haworthpress.com].

KEYWORDS. Lesbian studies, queer theory, genealogy, collaboration, homo/hetero binary, the personal, Ireland

. . . the concept 'queer' emphasizes the disruptive, the fractured, the tactical and contingent . . . any implication that queer theorization is itself a simple monolith would be hypocritical. Simply put, there is no 'queer' theory in the singular, only many different voices and sometimes overlapping, sometimes divergent perspectives that can loosely be called 'queer theories.' (Hall, 2003: 5)

In this position piece we will briefly introduce The(e)ories: Advanced Seminars for Queer Research, which we founded and have convened at University College Dublin in Ireland since January 2003.[1] We will do this in an effort to illustrate how the aims and development of The(e)ories have mirrored, but also deviated from the US/UK-centric model of Queer Theory, which (although largely a myth) continues to dominate discussions of sexuality.[2] In this, we endeavor to show how Queer Theory and Lesbian Studies, while not interchangeable, intersect with each other in important ways in our praxis in Ireland and thus, are not reducible to the "collision model" (Doan, this issue) forwarded by proponents and critics alike.

We have opted in the title of this piece to bring together the Anglo-Irish epithet, "*quare*" (Dolan, 1998: 211), and the Gaelic word for Ireland, "*Éire*," for several reasons. Firstly, because the word *quare*, which means odd, strange or eccentric, perfectly captures the difference in the way we practise Queer Theory in Ireland from the hegemonic bloc and thus, it is not easily subsumable under some globalizing framework. By extension, our formulation of Queer Theory cannot simply be subjected to the same critiques that are levelled against US/UK-centric models. Secondly, we deploy *quare* because it signals the doubleness of Queer Theory in Ireland and its various overlappings: The(e)ories is both queer *and* lesbian; queer *and* feminist. Joseph Valente explains a similar choice in his introduction to the collection, *Quare Joyce* (1998). While Valente uses *quare* to mark the oscillation and slippage between queer and straight in James Joyce's fiction, we employ it to unsettle the dichotomy between Queer Theory and Lesbian Studies (see also Johnson, 2001, 2003).

SLEEPING WITH THE ENEMY?
PROLIFERATING QUEER/LESBIAN GENEALOGIES

> ... any myth of origin suggests a linear (or we might say 'straight') path of development and implies a pure and singular starting point. (McRuer, 2002: 228)

A couple of genealogical myths have come to dominate discussions about the relationship between Lesbian Studies and Queer Theory (Dever, 1999). On the one hand, proponents claim that Queer Theory developed partly from Lesbian Studies, surpassing the field that spawned it with seemingly limitless inclusivity and the suaveness of its theoretical grammars; a post-lesbian position of sorts (Queen and Schimel, 1996; Warner, 1993; de Lauretis, 1991). On the other hand, critics bemoan the disappearance of Lesbian Studies under the queer moniker, fearing the loss of visibility, autonomy and credibility; a re-enactment of patriarchal hegemony (Walters, 1996; Kitzinger and Wilkinson, 1996; Jeffreys, 1997, 2003). Although engaging in radically different relations with the two fields, both positions figure Lesbian Studies in a state of weakness; the discarded (M)Other of the new poster-child of Critical Theory/Sexuality Studies (Beasley, 2005; Pellegrini, 2004). We are troubled by both of these linear trajectories of development, precisely because we have, in our work, both sought out and engaged in a polyamorous relationship with Lesbian Studies and Queer Theory. We do not claim here that the two fields are congruent (Giffney, 2004), neither do we wish to dilute their differences (Garber, 2001); rather, we insist that in our sampling of the pleasures of both fields, they have become a messy entanglement of shifting boundaries (Doan, 1994; Smyth, 1992; Halberstam, 1996). For us, there are more than simply two ways of understanding the complex interactions between these approaches to knowledge.

We come to this position piece as a 'lesbian-identified woman' and a 'straight-identified man,' both queerly-positioned and located in Ireland on the periphery of the US/UK hegemony. We say queerly-positioned rather than identified, because queer operates for us as an adverb and a verb rather than a noun; a doing rather than a being (Sullivan,

2003; Hall, 2003). The two, 'being' and 'doing,' should not be understood as the potential instantiation of a new binary or indeed as opposites, but rather as different positions (Lorde, 1984: 114-23). This focus on 'doing' queer rather than 'being' queer also elides unproductive debates about who is or is not identifiable under that sign: "the term 'queer' did not work because its very acknowledgement of plurality included all those deemed different from the norm, including young heterosexual people whose only claim to deviance is blue hair" (Khayatt, 2002: 497). Certainly, we concede that queer is useful as an identity category (LaGrace Volcano, 2005; Wilchins, 2002 a, 2002 b, 2004), however, it lacks the specificity to adequately describe our sexual identities (Khayatt, 2002). For Michael, queer connotes a theoretical, rather than a sexual, orientation (2005 c). For both of us, Queer Theory operates as a Deleuzoguattarian toolbox, which can be dipped into and out of as the need arises (Deleuze and Guattari, 1987). We do, however, utilize the term 'queer' in our work as an ontology relating to the output of research on sexualities and an umbrella descriptor to refer to members of the LGBTTIQA alphabet.[3] Having said that, it works best for us as an analytical tool (Butler, 1993; Burger and Kruger, 2001; Clarke, 2004; Doty, 2000) to point to the instability and elasticity of identity categories, while making visible, undermining and subverting (even if only conceptually) the system of compulsory heterosexuality (Hanscombe and Humphries, 1987; Babbit, 1999; Anonymous Queers; 1990; Kelly and Fiveash, 2001). According to Judith Halberstam:

> A queer methodology, in a way, is a scavenger methodology that uses different methods to collect and produce information on subjects who have been deliberately or accidentally excluded from traditional studies of human behaviour. The queer methodology attempts to combine methods that are often cast as being at odds with each other, and it refuses the academic compulsion toward disciplinary coherence. (2005: 13)

While freely admitting to the personal and strategic importance of our identifications–however loose–as 'lesbian' and 'straight' (Munt, 1997 a; O'Rourke, 2005), we are disturbed by the rigidity with which sexual-identity categories continue to be enforced and therefore disidentify with understandings of those categories as immovable (Butler, 1991; Thomas, 2000; Schlichter, 2004).[4] As 'lesbian' and 'straight,' we apparently occupy polar-opposite positions on the spectrum of sexuality; we are, in a sense, the embodiment of the homo/hetero binary (Fuss, 1991; Sedgwick, 1990).[5] In this, we are aware that our declarations as 'lesbian' and 'straight' respectively often provoke different reactions to our collaborative research in Queer Theory: while critiques are levelled against Michael's work, those same charges are laid at my feet with the collapsing of my research into its being seen merely as an extension of my 'lesbianism' (Munt, 1997 b; Freeman, 2005: 85). For example, Michael's colleagues have questioned the "intellectual substance" of his work and the title of one of his courses, 'An Introduction to Queer Theory,' was changed to 'An Introduction to the History of Sexuality' as departmental seniors feared that the original title would offend straight students. I, on the other hand, have been subjected to verbal abuse and hate mail, which conflated my work, my department and my identity. Thus, while Michael's work gets figured as abject, I am understood as abjection personified (Kristeva, 1982; Valentine, 1998). Our collaborative efforts have forced us to interrogate, sometimes uncomfortably, our identifications and the political ramifications of such positions individually and collectively, but also our investment in Queer Theory as a critical practice in our research and teaching (Wilson, 1997; Phelan, 1997) more generally.

When Suzanna Dunata Walters critically asks, "Why Can't a Woman Be More Like a Fag?" (1996), Sheila Jeffreys mourns "The Queer Disappearance of Lesbians" (1997), Celia Kitzinger and Sue Wilkinson write of "The Queer Backlash" (1996) or Heidi J. Nast warns us of "Queer Patriarchies, Queer Racisms, International" (2002), we hear and recognize their criticisms in what we have read, however, we cannot empathize wholeheartedly with their words, which do not accurately reflect what we are doing in Ireland. We are calling here for a greater contextualization of lesbian and queer theorizing and more reflexivity, as regards geographical location, on the part of those pointing to positive attributes and shortcomings. One of the main critiques of Queer Theory is that the term 'queer' tends to act as a synonym for 'gay male,' thus putting lesbians under erasure, so that the lesbian becomes "twice marginal and twice invisible" (Murray, 1996), an apparition (Castle, 1993) both in mainstream culture and the 'malestream' of Queer Theory.[6] This action results in, not only the silencing of lesbian detractors by distorting or ignoring their work (Zimmerman and McNaron, 1996; Zimmerman, 1997), but the focusing on topics relating to men primarily (Warner, 2000; Halperin, 2002) or masculinities more generally (Halberstam, 1998; Fraiman, 2003) to the detriment of other issues. We do, of course, recognize that queer is often collapsed into a substitute terminology for an often narrow understanding of gay-male subjectivity, identity and cultural production; what is more properly termed '(homo)Queer.'

Unlike queer, (homo)Queer does not function as a verb but only as a noun or adjective; it is descriptive–prescriptive even–rather than transformative. The appearance of homo in parentheses and my rendering of Queer with an upper-case Q is deliberate: in certain strains of Queer Theory and politics, as well as some representations of queer as an identity category or aesthetic, the word 'queer' functions merely as a reductive synonym for a narrow understanding of the term 'gay male,' e.g., white, middle-class, buff, able-bodied and so on. In this, (homo) Queer describes two things: the presentation of a commodified, naturalised image of *the* queer *as* gay man in shows, such as *Will and Grace, Queer Eye For the Straight Guy* and *Playing It Straight*, to name but three; Queer as brand (Klein, 2000). Secondly, it denotes the practice of using the term, 'queer,' in academic writings or community settings merely to appear cutting edge, subversive or hip when in fact all that is being forwarded is again a narrow conception of gay-male sexuality, without any recourse to lesbians, bisexuals, trans or intersex people, or indeed the vast majority of gay men.

Having said this, we would like to restate our earlier point that this is not how we do things with The(e)ories. The reason: a commitment to Feminism, which we think is imperative if Queer Theory is to survive and have continued relevance (Weed and Schor, 1997; Butler, 1992; Rudy, 2001). This is not a new argument, but one that needs continued reiteration, especially considering claims that we inhabit a postfeminist landscape; 'post' in this case meaning that an interest in Feminism is deemed to be no longer desirable, necessary or useful (Negra, 2004).[7]

THE(E)ORIES:
WORKING THROUGH THE LESBIAN STUDIES/
QUEER THEORY IMPASSE

Might Queer be nothing more than a smart career move on the part of an ambitious younger generation of theorists? (Jackson, 1999: 161)

The(e)ories: Advanced Seminars for Queer Research was conceived over a couple of cans of soft drinks, in a postgraduate computer room, on a hot afternoon in May 2002. Its title and call for papers were formulated at the back of a university examination hall, scribbled furtively on scraps of rough-work paper, while I supervised undergraduate exams. We began targeting potential speakers by e-mail, and distributing posters to university libraries, departments and LGBTIQ community centres long before we had secured any institutional support, not to mention funding. The series has been a labor of love for us; we did not figure it 'a smart career move' on our part, considering we neither had a career nor held much hope of acquiring one any time soon given how our work had been received by academics at University College Dublin. At the time, we were PhD students in Medieval History and English (Michael); the former department vehemently hostile, the latter ambivalent.

While seeking to fracture the unhelpful boundary that often prevents the chance of a productive encounter between Lesbian Studies and Queer Theory, Judith Halberstam envisages "a queer lesbian studies," which signifies the following:

> 'Queer' in this context performs the work of destabilizing the assumed identity in 'identity politics'. However, by continuing to use and rely upon the term 'lesbian', we acknowledge that identity is a useful strategy for political and cultural organizing. 'Lesbian' is a term that modifies and qualifies 'queer', and 'queer' is a term capable of challenging the stability of identities subsumed by the label 'lesbian.' (1997: 259)[8]

If, as Harriet Malinowitz states, "a lesbian Studies on the threshold of the twenty-first century needs to find ways of alchemising its apparent contradictions into new funds of knowledge" (1997: 268), then we think The(e)ories represents the cutting edge of a lesbian-feminist-queer engagement at the beginning of the new Millennium. In our work on The(e)ories and other projects, we have endeavored to foster a community of people interested in, and provide a forum for the discussion of, work on sexualities, by engendering a supportive and welcoming environment for speakers and attendees alike (Hemmings and Grace, 1999). We have done this partly by forming coalitions with other groups working in this area both within Ireland and abroad, such as the organizers of the annual Lesbian Lives conference or the conveners of the Dublin Queer Studies Group.[9] The(e)ories explores how a range of critical apparatuses (e.g., Postcolonial Theory, Psychoanalysis,

Feminism, Critical Race Theory, Disability Studies/Crip theory, Gerontology, Marxism) might be useful for examining sexuality and other identitarian systems governing race, ethnicity, nationality, class, gender, dis-ability and age. In this, we encourage multi-theoretical efforts and work that does not simply apply theory to a text or attempt to fit a text into a theoretical framework. Thus, we seek out research which challenges theoretical apparatuses as much as any other form of knowledge-production. We are interested in theory as an investigative tool, which means that Queer Theory must be, as Paul Strohm writes, "project oriented, aimed at explaining the text rather than its own vindication, uninsistent about its own status as a total explanatory system" (2000: xi). Thus, we agree with him, when he comments that "any deployment of a theory to overbear a text, to reduce it to 'more of the same,' to predestined conclusions already borne within the theory's initial assumptions, must be deplored" (xiv).

Our aim, more generally, is to challenge rigid mono-disciplinary formations and encourage multi-disciplinary and inter-faculty dialogue, in an effort to learn from the questions asked and approaches undertaken by various disciplines. In this, we constantly push the limits of what is considered to be acceptable in academia and reject hierarchies and traditional notions of academic etiquette.[10] For example, we have had a local drag-king troupe, the Shamcocks, perform in advance of a formal academic paper. In our events we seek to make visible and trace the ways in which norms relating to desire are constructed and embodied. We are not interested in transgression or subversion for their own sakes, but ask our participants to think practically about the political and ethical implications of challenging and attempting to deconstruct these norms. As such, we have a firm commitment to the contexts within which work on sexualities is produced, be they temporal, geographical, cultural or societal. To facilitate this, we invite speakers to be self-reflexive about their own identifications in their presentations and to ponder on what informs their praxis. We are well aware of both the potentialities and strictures involved in hosting a seminar series in an academic setting (Chinn, 1994: 244). In our efforts to facilitate maximal dialogue between presenters and attendees, we encourage speakers to present in a lively, entertaining fashion and display a clarity of thought by using accessible language, while being aware of the multi-disciplinary and community composition of audiences. This also means that we ensure that all locations are accessible in the physical sense, for example, by making sure that venues are wheelchair accessible and by offering sign-language interpretation.

Diana Fuss made the following remark in 1991 regarding Lesbian and Gay Studies:

> Perhaps what we need most urgently in gay and lesbian theory right now is a theory *of* marginality, subversion, dissidence, and othering. What we need is a theory of sexual borders that will help us to come to terms with and to organize around the new cultural and sexual arrangements occasioned by the movements and trans-mutations of pleasure in the social field. (1991: 5)

Over ten years later, we could adjust her statement to apply more closely to Queer Theory. To paraphrase Fuss: what we need most urgently in Queer Theory right now is a critical engagement with Queer Theory in its current manifestations. Practitioners must ruminate, more specifically, on queer's shortcomings, silences, hegemonies and exclusions, while thinking about the ways in which 'queer' has become a commodity as a term, concept and theory. What we need is a commitment to historicizing the field's development, as ahistoricism has the ironic effect of producing the very same mistakes as one's predecessors. This is not a call for linearity but merely an attendance to the fact that fields of knowledge do not simply materialize out of thin air. Queer continues to be a contentious term in LGBTI communities in Ireland. In this, we endeavor to remain open to criticisms of Queer Theory and the use of the term 'queer', thus incorporating them into our rationale for The(e)ories. Above all, our work in Ireland shows that Queer Theory is not simply a hip, young, radical, cutting-edge discourse, but plays an important role in educating people about heterosexual privilege; how our sexualities intersect with other facets of our identities; in addition to lesbophobia, homophobia, transphobia and biphobia by opening students up to considering diverse ways of living in the world. It is unfortunate but true that Queer Theory, with its pronouncements of aggressive inclusivity and universalism (Weinberg, 1996), often proves to be more palatable initially to students, who see Lesbian Studies as a minoritist discourse only relevant to self-identified lesbians. Thus, Queer Theory has the added function of being the grease which eases a student's passage into the pleasures and dangers of Lesbian Studies. In this, Queer Theory becomes not "The Monster that is Destroying Lesbianville" (Goldstein, 1997), but a conduit through which a diverse range of people come to learn about and respect lesbian lives, and are irrevocably changed by that encounter.

NOTES

This piece is based on a paper I presented at the "Queer(y)ing Psychology" symposium at the Open University, Milton Keynes, UK in June 2005. Michael and I are grateful to Meg Barker, Darren Langdridge and Lyndsey Moon for inviting us to share our work and to the audience for their helpful feedback, especially Peter Hegarty, Ian Hodges and Ani Ritchie. In addition to Michael for many fruitful discussions, I owe my thanks to Susan Bailey, Nicole Murray and Katherine O'Donnell for their pertinent suggestions on an earlier draft. There would be no The(e)ories without the continued support and generosity of participants and audience members: thank-you all. Michael and I are, as ever, indebted to Ailbhe Smyth, a radical lesbian feminist, who has been our most enduring supporter. For further information about The(e)ories: Advanced Seminars for Queer Research, visit URL www.theeories.com.

1. For an overview of lesbian lives and activism in Ireland see, for example, O'Donnell (2003); O'Toole (2000); Fox Roberts (2001); Crone (1988); Connolly and O'Toole (2005); O'Carroll and Collins (1995); Smyth (2000).

2. This US/UK-centric myth was especially evident at two recent conferences: 'Sexuality after Foucault,' University of Manchester, November 2003 and 'Queer Matters,' King's College, University of London, May 2004. What we mean by the US/UK-centric myth is the belief that all pioneering and interesting work is produced in Anglo-American contexts and other places are then converted or colonized by those efforts. We both draw on work from the US and the UK, while having a firm commitment to Feminism, Lesbian Studies and community-organized events.

3. Lesbian, Gay, Bisexual, Transgender, Transsexual, Intersex, Questioning, Affiliated.

4. "The primary social markers of a positioning as straight are the trappings of privilege . . . One's inclinations, if known will be enough for heterosexist society to grant one privilege, but to take one's heterosexuality on as a matter of identity is to endorse this granting of privilege and to make it central to one's life. Denying 'straightness', is a disavowal of such privilege . . . one might ask what a non-queer person is to say to the question whether they are straight or gay . . . We suggest that one follow the example of Oscar Wilde. When he was asked to state whether a certain passage in one of his books was blasphemous, Wilde, apparently, answered that 'blasphemy' was not one of his words. By extension, we recommend that those of us who are not gay, when asked whether we are straight, should insist that 'straight' is not one of our words" (Norris Lance and Tanesini, 2005: 183, 186). We agree with the position set out above to an extent, however, we both feel that Michael's embodying a 'straight' identity–his declaration of his libidinal desire for opposite-sex relations, while attempting to 'disavow' his unearned privilege as a 'heterosexual man' (Schacht, 2004)–is important if compulsory heterosexuality is ever to be unravelled. Heterosexuality continues to be all-pervasive and 'straight' persists in being a privileged position because it is a non-identity; as such, it is unmarked and not owned. If 'straights' are to become self-reflexive, they must firstly embody their identities as 'heterosexuals' and, in doing so, own the guilt that comes with the admittance to unearned privilege, in a system that is predicated upon the oppression of Others. In this, the declaration of a 'straight' identity becomes, not a defensive act ("I am straight and therefore not gay or bisexual"), but the beginning of a self-reflexive relationship with one's unearned privilege; only then can that privilege be disavowed and a 'straight' identity disowned.

5. Not to mention the obvious: our genders. In this, we are participating in a heterosocial (Maddison, 2000) rejection of hetero-patriarchy.

6. For example, Halperin (1995) did not take into account any feminist readings of Michel Foucault's work, while Gayle S. Rubin writes of the "amnesia about the past of Queer Studies" (2004: 9).

7. See, for example, the television shows, *Desperate Housewives, Ally McBeal, Sex and the City* and the film, *Bridget Jones's Diary*. Certainly there are many differences, indeed disagreements between Queer Theory and Feminism, which we think need another paper to tease out.

8. The meaning of the term 'lesbian' has always been subject to (sometimes furious) debate (Castle, 2003; Wilton, 1995).

9. Noreen co-organized 'Lesbian Lives, XI: Lesbian Lives, Studies and Activism since *The Lesbian Postmodern*' at University College Dublin in February 2004; we established the Dublin Queer Studies Group in 2001 and acted as moderators during 2001-2002.

10. In our work we continue to put all binaries under interrogation in an attempt to understand the shifting nature of identity categories and the richness of intersectional thinking (McCall, 2005): academic versus activist and community; humanities (as academic and in some way 'useless') versus the sciences as 'useful'; theory versus materiality; human versus nonhuman (Giffney and Hird, 2008; O'Rourke, 2005/2006).

REFERENCES

Anonymous Queers. "Queers Read This." Leaflet distributed at the Pride March, New York, July 1990. http://www.qrd.org/qrd/misc/text/queers.read.this

Babbit, Jami, dir. *But I'm a Cheerleader!* 1999.

Beasley, Chris. *Gender & Sexuality: Critical Theories, Critical Thinkers*. London: Sage, 2005.

Burger, Glenn and Steven F. Kruger, eds. *Queering the Middle Ages*. Minneapolis and London: University of Minnesota Press, 2001.

Butler, Judith. "Imitation and Gender Insubordination." In Diana Fuss, ed. *Inside/Out: Lesbian Theories, Gay Theories*. New York and London: Routledge, 1991: 13-31.

_____. *Bodies that Matter: On the Discursive Limits of 'Sex.'* New York and London: Routledge, 1993.

_____. "The Body You Want," an interview with Liz Kotz. *Art Forum*, November 1992: 82-9.

Castle, Terry. "Introduction." In Terry Castle, ed. *The Literature of Lesbianism: A Historical Anthology from Ariosto to Stonewall*. New York: Columbia University Press, 2003: 1-56.

_____. *The Apparitional Lesbian: Female Homosexuality and Modern Culture*. New York: Columbia University Press, 1993.

Chinn, Sarah. "Queering the Profession, or Just Professionalizing Queers?" In Linda Garber, ed. *Tilting the Tower: Lesbians/Teaching/Queer Subjects*. New York and London: Routledge, 1994: 243-50.

Clarke, Danielle. "Finding the Subject: Queering the Archive," *Feminist Theory*, 5(1), 2004: 79-83.

Connolly, Linda and Tina O'Toole. "Lesbian Activism." In Linda Connolly and Tina O'Toole. *Documenting Irish Feminisms: The Second Wave*. Dublin: The Woodfield Press, 2005: 171-95.

Crone, Joni. "Lesbian Feminism in Ireland," *Women's Studies International Forum*, 11(4), 1988: 343-7.

De Lauretis, Teresa, ed., "Queer Theory: Lesbian and Gay Sexualities," a special issue of *differences: A Journal of Feminist Cultural Studies*, 3(2), 1991.

Deleuze, Gilles and Félix Guattari. *A Thousand Plateaus: Capitalism and Schizophrenia*. Brian Massumi, trans. London and New York: Continuum, 1987.

Dever, Carolyn. "Either/And: Lesbian Theories, Queer Theories," *GLQ: A Journal of Lesbian and Gay Studies*, 5(3), 1999: 413-24.

Doan, Laura, ed. *The Lesbian Postmodern*. New York: Columbia University Press, 1994.

Dolan, Terence P., compiler and ed. *A Dictionary of Hiberno-English: The Irish Use of English*. Dublin: Gill and Macmillan, 1998.

Doty, Alexander. *Flaming Classics: Queering the Film Canon*. New York and London: Routledge, 2000.

Fox Roberts, Hayley. "'Always Keep a Lemon Handy': A Skeletal History of Lesbian Activism in Late Twentieth-Century Ireland," *The History Review*, 12, 2001: 113-27.

Fraiman, Susan. "Queer Theory and the Second Sex," *Cool Men and the Second Sex*. New York: Columbia University Press, 2003: 122-55.

Freeman, Elizabeth. "*Monsters, Inc.*: Notes on the Neoiberal Arts Education," *New Literary History*, 36(1), 2005: 83-95.

Fuss, Diana. "Inside/Out." In Diana Fuss, ed. *Inside/Out: Lesbian Theories, Gay Theories*. New York and London: Routledge, 1991: 1-8.

Garber, Linda. *Identity Poetics: Race, Class, and the Lesbian-Feminist Roots of Queer Theory*. New York: Columbia University Press, 2001.

Giffney, Noreen. "Denormatizing Queer Theory: More than (Simply) Lesbian and Gay Studies," *Feminist Theory*, 5(1), 2004: 73-8.

_____ and Myra J. Hird, eds. *Queering the Non/Human*. Aldershot: Ashgate, 2008.

Goldstein, Lynda. "Queer Theory: The Monster that is Destroying Lesbianville." In Beth Mintz and Esther Rothblum, eds. *Lesbians in Academia: Degrees of Freedom*. New York and London: Routledge, 1997: 261-8.

Halberstam, Judith. *Female Masculinity*. Durham and London: Duke University Press, 1998.

_____. "Queering Lesbian Studies." In Bonnie Zimmerman and Toni A.H. McNaron, eds. *The New Lesbian Studies: Into the Twenty-First Century*. New York: The Feminist Press, 1996: 256-61.

_____. *In a Queer Time and Place: Transgender Bodies, Subcultural Lives*. New York and London: New York University Press, 2005.

Hall, Donald E. *Queer Theories*. Basingstoke: Palgrave Macmillan, 2003.

Halperin, David M. *How to Do the History of Homosexuality*. Chicago and London: The University of Chicago Press, 2002.

_____. *Saint Foucault: Towards a Gay Hagiography*. Oxford: Oxford University Press, 1995.

Hanscombe, Gillian E. and Martin Humphries, eds. *Hetero Sexuality*. London: GMP Publishers Ltd., 1987.

Hemmings, Clare and Felicity Grace. "Stretching Queer Boundaries: An Introduction," *Sexualities*, 2(4), 1999: 387-96.

Jackson, Stevi. *Heterosexuality in Question*. London: Sage, 1999.

Jagose, Annamarie. *Queer Theory: An Introduction*. New York: New York University Press, 1996.

Jeffreys, Sheila. "The Queer Disappearance of Lesbians: Sexuality in the Academy," *Women's Studies International Forum*, 17(5), 1997: 459-72.

_____. *Unpacking Queer Politics: A Lesbian Feminist Perspective*. London: Polity, 2003.

Johnson, E. Patrick. "Strange Fruit: A Performance Piece About Identity Politics," *TDR: The Drama Review*, 47(2), 2003: 88-116.

_____. "'Quare' Studies or (Almost) Everything I Know About Queer Studies I Learned from my Grandmother," *Text and Performance Quarterly*, 21(1), 2001: 1-25.

Kelly, Deborah and Tina Fiveash. *Hey, Hetero!*, a public-art installation, 2001.

Khayatt, Didi. "Toward a Queer Identity." *Sexualities*, 5(4), 2002: 487-501.

Kitzinger, Celia and Sue Wilkinson, "The Queer Backlash." In Diane Bell and Renate Klein, eds. *Radically Speaking: Feminism Reclaimed*. London: Zed Books, 1996: 375-82.

Klein, Naomi. *NO LOGO*. London: Flamingo, 2000.

Kristeva, Julia. *Powers of Horror: An Essay on Abjection*. New York: Columbia University Press, 1982.

LaGrace Volcano, Del. "Del Boy," an interview with Noreen Giffney and Michael O'Rourke. *Gay Community News*, 182, 2005: 10-11.

Maddison, Stephen. *Fags, Hags and Queer Sisters: Gender Dissent and Heterosocial Bonds in Gay Culture*. London: St Martin's Press, 2000.

Malinowitz, Harriet. "Lesbian Studies and Postmodern Queer Theory." In Bonnie Zimmerman and Toni A.H. McNaron, eds. *The New Lesbian Studies: Into the Twenty-First Century*. New York: The Feminist Press, 1996: 262-8.

McCall, Leslie. "The Complexity of Intersectionality," *Signs: Journal of Women in Culture and Society*, 30(3), 2005: 1771-1800.

McRuer, Robert. Review of *A Genealogy of Queer Theory* by William B. Turner, *NWSA Journal: A Publication of the National Women's Studies Association*, 14(2), 2002: 227-9.

Munt, Sally R. "The Personal, Experience, and the Self." In Andy Medhurst and Sally R. Munt, eds. *Lesbian and Gay Studies: A Critical Introduction*. London and Washington: Cassell, 1997 a: 186-97.

_____. "'I Teach Therefore I Am': Lesbian Studies in the Liberal Academy," *Feminist Review*, 56, 1997 b: 85-99.

Murray, Jacqueline. "Twice Marginal and Twice Invisible: Lesbians in the Middle Ages." In Vern L. Bullough and James A. Brundage, eds. *Handbook of Medieval Sexuality*. New York: Garland, 1996: 191-222.

Nast, Heidi J., ed. "Queer Patriarchies, Queer Racisms, International," a special issue of *Antipode: A Radical Journal of Geography*, 31(5), 2002.

Negra, Diane. "'Quality Postfeminism' Sex and the Single Girl on HBO," *Genders*, 39, 2004, URL genders.org.

Nestle, Joan, Clare Howell and Riki Wilchins, eds. *GenderQueer: Voices from Beyond the Sexual Binary*. Los Angeles and New York: Alyson Books, 2002.

Norris Lance, Mark and Alessandra Tanesini. "Identity Judgements, Queer Politics." In Iain Morland and Annabelle Willox, "Introduction." In Iain Morland and Annabelle Willox, eds. *Queer Theory*. Basingstoke: Palgrave Macmillan, 2005: 171-86, 210-12.

O'Carroll, Íde and Eoin Collins, eds. *Lesbian and Gay Visions of Ireland: Towards the Twenty-First Century*. London: Cassell, 1995.

O'Donnell, Katherine. "Lesbianism". In Brian Lalor, ed. *The Encyclopedia of Ireland*. Dublin: Gill and Macmillan, 2003: 623-4.

O'Rourke, Michael. "On the Eve of a Queer-Straight Future: Notes Toward an Antinormative Heteroerotic," *Feminism & Psychology*, 15(1), 2005: 111-16.

_____, ed. "The Becoming-Deleuzoguattarian of Queer Studies," a special issue of *Rhizomes: Cultural Studies in Emerging Knowledge*, 11/12, 2005/2006.

_____. "Queer Theory's Loss and the Work of Mourning Jacques Derrida," *Rhizomes: Cultural Studies in Emerging Knowledge*, 10, 2005. URL rhizomes.net

O'Toole, Tina. "Ireland." In Bonnie Zimmerman, ed. *Lesbian Histories and Cultures: An Encyclopedia*. New York: Garland Publishing, Inc., 2000: 402-3.

Pellegrini, Ann. "Mind The Gap?" *GLQ: A Journal of Lesbian and Gay Studies*, 10(4), 2004: 637-9.

Phelan, Shane. "Introduction." In Shane Phelan, ed. *Playing With Fire: Queer Politics, Queer Theories*. New York and London: Routledge, 1997: 1-8.

Queen, Carol and Lawrence Schimel, eds. *PoMoSexuals: Challenging Assumptions about Gender and Sexuality*. San Francisco, CA: Cleis Press, 1996.

Rubin, Gayle S. "Geologies of Queer Studies: It's Déjà Vu All Over Again," *CLAGS News*, 14(2), 2004: 6-10.

Rudy, Kathy. "Radical Feminism, Lesbian Separatism, and Queer Theory," *Feminist Studies*, 27(1), 2001: 190-222.

Schacht, Steven, P. "Teaching About Being an Oppressor: Some Personal and Political Considerations," *Men and Masculinities*, 4(2), 2004: 543-64.

Schlichter, Annette. "Queer at Last: Straight Intellectuals and the Desire for Transgression," *GLQ: A Journal of Lesbian and Gay Studies*, 10(4), 2004: 543-64.

Sedgwick, Eve Kosofsky. *Epistemology of the Closet*. Durham: Duke University Press, 1990.

Smyth, Ailbhe. "Queers March in Dublin, Queers March in Cork, Why Can't Queers March in New York? The ILGO St Patrick's Day Protest," *International Journal of Feminist Politics*, 2(3), 2000: 414-23.

Smyth, Cherry. *Lesbians Talk Queer Notions*. London: Scarlet Press, 1992.

Strohm, Paul. *Theory and the Premodern Text*. Minneapolis and London: University of Minnesota Press, 2000.

Thomas, Calvin, ed. *Straight With a Twist: Queer Theory and the Subject of Heterosexuality*. Urbana: University of Illinois Press, 2000.

Valente, Joseph, ed. *Quare Joyce*. Ann Arbor: University of Michigan Press, 1998.

Valentine, Gill. "'Sticks and Stones May Break My Bones': A Personal Geography of Harassment," *Antipode: A Radical Journey of Geography*, 30(4), 1998: 305-32.

Walters, Suzanna Danuta. "From Here to Queer: Radical Feminism, Postmodernism, and the Lesbian Menace (or, Why Can't a Woman Be More Like a Fag?),". *Signs: Journal of Women in Culture and Society*, 21(4), 1996: 830-69.

Warner, Michael. *Fear of a Queer Planet: Queer Politics and Social Theory*. Minneapolis and London: University of Minnesota Press, 1993.

_____. *The Trouble with Normal: Sex, Politics and the Ethics of Queer Life*. Cambridge, MA: Harvard University Press, 2000.

Weed, Elizabeth and Naomi Schor, eds. *Feminism Meets Queer Theory*. Bloomington and Indianapolis: Indiana University Press, 1997.

Weinberg, Jonathan. "Things are Queer," 1996, URL theory.org.uk.

Wilchins, Riki. "A Continuous Nonverbal Communication." In Joan Nestle, Clare Howell and Riki Wilchins, eds. *GENDERqUEER: Voices from Beyond the Sexual Binary*. Los Angeles and New York: Alyson Books, 2002: 11-17.

_____. "It's Your Gender, Stupid!" In Joan Nestle, Clare Howell and Riki Wilchins, eds. *GENDERqUEER: Voices from Beyond the Sexual Binary*. Los Angeles and New York: Alyson Books, 2002: 23-32.

_____. *Queer Theory, Gender Theory: An Instant Primer*. Los Angeles and New York: Alyson Books, 2004.

Wilson, Angelia R. "Somewhere Over the Rainbow: Queer Translating." In Shane Phelan, ed. *Playing With Fire: Queer Politics, Queer Theories*. New York and London: Routledge, 1997: 99-111.

Wilton, Tamsin. *Lesbian Studies: Setting an Agenda*. London and New York: Routledge, 1995.

Zimmerman, Bonnie. "'Confessions' of a Lesbian Feminist." In Dana Heller, ed. *Cross-Purposes: Lesbians, Feminists, and the Limits of Alliance*. Bloomington and Indianapolis: Indiana University Press, 1997: 157-68.

_____ and Toni A.H. McNaron. "Introduction." In Bonnie Zimmerman and Toni A.H. McNaron, eds. *The New Lesbian Studies: Into the Twenty-First Century*. New York: The Feminist Press, 1996: xiii-xix.

doi:10.1300/J155v11n03_10

The Un/State of Lesbian Studies:
An Introduction to Lesbian Communities
and Contemporary Legislation in Japan

Claire Maree

SUMMARY. Although it would be safe to say that Lesbian Studies has never seriously been placed on the Japanese academic agenda, women-loving-women in Japan continue to individually and collectively desist from and resist heteronormative gender discourses. This paper first gives a brief overview of *rezubian* communities since the 1970s and then outlines the Basic Law for a Gender Equal Society and the Law Concerning Special Rules Regarding Sex Status of a Person with Gender Identity Disorder; two recent laws that demonstrate contemporary regulatory gender discourses. In closing, I stress that the paradox of contem-

Claire Maree is Associate Professor at Tsuda College in Japan. Her research interests focus on the intersections of language, gender and sexuality. She is currently researching *onê-kotoba* ('queens' language). She has been active in the Japanese queer community since 1990.

Address correspondence to: Dr. Claire Maree, Department of English, Tsuda College, 2-1-1 Tsuda-machi, Kodaira-shi, Tokyo 187-8577, Japan (E-mail: maree@tsuda.ac.jp).

The author's sincere thanks go to Izumo Marou and James Welker for their support and constructive comments on drafts of this piece. All errors of judgment, of course, lie completely with the author.

[Haworth co-indexing entry note]: "The Un/State of Lesbian Studies: An Introduction to Lesbian Communities and Contemporary Legislation in Japan." Maree, Claire. Co-published simultaneously in *Journal of Lesbian Studies* (Harrington Park Press, an imprint of The Haworth Press, Inc.) Vol. 11, No. 3/4, 2007, pp. 291-301; and: *Twenty-First Century Lesbian Studies* (ed: Noreen Giffney, and Katherine O'Donnell) Harrington Park Press, an imprint of The Haworth Press, Inc., 2007, pp. 291-301. Single or multiple copies of this article are available for a fee from The Haworth Document Delivery Service [1-800-HAWORTH, 9:00 a.m. - 5:00 p.m. (EST). E-mail address: docdelivery@haworthpress.com].

porary Japanese "lesbian studies," being almost nonexistent in the
academe *and* continuously in development in the community, is clear
only if we look at academic discourses alongside writings in both
commercial and community publications. doi:10.1300/J155v11n03_11

[Article copies available for a fee from The Haworth Document Delivery Ser-
vice: 1-800-HAWORTH. E-mail address: <docdelivery@haworthpress.com>
Website: <http://www.HaworthPress.com> © 2007 by The Haworth Press, Inc.
All rights reserved.]

KEYWORDS. Japan, *resubian/rezubian*, histories of communities,
mini-komi, basic law for a gender equal society, the law concerning special rules regarding sex status of a person with gender identity disorder

As a 38-year-old lesbian with a child, I have worked for the past
ten years or so to create a safer place for lesbians in Tokyo. It has
become easier for women to love women during these ten years,
because self-identified lesbians and bisexual women have
emerged to work on lesbian issues, whether in lesbian-only
groups, with gay men or in other women's groups. (Hara 1996:
129)

In July 2005 the fourteenth annual Tokyo Lesbian and Gay Film Festival was held in central Tokyo showing a collection of works from Japan and around the world. A month later the 2005 Lesbian and Gay
Parade returned to the metropolis after an absence of two years. In previous parades, as many as 5,000 people have marched through Shibuya
ward, one of the most popular shopping precincts in the central metropolis area (Sunagawa, 2002). The Nagoya Lesbian and Gay Revolution
was held annually in June, and the Sapporo Rainbow March took place
on the furrthernmost island in September 2005.[1]

Today, in 2007 LOUD (Lesbians of Undeniable Drive) continues to
run its community space after over ten years of operation; Regumi Studio (the first lesbian space in Japan) continues after twenty years; and
the Women's Only Weekend retreat this year celebrates its twentieth
year of weekend retreats for women. The Internet, too, boasts numerous
sites run by women-loving-women for women-loving-women. These
sites list clubs, pubs and other events run by and for women in major cities throughout Japan. Although events have come and gone, bars
opened and closed, magazines launched and withdrawn from publica-

tion, in the almost ten years since Hara Minako wrote, self-identified lesbians, queers, bisexual women and their friends continue working on lesbian issues here in Japan.[2] What of work that could be identified as 'Lesbian Studies'?

It would be safe to say that Lesbian Studies in the strict sense of the study of lesbian issues for lesbians by lesbians has never seriously been placed on the Japanese academic agenda. Rather, the critical study of same-sex female sexuality remains tentatively rocking between discussions on the validity of Gay/Lesbian Studies vis-à-vis identity politics and local reinventions of Queer Studies that lean towards masculinist desires. In contradiction to (or perhaps in support of) this, however, 'Lesbian Studies' (if it exists at all today in Japan), lives in shared histories of community events, in activism and in writings by woman-loving women. In its most critical form, it is found in community-study groups, translations (from mostly English language texts into Japanese) and activist agendas (Curran and Welker, 2005). Recently, it can be seen in calls for critical attendance to same-sex-partnership rights (Akasugi, 2004; Maree, 2004) and in a growing body of academic literature on queer women's histories and communities in Japan (Chalmers, 2002; Hiruma, 2003; Horie, 2004; Iino, 2004; McLelland, 2004; Watari, 2004; Welker, 2004). I will begin by outlining contemporary lesbian histories and then introduce two recent laws that underscore the heteronormative basis of gender regulation. In closing, I stress that one can understand the paradox of 'Lesbian Studies' being almost nonexistent in the Japanese academe *and* continuously in development in the community only if we look at academic discourses alongside community activism, social events and writings in both commercial and community publications.

FORMING COMMUNITIES

As with all communities, there is no one monolithic *rezubian* (lesbian) community in Japan, rather women-loving-women and their supporters have come together to create spaces and events reflective of their needs and/or desires.[3] Although women-loving-women have been active in Japanese Feminism and other social activism for many decades, it wasn't until the 1970s and the rise of Lesbian Feminism and activism that self-identified *rezubian* (lesbian(s)) began to form social clubs and to network together as self-identified lesbians (Hiruma, 2003; Watanabe, 1998; Izumo, 2000; Odaira, 2002; McLelland, 2004; Curran Welker, 2005).

Wakakusa no kai (Young Grass Club) is widely cited as the first documented lesbian social club formed in Japan (Izumo et al., 1997; Tomioka and Hara, 1996).[4] Since it was founded in 1971, it is reported to have attracted a total of 500 members to its monthly private parties. It went on to run for fifteen years (Tomioka and Hara, 1996), by which time, monthly women's-only bars had begun operating in Shinjuku *ni-chôme*, central Tokyo's so-called gay town. In fact, by 1984, Sunny's, the first women's bar in Shinjuku ni-chôme, was in operation.[5]

In the mid-1970s to early-1980s Lesbian Feminism emerged from the Women's Liberation Movement (Buckley, 1994; Mackie, 2003). Women who met though student organizations and women's lib groups went on to form their own collectives, produce *mini-komi* magazines, declare a 'lesbian manifesto,' organize the Lesbian Feminist Centre and run consciousness-raising workshops (Izumo et al, 1997; Mackie, 2003).[6] In the 1970s 'zines called *Subarashii onnatachi* (Wonderful Women), *Za daiku* (The daiku) and *Hikari guruma* (Shining Wheel) emerged and then quickly faded.[7]

As networks formed, women organized monthly parties and feminist gatherings. For example, lesbian weekend retreats were formed by an alliance of international and Japanese feminists in 1985. These weekends were initially composed of mostly expatriate (white) women, but gradually attracted more and more Japanese women. After an incident in which organizers of the retreats were verbally harassed by the parents of a participant, *Regumi Sutajio* (Regumi Studio) opened the first lesbian community office in Tokyo in an effort to provide lesbians with a neutral safe space (Izumo et al., 1997: 64). Despite the to-be-expected member changes and internal politics, this space continues today along with the *mini-komi Regumi Tsûshin* (Regumi Report).[8]

PERSONAL HERSTORIES: LESBIAN MEMOIRS, COMING-OUT STORIES

While the 1970s and 1980s saw the emergence of numerous group *mini-komi*, lesbian spaces and lesbian weekend retreats, in the so-called *gei bûmu* (gay boom) years of the early 1990s self-identified lesbian and bisexual women organized on a larger and more public scale.[9] One offspin of this was the publication by commercial presses of books and articles by and about lesbian issues. The precursor of this wave of commercial publications was undoubtedly *Onna wo aisuru onna no monogatari* (Stories of Women who Love Women), a groundbreaking volume initiated by a member of Regumi Studio, that enabled women in rural areas to get vital information about lesbian networks and events. It wasn't until Kakefuda Hiroko's *'Rezubian' de aru to iu koto* (On Being 'Lesbian'; 1992) that the next major lesbian publication was printed. Following closely was Izumo Marou's *Manaita no ue no koi* (Love Upon the Chopping Board; Izumo and Maree, 2000). These were two very different volumes which generated an increase in lesbian visibility within mainstream media and feminism.

In the 1990s lesbian women began to 'come-out' on a more public scale. In 1995, singer Sasano Michiru released her memoir, *Coming OUT*, and CD, *girl meets girl*, in quick succession. From the mid-1990s onwards, visibility increased as did access to both traditional and new media. The first commercial magazine for lesbian and queer women, *Furîne (Phryné)*, started publication in 1995, only to quickly fold and then re-emerge as *Anîsu (Anise)* from 1996-7, and again from 2001-3. The mid-1990s saw the establishment of the Lesbian and Gay Parade, the Lesbian and Gay Film Festival, and joint club events. Stronger bonds between the gay, lesbian and bisexual communities were formed and women were the driving force behind many new community events. Queer women also became deeply involved in HIV/AIDS activism. The English language volume, *Queer Japan*, was released in 1998, while 1999 saw the publication of Ikeda Kumiko's *Sensei no rezubian sengen* (A Teacher's Lesbian Declaration).

The 1990s also saw a marked increase in academic writings on sexuality. Contemporary academic journals were published featuring translations of seminal gay/lesbian/queer work and essays and roundtables by self-identified lesbian, gay and queer activists/academics (*Imago* "Lesbian" edition, 1991; "Gay Liberation" edition, 1995; *Gendai Shisô* "Lesbian/Gay Studies" edition, 1997). Two volumes entitled *Queer Studies* appeared in 1996, 1997 and then *Queer Japan*, a journal devoted to the discussion of queer community issues began being published in 1999 (Sunagawa, 1999). A survey of 310 non-heterosexual women undertaken by the *mini-komi Labrys* was compiled as a single volume (1998), and sociologist Yajima Masami published work on the life histories of "female homosexuals" (1999).[10]

CONTEMPORARY CONTEXTUALIZATION

These events have not unfolded in a social vacuum. The period since the 1970s has been one of great social and political change. Equal opportunity legislation has meant greater participation by women in the workplace and increased media attention on queer lives has engendered greater visibility. In the context of an economy in recession and the much-published fall in birth rates, recently enacted laws also underline the complexities of envisioning gender and sexuality studies in Japan. I will briefly consider two such laws below: firstly, the Basic Law for a Gender Equal Society 1999 and secondly, the Law Concerning Special Rules Regarding Sex Status of a Person with Gender Identity Disorder.[11]

According to its preamble, the Basic Law for a Gender Equal Society was:

> ... established in order to clarify the basic principles with regard to formation of a Gender-equal Society, to set a course to this end, and to promote efforts by the State and local governments and citizens with regard to formation of a Gender-equal Society comprehensively and systematically. (Gender Equality Bureau, 1999)

This law has led to the enactment of the Law for the Prevention of Spousal Violence and the Protection of Victims, and measures known as "Support Measures for the Balancing of Work and Child Raising" and "Measures to Support Women's Challenges."[12] According to the Law Concerning Special Rules Regarding Sex Status of a Person with Gender Identity Disorder, it is now possible for Japanese nationals to apply to change their registered sex as long as:

1. An applicant should be of or above the age of twenty years.
2. An applicant should be unmarried at present.
3. An applicant should not have a child at present.
4. An applicant should not have gonad or should be in permanent loss of gonadal function.
5. An applicant should have a part of body which assumes the external genital features of the opposite sex (Onoo, 2004:188).

In other words, unmarried, childless adult nationals who have undergone sex-reassignment surgery can now alter their registered gender on legal documents.

These two laws signal immense change on the national level. They also underwrite static notions of gender, however, that are intrinsically linked to the family. In regards to the gender-equality law, "women" and "men" are presented as fixed categories from which individuals form unions only in the realm of the family. As the act regarding changing one's registered sex indicates, it is now possible for individuals to enter these categories afresh, however, the state will only recognize this in accordance with specific regulations. Furthermore, the conditions preventing married persons and/or those with children from changing their registered sex effectively prescribes a rigid semantics to 'wife' and 'husband,' 'mother' and 'father.'

In other words, ways of understanding gendered bodies are confined to the binary of woman/man and set within the limits of heteronormative marriage and parenthood. Paradoxically, same-sex sex is imagined within this feminine/masculine binary that positions gay men as feminine and lesbian women as masculine. Whereas the image of the effeminate gay male is circulated in popular culture, however, the image of the lesbian (whether masculine or otherwise) is more difficult to imagine. As Sharon Chalmers states so succinctly:

> ... within mainstream representations, lesbian desire becomes the quintessential 'imaginary anatomy' for despite the fact that they do not rely on a position in relation and subordinate to male desire, lesbians are generally marked by male desire. These images are disseminated through popularised cultural myths. (Chalmers, 2001)

While I in no way wish to negate the very real experiences of transsexual individuals in Japan, or diminish the work of Japanese feminists with regard to laws on gender equality, I sit these two laws side by side here to identify contemporary gender regulation, and the way in which this sidesteps issues of state enforced heteronormativity. For, while at first seeming to simultaneously embrace the queer *and* to engage in gender equality, these very laws circumvent alternative discourses on gender and sexuality. I would argue that a similar position is echoed in much research done in the name of feminism and gender and/or sexuality studies.

QUEERYING THE ACADEME, OR, WHERE ARE THE GRRRRLS?

A search through the national Directory Database of Research and Development Activities (READ) results in a listing of twenty-six academics registered who have the word 'lesbian (*rezubian*)' in either their listing of published works or in the description of their current research interests. A similar search for 'female/woman, homosexual (*onna, dôseiai*)' gives two hits, 'homosexual (*dôseiai*)' eighty-one hits, 'queer (*kuiâ*)' nine hits, 'sexuality (*sekushuaritî*)' returns a whopping 237.[13] Interestingly, a search of Japanese language journals published between 1983-2005 and held at the National Diet Library gives 114 papers with the word '*rezubian*' in the title.[14] Apart from the special 'Gay/Lesbian Studies' edition of *Gendai Shisô* mentioned above, the listing includes a twenty-piece series by Horie Yuri in *Fukuin to Sekai* (Gospel and World) from 2003-4, entitled 'Rezubian to iu ikikata (A Way of Life Called Lesbian)', the 'lesbian studies' and 'Lesbian/Gay Studies' special issues of *Kaihôshakaigaku kenkyû* (The Liberation of Humankind: A Sociological Review 2003, 2004) and a six-part series by Takemura Kazuko entitled the 'Rezubian Kenkyû no kanôsei (The Possibility of Lesbian Research)' in the English studies journal, *Eigo Seinen* (1996).

These results reflect the current state in the Japanese academe. Firstly, we can see that studies of sexuality outnumber those of specific sexual minorities. Furthermore, a small number of scholars continue to work on issues of gender and sexuality. Coupled with the community histories outlined above, it is clear that activism and academia converge and diverge in academic, community and *mini-komi* publications. In response to the seemingly simultaneous engagement of the queer and circumvention of critiques of heteronormativity, what could be understood as 'lesbian studies' has grown in the form of alternative discourses (*mini-komi*, commercial magazines, translations, memoirs and declarations) from within communities of diverse women.

Given this, the question, 'what is the un/state of lesbian studies in Japan?' seems a relatively useless one to pose. Lesbian studies cannot survive in the academy if it is understood to presuppose a utopian sameness always already too narrow to accommodate multiple lived experiences of woman/female-to-woman/female-for-woman/female desire. Paradoxically, it continues to live on because individuals who experience the regulation of their gender and sexuality work both individually and collectively to resist that regulation by forming communities, being politically active, and/or socially connected via spaces, events and publications (including translations). As we have seen, the paradox of 'Lesbian Studies' being both simultaneously nonexistent *and* continuously in development is clear only if we look at academic discourses alongside writings found in *mini-komi* magazines and other alternative and/or popular media in Japan.

NOTES

1. The Nagoya Gay and Lesbian Revolution commenced as a gay event in 2001, the following year it was renamed.

2. All Japanese names are written according to the Japanese convention of surname followed by given name.

3. For a discussion on the words 'resubian' and 'rezubian' see Curran and Welker (2005).

4. It is necessary to stress that Wakakusa no kai is the first documented social group, not necessarily the first ever group.

5. Space restrictions prevent a discussion of either the bar/entertainment industry prior to the emergence of 'women's bars', or of bars that existed in areas other than *ni-chôme*.

6. *Mini-komi* are the equivalent to newsletters or current day zines. Buckley notes the importance of *mini-komi* to women's liberation and other feminist movements (1994).

7. The characters used for this publication *daiku* mean 'carpenter' the pronunciation of which is identical to the Japanese pronunciation of the English 'dyke'.

8. The name 'Regumi' is formed by taking the first sound 're' from 'rezubian' (lesbian) and adding 'kumi' (group).

9. While this 1990s is often referred to as the 'gay boom' era, it is not the only documented period where homosexuality or gay/lesbian issues have been the focus of widespread media attention. While there is still much work to be done in this area, for recent scholarship see Hiruma (2003); McLelland (2004); Curran and Welker (2005).

10. This is a companion to Yajima's earlier volume on life histories of 'male homosexuals' (1997).

11. In Japanese it is: *seidôitsusei shôgai no seibetsu no tori atsukai no tokurei ni kansuru hôritsu*. A translation of this law appears in Onoo 2004; a manual regarding the law overseen by Member of the House of Councilors, Onoo Chieko and with commentary by medical and legal professionals.

12. The Basic Law for a Gender Equal Society is comprised of five basic principles: 1. Respect for the human rights of women and men; 2. Consideration to social systems and practices; 3. Joint participation in planning and deciding policies; 4. Compatibility of activities in family life and other activities; 5. International co-operation. The most recent report published by the Gender Equality Bureau states that "the Japanese government puts emphasis on increasing the percentage of female leaders to at least 30% in every field of society by the year 2020 as the priority target."

13. This search of the READ (Directory of Research and Development Activities) database was conducted in April 2005.

14. The National Diet Library has the largest holding of journals published in Japan. The on-line electronic database dates back to 1983 and can be searched online. NDL-OPAC (journal) search was conducted in April 2005.

REFERENCES

AMPO-Japan Asia Quarterly Review, ed. *Voices from the Japanese Women's Movement*. Armonk, New York and London: M.E. Sharpe, 1996.

Anîsu (Anise), 1996.

Akasugi, Yasunobu, Tsuchiya Yuki and Tsutsui Makiko, eds. *Dôsei pâtonâ: Dôseikon/DP-hô wo shiru tame ni* (Same-Sex Partners: To Learn of Same-Sex Marriage and DP Laws). Tokyo: Shakaihihyô-sha, 2004.

Bessatsu Takarajima, 64. *Onna o aisuru onnatachi no monogatari* (Stories of Women Who Love Women). Tokyo: JICC Shuppankyoku, 1987.

Buckley, Sandra. "A Short History of the Feminist Movement in Japan." In Joyce Gelb, Marian Lief Palley, eds. *Women of Japan and Korea: Continuity and Change.* Philadelphia: Temple University Press, 1994: 150-86.

Chalmers, Sharon. "Tolerance, Form and Female Dis-ease: The Pathologisation of Lesbian Sexuality in Japanese Society," *Intersections*, 6, 2001. URL sshe.murdoch. edu.au/intersections/issue6/chalmers.html#n100.

_____. *Emerging Lesbian Voices from Japan.* Richmond, UK: Curzon, 2002.

Curran, Beverley, and James Welker. "From *The Well of Loneliness* to *Akarui rezubian.*" In Mark McLelland and Romit Dasgupta, eds. *Genders, Transgenders, and Sexualities in Japan.* London and New York: Routledge, 2005: 65-80.

Directory Database of Research and Development Activities. 17 April 2005, URL read.jst.go.jp.

Faderman, Lillian. R*esubian no rekishi* (Odd Girls and Twilight Lovers: A History of Lesbian Life in Twentieth Century America), trans. Tomioka Akemi and Hara Minako. Tokyo: Chikuma Shobô, 1996.

Furîne (Phryné), 1995.

Gendai Shisô. Rezubian/gei sutadeîzu (Lesbian/Gay Studies), 25-6, 1997.

Gender Equality Bureau, Cabinet Office. The Basic Law for a Gender-equal Society (Law No. 78 of 1999). 17 April 2005, URL gender.go.jp.

Hara, Minako. "Lesbians and Sexual Self-determination," AMPO-Japan Asia Quarterly Review, 1996: 129-32.

Hiruma, Yukiko. "Kindai Nihon ni okeru josei dôseiai no 'hakken' ('Discovery' of Female Homosexuality in Modern Japan)," *Kaihôshakaigaku kenkyû*, 17, 2003: 9-32.

Horie, Yuri. "Rezubian to iu ikikata (A Way of Life Called Lesbian)," *Fukuin to sekai* (Gospel and World), 58(1)-59(12), 2003-4.

_____. "Rezubian no fukashisei (Invisibility of Lesbians: On the Case of the United Church of Christ in Japan)," *Kaihôshakaigaku kenkyû*, 18, 2004: 39-60.

Iino, Yuriko. "Nihon no rezubian-feminisuto no sutôrî o yominaosu (Re-Reading Stories by Lesbian-Feminists in Japan)," *Kaihôshakaigaku kenkyû*, 18, 2004: 18-38.

Ikeda, Kumiko. *Sensei no rezubian sengen: Tsunagaru tame no kamuauto* (Teacher's Lesbian Declaration: Coming-Out to Connect). Kyoto: Kamogawa Shuppan, 1999.

Imâgo. Rezubian (Lesbian), 2-8, 1991.

_____. Gei riberêshon (Gay Liberation), 6-12, 1995.

Izumo, Marou. *Manaita no ue no koi* (Love Upon the Chopping Board). Tokyo: Takarajima-sha, 1993.

_____, Hara Minako, Tsuzura Yoshiko and Ochiya Kumiko. "Nihon no rezubian mûbumento (The Japanese Lesbian Movement)," *Gendai Shisô*, 25(6), 1997: 58-83.

_____ and Claire Maree. *Love Upon the Chopping Board.* Melbourne: Spinifex Press, 2000.

Kakefuda, Hiroko. *'Rezubian' de aru to iu koto* (On Being 'Lesbian'). Tokyo: Kawade Shobô Shinsha, 1992.·

Kokuritsu Kokkai Toshokan (National Diet Library), Zasshi kiji sakin (Index of journal articles), 17 April 2005, URL opac.ndl.go.jp

Mackie, Vera. *Feminism in Modern Japan.* Melbourne: Cambridge University Press, 2003.

Maree, Claire. "Same-Sex Partnerships in Japan: Bypasses and Other Alternatives," *Women's Studies*, 33(4), 2004: 541-9.

McLelland, Mark. "From Sailor-Suits to Sadists: 'Lesbos Love' as Reflected in Japan's Postwar 'Perverse pPress'," *US-Japan Women's Journal*, 27, 2004: 3-26.

Nagoya Gay and Lesbian Revolution. Nagoya Gay and Lesbian Revolution 2005. 17 April 2005. URL aln-nlgr.cside.com/ nlgr2005/js/purpose.htm

Odaira, Maiko. "Keredo anata! Bungaku o sutete wa shinai desho ne," *"Joshi bundan aidokuisha-jô to yokubô suru anetachi,"* *Bungaku,* 3(10), 2002: 134-47.

Onoo, Chieko, ed. *(Kaisetsu) Seidôitsuseishôgaisha seibetsu toriatsukai tokureihô* (Manual: Exemption Law for the Sex Status of People with Gender-Identity Disorder). Tokyo: Nihon Kajo Shuppan, 2004.

Queer Japan, 1, 1999.

Kuia sutadîzu henshû iinkai, eds. *Queer Studies '96.* Tokyo: Nanatsumori shokan, 1996.

_____, eds. *Queer Studies '97.* Tokyo: Nanatsumori shokan, 1997.

Sasano, Michiru. *Coming OUT!* Tokyo: Gentôsha, 1995.

_____. *Girl Meets Girl.* Victor, 1995.

Sawabe, Hitomi. *Yuriko dasuvidâniya: Yuasa Yoshiko no seishun* (Yuriko, do syvidanya: Yuasa Yoshiko's Youth). Tokyo: Bungeishunjû, 1990.

Sei ishiki chôsa gurûpu, eds. *310nin no seiishiki: Iseiaisha de wa nai onnatachino ankêto chôsa* (The Sexual Consciousness of 310 people: A Survey of Women Who Are Not Heterosexual). Tokyo: Nanatsumori Shokan, 1998.

Summerhawk, Barbara, Cheiron McMahill and Darren McDonald, trans. and eds. *Queer Japan: Personal Stories of Japanese Lesbians, Gays, Bisexuals and Transsexuals.* Norwich: New Victoria Publishers, 1998.

Sunagawa, Hideki. *Parêdo: Tokyo rezubian and gei parêdo 2000 no kiroku* (Parade: A Record of the Tokyo Lesbian and Gay Parade 2000). Tokyo: Potto Shuppan, 2001.

_____. "Nihon no gei/rezubian studies (Japanese Gay/Lesbian Studies)," *Queer Japan,* 1, 1999: 135-51.

Takemura, Kazuko. "Rezubian Kenkyû no kanôsei (The Possibility of Lesbian Research)," *Eigo seinen,* July-December, 1996.

Tsutsui, Makiko. "Transgender to pâtonâshippu: iseiaishugi to seibetsu nigensei wo koete (Transgender and Partnership: Surpassing Heterosexism and Sex Binarism," Akasugi: Tsuchiya and Tsutsui, 2004: 206-23.

Watanabe, Mieko. *"Seitô ni okeru rezubianism (Lesbianism in Seitô)."* In Shin feminizumu hihyô no kai, eds. *Seitô o yomu* (Reading *Bluestocking*). Tokyo: Gakugei Shorin. 1998.

Watari, Akeshi. "Rezubian sutadeîzu to shakaigaku (Lesbian Studies and Sociology)," *Kaihôshakaigaku kenkyû,* 18, 2004: 10-12.

Welker, James. "Telling her story: Narrating a Japanese Lesbian Community." In Andrea Germer and Andreas Moerke, eds. *Grenzgänge–(De-) Konstruktion kollektiver Identitäten in Japan (Crossing Borders–[De-] Construction of Collective Identities in Japan), Japanstudien: Jahrbuch des Deutschen Instituts für Japanstudiesn 16.* Munich: Iudicium, 2004: 119-44.

Yajima, Masami, ed. *Dansei dôseiaisha no raifu hisutorî* (Life Histories of Male Homosexuals). Tokyo: Gakubunsha 1997.

_____, ed. *Josei dôseiaisha no raifu hisutorî* (Life Histories of Female Homosexuals). Tokyo: Gakubunsha 1999.

doi:10.1300/J155v11n03_11

Peripheral Perspectives:
Locating Lesbian Studies in Australasia

Sara MacBride-Stewart

SUMMARY. In this paper I identify the key differences and similarities between New Zealand and Australian Lesbian Studies. Until recently, Australian and New Zealand perspectives have been viewed separately. The possible reasons for these differences are discussed and local understandings about diversity that have played a role in the destabilization of Lesbian Studies are considered. I proceed to consider the influence of Queer Theory on teaching and research in Lesbian Studies. doi:10.1300/J155v11n03_12 *[Article copies available for a fee from The Haworth Document Delivery Service: 1-800-HAWORTH. E-mail address: <docdelivery@haworthpress.com> Website: <http://www.HaworthPress.com> © 2007 by The Haworth Press, Inc. All rights reserved.]*

Sara MacBride-Stewart is a Lecturer in the School of Social Sciences at Cardiff University, Wales. She is currently working on projects on "Women's Experiences of Pelvic Pain" and "Professionalism, Feminisation and Medicine." Her research work and related publications are in the areas of heteronormativity and cervical screening, dental dams, and discourses of lesbian health.

Address correspondence to: Dr. Sara MacBride-Stewart, School of Social Sciences, Cardiff University, Glamorgan Building, King Edward VII Avenue, Cardiff, CF10 3WT, Wales (E-mail: macbride-stewarts@cardiff.ac.uk).

Many thanks to Victoria Clarke, Merryn Smith, Hernan Camilo Pulido-Martinez and other reviewers for their comments on an earlier version of this paper.

[Haworth co-indexing entry note]: "Peripheral Perspectives: Locating Lesbian Studies in Australasia." MacBride-Stewart, Sara. Co-published simultaneously in *Journal of Lesbian Studies* (Harrington Park Press, an imprint of The Haworth Press, Inc.) Vol. 11, No. 3/4, 2007, pp. 303-311; and: *Twenty-First Century Lesbian Studies* (ed: Noreen Giffney, and Katherine O'Donnell) Harrington Park Press, an imprint of The Haworth Press, Inc., 2007, pp. 303-311. Single or multiple copies of this article are available for a fee from The Haworth Document Delivery Service [1-800-HAWORTH, 9:00 a.m. - 5:00 p.m. (EST). E-mail address: docdelivery@haworthpress.com].

KEYWORDS. New Zealand, Australia, lesbian studies, queer studies, identity

LOCATION AND RELATION IN AUSTRALASIA

At the request of the special issue editors I have drawn together New Zealand and Australian perspectives. While the reference to New Zealand/Australia assumes a set of shared histories, geographies, institutions, economies, effects of colonization and im/migration, in actuality, the political and social histories of these two countries are diverse. For example, the population of both countries is small, but New Zealand's approximately 4,000,000 residents are overshadowed by Australia's 200 million. Despite both nations still existing as formal members of the British Commonwealth, in Australia public support for independence from the British Crown is stronger than in New Zealand. Both countries are democracies, with New Zealand currently represented as having a more liberal political structure and government, in comparison to the conservative political structure and government that exist in Australia. The distinctions do not end here. While academics from North America and the UK possibly overemphasise the similarities between New Zealand and Australia, local academics and historians in particular often fail to give due credit to the influence that New Zealand and Australia have on the other. As the idea of globalization has taken force, the eighteenth-century term, 'Australasia,' has resurfaced both locally and internationally, as a reference to the relations between New Zealand and Australia; Australasia has emerged as a political and cultural entity which shares a history of being settled by Europeans at a similar time in the late 1700s (Mein Smith and Hempenstall, 2003).

Studying both nations' stories together is a new task for many academics, and in Lesbian Studies few publications highlight the relations between both places (Riggs and Walker, 2004; Robinson et al, 2002). Riggs and Walker, in particular, argue for the importance of exploring the contexts that have shaped research in both places. They suggest that this work requires paying attention to broader disciplinary approaches for organizing sexuality and gender, while considering the ways such approaches have been taken up in New Zealand and Australia. They conclude that differences in Gay and Lesbian Psychology in New Zealand and Australia are shaped by New Zealand's smaller size, lack of a specific psychological code of ethics and the existence of an institutional culture that emphasizes diversity.

There are important distinctions between the two nations' perspectives on diversity that must be considered before I proceed. In New Zealand, understandings about how individuals come to experience their ethnicity emerge out of a discourse of bicultural politics, which is based on making a distinction between, what I will simply refer to here as, indigenous Maori and settler (mainly British and European) identities. In the 1980s, New Zealand officially became a bicultural nation formed in the idea that the cultural identity of either group would be accommodated and protected in all areas of their lives. An originary treaty in 1840 between the British Crown and Maori representatives is a primary means for organizing the apparent protections offered by biculturalism. As a legal document it is incorporated into many policy frameworks, and it continues to inform cultural understandings about how the relationships between the dominant and minority ethnic groups in New Zealand should be organized. In Australia, understandings about ethnicity are organized in a different way, around a discourse of multiculturalism which is based on a set of beliefs about the right of individuals to have and express their cultural diversity. There is no expectation, however, that any group should be included or that they will be protected. Consequently, different versions of diversity as a legal, political and social discourse for understanding ethnicity have predominated.

LESBIAN STUDIES IN AUSTRALASIA

The strongest ties between New Zealand and Australian Lesbian Studies reflect the influence of ideas from North America and England. There has been nothing distinct about an Australasian perspective that has produced alternative definitions to those from North America or the UK. Zimmerman argues that the development of Lesbian Studies was deeply influenced by Feminism:

> . . . the field was strongly and unmistakably flavoured by . . . Lesbian feminism which is rooted in the specificity of lesbians. It assumes that lesbians differ from heterosexual women and gay men [sharing] a common border with lesbian separatism. (1996: 270)

As will become evident, Lesbian and Gay Studies made a greater impact in Australia, than did Lesbian Studies. The distinctions between the two fields can be understood in relation to concerns about gender. Lesbian Studies views 'lesbian' as a meaningful category which, for les-

bian feminists, provides the basis for an analysis of patriarchal social
structures and institutions; it distinguishes itself from Lesbian and Gay
Studies which, in contrast, is argued to be unconcerned with the effects
of gender (Jagose, 1996).

Lesbian Studies began informally in New Zealand and Australia during the early 1970s. As elsewhere, the origin of Lesbian Studies lay in
the consciousness-raising movements of women's rights and became
institutionalized in university-teaching programmes often as part of
Women's Studies programmes (Jagose, 1996, Laurie, 2001). There are
a number of Australasian anthologies that have detailed the accomplishments that mark lesbian studies as a discipline. Reproducing the style of
anthologies such as Bonnie Zimmerman and Toni McNaron's *The New
Lesbian Studies* (1996), Australasian efforts attempt to reflect the specific and local contexts of Australia and New Zealand (Laurie, 2001;
Willett, 2001).

Susan Sayer (1996), in her account of Lesbian Studies in Aotearoa/
New Zealand, listed conferences and university courses (many now re-
dundant), academics, publications, literary work and graduate research
projects. Other accounts identify lesbian archives and organizations
(Laurie, 2001). These accomplishments mainly highlight local interests, for example, by tracing personal archives of regional lesbian newsletters. Some of the information included in the anthologies does,
however, represent wider interests and includes information, for example, about national historical lesbian and gay archives such as the Lesbian and Gay Archives of New Zealand (owned by a trust and housed in
the National Library of New Zealand), or the substantial and volun-
tarily-run, Australian Lesbian and Gay Archives Services, which is
based in Melbourne. The recent New Zealand Lesbian Studies anthology (Laurie, 2001) focussed on local historical figures (such as male-
impersonators, Amy Brock and Mr X, and artist, Francis Hodgkins),
and included some research on social issues (such as parenting, coming
out and family law) and literary texts (the novels by Annamarie Jagose).

Australia has a much stronger tradition of Lesbian and Gay studies,
or Lesbian, Gay, Bisexual and Transgender (LGBT) Studies compared
to New Zealand. Willett's (2001) text is a historical account of the last
thirty-plus years of gay and lesbian activism in Australia. It has been
suggested that his account has considered the impact of Lesbian Feminism and activism only where it occurs in relation to what gay men have
achieved (Baird, 2001). This stronger emphasis on Lesbian and Gay
studies is also evident in the organization of events, such as the program
of academic and activist conferences, which occurred during the 2002

Sydney Gay Games, and as well as in academic publications (Riggs and Walker, 2004). In their introduction to *Out in the Antipodes*, Damien Riggs and Gordon A. Walker (2004) give an example of how the Australian Psychological Society has membership structures, such as the Interest Group for Gay and Lesbian Issues in Psychology, which produces resources like the *Guidelines for Psychological Practice with Lesbian, Gay and Bisexual Clients* and a fact sheet on *Sexual Orientation*; the same initiatives do not exist in New Zealand. Despite this, Lesbian and Gay Studies in New Zealand has always been significantly influenced by ideas coming from Australia, highlighting an apparent expansion of academic work out from its centres in the UK and North America. The historical accounts make no comments about whether Lesbian and Gay Studies and politics in Australasia has made any significant impact in the reverse, that is, upon scholarship in the UK and North America.

CRITIQUE OF LESBIAN STUDIES

I want to briefly reflect on the impact that debates about diversity have made on the current status of Lesbian Studies in Australasia. During the 1980s and '90s, the attempt by lesbian feminists to produce a coherent account about what it means to be a lesbian generated some awareness that the category 'lesbian' may not reflect the experiences of all women. This was particularly so for (indigenous) Maori women in New Zealand. New identity terms like 'wahine takataapui' (Maori reference to lesbian, gay and/or transgendered) were brought into parlance during the 1990s by Maori lesbians publicly involved in lesbian community politics and Lesbian Studies (Sayer, 1996). The production of these new identity categories in New Zealand, and the relative silencing of indigenous women in Australia, served to further emphasize the exclusiveness of lesbian as an identity category.

Jagose (1996) has argued that accounts like those published by Maori academics, Michelle Erai and Ngahuia Te Awekotuku (1992) about their perspectives as Maori lesbians can contribute to representations of lesbian diversity. She argues that they remain insufficient for destabilizing the notion of a unitary lesbian identity that was so popular within Lesbian Feminism. It may seem obvious to state this, but the implications of a bicultural politics are important. The understanding of diversity that gets represented here is one of 'equal but different.' The expectation that Maori women have of mainstream feminist politics is that 'inclusion' occurs on a basis that it is self-determining, that is, Maori women have the right to determine how and why they are represented. There are similarities to Lesbian Feminism with what Jagose describes as an 'ethnic' model of identity, which promotes the "'equal but different' logic of the civil rights movement" (1996: 61). Jagose goes on to argue that, "despite its origins in a race-based politics, the ethnic model's gay and lesbian subject is white . . . the ethnic model could only theorise race as an insubstantial or, at best, an additional category of identification" (1996: 62-3). So despite the possibilities of biculturalism or Lesbian Feminism, new ways of theorizing relationships between sexuality and ethnicity have been sought.

More recently, Maori and Australian indigenous lesbians have attempted to re-theorize sexuality and gender by drawing on frameworks emerging from their own cultural perspectives, with the consequence of providing possible alternatives to what is known, even in New Zealand and Australia, as a Western model of sexuality. As Jagose argues, the possibility that lesbians have not been able to represent themselves as a coherent community deteriorated into frustration "with the categories of identification themselves and a questioning of their efficacy for political intervention" (1996: 71).

LESBIAN QUEER STUDIES

The organization of Lesbian Studies around the concerns of gender meant that it has also been particularly affected by the recent loss of many Women's and Gender Studies programmes at Australasian universities. Women's Studies programmes, like those at Canterbury University which had been in existence for up to 15 years, have been substantially restructured, partly as a result of the move to operate publically-owned New Zealand universities on a business model. As many Gender Studies departments in New Zealand are restructured into a programme of study taught by affiliated rather than dedicated staff members, Gender Studies has come to reflect the disciplinary and individual contributions of the staff attached to each of these programmes, including Sociology, Literature, Philosophy, Critical Race Studies, Visual Culture, Postcolonial Theory, Cultural History and Queer Theories. The development of dedicated courses in Sexuality Studies in New Zealand and Australia has not guaranteed the inclusion of Lesbian Studies or Queer Lesbian Studies perspectives. Where it does occur, such courses are likely to offer a historicized critique of lesbian identity politics or subsume gay and lesbian issues together.

Although I have argued that Lesbian Studies in Australasia has had little influence on North America and the UK, the same cannot be said of Queer Theories. Academics based in New Zealand or Australia have made substantial contributions to writing histories of Queer Theory, such as the internationally recognized introductory texts by Annamarie Jagose (1996; see also 1994) and Nikki Sullivan (2003). Certainly, the impact of other sexuality theorists who live or have lived in Australia and who have produced influential works to rival anything from that of the Anglo-American hegemony can not go unmentioned, for example, Shelia Jeffreys, Elizabeth Grosz, Elspeth Probyn and Barbara Creed, as well as David Halperin, Barry D. Adam, Alan McKee and Robert Altman. Notably Queer Theories in New Zealand and Australia are both located in and inform a particularly Antipodean version of Cultural and Critical Studies or Gender Studies, marked by events or topics which reflect the regionality of sexuality and gender, such as the Sydney Mardi Gras or Western imaginings about sexuality amongst Pacific peoples (Wallace, 2003).

Queer Studies represents different ideological positions for theorizing sexuality and its relationship to gender in comparison with Lesbian Studies. While Lesbian Studies focuses on the importance of sexual identity for understanding our sexual desires and relationships, Queer Theory questions taken-for-granted assumptions about sexual identity, including its perceived importance and the means by which it comes about. As Nikki Sullivan explains:

> . . . sexuality is not natural, rather it is discursively constructed . . . experienced and understood in culturally and historically specific ways. Thus we could say that there can be no true or correct account of heterosexuality, of homosexuality, of bisexuality, and so on, [and that] contemporary views of particular relationships and practices are no more enlightened or any less symptomatic of the times than those held by previous generations. (2003: 1)

Sullivan provides an account of how queer texts from Australasia may be read and interpreted in numerous ways by local and non-local audiences. For example, she discusses how Australasian references like 'sticky rice' act as a label to describe relationships between Australian-Asian same-sex couples, while also identifying how sexual practices get modelled on sexual relations as they are lived.This term highlights how sexual relations in Australasia are based upon the expectations of a globalized and disaporic regionality that also includes South East Asia and the Pacific (2003: 74).

Judith Halberstam suggests that such an alternate pedagogical approach to Lesbian Studies could be referred to as Queer Lesbian Studies. A characteristic of Queer Lesbian Studies is a concentration on the importance of historical analysis, "emphasizing the historical shifts within the social meaning of sexuality and also in terms of remaining aware of the history of lesbian studies and women's studies" (1996: 260). Although the term, 'Queer Lesbian Studies' is not often used in New Zealand or Australia, there are examples of work which represents what Halberstam is attempting to reference here (Alice and Star, 2004). Notably, there are also critiques of Queer Studies, on the basis that it does not adequately address the specificity of lesbian experiences (Jeffreys, 2003).

The approaches described here (lesbian feminist, queer lesbian, LGBT) reflect the dominant mode in which Lesbian Studies is taught in New Zealand and Australia. Lesbian Studies does not currently hold prominence in either country. This situation is not unique to New Zealand or Australia; it reflects the academic discourse currently witnessed in North America and the UK, concerning the limitations of managing diversity, the difficulties of teaching Lesbian Studies and concerns that Queer Theory has abandoned a focus on the specificities of women's sexualities. In contrast, Queer Studies in Australasia seems to have a broader significance in relation to the extensive ways in which sexuality and gender impact culturally upon everyday lives.

REFERENCES

Alice, Lynne and Lynne Star, eds. *Queer in Aotearoa New Zealand*. New Zealand: Dunmore Press, 2004.

Baird, Barbara. "Living Out Loud: A History of Gay and Lesbian Activism by Graham Willett," *Australian Humanities Review*, April 2001, http://www.lib.latrobe. edu.au/AHR/archive/Issue-April-2001/baird.html (8 May 2005).

Brickell, Chris. "Heroes and Invaders: Gay and Lesbian Pride Parades and the Public/ Private Distinction in the New Zealand Media Accounts." *Gender, Place and Culture*, 7 (2000): 163-78.

Halberstam, Judith. "Queering Lesbian Studies." In Bonnie Zimmerman and Toni McNaron, eds. *The New Lesbian Studies: Into the Twenty-First Century*. New York: The Feminist Press, 1996: 256-61.

Jagose, Annamarie. *Queer Theory: An Introduction*. New York: New York University Press, 1996.

_____. *Lesbian Utopics*. New York: Routledge, 1994.

Jeffreys, Shelia. *Unpacking Queer Politics: A Lesbian Feminist Perspective*, Cambridge: Polity Press, 2003.

Laurie, Alison, J. "Foreword," *Journal of Lesbian Studies*, 5 (1/2), 2001: xxv-xxxii.

_____, ed. *Lesbian Studies in Aotearoa/New Zealand*. New York: Harrington Park Press, 2001.

Mein Smith, Philippa and Peter Hempenstall. "Australia and New Zealand: Turning Shared Pasts into a Shared History," *Literature Compass*. Oxford: Blackwell, 2003: http://www.history-compass.com/splash/default.htm (7 May 2005).

Riggs, Damien, W. and Gordon A. Walker, eds. *Out in the Antipodes: Australian and New Zealand Perspectives on Gay and Lesbian Issues in Psychology*. Bently, WA: Brightfire Press, 2004.

Robinson, Kerry, Jude Irwin and Tania Ferfolja, eds. *From Here to Diversity: The Social Impact of Lesbian and Gay Issues in Education in Australia and New Zealand* Binghamton, NY: Harrington Park Press, 2002.

Sayer, Susan. "'Out of the Blue': Lesbian Studies in Aotearoa/New Zealand." In Bonnie Zimmerman and Toni A.H. McNaron, eds. *The New Lesbian Studies: Into the Twenty-First Century*. New York: The Feminist Press, 1993, 240-6.

Sullivan, Nikki. *A Critical Introduction to Queer Theory*. Edinburgh: Edinburgh University Press, 2003.

Te Awekotuku, Ngahuia. "Kia Mau, Kia Manawanui: We Will Never Go Away: Experiences of a Maori Lesbian Feminist." In Rosemary Du Plessis et al., eds. *Feminist Voices: Women's Studies Texts for Aotearoa/New Zealand*. Auckland: Oxford University Press, 1992: 278-89.

Wallace, Lee. *Sexual Encounters: Pacific Texts, Modern Sexualities*. Cornell: Cornell University Press, 2003.

Willett, Graham. *Living Out Loud: A History of Gay and Lesbian Activism in Australia*. Sydney: Allen and Unwin, 2000.

Zimmerman, Bonnie and Toni A.H. McNaron. "Introduction." In Bonnie Zimmerman and Toni A.H. McNaron, eds. *The New Lesbian Studies: Into the Twenty-First Century*. New York: The Feminist Press, 1996: xiii-xix.

_____. "Placing Lesbians." In Bonnie Zimmerman and Toni A.H. McNaron, eds. *The New Lesbian Studies: Into the Twenty-First Century*. New York: The Feminist Press, 1996: 269-76.

doi:10.1300/J155v11n03_12

'Russian Love,'
or What of Lesbian Studies in Russia?

Nadya Nartova

SUMMARY. This piece discusses the problems attending to the development of Lesbian Studies in Russia. doi:10.1300/J155v11n03_13 [Article copies available for a fee from The Haworth Document Delivery Service: 1-800-HAWORTH. E-mail address: <docdelivery@haworthpress.com> Website: <http://www.HaworthPress.com> © 2007 by The Haworth Press, Inc. All rights reserved.]

KEYWORDS. Homosexuality, lesbian studies, Russia, gender

RUSSIA IN 2005

One can see Russian lesbian internet sites, in some towns there are lesbian discos, in big cities lesbian couples can be seen hugging, while

---

Nadya Nartova is conducting sociological research in the Centre for Independent Social Research in St. Petersburg, Russia, and is a PhD student at the European University in St. Petersburg. Her research interests include Feminist Theory, Gender Studies, sociology of sexuality, Gay/Lesbian Studies. Her recent publications include "'Freaks and People': Heterosexuality and Lesbianism." *Gender Studies*, 10, 2004: 197-206 (rus); and "Lesbian Families: Reality Behind the Wall of Silence." In S. Oushakin, ed. *Wedlock: Construction Models*, vol. 1. Moskow: NLO, 2004: 292-315 (rus).

Address correspondence to: Nadya Nartova, P.O. Box 193, St. Petersburg, Russia 191040 (E-mail: nadich@eu.spb.ru).

[Haworth co-indexing entry note]: "'Russian Love,' or What of Lesbian Studies in Russia?" Co-published simultaneously in *Journal of Lesbian Studies* (Harrington Park Press, an imprint of The Haworth Press, Inc.) Vol. 11, No. 3/4, 2007, pp. 313-320; and: *Twenty-First Century Lesbian Studies* (ed: Noreen Giffney, and Katherine O'Donnell) Harrington Park Press, an imprint of The Haworth Press, Inc., 2007, pp. 313-320. Single or multiple copies of this article are available for a fee from The Haworth Document Delivery Service [1-800-HAWORTH, 9:00 a.m. - 5:00 p.m. (EST). E-mail address: docdelivery@haworthpress.com].

in bookstores one might find a translation of *The Lesbian Body* (1975) by Monique Wittig or *Epistemology of Closet* (1990) by Eve Kosofsky Sedgwick. What would someone interested in Lesbian Studies find? In the last four years five empirical articles have been published in Russian. This seems very little. Perhaps Gay or Queer Studies more generally are in progress? These studies are more numerous, but I would rather not say that this school is more successful or that it overtakes Lesbian Studies. To understand what is going on, I suggest reviewing the development of the study of homosexuality in Russia, beginning with the Soviet period. It is important to emphasize now that I am focusing on studies in Russia, in Russian and so will not be including foreign research on Russia.[1] Moreover, taking into account the objectives of this collection of essays, I will focus my study of homosexuality on lesbianism, thus excluding transsexualism, drag and bisexuality.

During almost the whole Soviet period, homosexuality among men was a criminal offense and therefore it was constructed/produced, regulated and controlled in a specific way by the legal discourse that included legislative codification and adjudicative practice. The production of men's homosexuality as a criminal offense led not only to control over homosexual practices, but also to control over other spheres, for example, in the field of Science through an informal taboo on alluding to homosexuality and homoeroticism even in studies of ancient cultures (Kon, 1997: 355). Homosexuality among women was not criminalized, but was under the control of another discourse, that of medicine:

> "Homosexualism is a strong defect. At that a lot of people suffer from their pathology, feel unhappy, become unstable to different psychotraumatic kinds of impact . . . still, a considerable group of patients don't consider their state abnormal and don't want to be treated." (Sviadosch, 1998: 144-5)

Lesbianism was pathologized as a psychiatric disease which was to be treated in different ways, for example, with drugs (Sviadosch, 1998). Placed in the context of medicine and criminal law, homosexuality was a closed topic for the public.

Transformations beginning in Russia in the 1980s/1990s, have led to changes in all spheres of society: from the political to the private. Many topics that had been taboo before entered the public domain, among them sexuality and homosexuality. Notwithstanding the fact that for the mass media homosexuality was an exciting topic, the changed conditions allowed questions to be raised about decriminalizing male homosexuality. I. Kon, who studied sexuality in Russia, writes that researchers and human rights advocates wrote in newspapers and magazines in favor of the repeal of criminal penalties from the standpoint of human rights (1997: 354). In academic discourse the decriminalization of men's homosexuality continued to be seen as possible only via its transformation from a 'crime' into a medical pathology. At the beginning of the 1990s work on men's homosexuality was written by medical doctors, published in medical journals, which considered homosexuality a pathology that required treatment (Derevianko, 1991; Isaev, 1991, 1992 a, 1992 b). Lesbianism remained a psychiatric problem; 'a sexual deviation.' It is possible to find evidence of this attitude in studies of 'sexual perversions' (lesbianism is named the main one) among convicted and sentenced women (Volkov, 1992).

At the same time the first gay/lesbian organizations, initiatives and newspapers appeared at this time. Their collective goal has been to normalize homosexuality, both in terms of the heterosexual majority and also within the homosexual community, as well as to fight for the repeal of criminal penalties for engaging in 'homosexual' behavior.[2] The first organizations were 'coalitional,' that is they united both gays and lesbians, although, according to researchers, it soon became clear that mainly men directed the movement. Notwithstanding the fact that in the cradle of the movement there were lots of women, the first homosexual organizations didn't try to fight the psychiatric designation of homosexuality or fight for legal rights for lesbian mothers; instead they concentrated all their efforts on issues relating to HIV/AIDS and the repeal of criminal penalties for pederasty. As a result lots of women began to think that homosexual organizations did not fully represent their lives and interests (Essig, 1999). Thus, separatist lesbian organizations, groups and initiatives started to appear. In this, a relatively autonomous lesbian sphere began to form.

Sociologist I. Kon published a book about sexual culture in Russia in 1997. One of its articles was dedicated to homosexuality and lesbianism. This was the first Russian academic publication normalizing homosexuality not only as regards Russian society generally, but also as a subject in social studies. In 1998 a book by the same author appears wholly dedicated to problems of same-sex love (Kon, 1998). Both books belong to History and Cultural Studies, and are considered to be 'the classics' of Homosexuality Studies in Russia.

In the second half of the 1990s public interest in homosexuality decreased and the political activity of gay and lesbian initiatives changed from directing their energies at the mainstream to concentrating on the community: seminars were organized, brochures and information sheets were published and a variety of social events were organized. Olga Zhuk, a lesbian activist, published 500 copies of *Russian Amazons* in 1998. The first part of the book concentrates on the Silver Age of Russian culture and those women who constituted, according to the author, *the* lesbian culture in Russia at the beginning of the Twentieth Century. The second part of the book depicts the Soviet period, or the prison and camp lesbian culture in the Soviet Union, to be more precise. The book is an important one for lesbian women and for the heterosexual majority, because it showed lesbianism to be an integral part of the history of culture.

At the beginning of the year 2000 a strange situation developed in Russia. Lesbianism, which had already been excluded from the list of psychiatric disorders, was forced into a 'comfortable closet'—a specific and relatively autonomous field of culture that included both public (clubs, sites, printed editions) and private (one's own personal relationships, networks of friends and acquaintances) institutions. Inside of this space a person might acquire and produce information, look for support, represent and bring into effect the lesbian way of life, that is 'be a lesbian.' The topic of homosexuality outside this field is problematic however: Russian society, although recognizing homosexuality as a fact of life, has not accepted it as a norm equal to heterosexuality. Rare public discussions are dedicated, not to the problem of human rights or the defense of same-sex partners, but rotate around such purely homophobic topics as, for instance, "Should they be given the right to live among us or rather be locked in a ghetto"? The intensification of the Russian Orthodox Church has helped to engender this homophobia. Thus, one can be a lesbian in one's private life or in a club, but one must not mention it in public.

In the academic sphere an ambiguous situation has developed as well. On the one hand, it still turns out to be possible to make declarations about the incompetence of Homosexuality Studies. Thus, the authors who compiled a bibliography of publications on sexuality that appeared in Russia from 1991-2000 point to homosexuality and lesbianism in their introduction.

> ... different topics are unequally paid attention to; thus homosexuality (including lesbianism), women prostitution and different forms of violence (to children and in the family) is paid a lot of attention to; moreover, it increases with each year. On the contrary, other topics that are not less important are 'in the shadow'—for ex-

ample, the fact that the institution of wedlock lost its monopolistic control over sexuality . . . Apparently, such 'mistakes' are caused by their innocuity on the one hand and their sensational character on the other. (Golod and Kuznetsova, 2002: 7)

On the other hand, some concrete, even if not very substantial, empirical studies of homosexuality are currently being carried out. In the last four years several articles and monographs were published: two studies on the legal status of homosexuals and same-sex partners (Alexeev, 2002 a, 2002 b), articles on homophobia among youngsters (Omelchenko, 2002 a, 2002 b), on homodebut or coming-out (Omelchenko, 2004), on male same-sex couples (Vorontsov, 2004), on homosexual families (Kupriyanova, 2002) and on discourses of homosexuality in literature at the beginning of the Twentieth Century (Etkind, 2002).

In regards to lesbianism, an article by a Finnish researcher, A. Rotkirkh, appeared in 2002, which described lesbian relationships in the late Soviet period (Rotkirkh, 2002). I. Kupriyanova published a piece on violence in relation to homosexual women (Kupriyanova, 2003) and O. Gurova wrote a paper on the representation of female homosexuality in modern Russian mass culture (Gurova, 2003). Two of my articles on lesbian families and on the construction of lesbianism in the mass media were published in 2004 (Nartova, 2004 a, 2004 b). So does Lesbian Studies exist in Russia? As far as publications are concerned: yes. Are we correct in saying there are discussions of Gay/Lesbian Studies in Russia? No. The published works are of a local character; they are pointlike and devoted to different topics, embodying different theoretical approaches. They are like scattered stars in the sky forming neither the Milky Way nor even smaller constellations.

The fact that in the last fifteen years fewer than ten studies have been published shows a lack of academic interest rather than signifying 'the beginning of a field.' Why so? On the one hand, the absence of public discussions and public political activities of lesbian and gay/lesbian initiatives mean that homosexuality continues to be seen as unimportant, thus there is no call from the Social Sciences or the Humanities for studies to be carried out. On the other hand, one might expect that interest in lesbianism (and more widely in homosexuality) could emerge and develop within the framework of Gender Studies, existent in Russia since the 1990s, in many regards due to Western academic, theoretical and financial investments. The 'gender' category is legitimate and popular in Russian academic contexts, but it has changed from a separate category of analysis to one dovetailing with 'sex.' 'Gender' in Russia is a respected category that could include studies which are not regarded as scientific in mainstream of Social Studies. On the other hand it suspends any hint of the political biases of Feminism. 'Gender Studies' in Russia functions as an umbrella term, which includes all imaginable perspectives from biological determinism to post-structuralist criticism, from Women's and Men's Studies to Feminist Theory. As the usage of 'gender' as a term does not offend either the philistine or the researcher, it does not prompt questions to be asked about the construction of 'sex' as a category, as well as about the production of masculinity and femininity. Questions about the production of heterosexuality, homosexuality, and heteronormativity can be avoided as well. This, of course, might be just one possible interpretation for why there is no Lesbian Studies in Russia.

So, does it look likely that Lesbian Studies is going to develop in Russia? It is even more difficult to answer this question, and so I would rather try not to answer it at this time. The only thing I would like to stress is that a new category, 'queer,' has appeared in Russian discourse relating to sexuality both in academia and in the public sphere. For example, a well-known gay magazine published in Moscow is named *Queer*. I'm afraid that 'queer' as a category might have the same fate as the 'gender' category. That is, having avoided any intellectual strains, it would successfully become a legitimate umbrella notion for nominating and studying anything.

In conclusion, I assert that today in Russia homosexuality is recognized as existing but is not considered to be 'normal' or equal to heterosexuality. Although lesbian clubs, Internet sites and publications exist, any public discussion of homosexuality is marginalized. As regards the Academy, there is neither an institutionalized field of 'Lesbian Studies,' nor even the rudiments of a discussion. Rare publications are not enough for a full description and understanding of what is going on in Russia, not to mention the development of theory. One can only guess what will happen next. Altogether, one can love in Russia, but studying that love is problematic.

NOTES

1. By all means, the Soviet Union and Russia are of great interest to Western researchers, including those working on homosexuality. I consider foreign studies interesting and important; some of them are translated into Russian, some were written especially for Russian editions. The majority of these studies, however, can't be found in Russian university libraries. Western authors and their work remains part of the

Western debate about sexuality, so I don't consider them in this article. Still it is important to pay attention to the following unique studies: Healey (2001); Essig (1999); Burgin (1994).

2. In 1993 the section of the Penal Code penalizing 'voluntary pederasty' was revoked.

3. (rus) indicates that the title has been translated from Russian into English; all translations are the author's.

REFERENCES

Alexeev, N. *Juristic Regulation of the Lives of Sexual Minorities: Russia in the Light of International Organizations, Practice and National Legislation of Different Countries of the World.* Moskow: Bek, 2002 a (rus).[3]

_____. *Gay Marriage: Family Status of Same-Sex Couples in International, National and Local Legislation.* Moskow: Bek, 2002 b (rus).

Burgin, D.L. *Sophia Parnok: The Life and Work of Russian Sappho.* New York University Press, 1994.

Derevianko, I.M. *Homosexuality.* Moscow: Znanie (Issue "Medicine"), 1991 (rus).

Etkind, A. "Secret Code for a Stray Sex: Literature Discourse on Homosexuality Since Rozanov Till Nabokov." In E. Zdravomyslova and A. Temkina, ed. *Search for Sexuality.* SP: Dmitry Bulanin, 2002: 79-95 (rus).

Essig, L. *Queer in Russia: A Story of Sex, Self, And The Other.* Duke University Press, 1999.

Golod, S. and L. Kuznetsova. *Social Problems of Sexuality: Annotated Bibliography (1990s).* SPb: Social Society n.a. M.M. Kovalevsky, 2002 (rus).

Gurova, O. "'Tatu' or the Representation of Female Homosexuality in Modern Russian Mass Culture," *Gender Studies,* 9, 2003: 194-200 (rus).

Healey, D. *Homosexual Desire in Revolutionary Russia. The Regulation of Sexual and Gender Dissent.* Chicago and London: The University of Chicago Press, 2001.

Isaev, D.D. "Characteristics of Sexual Identity of People with Homosexual Attraction Habits," *Psychiatry and Medical Psychology Review,* 2, 1992 a: 56-7.

_____. "Characteristics of Homosexual Orientation by Inherited and Aquired Homosexuality," *Psychiatry and Medical Psychology Review,* 3, 1992 b: 70-1 (rus).

_____. "Homosexuality and its Etiological Models," *Psychiatry and Medical Psychology Review,* 2, 1991: 50-60.

Kon, I.S. *Sexual Culture in Russia: Strawberry on a Birch-Tree.* Moskow: OGI, 1997 (rus).

_____. *Moonlight at the Dawn. Fronts and Masks of Same-Sex Love.* Moskow: Olimp; OOO "Editing Company 'AST'," 1998 (rus).

Kupriyanova, I. "Same-Sex Families in Modern Society: The Problems of Normalization," *Problems of the Norm and Pathology: Modern Discourse Practices.* Sartov: Publishing House of SSMU, 2002 (rus).

_____. "Violence towards Homosexual Women: Everyday Experience," *Violence and Social Changes.* Moskow, 2003 (rus).

Nartova, N. "Lesbian Families: Reality Behind a Wall of Silence." In S. Oushakin, ed. *Wedlock: Construction Models,* vol. 1. Moskow: NLO, 2004 a: 292-315 (rus).

_____. "'About Monsters and People': Heterosexuality and Lesbianism," *Gender Studies*, 10, 2004 b: 197-206 (rus).

Omelchenko, E. "'We Don't Like Gays': Youth Homophobia in Rural Areas." In S. Oushakin, ed. *About Masculinity*. Moskow: NLO, 2002 a: 582-609 (rus).

_____. "Studying Homophobia: Mechanisms of Exclusion of the 'Other' Sexuality in the Rural Youth Environment." In E. Zdravomyslova and A. Temkina, eds. *Search for Sexuality*. SPb: Dmitry Bulanin, 2002 b: 469-508 (rus).

_____. "Vague Origin: Homodebut/Coming-Out in the Context of Sexual Scenario," *INTER*, 2-3, 2004: 74-86 (rus).

Rotkirkh, A. "Love With Words and Without: Experience of Lesbian Relationships in the Late Soviet Period." In E. Zdravomyslova and A. Temkina, eds. *Search for Sexuality*. SPb: Dmitry Bulanin, 2002: 452-69 (rus).

Sedgwick, Eve Kosofsky. *Epistemology of the Closet*. Berkeley: University of California Press, 1990.

Sviadosch, A.M. *Female Sexual Pathology*. Moskow: Medicine, 1988 (rus).

Volkov, V., S. Kalinichenko and A. Pischelko. *Sexual Perversions among Convicted and Sentenced Women: Educational Guidance*. Domodedovo: MIPK for OVD Workers, 1992 (rus).

Vorontsov, D. "'Family Life Is Not For Us': Myths and Values of Male Homosexual Couples." In S. Oushakin, ed. *Wedlock: Construction Models*, vol. 1. Moskow: NLO, 2004: 576-601 (rus).

Wittig, Monique. *The Lesbian Body*, trans. David Le Vay. New York: Morrow, 1975.

Zhuk, Î. *Russian Amazons: History of the Lesbian Subculture in Russia: XX Century*. Moskow: Glagol, 1998 (rus).

doi:10.1300/J155v11n03_13

Queerying Borders:
An Afrikan Activist Perspective

Bernedette Muthien

SUMMARY. This article offers an overview of academic work that focuses on queer sexualities in Africa and argues that binary categories, particularly those imported from outside Africa, are not adequate for addressing African sexualities. doi:10.1300/J155v11n03_14 *[Article copies available for a fee from The Haworth Document Delivery Service: 1-800-*

Bernedette Muthien is a member of the pan-African gender network, Amanitare, as well as being an active member of the Executive Council of the International Peace Research Association 2000-2006. She also serves on a number of international advisory boards, including the international journals, *Human Security Studies* and *Queeries* (Africa Editor), as well as the International Resource Network of the Center for Lesbian and Gay Studies, City University of New York (CUNY). A former anti-apartheid activist who spent time in prisons during her adolescence due to youth and student leadership, Bernedette's life's work is centered on consciousness transformation in the intersecting areas of genders and sexualities, justice and peace. She believes in accessible research and writing, and has published both academic and creative writing (especially poetry) locally and abroad. She is founding Director of a registered NGO, Engender: URL: engender.org.za.

Address correspondence to: Bernedette Muthien, Engender, P.O. Box 12992, Mowbray, 7705, Cape Town, South Africa (E-mail: bmuthien@icon.co.za, info@engender.org.za).

The author expresses appreciation for the contributions of Yvette Abrahams, Lorna Israel, Mikki van Zyl, as well as Engender's financial and other supporters.

[Haworth co-indexing entry note]: "Queerying Borders: An Afrikan Activist Perspective." Muthien, Bernedette. Co-published simultaneously in *Journal of Lesbian Studies* (Harrington Park Press, an imprint of The Haworth Press, Inc.) Vol. 11, No. 3/4, 2007, pp. 321-330; and: *Twenty-First Century Lesbian Studies* (ed: Noreen Giffney, and Katherine O'Donnell) Harrington Park Press, an imprint of The Haworth Press, Inc., 2007, pp. 321-330. Single or multiple copies of this article are available for a fee from The Haworth Document Delivery Service [1-800-HAWORTH, 9:00 a.m. - 5:00 p.m. (EST). E-mail address: docdelivery@haworthpress.com].

HAWORTH. *E-mail address: <docdelivery@haworthpress.com> Website:
<http://www.HaworthPress.com> © 2007 by The Haworth Press, Inc. All rights
reserved.]*

KEYWORDS. Africa, activism, inbetweenities, fluidities, bisexuality,
lesbian, queer, transformation

planetary piss?[1]	neutron? (2005)
i yearn to float with ducks on open air waves nip pluck tuck everywhere neither here nor there i am both none inbetween kiss her fuck him desire only a dream sitdowncomic pencilling shower songs thru unwooded electrical storms	i am an infinite ravine engorged rivers erode my scar tissue lickmarbling the craters on all sides nations in-habit my being as i moisten for his mastery and fingertip her open-legged vulnerability all the while aware of all our innocence made of nothing but air +/- i am charged with no sides

Any field of study only has relevance if actual people, and communities of people specifically, are able to use it in concrete ways. Hence theorizing entirely for theory's sake, however intellectually stimulating to
some of us, has absolutely no relevance to the daily, lived realities of
grassroots (or 'ordinary') people. Scholar-activist Lorna Israel cautions
us about this on dualistic view, a view derived from lived experience in
both activist and academic (rarely intersecting) environments: "It's as if
'ordinary' people [are not seen] to be 'theoretical' about their 'experience' and the theoreticals hopelessly devoid of being experiential– flu-
idly speaking, an experience is as theoretical in as much as the
theoretical is very much experiential. They should not be put on
oppositional grounds."[2] While I agree with Israel entirely, especially to
avoid dichotomizing theorizing and experience, the inextricable experi-
ence-theory dance is not often slow and close, but rather loose and jag-

ged, and often exploitative, rather than co-creational. Hence my own passionate commitment to participatory, action-based research methodologies, that seek mutual skills exchange.

In the broader African context, and particularly in South Africa ten years into democracy, systemic transformation is of critical importance. Questions relating to how one transforms societies from inequality, injustice and systemic violence into societies of reconciliation, diversity, justice and non-violence, are issues most pertinent to many of us. Violence is a daily, lived reality for non-heteronormative people the world over, and especially in Africa, but even closer to home in South Africa specifically. Here, as is the case everywhere, lesbians are subject to what this author calls "curative rape," the rape of women perceived of as lesbian by men as an ostensible 'cure' for their (aberrant) sexualities.[3] Other men also, even more ironically, subject some gay men to this 'curative rape.'[4] Hence theorizing about non-heteronormativity, and lesbianism in particular, cannot be divorced from the ordinariness of 'curative' rape for many lesbians the world over, and South Africa specifically.

Further questions to contemplate include how relevant a field of Lesbian Studies is to ordinary people, what is a Lesbian, and who defines Lesbianism? The word 'lesbian,' as are most of the concepts encompassed within the rainbow or alphabet soup of Greek letters LGBTQI, were coined and developed outside African realities. In South Africa Nguni speakers have long (erroneously) referred to homosexuals as *stabane* or 'hermaphrodite' (intersexed). The original inhabitants of Southern Africa, the Khoisan, were *not* heteronormative, and genders and sexualities were seen as fluid and dynamic, rather than as static binaries. This fluidity applies to most ancient indigenous peoples the world over, from Native American *berdache* to Indian *hijras*. Definitions usually work in negative terms, which define self in relation (and usually in opposition) to anOther. Hence, homosexual means not heterosexual, and lesbian thus non-heterosexual, or homosexual, woman.[5] Employing a linear definition of lesbian, however, may exclude the infinite varieties of sexuality choices that are inbetween and vary over time and with circumstances.

So how should one define lesbian? Many people I associate with define lesbian as the equivalent of gay homosexual, i.e., the opposite of heterosexual. While the construct queer embraces those who are non-heteronormative and includes the inbetween fluids. Thus, the construct lesbian does not necessarily include me, because I define myself as beyond binaries, as inbetween and fluid, dynamic and variable. Perhaps some may call me bisexual, but this term too subscribes to a notion of polarity, that I am both poles, when in fact I shift and change positions, not on a static linear continuum, but on an endlessly spiralling ellipse, that not ironically is ovoid, symbolic of female reproductive power. Is lesbian defined as orientation, or as preference? Are we victims of biology, or active agents with choice?

While I do respect those who identify as lesbian, we all know lesbians who sleep with men, and lesbians who, even if they don't act, enjoy sexual fantasies of men. The same applies to women who identify as heterosexual and, often silently, mentally or actually engage sexually with other women. Many African women outside South Africa, who might identify as lesbian elsewhere, are married with children, and/or practice their same-sex sexuality in silence, due to the violences of post-colonial patriarchal homophobia. For example, a leading African gender activist's house was bombed at least once, because she worked on sexualities broadly, and lesbian activisms specifically, apparently outside of the general public view. One of her tasks has been to establish discreet national networks for gay men and women respectively. It is these clandestine activisms relating to sexualities that directly resulted in the attacks on her, and which warrants such extreme caution on her part. A further example is prior attacks on Engender's intersexed Board member, Sally Gross, which necessitates similar personal safety measures. Personal violences against non-heteronormative activists are closely tied to the generic societal violences against those perceived as not heterosexual, including the 'curative' rape of women perceived as lesbian, which is so prevalent that queer organizations in South Africa have entire projects dedicated to this form of gender violence specifically.[6]

It is precisely the imperatives of hetero-patriarchy that keep both lesbians and their straight sisters in the flimsy boxes of their binarized sexuality. How much simpler it is to find safety in a homogenous identity, even if all identities are more complex upon further investigation. For example, archeo-anthropology shows that humans have always migrated across continents throughout time, and hence the idea of a homogenous race or nationality is flawed at best. We are each, all, hybridized, without any definite certainty about origins. The only thing we can ever really be certain of, at this stage, is that we are all born human. Even as some ancient spiritual traditions, such as Hinduism and Jainism, refer to inter-species reincarnation.[7]

If we assume that sexuality, like any other identity, shifts constantly on the endless circumference of an infinite ovoid, then sexuality can never really be fixed; is not predetermined and primordial and does not hold us hostage physiologically. This is because the field of physiology itself evinces that chromosomes and hormones are by nature fluid, and both 'male' and 'female' exists in *all* human beings. So that static polar genders of male and female are not scientifically accurate, and merely serve the interests of hetero-patriarchy, to divide and rule, in similar ways that Science has been used to divide and conquer during colonial eras and under apartheid in South Africa.[8] As Stephen Batchelor puts it:

> Things are not as clear-cut as they seem. They are neither circum-scribed nor separated from each other by lines. Lines are drawn in the mind. *There are no lines in nature . . .* Everything emerges] from a matrix of conditions and in turn becomes part of another matrix of conditions from which something else emerges. (1997)

Is there such a construct as an African lesbian? Is the idea of an African in a globalized world possible? Mikki van Zyl reminds us that: "It may be worth mentioning the straddling of colonial boundaries by groups in each of more than 50 national (colonial) boundaries, and that as a conti-nent, Africa arguably has the world's most diverse cultural and historic legacies with more than 2000 languages spoken."[9]

Africa includes the range of Lesotho's lesbian-bisexual miners' wives in Cheryl Stobie's work to Ifi Amadiume's writings of women-to-women marriages in her native Nigeria.[10] Stobie critiques the book, *Boy-Wives and Female Husbands: Studies of African Homosexualities*, which offers a range of texts from the Eighteenth-Late Twentieth Cen-turies and examines a considerable number of sub-Saharan cultures, providing ample evidence of homosexual practices being indigenous over a long period. There is much fascinating material, including trans-lations of ethnographic accounts of pre-colonial and colonial times, court records of male homosexual 'crimes' in early colonial Zimbabwe, same-sex marriages, the concept of 'male lesbians' in Hausa (West Af-rica), adolescent same-sex sexual behaviour, cross-dressing, role rever-sal, and women who love women in Lesotho. Also of interest is an appendix with a list of fifty-odd African cultures with same-sex pat-terns, most of which have local terms for same-sex sexual practises or roles and there is evidence for same-sex erotic relationships between co-wives, and between (heterosexually) married women in Lesotho.

Speaking of his native Dagara people in Burkina Faso, Malidoma Some asserts that gender has very little to do with anatomy:

It is purely energetic. The whole notion of 'gay' does not exist in the indigenous world. That does not mean that there are not people who feel this way that certain people feel in this culture, that has led to them being referred to as 'gay' . . . The great astrologers of the Dogon are gay . . . Why is it that everywhere else in the world, gay people are a blessing and in the modern world they are a curse? It is self-evident. The modern world was built by Christianity. They have taken the gods out of the earth and sent them to heaven, wherever that is . . .

Sobanfu Some reflects on the *ordinariness* of Dagara women's sexual-spiritual intimacies:

Sexuality, including woman-to-woman sexuality, is so integrated into the spiritual life of the Dagarat that her people have no word to specify 'lesbian' or even 'sex' . . . Like many other Africans, the women of Dagara do not sleep with their men. Women need to sleep together, to be together to empower each other . . . then if they meet with men, there is no imbalance . . . We have a female father who gives us male energy. She looks like a male. Anything we feel or experience that we haven't dealt with is expressed. This women's group ritual balances their male/female energy. It is so we are not completely male or female.[11]

Alicia Banks cites an article entitled "Inside Gay Africa" (1986) to describe how the Watusi still have a reputation for bisexuality in the cities of East Africa, in which Zande women risked execution by pleasuring one another, sometimes with phalluses fashioned from roots and in this same part of Zaire, homosexuality had a mystical element to it while bisexuality is also quite common among the Bajun tribes of east Africa. So while the word lesbian may have ancient Greek origins, the practises it describes are certainly universal, and definitely includes Africa. What is clear from many of the citations above, however, is that sexualities are not necessarily divorced from spiritualities or other aspects of life and being human, as well as the fact that sexualities have always been fluid in especially pre-colonial Africa and many other ancient indigenous societies.

Rather than a narrow focus on lesbianism, and Lesbian Studies, it may serve Africa better if we re-historicize and re-claim pre-colonial fluidities, as at least one way of moving beyond the stranglehold of colonial, and still-prevalent, binaries, oppressions and violences. In this sense alone, Queer Studies broadly offers a more comfortable reception–rather than home–because it offers greater inclusivity, even as it suffers from the same dis-eases of power and exclusion as any other field of study. Lorna Israel refers to the irony of a notion of the pre-colonial, defined in relation to the colonial:

> As for going to the beginning of it all–especially the heavily ro-manticised notion that there was something unique, originary and therefore pure and integral during the pre-colonial period is just that: a very romantic notion because by ascribing to it a sense of time called pre-colonial you have exactly located its time zone within the bounds of the colonial period so it is theoretically and empirically impossible to disentangle the two–remember the one re-reading does not exactly belong to a pre-colonial moment and how will we ever know that there is such a time called pre-colonial when, precisely, such designation belongs to the very time that confines somebody designating it?![12]

To the question, "Are we now post-lesbian?" gender activist Mikki van Zyl replies:

> Post-what lesbian? We never even got started here, and maybe that is a good thing. There is such a thing as discourses being damag-ing. That doesn't mean I'm not a revolutionary . . . I believe les-bian studies are still based on a particular (Westocentric) paradigm of gender and heterosexuality. Our biggest 'enemy' is hetero-patriarchy, and that is where it must be located . . . [Sexuality Stud-ies] must be inclusive of all marginalized sexual identities, provided it is located in a dismemberment (!) of heteropatriarchy. To quote Marianne Thamm–I have nothing against the penis, it's the life support system that comes with it which I object to."[13]

Lesbian scholar-activist, Yvette Abrahams, offers this challenge: "How does the identity we choose help us to live in practice? What is the rele-vance of identity studies to daily life as a queer person, or for that matter to our struggle against homophobia, for full sexual health and freedom?" In one documentary short (at the Out in Africa Film Festival 2005 in Cape Town), Gail Smith says, "I don't even think we have begun to theorize how we undermine homophobia as a system. We need to approach it in the same way we analyze racism or sexism. And for South Africa that is perfectly true."[14] I believe that adopting and living any non-hetero-normative identity and lifestyle is a subversion of hetero-patriarchy, and hence contributes towards transforming society. If one's identities and lifestyles attempt to transcend status-quo binaries, it may prove to be all the more revolutionary, even as it may be more challenging to hold one's ground in opposition to the coerciveness of perceived polarities.

In her seminal essay, "The Master's Tools Will Never Dismantle the Master's House," the late Audre Lorde wrote:

> Those of us who stand outside the circle of this society's definition of acceptable women; those of us who have been forged in the crucibles of difference; those of us who are poor, who are lesbians, who are black, who are older, know that *survival is not an academic skill* [original emphasis]. It is learning how to stand alone, unpopular and sometimes reviled, and how to make common cause with those other identified as outside the structures, in order to define and seek a world in which we can all flourish . . . In a world of possibility for us all, our personal visions help lay the groundwork for political action. The failure of the academic feminists to recognize difference as a crucial strength is a failure to reach beyond the first patriarchal lesson. *Divide and conquer, in our world, must become define and empower* [emphasis added]. (1981: 98-101)

In walking the transformative talk, may this queerly fluid and inbetween activist, who identifies as polymorphously perverse for its ironically subversive and transformative potentials, leave you satisfied with the moment, fully aware that any authenticity is merely an ideal . . .

<u>I Q</u>

u're in the centre
of your war against conflict
and yet the silences of an entire
alphabet
around one Greek letter
closes the infinite spiral
of balkanisation
decapitating
this (in)voluntary bastard's
air
supply

31 august 2003
italy, for lepa

picture perfect

there's a thumbprint
on a face without a pupil
and lines of identity
circling the frame
greyscale
with some swatches
of peach
life's a finger supper
snap

NOTES

1. The poems reproduced here are by the author, and are an attempt to illustrate the interconnectedness and interdependence, of all things–creativity, activisms, and scholarship.

2. Email communication, 11 April 2005. Israel is based in the Philippines.

3. For example, at the international Women in Black Conference in Italy during 2003 a special lesbian parallel workshop was held, the best attended of that particular time-slot, where lesbians from different countries, amongst other topics, shared anecdotes of 'curative' rape in their respective countries, including the Balkans. The author also conducted participatory research on violence between and against lesbian and bisexual women in Cape Town during early 2004, and literature on the subject around the world is readily available from even a cursory internet search. The rapists are single assailants, sometimes arranged by family members, and/or gangs, with pregnancy, STI and HIV transmission further complicating the inevitable rape trauma.

4. When an ostensibly heterosexual man engages in sexual intercourse with an apparently homosexual man, it is the heterosexual man who is more homosexual (less heterosexual) during this encounter, hence the irony of 'curing' homosexual men through rape.

5. Lorna Israel offers the following, on the origins of othering sexualities as rooted in heterosexuality: "it might interest you to read Jonathan Katz' *The Invention of Heterosexuality*–it was the heterosexuals who were first stigmatised (because of the assumption they were engaged in sex outside the norms of pro-creativity). Later on, they would impute the same stigmaphobic ramifications to the homosexuals. Like you said, meanings/definitions are imbricated by negativities–from my reading of Katz, it might be worthy to revisit first heterosexuality and the discursive regimes that had constituted it as the norm, before we could even begin to historicise/re-historicise homosexuals in all their varying cultural, and historical designations. [Another] author argues that without the constitution of the heterosexuals, lesbians would not be able to begin the process of designating themselves–it was the het that co-extensively produced the homosexuals" (Email communication, 11 April 2005).

6. For example the Forum for the Empowerment of Women (FEW) in Johannesburg coordinates the Rose Has Thorns Campaign, dedicated to combating what they call 'corrective' rape, and Triangle Project in Cape Town is also attempting to address this societal scourge more recently.

7. The use of 'human' here is meant to transcend heteronormativity and other violences, since generic humankind precedes hetero-patriarchy, with its intrinsically binaried construction/s of genders and sexualities, by thousands of years.

8. For further explication, see Muthien (2005, 2004, 2003).

9. Email communication, 10 December 2004.

10. Stobie cites heterosexually married women having sexual relations with other women in Lesotho since at least the 1950s and refers to the practice of bisexuality since at least the 1920s in Namibia. It is also well documented that miners in apartheid South Africa (in men-only hostels) routinely engaged in homosexual practices, as is common in other forced same-sex environments like boarding schools throughout Africa and elsewhere, and prisons the world over.

11. For the curious, Malidoma (male) and Sobanfu (female) are spouses and reside in northern California. They have each published numerous books on African spiritual-

ity, and conduct workshops internationally, while maintaining close connections to their native Burkina Faso.

12. Email communication, 11 April 2005.
13. Email communication, 3 March 2005.
14. Email communication, 11 April 2005.

REFERENCES

Amadiume, Ifi. *Reinventing Africa: Matriarchy, Religion and Culture.* London: Zed Books, 1998.
_____ . *Male Daughters and Female Husbands: Gender and Sex in an African Society.* London: Zed Press, 1988.
Banks, Alicia. "Gay Racism: White Lies/Black Slander," *Fito,* feminist e-zine, 2005. URL fito.co.za
_____ . "Inside Gay Africa," *BlackOut,* Fall 1986.
Batchelor, Stephen. *Buddhism without Beliefs.* New York: Riverhead, 1997.
Lorde, Audre. "The Master's Tools Will Never Dismantle the Master's House" (1979). In Cherríe Moraga and Gloria Anzaldúa, eds. *This Bridge Called My Back: Writings by Radical Women of Color.* Watertown, MA: Persephone Press, 1981: 98-101.
Muthien, Bernedette. "Playing on the Pavements of Identities." In Mikki van Zyl and Melissa Steyn, eds. *Performing Queer. Shaping Sexualities 1994-2004,* Volume 1. Cape Town: Kwela Books, 2005: 41-73.
_____ . "Why Are You not Married Yet?!" *Fito,* feminist e-zine, 2004. URL fito.co.za
_____ . "Why Are You not Married Yet?! Heteronormativity in the African Women's Movement," *Women's Global Network for Reproductive Rights Newsletter,* 79, August 2003. URL wgnrr.org/frameset.htm (in English, Spanish and French).
Ochs, Robyn and Sarah E Rowley, eds. *Getting Bi: Voices of Bisexuals Around the World.* Boston, MA: Bisexual Resource Center, 2005.
Stobie, Cheryl. "Reading Bisexualities from a South African Perspective," *The Journal of Bisexuality,* 3(1), 2003: 33-52.
Some, Malidoma. "Gays: Guardians of the Gates," *M.E.N. Magazine,* 1993.
Some, Sobanfu. "The Lesbian Spirit," *Girlfriends Magazine,* July 1994. URL mask.org.za

doi:10.1300/J155v11n03_14

"Where Are the Lesbians in Chaucer?"
Lack, Opportunity
and Female Homoeroticism
in Medieval Studies Today

Michelle M. Sauer

SUMMARY. This article explores the study of lesbians in the Middle Ages and proposes that the unstable construct of lesbian poses a problem for traditional Medieval Studies that can lead to the development in Medieval Studies of more nuanced and productive theorizing. doi:10.1300/J155v11n03_15 *[Article copies available for a fee from The Haworth Document Delivery Service: 1-800-HAWORTH. E-mail address: <docdelivery@haworthpress.com> Website: <http://www.HaworthPress.com> © 2007 by The Haworth Press, Inc. All rights reserved.]*

Michelle M. Sauer is Associate Professor of English and Coordinator of Gender Studies at Minot State University (Minot, ND), and Managing Editor of *Medieval Feminist Forum*. She holds degrees in Medieval English Literature from Purdue University, Loyola University Chicago and Washington State University. Her edition of the *Wooing Group and A Discussion of the Love of God* is forthcoming from Boydell & Brewer Press. She has also published on anchoritism, mysticism, asceticism, Church History, Marlowe and Queer Theory. Additionally, she has served as Campus Diversity Chair, and has been invited to speak on women's rights, the status of GLBTQ individuals and sexual harassment in a variety of forums.

Address correspondence to: Professor Michelle M. Sauer, Department of English, Hartnett Hall 141W, Minot State University, Minot, ND 58707, USA (E-mail: michelle.sauer@minotstateu.edu).

[Haworth co-indexing entry note]: " 'Where Are the Lesbians in Chaucer?" Lack, Opportunity and Female Homoeroticism in Medieval Studies Today." Sauer, Michelle M. Co-published simultaneously in *Journal of Lesbian Studies* (Harrington Park Press, an imprint of The Haworth Press, Inc.) Vol. 11, No. 3/4, 2007, pp. 331-345; and: *Twenty-First Century Lesbian Studies* (ed: Noreen Giffney, and Katherine O'Donnell) Harrington Park Press, an imprint of The Haworth Press, Inc., 2007, pp. 331-345. Single or multiple copies of this article are available for a fee from The Haworth Document Delivery Service [1-800-HAWORTH, 9:00 a.m. - 5:00 p.m. (EST). E-mail address: docdelivery@haworthpress.com].

KEYWORDS. Medieval Studies, pre-modern sexuality, lesbian-like, defining lesbianism, masculine bias of homosexuality, lack

Recently, I had an editor comment on a draft of an article that she was concerned about "slippage" because of my reliance upon non-medieval sources to inform my discussion of woman-woman eroticism in medieval texts. My initial surprise gave way to annoyance–*what* medieval sources, I wondered? I had already used the only ones I could think of.[1] My response to her, "the use of ancient and Early Modern resources for explorations of woman-woman eroticism in the Middle Ages is standard and necessary," was at once both true and frustrating. That the standard practice of my professional field, that is Queer Studies of Medieval Literature, is to draw primarily from other eras is embarrassing, and obviously not understood beyond the narrow perspective of my fellow medievalists, if indeed even by them. In examining my discomfiture, I found myself reflecting on Jane Chance's introduction to her recently edited collection, *Women Medievalists in the Academy*. In it, Chance writes, "the reaction of shame by the (woman) reader over the apparent absence of women in history of medieval criticism would echo the reaction of Virginia Woolf in her famous polemical essay *A Room of One's Own* (1929)" (2005: xxiv). Although Chance was not specifically referring to the dearth of lesbian studies about the Middle Ages, her words about shame struck a note. It was incomprehensible to this editor that I not only was relying on texts that didn't 'match' my era (an unfortunate side effect of rigid periodization), but also that I 'should' be relying on those resources, since they are my only current options.[2] I wondered, too, at my defensiveness–did my insistence on the 'standards of my field' make me unwittingly complicit in this continued exclusion of lesbian history? Was I more concerned that I be taken seriously, following the standard advice given to medievalists, "better to be dull than 'unsound'" (or, presumably, uncooperative)? (Patterson, 1990: 102).

Maybe I shouldn't have been surprised by her surprise. After all, the medieval era as a whole has suffered its own obscurities.[3] Lee Patterson, among others, addressed this problem a decade ago. "In the current academic milieu," he writes, "medieval studies is a marginalized institution" (87). Similar comments are reiterated throughout the field. Robert Stein remarks that many see the Middle Ages as "an excluded territory, always situated antithetically to the modern" (1995: par. 3). More than just being marginalized, however, the Middle Ages is also the "rejected object" instead of a subject, "stigmatized" by "otherness" (Patterson, 1990: 99; 103). A further connection can be made here not only between woman as other and Medieval Studies, but also between lesbians as "other Others" and Medieval Studies. Penelope J. Engelbrecht points out that since the lesbian cannot, according to the existing patriarchal model, 'properly' occupy either the subject or object position, she is perpetually marginalized, "'outside' of everything that is . . . to be nonexistent" (1990: 89-90). According to Patterson et al., medieval studies also exist outside of everything, and are rapidly becoming practically non-existent. John Dagenais and Margaret R. Greer highlight this disappearance, putting forward the Middle Ages as a "gaping hole in history" (2000: 435). It is this "hole" and the subsequent accompanying marginalization that David Aers refers to as "systematic amnesia" on the part of modern historians (1992: 180-1). In short, the medieval is the "not-modern" as much as a woman is "not-man," and a lesbian is "not-woman." A medieval lesbian–or indeed a medievalist who studies lesbians–may as well dig the gaping hole herself (Chance, 2005: xxvii).

In her article, "Twice Marginal and Twice Invisible: Lesbians in the Middle Ages" (1996), Jacqueline Murray focuses on this match between Medieval Studies and Lesbian Studies. Like Patterson, she sees a future that has yet to be exploited: "The study of attitudes and ideas about lesbians in the Middle Ages is neither as anachronistic as some theorists might believe, nor as futile as traditional historians might think" (208), though she is particularly concerned with the history of sexuality. Despite the obstacles that must be overcome, there are some studies of medieval lesbians in existence; however, these are few in number, and limited in scope (although see Canadé Sautman, 2001; Lochrie, 2001; Murray, 2004). None addresses a major canonical text or body of literature; indeed, none take on Chaucer. There are, so far at least, no lesbians in Chaucer, and should we want to find some, the task will be difficult. Murray addresses this problem directly, beginning by admitting that "Any attempt to study lesbians in the Middle Ages is, from the outset, fraught with difficulties, both conceptual and evidential" (191). Those of us who wish to recover medieval lesbians are obliged to be creative. This resourcefulness can take many forms, but tends to settle into two distinct approaches–redefining lesbianism and "reading between the lines" (Frantzen, 1996).[4] Both can bring rewards, but both are laden with pitfalls.

Theoretically, in order to 'find' medieval lesbians, one must first define an indefinable state, and then uncover that which does not exist. For instance, in using the term 'lesbian' in my own article title and text, I might acknowledge that I am aware that using the term "lesbian" is anachronistic in reference to the Middle Ages, explaining its use as a way to better situate my discussion about current scholarly practices, particularly in relation to other eras. In such a discussion, it becomes clear that the only definition of lesbian is and can be the modern one (if there even is such a thing as that) because there was no medieval one. This is, of course, a problematic conclusion, particularly since as a culture, Western society still labors under the belief that the male experience is 'normal.' Apparently, the extension of male normalcy extends even into the homosexual realm. As readers and scholars, we are invited to 'do' the history of homosexuality, but only from the male perspective; our gaze is turned towards woman-as-object and away from woman-as-subject; thus, active creation of an identity, sexual or non-sexual, is a realm better suited for men, even gay ones, than for women (Halperin, 2000).[5]

Constructing a definition for medieval lesbianism is fraught with difficulties. Problematically, these definitions often teeter towards a reduplication of the heterosexual matrix, casting an active 'manly' woman as pursuing a passive, 'womanly' woman, instead of outlining a general term for women who have (or want to have) sex with women (de Lauretis, 1988). That is, one of the main problems with Medieval Studies today–as well as the examined texts–is the insistence on viewing sexual intercourse from a phallocentric point of view, and on categorizing gender roles dually as masculine and feminine, with little room outside that binary perspective. For instance, Bernadette J. Brooten purports to use "lesbian" in "its medieval sense of a woman who 'behaves like a man' (i.e., usurps the male cultural role) and 'is oriented toward female companions for sex'" (1996: 17). In doing so, she elides the later European Middle Ages with the [Mediterranean] Patristic era, combining cultures and geographic regions, as well as centuries. More than that, however, she places medieval lesbians in the category of 'not-quite-woman.' This perception is emphasized in Brooten's discussion of the verb 'lesbiazein' ('lesbizein'), which she reports as meaning, "to perform fellatio," and thus generally avoided by Classicists when discussing woman-woman eroticism (22). Her claim of resituating 'lesbian' by associating it with usurpation of the "male cultural role" does little to dispel this masculinizing image.

The idea that 'real' sex is penetrative in nature, if not strictly penile-vaginal, has plagued lesbians throughout history, but perhaps never so thoroughly as in the Middle Ages (Lochrie, 2001). Thus, the few studies that do address medieval lesbianism have almost unilaterally addressed medieval theologians' incredulity that two women could find 'something to do' with each other in bed, a perspective not limited solely to Christianity. Gail Labovitz reports that Jewish rabbinic texts "specify that female homoerotic activities are non-penetrative, but also nonetheless forbidden. The possibility of penetrative activity between women is not considered" (2003: 5). Similarly, the Qur'an is almost silent about female-female sexual activity, as pointed out by Kecia Ali, because "the legal effects of sexual activity attach to (vaginal or anal) penetration by a penis" (2002: par. 4). Where there is no penetration, there is little to discuss it seems, and many medieval literary scholars appear to agree. Indeed, while male homosexuals seem to have at least partially escaped the conflation of act with identity, lesbianism is still defined through sex acts. Penelope J. Engelbrecht invites us to reconsider this insistence on coupling lesbian with sexual practices, reminding scholars, "a woman need not be sexually active to consider herself a lesbian" (1990: 90). This concept has been expanded by Judith Bennett (2000) in her discussion of "lesbian-like" women, and should have been furthered by the advent of Queer Theory. Unfortunately, despite the popularity of gendered readings, lesbian studies of the Middle Ages still remain underrepresented.

Great strides have been made in the study of homosexuality in the Middle Ages; however, these studies, even those purportedly about same-sex relations in general, have tended to conflate 'homosexuality' with *male* homosexuality. Lesbians are consigned to footnotes, passing references and fleeting comments, or they are simply skipped altogether.[6] As Kathleen Coyne Kelly points out, "the word 'homoerotic' especially in the context of masculinity studies, is marked almost exclusively as masculine" (2002: 246). For example, David M. Halperin writes "I want to describe, very tentatively, some important prehomosexual discourses, practices, categories, patterns, or models . . . and to sketch their similarities with and differences from what goes by the name of homosexuality nowadays" (2000: 90). Intriguingly, none of these mysterious practices involve two women despite his re-genericization of the term. Karma Lochrie contends that this all-too-standard practice is an act of "presumptive sodomy." She goes on to define this concept: "like presumptive heterosexuality, presumptive sodomy has the effect of privileging a version of medieval sodomy that excludes women and gender and replicates the very misogyny of the medieval category" (1999: 296). Efforts to codify lesbianism are often the only mention of woman-woman eroticism in entire studies that supposedly explore homosexuality in general. Furthermore, when lesbians are mentioned in such inquiries, they are often defined in terms of lack–lack of sources about them, lack of threat to the patriarchy and lack of interest to scholars.

I am troubled by the insistence upon lack and exclusion as a central part of lesbianism and studies thereof, especially in relation to Medieval Studies. Women are categorized as lesbians because they exclude men from their sexual self (socially, emotionally, spiritually or psychologically). Men, however, are deemed 'homosexual,' or at least discussed in terms of homosexuality, not because they exclude women, but rather because they include men. Studies of male homosexuality in the pre-modern world address patricians who have political-pederast relationships with boys as well as monks who take advantage of novices, despite the fact that these men also (usually) engaged in heterosexual relations with women. At the same time, medieval lesbians are overshadowed because it is difficult to find evidence of women who exclusively preferred other women. Why do we feel exclusivity is a necessary component of [premodern] lesbianism, but not of male homosexuality? Medieval lesbians, if we say there were such women, did not really have the choice to exclude men from their sexual selves, as even cloistered virgins were married to Christ, and thus partnered off in a heterosexual relationship. Medieval men, on the other hand, did have the choice–albeit a dangerous one–to include other men, and even, perhaps, to exclude women from their sexual sphere. There is a lack here, but it is not necessarily the lack of men; rather, for the 'medieval lesbian,' it was lack of choice.

It is our insistence that is the anachronistic invader here, not the 'medieval lesbians' themselves. Presumptively, if not presumptively sodometric, we insist that women-identified-women of earlier eras conform to our perceptions of behavior. In her provocative discussion of Alan Bray's final work, *The Friend*, Valerie Traub makes an excellent, and uplifting, point:

> If we shift our focus from what Bray says about women to what his work makes available to those of us working on women, however, a more enabling set of procedures emerges. Adoption of Bray's insights about the unstable nature of erotic signification and consideration of the ontological and epistemological issues raised by his work, for instance, would greatly nuance scholarship in this field, which has tended to presuppose a certain knowingness about what constitutes sexuality. (2004: 354)

Of course, Traub's work is about the Early Modern Era, so I 'shouldn't' even be referencing it. Nevertheless, she makes an excellent point— modern Gender Theory can help us read the past, but modern gender identities may not be able to. Ulrike Wiethaus concurs, suggesting, "the current perception of a lack of source materials [about medieval female homosexuality] is influenced by our search for descriptions of esthetics and relations that fit contemporary models of homoeroticism" (Wiethaus, 2003: 289). In order to reclaim a lesbian history within the Middle Ages, it seems logical for our next step to be an examination of our own presumptions about female-female desire. When we are able to suspend our reliance upon the gender patterns and discourses of desire that we are immersed in, then we might be able to dispassionately examine the potential gendered identities of others.

The scholars who have undertaken investigations of medieval lesbianism often extend their efforts to establishing parameters, taking their cue from postmodern theory, and relying on varying degrees of social/ emotional/sexual ties as parameters of lesbianism, and usually involving some measure of choice or self-identification (Sheingorn and Sautman, 1997; Ferguson, 1981). Yet, relying too heavily on self-identification is problematic in medieval society, which allowed little choice for any woman to self-define. Kelly attempts to mitigate this idea of self-identification by softening it to "attention". She believes the medieval lesbian to be "a woman whose attention is focused on another woman or on other women in such a way that she demonstrably threatens the patriarchal, heteronormative order" (2002: 250). Utilizing expanded perceptions such as this opens up opportunities to "read the blanks" (Schibanoff, 1992). Tracing those blank spaces can be a challenging yet rewarding pursuit, one that should be pursued more vigorously.

Of course, reading between the lines creates its own problems, particularly for critics who insist upon purely historical readings of sexuality. Still, without such creative recovery, queer history in general, and lesbian history more specifically, would remain shrouded in darkness. Thus, some scholars have chosen to locate these 'blanks' both textually and physically. Judith Bennett, in a much-discussed article, suggests that in order "to approach the social history of lesbianisms in the Middle Ages . . . we try broadening our perspective to include women whom I have chosen to call 'lesbian-like'" (2000: 9). Including these women, such as cross-dressers, prostitutes, and others, opens up spaces for investigation while providing resistance to heterosexist and masculinist biases. Diane Watt, for example, provides a careful reading of the

French romance *Yde et Olive*, which contains the story of two women who are married to each other. Watt points out that:

> . . . the language that the narrator uses to describe Yde's procrasti- nation [of the consummation] may even suggest that she could have used a prosthetic had she so wished: "And Yde lay with her/ his wife, S/he didn't . . . jab or touch her in her nether regions" . . . Even if the narrator denies that it has taken place, the possibility of intercourse is certainly raised." (1998: 279-80)

What is left for us is to fill in the blanks, and envision the possibility of non-penetrative sex and sexually fulfilling homoeroticism between women. Though such actions are not explicit, the narrative allows for this interpretation because of the textual gap, the space between the lines. In this same vein, Carolyn Dinshaw provides us with a blank, rather than filling one, in her discussion of *Sir Gawain and the Green Knight*. As she points out, it is not that the possibility of female-female desire could not exist in the Middle Ages; rather, it was so incompre- hensible to men–it was such a large 'blank'–that it could not be represented (Dinshaw, 1997; 1999: 88-94).

Other scholars have focused on created ('creative') spaces–places between the lines–that could allow for woman-woman erotic encoun- ters. Mary Anne Campbell suggests that "'Holy maidenhood' provided for medieval women not only a rejection of physical heterosexuality but also a rejection of spiritual heterosexuality–in favor of women-only physical spaces and women-identified spirituality" (1992: 15). The homoeroticism of religious women is a lesbian structure addressed some time ago by E. Ann Matter, who acknowledges that "an inquiry into the history of lesbians in medieval Christian Europe . . . [is] a ven- ture into a realm of silence and contradiction" (1989: 51). Examining the cloisters and the words created within them, Matter suggests that mystic visions, spiritual letters, and Church rituals provided a place for woman-woman eroticism, whether expressed physically or not. Like- wise, in my work, I posit that in the early Middle Ages, "both the regula- tions for and the structure of the anchoritic cell could provide the necessary space and conditions to create a 'lesbian void,' in which the anchoress could explore woman-woman erotic possibilities. Further, this void was supported not only by the cell's configuration, but also through the religious Rule for anchoresses as well as by medieval theo- logical concepts about 'lesbian' acts" (2004: 70; see also Jankowski, 2000). The concept of the lesbian void integrates well with Bennett's position that we should look for "lesbian-like" women and the notion that we should be filling in the blanks. What these ideas do is take for granted that lesbian desire existed. The lack, then, was not women's sexuality or desire, but rather a 'woman-friendly' (a 'lesbian') space. This space, as explored, is both literary and physical.[7]

If Queer Theory, rightfully or not, is concerned with investigating previously overlooked spaces, it stands to reason that studies of medieval lesbianism should be an increasing focus of sustained investigations. Regrettably, however, Queer Theory, which has done much to expand examinations of all non-heteronormative sexualities, has seemingly not advanced the state of Lesbian Studies. Studies of same-sex relations have focused on male-male relations while Queer Studies have looked at other sexualities beyond same-sex eroticism. Both options, while laudable, dishearteningly exclude the lesbian. This is a position shared by Murray:

> While women in general have attracted increasing attention from medievalists, lesbians remain ignored as subjects. Thus medieval lesbians have been twice marginalized. Mainstream women's history has elided them under the rubric 'homosexual', while studies of medieval homosexuality focus on men and elide lesbians into the category 'women'. Medieval lesbians are rendered invisible, . relegated to footnotes and tangential references in the works of historians of women and of male homosexuality. (1996: 193)

Returning to my initial quandary, it is this very refusal by scholars to pursue medieval notions of lesbianism that make it necessary for those of us who work on representations of woman-woman eroticism and the Middle Ages to work backwards from Early Modern Studies and forward from Classical and Patristic Studies. Meanwhile, scholarship about medieval male-male eroticism flourishes.[8]

Another noticeable lack–which provides an excellent opportunity–is the scarcity of investigations into female homoeroticism in medieval Britain. As the title of this article suggests, when it comes to finding lesbians in Chaucer, one is hard-pressed to find any. In fact, with the rise of Queer Theory, it might seem that this is the place where multiple, conflicting, and overlapping concerns about marginalization should converge. Indeed, the rise in 'queer Chaucer' studies brought me hope. Unfortunately, that hope was quickly dashed. Steven F. Kruger's article, "Claiming the Pardoner: Toward a Gay Reading of Chaucer's *Pardoner's Tale*" (1994), was a groundbreaking study, and while it focused on male homosexuality, the groundwork for other studies was seemingly laid out. Since then, however, the shortage of studies about female homoeroticism has not only continued, but also become more obvious. Queer readings of Chaucer, the touchstone figure of medieval culture, have remained an 'all-boys club' for the most part. Glenn Burger's *Chaucer's Queer Nation* (2003) typifies this scholarly trend. In it, he addresses the issue of female masculinity, but doesn't extend this to woman-woman eroticism, or touch upon the possibility thereof. Indeed, he becomes a purveyor of presumptive sodomy in his discussion of Eve Kosofsky Sedgwick's concept of 'homosexual panic,' concluding that:

> . . . certainly there are analogies between medieval sodomite and modern homosexual as subject categories constituted as negatives by dominant culture . . . But at the same time, neither 'the homosexual', nor his more optimistic 'gay' younger brother will likely be found reproduced exactly in medieval systems of representation. (2003: 126; see also Sedgwick, 1990: 182-212)

That is likely true; however, it seems that the female homosexual and her younger 'gay' sister, are not found in either medieval *or* modern systems of representation. Lochrie suggests that in order to undo the practice of presumptive sodomy that such studies need to be "situate[d] within the natural/unnatural matrix, in alignment with–rather than in opposition to–so-called heterosexuality . . . In the process, too, women and gender would cease to be excluded by the presumptions of medieval scholarship" (1999: 307). Even when gender has been the major focus of Chaucerian studies, female homoerotic potential is still often overlooked. Both Elaine Tuttle Hansen's *Chaucer and the Fictions of Gender* (1992) and Carolyn Dinshaw's *Chaucer's Sexual Poetics* (1989), admittedly two revolutionary volumes, exclude, for the most part, lesbian possibilities from their discussions, although alternate sexual identities figure prominently in their discussions. In her latest book, *Getting Medieval: Sexualities and Communities, Pre- and Postmodern*, Dinshaw addresses the difficulties of queer readings finding reception among medieval scholars, while at the same time endorsing the combination of activism and scholarship, particularly lesbian scholarship, and particularly in Medieval Studies. The consequences, she admits, may be heavy:

We are not all safe . . . while I am mindful of my privilege as a tenured professor at an elite university I know also that privilege does not guarantee my safety: I am a lesbian teacher of queer histories, and such teachers are extraordinarily vulnerable. (1999: 37)

Studies of male homosexuality are becoming a part of the standardized elite–their dominance in Chaucer studies alone indicates their acceptance into 'mainstream' academia. Numerous studies of male homosexuality discuss the British Isles. Within the limited number of studies about medieval lesbians and lesbianism, however, few have been focused on the British Isles, while a large number of the Early Modern lesbian studies have been.

It seems that the true lesbian void, then, is the dearth of scholarship on woman-woman eroticism in the Middle Ages, especially in studying Britain and in examinations of canonical figures such as Chaucer. This lack is noted even in non-academic resources, such as the *glbtq* encyclopedia entry on medieval English literature: "And for lesbians attempting to understand why they have been silenced for much of the English tradition, it is with the silence of medieval English texts that they should begin" (Boyd, 2002: 3). Unfortunately, the author is guilty of this same offense himself. The rest of the article is devoted almost exclusively to an overview of perceptions of sodomy and male homoeroticism. It is time, perhaps, for lesbians–and others–who are attempting to understand why they have been silenced to also blame the critics.

Returning for a moment to Murray's now-infamous claim that medieval lesbians are "twice marginalized and twice invisible," I suggest that this catchphrase be slightly modified to account for the lack in our own field of study. In reality, medieval lesbians and the scholars who pursue them are really 'thrice marginalized and thrice invisible,' being excluded on the basis of being a non-heteronormative woman historically situated in the 'dark ages.' Nevertheless, while I have discussed the inadequacy of lesbian criticism in today's Medieval Literary Studies and may appear overly pessimistic, I also hope that I have at least implicitly addressed the opportunities within the field. It is precisely because of the lack of obviously available (or even available) primary sources that there can be considerable possibilities for secondary criticism and for re-gendered readings of existing materials. Though marginalized, medieval lesbians–and medieval scholars of lesbianism–do not have to be invisible. In the meantime, however, we scholars may still have to rely on other eras for support.

NOTES

1. This article was completed prior to the publication of two texts that address these issues, at least to some extent. The first is Karma Lochrie's *Heterosyncracies: Female Sexuality when Normal Wasn't* (U Minnesota P, 2005). Concentrating on dismantling 'normal,' she examines various medieval texts–including the *Canterbury Tales*–in an effort to destabilize traditional hetero-dominated discourses of female sexuality that rely upon a binary. The other work, *History Matters: Patriarchy and the Challenge of Feminism* by Judith M. Bennett (U Penn Press, 2006), includes a chapter on the 'L-Word in Women's History.' In this chapter, Bennett deepens her previous discussion of the 'lesbian-like' woman, stating at one point, '[r]esponding to the sparse evidence for actual lesbian practices, medievalists have mostly adopted intellectual or cultural approaches, not social history' (111).

2. In my perusal of fellow scholars' bibliographies, I noted that the majority of articles cite (as had I) such 'non-medieval' texts as Bernadette J. Brooten (1996), which covers the Classical and Patristic eras, along with Judith Brown (1986); Valerie Traub (2002), both of which focus on the Early Modern period.

3. I am following the accepted standards of periodization in my discussion: Patristic era 1st-5th centuries; Middle Ages 449-1485 CE; early modern era 1485-1660 CE. Technically, the British Middle Ages includes both the Anglo Saxon era (449-1066 CE) and the Middle English era (1066-1485 CE), also known as the High Middle Ages. Similarly, the early modern era (formerly called the Renaissance) encompasses the early Tudor period (1485-1558 CE), the Elizabethan era (1558-1603 CE), the Jacobean age (1603-1625 CE), and the Carolingian period (1625-1649 CE). While I thank the *Journal of Lesbian Studies* reader who indicated that it would be helpful to my audience to distinguish among these literary/historical time periods, I can't help but wonder why it is that I both know and am expected to know, for example, when the Victorian era was, but my colleagues are not reciprocally responsible for knowledge about the medieval era.

4. In this piece, Frantzen forces lesbians to read between *his* lines in order to reclaim their own history of homosexuality, as he mentions female homoeroticism only twice outside of the footnotes.

5. Halperin identifies his perspective quite specifically in his title–he will only be concerned with the male homosexual experience–but soon collapses his term to simply 'homosexuality,' while restricting his discussion solely to the male experience.

6. For example, David E. Greenberg's *Constructions of Homosexuality* (1988), a 635-page tome, contains only 26 references to lesbianism, two of those longer than a single sentence, and three of those in footnotes. The jacket praise includes comments such as "a penetrating cross-cultural and transhistorical account of the ways in which societies perceive and respond to homosexuality", demonstrating the overwhelming acceptance of using the term 'homosexuality' exclusively in regards to male-male same-sex experiences.

7. The LGBT Religious Archives Network and the Chicago Theological Seminary awarded this article the 2005-06 LGBT Religious History Award. It is noticeable, and significant, that the committee listed "L" first in the award's name.

8. For instance, the recent collection *Queering the Middle Ages* (2001) reflects this trend. The table of contents boasts an impressive line up of well-known and well-respected scholars, features two excellent editors, and features a variety of texts and contexts. The volume is divided into three sections of essays, each featuring a respondent as well. However, of these thirteen essays, none address medieval lesbianism, although other queer sexualities, including bestiality, chastity, and fetishism, are examined. Furthermore, of these thirteen essays, only two focus primarily on English texts.

REFERENCES

Aers, David. "A Whisper in the Ear of Early Modernists; or Reflections on Literary Critics Writing the 'History of the Subject'." In David Aers, ed. *Culture and History, 1350-1600: Essays on English Communities, Identities, and Writing.* Detroit: Wayne State University Press, 1992: 177-203.

Ali, Kecia. "Same-Sex Sexual Activity and Lesbian and Bisexual Women," Special Focus: Islam. In Bernadette J. Brooten, dir. *The Feminist Sexual Ethics Project.* Brandeis University, 10 December 2002. URL brandeis.edu/projects/fse/Pages/femalehomosexuality.html.

Bennett, Judith M. "'Lesbian-like' and the Social History of Lesbianism," *Journal of the History of Sexuality,* 9, 2000: 1-24.

Boyd, David Lorenzo. "English Literature: Medieval," *glbtq: An Encyclopedia of Gay, Lesbian, Bisexual, Transgender, and Queer Culture.* New England Publishing Associates, 29 February 2004. URL glbtq.com/literature/eng_lit1_medieval.html.

Brooten, Bernadette J. *Love Between Women: Early Christian Responses to Female Homoeroticism.* Chicago: University of Chicago Press, 1996.

Brown, Judith. *Immodest Acts: The Life of a Lesbian Nun in Renaissance Italy.* Oxford: Oxford University Press, 1986.

Burger, Glenn. *Chaucer's Queer Nation.* Minneapolis and London: University of Minnesota Press, 2003.

_____ and Steven F. Kruger, eds. *Queering the Middle Ages.* Minneapolis and London: University of Minnesota Press, 2001.

Campbell, Mary Anne. "Redefining Holy Maidenhood: Virginity and Lesbianism in Late Medieval England," *Medieval Feminist Newsletter,* 13, 1992: 14-15.

Chance, Jane. "Introduction: What has a Woman to do with Learning?" In Jane Chance, ed. *Women Medievalists in the Academy.* Madison: University of Wisconsin Press, 2005: xxiii-xxxvii.

Dagenais, John and Margaret R. Greer. "Decolonizing the Middle Ages: Introduction," *Journal of Medieval and Early Modern Studies,* 30(3), 2000: 434-46.

De Lauretis, Teresa. "Sexual Indifference and Lesbian Representation," *Theater Journal,* 40, 1988: 155-77.

Dinshaw, Carolyn. "Chaucer's Queer Touches/A Queer Touches Chaucer," *Exemplaria,* 7(1), 1995: 75-92.

_____. *Getting Medieval: Sexualities and Communities, Pre- and Postmodern.* Durham: Duke UP, 1999.

_____. "Getting Medieval: *Pulp Fiction,* Gawain, Foucault." In Dolores W. Frese and Katherine O'Brien O'Keefe, ed. *The Book and the Body.* Notre Dame: University of Notre Dame Press, 1997: 116-63.

Ferguson, Ferguson. "Patriarchy, Sexual Identity, and the Sexual Revolution," *Signs: Journal of Women in Culture and Society,* 7(11), 1981: 158-72.

Frantzen, Allen J. "Between the Lines: Queer Theory, the History of Homosexuality, and Anglo-Saxon Penitentials," *Journal of Medieval and Renaissance Studies* 26(2), 1996: 255-96.

Greenberg, David E. *Constructions of Homosexuality.* Chicago: University Chicago Press, 1988.

Halperin, David M. "How to Do the History of Homosexuality," *GLQ: A Journal of Lesbian and Gay Studies*, 6(1), 2000: 87-124.

Holsinger, Bruce Wood. "The Flesh of the Voice: Embodiment and the Homoerotics of Devotion in the Music of Hildegard of Bingen," *Signs: Journal of Women in Culture and Society*, 19(1), 1993: 92-126.

Jankowski, Theodora A. ". . . in the Lesbian Void: Woman-Woman Eroticism in Shakespeare's Plays." In Dympna Callaghan, ed. *A Feminist Companion to Shakespeare*. Malden, MA: Blackwell, 2000: 299-319.

Kelly, Kathleen Coyne. "The Writable Lesbian and Lesbian Desire in Malory's *Morte Darthur*," *Exemplaria*, 14(2), 2002: 239-70.

Kruger, Steven F. "Claiming the Pardoner: Toward a Gay Reading of Chaucer's *Pardoner's Tale*," *Exemplaria*, 6(1), 1994: 115-40.

Labovitz, Gail. "Female Homoerotic Sexual Activity–Sources (Judaism)." In Bernadette J. Brooten, dir. *The Feminist Sexual Ethics Project*. Brandeis University. URL brandeis.edu/projects/fse/Pages/femalehomosexuality.html

Lochrie, Karma. "Presumptive Sodomy and its Exclusions," *Textual Practice*, 13(2), 1999: 295-310.

_____. "Between Women." In Carolyn Dinshaw and David Wallace, eds. *The Cambridge Companion to Medieval Women's Writing*. Cambridge: Cambridge University Press, 2001: 70-88.

_____. "Presidential Improprieties and Medieval Categories: The Absurdity of Heterosexuality." In Glenn Burger and Steven F. Kruger, eds. *Queering the Middle Ages*. Minneapolis and London: University of Minnesota Press, 2001: 87-96.

Matter, E. Ann. "My Sister, My Spouse: Woman-Identified Women in Medieval Christianity." In Judith Plaskow and Carol P. Christ, eds. *Weaving the Vision: New Patterns in Feminist Spirituality*. New York: Harper Collins, 1989; reprinted *Journal Feminist Studies in Religion*, 2(2), 1986: 81-93.

Murray, Jacqueline. "Twice Marginal and Twice Invisible: Lesbians in the Middle Ages." In Vern L. Bullough and James A. Brundage, eds. *Handbook of Medieval Sexuality*. New York: Garland, 1996: 191-222.

_____. "Lesbians in the Middle Ages." In Katherina M. Wilson and Nadia Margolis, eds. *Women in Middle Ages: An Encyclopedia*. Greenwood, 2004: 556-60.

Sauer, Michelle M. "Representing the Negative: Positing the Lesbian Void and Medieval English Anchoritism," *thirdspace*, 3(2), 2004: 70-88 URL thirdspace.ca/articles/3_2_sauer.htm

Sautman, Francesca Canadé and Pamela Sheingorn, "Charting the Field." In Francesca Canadé Sautman and Pamela Sheingorn, eds. *Same Sex Love and Desire Among Women in the Middle Ages*. Basingstoke: Palgrave Macmillan, 2001: 1-47.

Schibanoff, Susan. "Chaucer's Lesbians: Drawing Blanks," *Medieval Feminist Newsletter*, 13, 1992: 11-14.

Sedgwick, Eve Kosofksy. *Epistemology of the Closet*, Berkeley: University of California Press, 1990.

Sheingorn, Pamela and Francesca Canadé Sautman, "Same-Sex Love and Desire among Women in the Middle Ages: A Report on the State of the Field," *Society for the Study of Homosexuality in the Middle Ages Newsletter*, January 1997: 1-3.

Stein, Robert. "Medieval, Modern, Postmodern: Medieval Studies in a Post Modern Perspective." Unpub. paper, Georgetown University; Washington, DC, 1995. URL georgetown.edu/labyrinth/conf/cs95/papers/stein.html

Traub, Valerie. "Friendship's Loss: Alan Bray's Making of History," *GLQ: A Journal of Lesbian and Gay Studies*, 10(3), 2004: 339-65.

_____. *The Renaissance of Lesbianism in Early Modern England*. Cambridge: Cambridge University Press, 2002.

Watt, Diane. "Behaving like a Man? Incest, Lesbian Desire, and Gender Play in 'Yde et 'Olive' and its Adaptations," *Comparative Literature*, 50(4), 1998: 265-85.

Weithaus, Ulrike. "Female Homoerotic Discourse and Religion in Medieval Germanic Culture." In Sharon Farmer and Carol Braun Pasternack, eds. *Gender and Difference in the Middle Ages*. Minneapolis and London: University of Minnesota Press, 2003: 288-321.

Wolfthal, Diane. "An Art Historical Response to 'Gay Studies and Feminism: A Medievalist's Perspective'," *Medieval Feminist Newsletter*, 14, 1992: 16-19.

doi:10.1300/J155v11n03_15

Index